Colophon

Sanders Kleinfeld and Dawn Frausto provided quality control for *QuickBooks 2008: The Missing Manual*. Valerie Perry wrote the index.

The cover of this book is based on a series design originally created by David Freedman and modified by Mike Kohnke, Karen Montgomery, and Fitch (*www.fitch.com*). Back cover design, dog illustration, and color selection by Fitch.

David Futato designed the interior layout, based on a series design by Phil Simpson. This book was converted by Abby Fox to FrameMaker 5.5.6. The text font is Adobe Minion; the heading font is Adobe Formata Condensed; and the code font is LucasFont's TheSans Mono Condensed. The illustrations that appear in the book were produced by Robert Romano and Jessamyn Read using Macromedia FreeHand MX and Adobe Photoshop CS

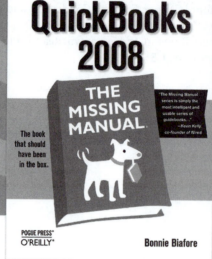

Diversity, Oppression, and Social Functioning

Person-in-Environment Assessment and Intervention

SECOND EDITION

George A. Appleby

Southern Connecticut State University

Edgar Colon

Southern Connecticut State University

Julia Hamilton

Southern Connecticut State University

PEARSON

Boston • New York • San Francisco
Mexico City • Montreal • Toronto • London • Madrid • Munich • Paris
Hong Kong • Singapore • Tokyo • Cape Town • Sydney

Senior Series Editor: *Patricia Quinlin*
Series Editorial Assistant: *Sara Holliday*
Marketing Manager: *Laura Lee Manley*
Production Editor: *Roberta Sherman*
Editorial-Production and Composition Services: *Stratford Publishing Services*
Composition Buyer: *Linda Cox*
Manufacturing Buyer: *JoAnne Sweeney*
Photo Research: *Stratford Publishing Services*
Cover Administrator: *Elena Sidorova*

For related titles and support materials, visit our online catalog at www.ablongman.com.

Between the time website information is gathered and then published, it is not unusual for some sites to have closed. Also, the transcription of URLs can result in typographical errors. The publisher would appreciate notification where these errors occur so that they may be corrected in subsequent editions.

Library of Congress Cataloging-in-Publication Data

Appleby, George A.
    Diversity, oppression, and social functioning: person-in-environment assessment and intervention / George A. Appleby, Edgar Colon, Julia Hamilton. —2nd ed.
        p. cm
    Includes bibliographical references and index
    ISBN 0-205-38662-8
  1. Social work with minorities.   2. Person-in-environment system.   I. Colon, Edgar.
II. Hamilton, Julia.   III. Title.
    HV3176.A77 2007
    362. 84—dc22   2005036332

Printed in the United States of America

10 9 8 7 6 5   10 09 08

Contents

5 *Racism: African Americans*
and Caribbean Islanders   *68*

Julia Hamilton

Foreword

Discrimination. Oppression. Exploitation. These are fighting words to the professional social worker. Dr. Appleby and his colleagues in this text provide us with a more scientific approach to understanding the problems related to diversity than is available in most literature on the subject. And in utilizing the NASW-developed person-in-environment (PIE) system in a creative and inventive way, the authors are able to help us understand the many problems related to diversity and to help us find solutions and remedies.

Now, diversity is a beautiful thing. I remember seeing a vast field of spring wild flowers in a mountain valley in France. The beauty of it still lingers in my memory. There were thousands of flowers, dozens of varieties all blooming and growing. I'm not a botanist, and I can't tell you what kinds of flowers these were or what was going on amongst them. I suppose some were getting more sun or rain than others, and some were growing around rocks that made their prospects less bright than their neighbors'. Maybe others were affected by contaminants in the soil or air. I'm not sure if the pink flowers felt superior to the blues or the multipetaled dominated their single-petaled neighbors. I'm sure some were more attractive than others in the process of reproduction. The overall impact, though, was of the beauty in diversity and the pleasure it gave to see it in existence.

Whenever I return from a trip out of our country and see our people living and working around me here, I marvel at the miracle that is the United States. Unlike almost any other country in the world, we have people of different color, ethnicity, culture, religion, and lifestyle actually living side by side. This does not occur without some difficulty, but we do have more diversity and on a larger scale than any place in the world. This diversity has been the engine for our country. It has provided the energy and creativeness for which we are recognized around the world.

However, not everyone sees beauty in diversity. Like in that field of flowers, people in our communities often have difficulties interacting with each other. Many fear diversity or feel threatened by the presence of people different than themselves. Discrimination, oppression, victimization, and exploitation are its concomitants. Whatever the cause of these behaviors—be it fear of others different than ourselves, ancient hatreds, scarcity of resources, or any of the other dozen or so reasons often cited—it is the presence of these negative conditions that stirs the consciences of social workers.

For social workers, more than other professionals, are steeped in a tradition of working for social justice. Our dream is of a society prospering in its diversity and free of discrimination and oppression. Indeed, the profession of social work was born a hundred years ago partly out of concern for the diverse ethnic groups then arriving in our country. Social workers sought to deal with the abuses experienced by the individuals and families arriving on our shores. The task of social work then, as now, was to ensure that all individuals had an equal opportunity to develop their talents and to enjoy their lives as fully as possible. Social work is aware of each person's uniqueness, of the beauty and value in diversity, and of the negative effects of prejudice and stereotyping. Social work still strives to establish a society in which all people can live in harmony.

Over the years, the profession has developed a range of approaches and techniques to assure those it serves that as many as possible are able to enjoy the fruits of their labor and have as full and rich a life as possible. The social work profession has produced the micro-level social worker—the caseworker or the clinical social worker—to deal with the problems presented by clients in their social roles. And the macro-level worker—the community organizer or the social change agent—was created to address the problems in the society that were depriving the individual of an equal opportunity. The authors of this book bring us up to date on problems and issues in these practice areas as well as on the techniques and intervention strategies useful in practice.

The use of the person-in-environment (PIE) system (*Person-in-Environment System*, NASW Press, 1995) in this text is an innovative feature and is noteworthy. For those not yet familiar with the PIE system, it is, in brief, a social work theory-based system for describing, classifying, and coding the common problems of the clients of social workers. It is a four-factor system that describes in succinct terms the problems that clients are experiencing in their social roles, their environment, and with their physical and mental health. This multidimensional holistic approach to assessment provides social work with a tool that clearly identifies problems that clients are experiencing. PIE not only identifies problems in relationships but also problems in the community—the environment. The system requires the social worker doing an assessment to note if discrimination is present and, if so, to recommend correction or remedy.

Social work also has its problems with diversity within its ranks. Susan Dworak-Peck, past president of NASW and IFSW, writes: "Despite our commitment to common values and principles the profession of social work has suffered from the lack of a unifying framework that might bring together the diverse areas of expertise within the profession. PIE helps to strengthen and unify social workers in our diversity. This system furnishes a new frame of reference for experts in all areas of social work and links the fields of practice, research, education and administration" (*Person-in-Environment System*, p. ix).

I would like to commend Dr. Appleby and his colleagues for their unique contribution to the social work literature on this most important subject. And I compliment them for their innovative use of the person-in-environment system. Those who read and study this text will certainly be wiser and more effective social workers for their effort.

James M. Karls, Ph.D., LCSW, ACSW
Co-Director, Person-in-Environment Project
Clinical Associate Professor, University of Southern California, School of Social Work

Preface

The historic mission of social work and the revised National Association of Social Workers' (NASW) *Code of Ethics* require cultural competence and a renewed commitment to practice with society's most vulnerable groups (NASW, 1996). Cultural Competence and Social Diversity (Section 1.05) states that social workers should understand culture and its function in human behavior and society, recognizing the strengths that exist in all cultures. Social workers should have a knowledge base of their clients' cultures and be able to demonstrate competence in the provision of services that are sensitive to clients' cultures and to differences among people and cultural groups. Social workers should obtain education about and seek to understand the nature of social diversity and oppression with respect to race, ethnicity, national origin, color, sex, sexual orientation, age, marital status, political belief, religion, and mental and physical disability (p. 9).

The *Code of Ethics* (1996, p. 22–23), when identifying social workers' ethical responsibility as professionals under Competence (Section 4.01), states that they "should strive to become and remain proficient in professional practice and the performance of professional functions." Discrimination (Section 4.02) states that they "should not practice, condone, facilitate, or collaborate with any form of discrimination on the basis of race, ethnicity, national origin, color, sex, sexual orientation, age, marital status, political belief, religion, or mental or physical disability."

The standards set by the Council on Social Work Education (CSWE) in 1988 and 1993 for BSW and MSW curricula have attempted greater clarity in guiding social work educators in the preparation of students for practice that reflects the profession's values and commitments. The *Educational Policy and Accreditation Standards* (2002), Part 4, 4.1 states that programs in social work education must provide content related to "oppression and to the experiences, needs, and responses of people who have been subjected to institutionalized forms of oppression. . . . The curriculum must provide content on ethnic minorities of color and women . . . groups that have been consistently affected by social, economic and legal bias or oppression . . . those distinguished by age, religion, disablement, sexual orientation, and culture" (p. 111).

The traditional domains of social work practice—services for children and families in the home, child welfare, schools, services for the physically and mental disabled, within criminal justice, mental health, family violence, substance abuse service systems, occupational services, the health care industry, and the elder care service systems—have been affected by these shifts in client demographics. Practice in each of these domains, then, requires a reevaluation of the usefulness of normative client system assessment processes and those normative intervention strategies whether targeting the individual, the family, the small group, the community, or the social welfare agency, as well as those designed to bring about cultural and societal transformation. Practice effectiveness with new person-in-environment situations must be explored, refined, and evaluated systematically.

The revised text is organized into three sections: Power (Chapters 1–4), Identity (Chapters 5–15), and Change (Chapter 16). It is designed to focus on similarities and differences between and among forms of oppression and to emphasize ways in which issues of race, class, gender, sexuality, and difference intersect. These issues are addressed throughout the book, drawing parallels, repeating themes, and offering another analytic perspective. A new chapter on ethnic identity development broadens the discussion of various psychological models that clarify the dynamics of personal growth.

Power is a common conceptual framework for understanding the experience of minority and other vulnerable populations. In the chapters on power, the concepts *oppression* and *power* are introduced to help the practitioner systematically center the client's experience in a social environment with real and potential social and psychological barriers. The client's personal, reference group, or cultural adaptation to these toxic, non-nutrient environments will be incorporated methodically into assessment.

The chapters on identity explore theories for practice (Longres, 1996), specifically the empirical knowledge of vulnerable populations that informs client system assessment. These include people of color; women; Hispanics/Latinos; Native Americans; Asian Americans; religious minorities; lesbian, gay, bisexual, and transgender people; immigrants; and people challenged physically, mentally, and emotionally. There are new chapters on practice with immigrant and appearance discrimination. This theoretical knowledge related to a wide range of culturally diverse and oppressed populations has received too little attention in other major social work practice texts. While normative theory will continue to inform most practice, culturally specific content, as presented in this text, will give greater depth to assessment and intervention.

The integration of all relevant theory is intellectually demanding; thus our task is to turn professional analysis into something more manageable for both the instructor and the learner. A specific framework will be used to limit the conceptual parameters; that is, a focus on the clients' problems in social roles functioning in difficult environments. This will be operationalized by using Factors I and II of the classification system developed by Karls and Wandrei's (1994) person-in-environment (PIE) system, designed to describe and code client problems in social functioning in terms of role performance (family, occupation, interpersonal, and life situational roles) as influenced by problems in the environment (economic/basic needs system; educational/training system; judicial/legal system; health, safety, and social services system; voluntary association system; and affectional support system).

The last chapter presents knowledge related to what social workers do to influence client systems and to change those social arrangements and institutions with which vulnerable groups interact. Theories of practice with vulnerable populations will be explored from the standpoint of new skills needed for effective intervention. This exploration will be grounded in an ecological framework (Germain & Gitterman, 1996) and a strengths or empowerment perspective of practice (Dubois & Miley, 1992). These contextual theories best inform social work's problem-solving activities with client systems of various sizes (foundation practice) focusing primarily on problems of living, social functioning, coping, and adaptation. The assessment and intervention scope of this text will not include clinical practice with profound psychiatric problems nor administrative or policy practice with complex organizations and highly technical policy choices.

The text will explore minority and other vulnerable group-specific social work practice related to problems of social role functioning influenced by an oppressive social context or environment. The use of the person-in-environment (Karls & Wandrei, 1994) classification system as an overall framework makes this text unique. You will learn to codify clients' problems in social functioning and problems in the environment. This classification system has the potential of establishing a common language for the profession of social work. This assessment system will be used as a means for ordering the broad theoretical data available to social workers related to Factor I, client functioning in his or her core social roles in the family, the occupational setting, or other interpersonal or life situations. Problems in functioning will be categorized by type, severity, duration, and coping index. The institutional or environmental context will be the second point for analysis, Factor II. Minorities and other vulnerable groups often experience problems in their environments (economic/basic needs system; educational/training system; judicial/legal system; health, safety, and social services system; voluntary association system; and affectional support system) because of discrimination and other institutional barriers. These social arrangements may be defined as an "ism": racism, sexism, ethnocentrism, heterosexism, ableism, classism, religious bigotry, and xenophobia. These will be explored as environmental problems—objective and subjective barriers to social functioning. This discussion will establish as its conceptual context a thorough review of power, privilege, and control resulting in oppression, stigmatization, marginalization, and discrimination, which is then experienced psychologically as alienation, powerlessness, and social isolation and individually as shame, guilt, anger, rage, and the internalization of oppression. These social processes are experienced differently by each marginal group and are manifested in varying levels of social role functioning.

The broader theoretical framework, symbolic interaction, and individual and group identity development and resiliency will help unify the wide-ranging content found in the various chapters. The text will then present knowledge for use, that is, practice knowledge in a highly structured manner, avoiding the confusion often associated with the compilation of loosely connected articles. Each population-specific chapter will present assessment and intervention theory within a context of an ecological framework and a strengths or empowerment perspective. This will be followed by a case study to reinforce cultural theory related to assessment and intervention. Each contributor will discuss those social work interventions that support resiliency and are associated with typical person-in-environment situations encountered by the individual, the family, the small group, and the community, as well as those general problems or concerns that must be addressed at the cultural or the societal level.

The summary chapter will explore affirmative practice principles, techniques, and models appropriate for clients from culturally diverse and oppressed populations. Several principles important to affirmative practice are discussed, which require the practitioner to embrace the richness and challenge of diversity as presented throughout this text. The practitioner is also reminded of the importance of continual self-exploration and evaluation when engaged in culturally competent practice. You are urged to work toward becoming culturally competent.

G. A. Appleby
E. Colon
J. Hamilton

Acknowledgments

We would like to acknowledge the following reviewers: Lessie Bass, East Carolina University; Michael Coconis, Ohio Dominican College; and Gary L. Villereal, University of Texas Pan American.

References

Council on Social Work Education (CSWE), Commission on Accreditation. (2002). *Educational Policy and Accreditation Standards*. Washington, DC: CSWE.

DuBois, B., & Miley, K. K. (1992). *Social work: An empowering profession*. Boston: Allyn & Bacon.

Germain, C. B., & Gitterman, A. (1996). *The life model of social work practice*. New York: Columbia University Press.

Karls, J. M., & Wandrei, K. E. (1994). *Person-in-environment system: The PIE classification system for social functioning problems*. Washington, DC: NASW.

Longres, J. F. (1996). *Human behavior in the social environment* (2nd ed.). Itasca, IL: F. E. Peacock.

National Association of Social Workers (NASW). (1996). *Code of ethics*. Washington, DC: NASW.

1

Framework for Practice with Diverse and Oppressed Clients

George A. Appleby

This text meets a specific need in professional education—materials that address the knowledge and skill requirements for generalist social work practitioners who assist the poor; people of color; women; gay men, bisexuals, and lesbians; ethnically and religiously diverse clients; the chronically ill; those who are physically and mentally challenged; immigrants; the aging; and others who are oppressed. Social workers, as well as other professionals working in the health and human services, need population-specific knowledge and culturally sensitive interaction skills to work effectively with changing client populations.

An educational text such as this is justified because of social work's historic mission, the ethical mandates for the profession, the changing demographics of the populations being served by social service agencies, and lastly, the accreditation standards for social work educational programs in the United States.

The America that existed at the birth of the profession of social work a century ago is a far cry from the America in which we live today or in which we will live in the future. The typical American was thought to be white and middle class, speaking English, and living in a nuclear family where father, the head of the house, went to work every day, while mother shopped, cleaned, and baked. This image was somewhat truthful: In 1950, white English speakers dominated all social institutions, and 78% of all households consisted of married couples. Even then, however, the nation was more diverse than these facts suggest.

This is not America today. Our skin color is quite varied. One out of every four of us now identifies ourselves as Hispanic or non-white. One out of every two or three marriages ends in divorce, and more unmarried women who get pregnant keep their babies. Unmarried females head more than one quarter of all families with children under eighteen. Married couples comprise little more that half of all households. Today 60% of all women work outside the home. It is commonly accepted that 10% of the population is gay or lesbian.

The future is likely to reflect even greater change. It is projected that by the beginning of the next century, white males will account for approximately 10% of new entrants in the workforce. Women will account for two-thirds of the growth in employment, with minority and immigrant males making up the rest. By mid-century, the average American will no longer be a non-Hispanic white.

The traditional domains of social work practice—services for children and families in the home; child welfare; schools; services for the physically and mental disabled; within criminal justice, mental health, family violence, substance abuse service systems; and the not-so-quiet revolution in the occupational services, the health care industry, and the elder care service systems—have been affected by these shifts in client demographics. These then require a reevaluation of the usefulness of normative client assessment processes and those normative intervention strategies targeting the individual, the family, and the community, as well as those designed to bring about cultural and societal transformation. Practice effectiveness with new person-in-environment situations must be explored, refined, and evaluated systematically.

The people we will study in this text have demonstrated profound social, psychological, and political resiliency throughout an almost universal history of violence and discrimination. However, in the course of the life cycle, some of these people will find the need for mental health or social services. This text is designed to prepare social workers and other health and human service professionals to better assess the concerns, problems, and issues presented by culturally diverse and oppressed clients and then to more effectively intervene with the widest possible array of interpersonal and social change methods appropriate to the presenting problem. Because social workers comprise the largest professional discipline in the mental health and social service systems, they must be well prepared to deal effectively with these needs.

It has been well documented that the population we will focus on has experienced oppression at the behest of religion, culture, and civil and criminal legal codes. As targets of institutionalized discrimination, they continue to be at risk of stigmatization and violence. Therefore, it is understandable that the most vulnerable clients appear in the full range of social work agencies and programs. While most have the same needs as their non-stigmatized counterparts, their socially constructed differences may have an impact on the perception of the problem, how the problem is sustained in the social environment, and the availability of formal and informal resources to help resolve the problem.

Social work has a long tradition of concern and advocacy for various minorities and oppressed groups. The historic mission of social work and the revised National Association of Social Workers' (NASW) *Code of Ethics* requires cultural competence and a renewed commitment to practice with society's most vulnerable groups (NASW, 1996). Cultural Competence and Social Diversity (Section 1.05) states that social workers should understand culture and its function in human behavior and society, recognizing the strengths that exist in all cultures. Social workers should have a knowledge base of their clients' cultures and be able to demonstrate competence in the provision of services that are sensitive to clients' cultures and to differences among people and cultural groups. Social workers should obtain education about and seek to understand the nature of social diversity and oppression with respect to race, ethnicity, national origin, color, sex, sexual orientation, age, marital status, political belief, religion, and mental and physical disability (p. 9).

NASW reaffirmed in 1993 and again in 1996 its commitment to working against discrimination and to improving access to health and human services for all people. Its most recent landmark social policy statement addressed the profession's concern for the political and psychosocial status of vulnerable groups (NASW, 1977, 1997). As an example, in its social policy statement, Lesbian, Gay and Bisexual Issues, the profession clearly recognizes that homosexuality, as well as gay, bisexual, and lesbian cultures, has existed throughout history, a history characterized by persistent social condemnation and discrimination (NASW, 1997). Similar attention was directed toward the concerns of women and African Americans at the 1996 Delegate Assembly. The association also has identified the elderly, the poor, immigrants, the physically and mentally disabled, and ethnic groups for policy refinement at the 1999 Delegate Assembly. The *Code of Ethics* (1996, pp. 22–23), when identifying social workers' ethical responsibility as professionals under Competence (Section 4.01), states that they "should strive to become and remain proficient in professional practice and the performance of professional functions." Discrimination (Section 4.02) states that they "should not practice, condone, facilitate, or collaborate with any form of discrimination on the basis of race, ethnicity, national origin, color, sex, sexual orientation, age, marital status, political belief, religion, or mental or physical disability."

The standards set by the Council on Social Work Education (CSWE) in 1988 and 1993 for BSW and MSW curricula have attempted greater clarity in guiding social work educators in the preparation of students for practice that reflects the profession's values and commitments. *Education Policy and Accreditation Standards* (2002), 4.1, states that programs in social work education must provide content related to "oppression and to the experiences, needs, and responses of people who have been subjected to institutionalized forms of oppression. . . . The curriculum must provide content on ethnic minorities of color and women . . . groups that have been consistently affected by social, economic and legal bias or oppression . . . those distinguished by age, religion, disablement, sexual orientation, and culture" (CSWE, 2002, p. 111). Now that we have established justification for professional preparation related to cultural diversity and oppressed populations, the goals for this project can be stated.

The primary goal of this book, then, is to present information to students and professionals designed to improve the delivery of health, mental health, and human services to culturally diverse and oppressed people, their families, and their communities. Specifically, the text will present theories for practice, which will inform multicultural understanding necessary for a person-in-environment assessment of culturally diverse and oppressed clients. Theory related to gender, ethnicity, race, culture, sexual orientation, class, aging, disability, and religion, as well as individual and group identity development and social conflict, will be drawn from the social work literature and the empirical work of the foundation disciplines of anthropology, sociology, social psychology, political science, psychology, and multicultural studies. The use of this social science knowledge base expands the parameters of the practitioner's understanding of social systems and environmental factors.

Most clients of social workers present themselves or are referred for help because they are having difficulties in their social role function, such as their relationships with others in their family, at work, at school, or in the community. The social functioning is a person's overall performance in his or her social roles.

A second goal is to present an analytic framework from which to assess problems in the client's environment. The dynamics of oppression will become clear to the practitioner after an exploration of the concepts of culture, power, control, privilege, and stratification. These are explicit in racism, ethnocentrism, sexism, classism, ableism, heterosexism, ageism, xenophobia, and religious bigotry. The "isms" are the social arrangements that become toxic or problematic in the client's social environment. Concepts of individual and group identity and related notions of shame, guilt, and internalized oppression, as well as social stereotype, isolation, marginalization, and stigmatization, will be presented as foundation knowledge. In social work, a person and his or her environment are regarded as interacting, each influencing and shaping the other. The aforementioned theories suggest environmental problems, which are factors outside of the client, that affect social functioning and well-being.

A third goal is to present theories of practice that emphasize cultural strengths and individual and group resiliency, which will inform effective intervention with culturally diverse and oppressed people, also with their impinging environments (social arrangements and institutions). Practice will include interventions with the individual, families, small groups, and communities. Models of practice with specific vulnerable groups will be analyzed for the utility with other oppressed populations.

The fourth goal is to encourage the systematic evaluation of proposed practice assessment and intervention strategies with culturally diverse persons in various environmental situations, as well as in a managed care environment.

The objectives are practice oriented and quite specific: to increase skills in biopsychosocial assessment and the effectiveness of psychosocial interventions. Ultimately, this is an effort to help social workers minimize the influences of racism, classism, sexism, and other oppressions in their practice and, over time, in the environments in which their clients function. Because this text is designed to supplement the rich literature related to generalist and advanced practice and to our expanding knowledge of human diversity in general, the authors will not attempt to introduce, elaborate, or summarize the general foundation knowledge, values, and skills commonly associated with social work practice. Rather, the emphasis is on the knowledge, values, and skills needed for practice with these specific populations.

Social workers are uniquely situated to serve the most vulnerable. Social work emphasizes the dual focus on the individual and his or her social environment. Social work interventions are directed at the interaction between people and society. This work at the interface involves helping individuals understand and cope with their environments, as well as advocating for social change aimed at improving opportunities and the quality of people's lives.

This text focuses on typical problems and treatments for psychological and life stage issues but does not discuss major psychiatric problems. The problems selected for discussion exclude those with gross social disorganization or serious psychopathology requiring intensive psychiatric intervention. The issues covered include internalized oppression and guilt and shame; lack of integrated positive minority identity; family conflict; relationship difficulties; substance abuse; violence; AIDS; role and status changes over time; and the impact of their marginal status on the access to health and social services, the development of community, and the recognition of social, political, and legal rights. The interventions included are designed to maximize human potential, improve psychological and interpersonal functioning (specifically social role functioning), and develop a positive self-identity, group consciousness and identity development, community and institution building, as well as institutional change to sustain supportive and nurturing social environments. This is a demanding task, one in which the practitioner is required to understand a range of social science and practice theoretical frameworks, and then a range of mid-level assessment and intervention frameworks, and lastly specific skills and knowledge.

The process of moving from a commitment to culturally sensitive practice to professional tasks and methods is not simple. This vast body of psychosocial and cultural knowledge must be channeled into knowledge for use. We must decide what is necessary and appropriate information to inform the development of an assessment and the implementation of an intervention that is empirically grounded. The following discussion of frameworks will help us focus on specific bodies of knowledge.

Theory for Practice

The groundwork for this proposed change-oriented practice with diverse people is laid by distinguishing among three kinds of theory: a theory of practice, a theory for practice, and a theory of caring. Robert Vinter (1967) describes a theory of practice as consisting of "a body of principles, more or less systematically developed and anchored in scientific knowledge, that seeks to guide and direct practitioner action" (p. 245). These principles are "directed not at understanding reality, but at achieving control over it" (p. 432). Observing social workers as they go about their work with culturally diverse and oppressed clients and then codifying what they are doing could formulate a theory of practice. From these observations, it should be possible to specify what social workers do and what results they get. A theory constructed from observations may describe present practices, but it has a limited ability to improve it or to bring about change. In addition, psychosocial interventions specifically designed for many of these vulnerable clients have had too variable a history for systematic observation. Contemporary theories of practice, especially the ecological model (Meyer, 1993; Hepworth & Larsen, 1993; Germain, 1991; Compton & Galaway, 1989), supported by a diversity framework and the strengths and empowerment perspectives (Solomon, 1982; Saleeby, 1992), appear to be effective in addressing the needs of this population. This is the theory of practice advanced in this text.

A theory for practice is a system of ideas or statements that explain social work practice. It provides for the development of practice models and principles out of which actual practice might evolve. Rather than being based on the norms and roles of the profession, it is more likely to be indebted to the social, behavioral, and biological sciences. A proposed theory for practice could be developed from the ideas and content in this book, but only after it is bolstered with the clinical and empirical research of practitioners. Longres (1995) suggests that "a theory for practice is a prerequisite for the development of a practice theory . . . it can be understood as a system of statements intended to explain human behavior and make it comprehensible, toward the ultimate purpose of learning how to control human behavior" (p. 3). The discussions that follow are structured to make the life experience of diverse populations comprehensible to the social work practitioner. The authors seek to contribute to practice theory by synthesizing a body of theory related to each population from a social systems perspective.

The purpose or function served by social workers is to help people out of their predicaments. In the process of doing this, it is hoped, a better society will result. Behind these vague general statements lie many contradictions and complexities. Does practice help the client by helping her adjust and cope with the realities and demands of the larger society? Does practice help the client by championing her cause and insisting that society accommodate her needs? These questions are the core of an age-old dilemma within the profession, whether the function of social work is social control or social change. In practice it is not always easy to distinguish between these philosophies. Longres (1981, pp. 55–56) suggests that in reality most practice is oriented somewhere in between: ". . . it follows what might be called a liberal philosophy, accepting a certain degree of conformity while working for a certain degree of within-system change."

Longres (1981) further notes that social workers by tradition operate on the basis of a theory of caring. While theories *of* practice and *for* practice strive to be empirical and therefore free of values, a theory of caring is value dominated. Practitioners adopt the value that it is good to show care, and they support their practice with political and ideological values concerning the best ways to show care. While this is both necessary and good, practice cannot be based solely on values. However, a value stance that discrimination and prejudice directed against any group are damaging to the social, emotional, and economic well-being of the affected group and of society as a whole leads to a commitment to advancing policies and practices that will improve the status and well-being of all people, but specifically "to prevent and eliminate domination of, exploitation of, and discrimination against any person, group, or class on the basis of race, ethnicity, national origin, color, sex, sexual orientation, age, marital status, political belief, religion, or mental or physical disability"

(NASW, 1997, p. 351). In this book we develop a perspective on practice with these populations that combines a theory for practice with a theory for caring, that is, a particular set of underlying values. As we present theories of human behavior, we will evaluate them from a social work value perspective of concern for human dignity and social justice.

Ecological Framework for Practice

Contemporary social work views human needs and problems as generated by the transactions between people and their environments. The goal of practice is to enhance and restore the psychosocial functioning of persons or to change the oppressive or destructive social conditions that negatively affect the interaction between persons and their environments. The ecological model of practice (Meyer, 1993; Hepworth & Larsen, 1993; Germain, 1991; Compton & Galaway, 1989), the framework used in this text, consists of five interconnected domains or levels: (1) historical, (2) environmental-structural, (3) cultural, (4) family, and (5) individual. The lives and social conditions of clients should be assessed in relation to each of these domains.

The ecological model of practice recognizes that transactions between the individual and the environment are products of all these domains and thus complex and disruptive of the usual adaptive balance or goodness-of-fit, often resulting in stress. This approach to practice emphasizes the adaptive, evolutionary view of human beings in constant interchange with all elements of their environment (Meyer, 1993; Hepworth & Larsen, 1993; Germain, 1991; Compton & Galaway, 1989). Adaptation, a key concept in this framework, refers to the exchanges of information, energy, and matter between persons and environments. This is an active, dynamic, and often creative process, wherein each element of the ecosystem shapes the other. The practitioner's task may be to assist directly or indirectly in the process of developing a positive self and group identity, to manage the information around the stigmatized identity, and to advocate for more nurturing (nondiscriminatory) environments. In this model, the worker's attention is directed to people's problems of living, and the importance of client strengths is readily apparent.

The history of positive and noxious factors in the experience of people sets the context for understanding any presenting problem. The history of group oppression and exploitation should be noted. Oppression has taken form in religion, culture, law, and social stratification. U.S. society, strongly influenced by interpretations of Judeo-Christian moral codes, is conflicted when confronted with difference. While change is in fact occurring, not one of these social structures could be characterized as nurturing. At best, they are benign (Appleby & Anastas, 1992).

The ecological model of practice also deals with the processes that give rise to stress and problems in living. Germain and Gitterman (1980) define stress as a psychosocial condition "generated by discrepancies between needs and capacities, on the one hand, and environmental qualities on the other. It arises in three interrelated areas of living: life transitions, environmental pressures, and interpersonal processes" (p. 7). New responses are required by the changing demands associated with life transitions. All life transitions require cognitive, affective, and behavioral or relational shifts because of changes in the capacities, self-image, worldview, uses of environmental resources, and the development of new goals. All these shifts require the restructuring of one's life space. For example, the lesbian or gay client often experiences major shifts in confronting the life transitions of coming out, pairing with a life partner, having children, or aging. Stress is likely to be especially great if the change is sudden and unexpected, whereas gradual change affords time for advanced preparation.

Environments can be the source of stress depending on whether they support or interfere with life transitions. Opportunity structures may be closed to marginalized groups. The presence of well-organized hate groups, such as the Ku Klux Klan, Society for the Advancement of Straight People, or English Only Councils, as well as state statutes that promote discrimination, will cause stress in even the most well-adjusted individual. Even organizations designed to meet adaptive needs, like health, mental health, and social service agencies, may have stressful policies and procedures. Social networks, such as coworker and professional associations, may be unresponsive so that isolation or conflict results. Even physical settings may be unsuitable and lead to stress.

Interpersonal processes can also lead to adaptive challenges. Primary groups, such as family and friends, in dealing with life transitions or unresponsive environments, may experience added stress because of relationship patterns within the group itself. Maladaptive processes such as inconsistent mutual expectations, exploitive relationships, and blocks in communication are sources of stress to individual members and to the family or group itself (Germain, 1991).

Interpersonal interventions should address client powerlessness by using strategies that enable clients to experience themselves as competent, valuable, and worthwhile individuals and members of their cultural group. The practitioner must use his or her professional power to facilitate a cognitive and behavioral shift in clients' sense of being trapped in a subordinate role, to counter the myths and stereotypes about their marginal status, to avoid the internalization or acting out of stereotypes, to change negative cultural identity and self-perception of being powerless and victims, and to learn new strategies for not colluding in their own victimization. These strategies are often referred to as stigma management, a lifelong process of information management concerning social stratification and identity. It is a process of carefully controlling what others know about them. The practitioner may assist the client to share her identity or to conceal it depending on the particular situation. These strategies, according to Cain (1991), actually involve complex interactional negotiations. Disclosure often entails careful planning and execution, and concealment requires close attention to many details of social presentation. Herdt and Boxer (1991) would argue, however, that common practice remedies represent an older, more traditional social service model, wherein pathology, stigma, contaminated self, and stigma management are core constructs, and therefore are off the mark. In reference to gay and lesbian people, they would advocate for a "queer" model that emphasizes building a "queer" community, positive "queer" identity, and radical social action. The practice interventions would include community development, community and public education, consciousness-raising and self-help groups, political mobilization, and coalition building with other oppressed groups with the intent of transforming society. This controversy reflects an age-old macro-versus-micro practice debate or the either/or position of social transformation versus reform and remedial change. The profession historically has moved back and forth between these two positions. Many practitioners attempt to combine both approaches, leaving the philosophical and theoretical debate to social work faculty.

However, the perspective of this text suggests that the psychosocial forces previously discussed be reframed so as to inform social work practice that focuses on policy and community change. Practitioners must understand and direct their energies to environmental pressures (discrimination, violence, prejudice, and the lack of civil rights protections) into action that influences society's definition of and response to social problems, needs, or concerns of the community. Practitioners must be skilled in mobilizing the political and collective will so as to transform private troubles into public issues. Finally, practitioners should design and implement, with extensive input from oppressed clients, effective laws, program policies, and community-based institutions and services. These should reflect the values of the profession and be based on sound knowledge about each of the vulnerable people as presented in this text.

Diversity and Strengths Perspective

The task ahead is to better understand the life transitions, environmental pressures, and interpersonal processes that are unique to each target group. While this general model of intervention moves us in that direction, it becomes more complicated in the specifics. If the practitioner were to draw on normative theories of human functioning associated with the five levels of assessment noted or the three processes in living just described when assisting a marginalized client, the psychosocial assessment and the interventions made might be well off the mark. The assumptions made by the clinician would fail to recognize the specific cultural context within which the client functions, his strengths, his adaptations as a result of little-known community resources, or his effective coping strategies typical of most minorities.

This failure to recognize the client's strengths would be partially due to the societal norm of cultural blindness, or the melting pot ethos. The yardstick for understanding and delivering services is white, middle class, and heterosexual (Pinderhughes, 1989). Effective practitioners act on the social work commitment to respect human diversity by placing all clients in their own cultural context and then drawing on a strengths perspective (Saleebey, 1992) wherein it is assumed that all clients possess untapped reserves of mental, physical, and emotional resources that can be called on to help them develop, grow, and overcome their problems. The social work literature related to feminist practice (Van Den Bergh & Cooper, 1986) or work with people of color (Pinderhughes, 1989; Solomon, 1982; DeVore & Schlesinger, 1981) offers a clarity of perspective on assessment as well as a range of empowering interventions appropriate for other culturally diverse groups.

An ecological perspective, which is supported by a diversity framework, can help the worker to get beyond the ethnocentric, sexist, class-biased, heterosexist formulations of normative theories. The client's perception of his or her life problem or stress, as well as the worker's understanding of that perception, must be seen as complex and variable. All people do not necessarily experience particular events or processes in the same way as either negative or positive. Other factors, such as social supports/networks (Maguire, 1983; Waters, 1994), hope (Snyder, 1994), or a sense of coherence (Antonovsky, 1987) may intervene in significant ways. Age, gender, sexual orientation, race, social class, spirituality/religion, ethnicity, abilities, lifestyle and culture, health status, experience, attitudes, vulnerability, and other personality features will affect whether an event, status, or process will be experienced as stressful.

It is important to remember that there is often as much diversity within a particular group as between groups. Therefore, any client should be asked to differentiate his or her own individual experiences as a member of a particular diversity or reference group as a cautionary step against working from stereotypic assumptions (Greene, 1994).

Just as there is an extensive literature related to ecological and empowerment models of social work practice, the recent attention given to cross-cultural or diversity practice has been impressive. There seems to be a consensus that practitioners should, at a minimum, start with an awareness of their own culture; be open to cultural difference; be committed to a client-oriented, systematic learning style; use cultural awareness; and acknowledge the integrity of culture. Greene (1994) in her summary of this literature notes that it is impossible to gain intimate, comprehensive, detailed knowledge on all groups, thus it seems improbable that an overarching model will emerge. However, it is clear that for multicultural practice to be effective, the client (his or her experience and meaning) must be put at the center of the helping process. This involves an attitude of respect for the client's experiences and lifestyle, an appreciation of the client's right of self-determination, knowledge about the client's group's life, skill in helping, and knowledge of human behavior.

Value Base for Practice

The value base for practice with diverse and oppressed populations is a theory of caring based on values of justice, independence and freedom, the importance of community life, client self-determination, and social change. Justice must be accessible to all on an equal basis; it must be impartially applied. Social conditions must be just. People want to feel a sense of self-importance and have a real ability to make decisions that affect their own lives. Independence and freedom are needed to experiment, reflect, and change. People generally want to create their own communities, to have a chance to experience support and a feeling of belonging, to have greater power over their lives, and to find ways of resolving problems. On the other hand, when people are isolated, they may become victims of exploitation and alienation and feel powerless, vulnerable, and unimportant. People want a chance to affect their own future, to make choices. A sense of accomplishment comes from engaging in action, not from being acted on. Products of change are all around us, and it is these that feed our sense of optimism (Appleby & Anastas, 1998). These values often conflict with those of the broader society.

Zimmerman (1995) reminds us that the value traditions that emerged as dominant in the United States when this country was founded were individualism, private property, and minimal government. These value traditions became the basis for legitimizing society's institutional structures, normative framework, and system of social control. These values also are the traditions that form the basis for how members of the society have come to view families, government, the economy, and their relationship to each other, and for how they think it ought to be. These values present problems for many of the populations studied in the text.

Assessment and Intervention Framework

The text will explore theories for practice (Longres, 1995), specifically the empirical knowledge of vulnerable populations that informs client system assessment. This theoretical knowledge related to a wide range of culturally diverse and oppressed populations has received too little attention. While normative theory will continue to inform most practice, culturally specific content, as presented in this text, will add greater depth to assessment and intervention. Oppression will be a common conceptual framework for understanding the experience of minority and other vulnerable populations. This will help the practitioner to systematically center the client's experience in a social environment with real and potential social and psychological barriers. The client's personal, reference group, or cultural adaptation to these toxic, non-nutrient environments will be incorporated methodically into assessment.

The integration of all relevant theory is intellectually demanding, thus our task is to turn professional analysis into something more manageable for both the instructor and the learner. A specific framework will be used to limit the conceptual parameters, that is, a focus on the clients' problems in social role functioning in difficult environments. This will be operationalized by using Factors I and II of the classification system developed by Karls and Wandrei (1994a). The person-in-environment (PIE) system is designed to describe and code client problems in social functioning in terms of role performance (family, occupation, interpersonal, and life situational roles) as influenced by problems in the environment (economic/basic needs system; educational/training system; judicial/legal system; health, safety, and social services system; voluntary association system; and affectional support system). The practitioner is encouraged to become familiar with the PIE system, which is in both text and manual form.

Without some way of classifying client problems (emotional, mental, or social), social workers, as is true with other human service professionals, must rely on descriptive statements that may or may not convey essential factors, and may vary in format, focus, and language from worker to worker and from agency to agency. It is important not only to have classification systems but also to have systems that lead to intervention decisions that produce the results expected by both the client and the funders of services. Karls and Wandrei (1994b) developed a classification system that addresses social work's need to integrate and understand the interrelationship of the person and his or her situation and the environment. This system will be used extensively by social workers in the future.

The PIE system starts with the premise that social workers draw on four classes of information to describe their clients: social functioning, environmental problems, mental health problems, and physical health problems. While the four factors are discrete, in that each stands for one facet of the client's problem, the complexity and interactiveness of all factors are understood. The four factors are as follows:

Factor I: Social Role Problem Identification
Factor II: Environmental Problem Identification
Factor III: Mental Health Problem Identification
Factor IV: Physical Health Problem Identification

Factors I and II are unique to social work practice and commonly associated with generalist practice. Factor III borrows that which is useful for social work practice from the DSM-IV system: Axes I and II. Factor IV is a listing of physical health problems, using the *International Classification of Diseases, Ninth Revision, Clinical Modification* (ICD-9-CM; U.S. Department of Health and Human Services, 1991). All four factors cover the attention of advanced or clinical practice. Karls and Wandrei (1994a) note, "by identifying primacy of social work in social intervention and environmental areas, PIE clearly helps differentiate the role of the social worker from that of other mental health and health professionals" (p. 24). From the standpoint of this text, using this framework we are able to order our knowledge so as to better understand the nature of social functioning and environmental problems of culturally diverse or oppressed clients. Our task is to identify theory and empirical knowledge associated with social functioning, specifically social role performance related to *family roles* (parent, spouse, child, sibling, other family roles, or significant other role), *interpersonal roles* (lover, friend, neighbor, member, other interpersonal), *occupational roles* (worker-paid, worker-home, volunteer, student, other occupational role), and *special life situation roles* (consumer, inpatient client, outpatient client, probationer/ parolee, prisoner, immigrant–legal, immigrant–undocumented, immigrant–refugee, other special life situation role). (See Table 1.1.) These roles can be defined in terms of fulfilling a recognized and regulated position in society. Tradition, law, and societal and family values define the content of roles. While the functions related to each role are the same across cultures, the way the functions are achieved may vary from culture to culture or from individual to individual within a specific culture. The worker identifies the social roles with which the client is experiencing difficulty and then the type of interactional difficulty: power, ambivalence, responsibility, dependency, loss, isolation, victimization, mixed, other. The listing of types of problems attempts to provide standardized terminology to describe the most commonly observed types of interactional difficulty (Karls & Wandrei, 1994a). The problem is then analyzed from the perspective of level of severity (no problem, low, moderate, high, very high, catastrophic), the duration of the problem (more than five years, one to five years, six

TABLE 1.1   *Factor I: Social Role Problem Identification*

Roles

1. Family
   a. Parent
   b. Spouse
   c. Child
   d. Sibling
   e. Other Family Role
   f. Significant Other
2. Interpersonal
   a. Lover
   b. Friend
   c. Neighbor
   d. Member
   e. Other Interpersonal
3. Occupational
   a. Worker–Paid
   b. Worker–Home
   c. Volunteer
   d. Student
   e. Other Occupational

4. Special Life Situation
   a. Consumer
   b. Inpatient Client
   c. Outpatient Client
   d. Probation/Parolee
   e. Prisoner
   f. Immigrant—Legal
   g. Immigrant—Undocumented
   h. Immigrant—Refugee
   i. Other Special Life Situation

months to one year, one to six months, two weeks to one month, less than two weeks), and the client's ability to cope with the problem (outstanding, above average, adequate, somewhat inadequate, inadequate, no coping skills). All responses are coded, and all recommended interventions should be listed.

Factor II draws our attention to six environmental problem areas: economic/basic needs system; education and training system; judicial and legal system; health, safety, and social services system; voluntary association system; and affectional support system. Specific problems within each system are identified; these then are analyzed from the perspective of severity, duration, and coping ability of the client. The codes for these systems are listed in Table 1.2. Just as it was noted that culture and intergroup differences might have an impact on social role functioning, problems with environmental systems may also be related to the client's culture or an expression of the dominant culture. The worker's understanding of diversity literature is crucial here. See the Evaluation Forms for Factors I and II in the appendix.

TABLE 1.2 *Factor II: Problems in the Environment*

Environmental Systems	*Codes*
1. Economic/Basic Needs System	5000.XX
Food/Nutrition	5100.XX
Shelter	5200.XX
Employment	5300.XX
Economic Resources	5400.XX
Transportation	5500.XX
Discrimination in Economic/Basic Needs System	5600.XX
2. Education and Training System	6000.XX
Education and Training	6100.XX
Discrimination in Education/Training System	6200.XX
3. Judicial and Legal System	7000.XX
Judicial and Legal	7100.XX
Discrimination in Judicial/Legal System	7200.XX
4. Health, Safety, and Social Services System	8000.XX
Health/Mental Health	8100.XX
Safety	8200.XX
Social Services	8300.XX
Discrimination in Health, Safety, and Social Services System	8400.XX
5. Voluntary Association System	9000.XX
Religious Groups	9100.XX
Community Groups	9200.XX
Discrimination in Voluntary Association System	9300.XX
6. Affectional Support System	10000.XX
Affectional Support	10100.XX
Discrimination in Affectional Support System	10200.XX

Source: Copyright 1994, National Association of Social Workers, Inc., *PIE Manual: Person-in-Environment: The PIE Classification System for Social Functioning Problems.* By J. M. Karls & K. E. Wandrei (p. 51).

Conclusion

This chapter has presented a broad justification for developing culturally sensitive practice competence with the ever-expanding diverse client populations served by social workers. A process for selecting an appropriate body of theoretical and empirical knowledge was considered. The outcome of this text is, then, to present information about specific oppressed groups that will improve the quality of social work assessment and the array of social work interventions. In the next chapter, we will discuss sociocultural theories related to all oppressed groups and psychosocial knowledge related to marginalized individual and group adaptation, coping, and change.

References

Antonovsky, A. (1987). *Unraveling the mystery of health: How people manage stress and stay well.* San Francisco: Jossey-Bass.

Appleby, G., & Anastas, J. (1992). Social work practice with lesbians and gays. In A. Morales & B. Sheafor (Eds.), *Social work: A profession with many faces* (pp. 347–381). New York: Allyn & Bacon.

Appleby, G., & Anastas, J. (1998). *Not just a passing phase: Social work with gay, lesbian and bisexual people.* New York: Columbia University Press.

Cain, R. (1991). Stigma management and gay identity development. *Social Work, 36*(1), 67–73.

Compton, B. R., & Galaway, B. (1989). *Social work processes.* Belmont, CA: Wadsworth.

Council on Social Work Education (CSWE), Commission on Accreditation. (1988, 1993, 2002). *Educational policy and accreditation standards.* Washington, DC: CSWE.

———. (1992). Curriculum policy statement for master's degree programs in social work education. Washington, DC: CSWE.

DeVore, W., & Schlesinger, E. (1981). *Ethnic sensitive social work practice.* St. Louis, MO: C. V. Mosby.

Germain, C. B. (1991). *Human behavior and the social environment: An ecological view.* New York: Columbia University Press.

Germain, C. B., & Gitterman, A. (1980). *The life model of social work practice.* New York: Columbia University Press.

Greene, R. R. (1994). *Human behavior theory: A diversity framework.* New York: Aldine De Gruyter.

Hepworth, D. H., & Larsen, J. (1993). *Direct social work practice: Theory and skills.* Pacific Grove, CA: Brooks/Cole.

Herdt, G., & Boxer, A. (1991). Ethnographic issues in the study of AIDS. *Journal of Sex Research, 28*(2), 171–188.

Karls, J. M., & Wandrei, K. E. (Eds). (1994a). *Person-in-environment system: The PIE classification system for social functioning problems.* Washington, DC: NASW.

Karls, J. M., & Wandrei, K. E. (1994b). *PIE manual: Person-in-environment system: The PIE classification system for social functioning problems.* Washington, DC: NASW.

Longres, J. F. (1981, 1995). *Human behavior in the social environment* (2nd ed.). Itasca, IL: F. E. Peacock.

Maguire, L. (1983). *Understanding social networks.* Beverly Hills, CA: Sage.

Meyer, C. (1993). *Assessment in social work practice.* New York: Columbia University Press.

National Association of Social Workers (NASW). (1977). Gay issues. *Social work speaks: NASW policy statements.* Washington, DC: NASW.

———. (1996). *Code of ethics.* Washington, DC: NASW.

———. (1997). Lesbian, gay, and bisexual issues. *Social work speaks: NASW policy statements.* Washington, DC: NASW Press.

Pinderhughes, E. (1989). *Understanding race, ethnicity, and power.* New York: Free Press.

Saleebey, D. (1992). *The strengths perspective in social work practice.* New York: Longman Publishing Group.

Snyder, C. R. (1994). *The psychology of hope*. New York: Free Press.

Solomon, B. (1982). The delivery of mental health services to Afro-American individuals and families: Translating theory into practice. In B. Bass, G. Wyatt, & G. Powell (Eds.), *The Afro-American family: Assessment, treatment and research issues*. New York: Grune & Stratton.

U.S. Department of Health and Human Services. (1991). *International classification of diseases— 9th revision—clinical modification* (4th ed.). Washington, DC: U.S. Government Printing Office.

Van Den Bergh, N., & Cooper, L. B. (Eds.). (1986). *Feminist visions for social work*. Silver Spring, MD: NASW.

Vinter, R. D. (1967). Problems and processes in developing social work practice principles. In E. J. Thomas (Ed.), *Behavioral science for social workers* (pp. 425–432). New York: Free Press.

Waters, M. (1994). *Modern sociological theory*. London: Sage.

Zimmerman, S. L. (1995). *Understanding family policy: Theories and applications* (2nd ed.). Thousand Oaks, CA: Sage.

2

Culture, Social Class, and Social Identity Development

George A. Appleby

Social workers seek to understand a client in the context of person-in-environment. This framework emphasizes the interdependency of the individual and the environment: the environment's influence on the individual and his or her ability to influence the environment. People attempt to achieve a balance between their psychosocial capacities and the demands of their environment. Those whom society values have an easier time reaching this balance, while those whom society devalues often experience problems in social functioning and with environmental systems support. It is well documented in the profession's literature that society is separated into social groups, which possess different levels of power and prestige, and that dominant groups are at liberty to define the overall social status quo.

In this text, we specifically focus on populations who are members of subordinate cultures, who have been marginalized by the dominant culture, and thus who are at risk of discrimination and other forms of oppression. These are defined groups of people who are targets of hate crimes, derision, social exclusion, and bias. These are populations who have limited access to society's resources because of our hierarchies of power and whose social functioning may be affected by their often toxic environments. Social sciences provide us with an array of theoretical explanations for how people interact with their environments and why people may be mistreated, yet still find the strength to grow and survive.

In this chapter, we will discuss culture as an important conceptual foundation for understanding social behavior. We will explore social class as a significant societal adaptation in distributing power and privilege. These discussions will help us to better understand how the individual, from a dissimilar background than that of the dominant group, develops both personal and group identities. The theories presented will be theories for practice. Finally, we will connect this broad understanding to an implementation of the Person-in-Environment classification system, as an aid to social work assessment and intervention.

Anthropologists define culture as all the ideas, knowledge, and objects that are transmitted from generation to generation in a society. The patterns of behavior that form the basis of any culture are established and enforced by the norms, folkways, mores, and laws. We will look at culture in a general sense first and then explore select components of culture in greater detail.

Generally, each society's norms or rules vary in the degree of feelings they arouse and in the response to their violation. Folkways govern our everyday activities and are the weakest of all norms; their violation meets only with mild disapproval. Mores, the strongest norms, define a culture's basic morality. Societies often feel that certain folkways or mores merit formalization, and so laws are written and legally enforced. A society's norms reflect its values, which are those qualities a society considers good and desirable for its members to possess.

Human culture is maintained and transmitted chiefly through language. The linguistic relativity hypothesis suggests that each language shapes its speakers' view of the world in unique ways that reflect specific aspects of its culture. Change occurs constantly, but not evenly, in a culture as environmental forces continually shift. Cultures tend to be conservative, or resist change. The theory that material culture determines nonmaterial culture, which in turn serves to maintain and perpetuate the material aspects, is called material determinism.

Though less well integrated than earlier, traditional societies, modern societies are better able to absorb change and thus stand a better chance of survival. Cultural strain may arise from various sources, particularly when ideal culture differs from real culture, and when a society's norms and values are outmoded and inappropriate for events in the real world. Large modern societies show much internal variation and often are composed of numerous smaller groups whose lifestyles vary. A subculture is a group whose beliefs, values, and norms differ from those of the larger society; subcultures that consciously oppose and reject features of the larger culture are known as countercultures.

The United States is made up of many subordinate cultures and several dominant cultures, which exist next to one another always with stress, often with minimal social tension, but sometimes with major disruption. Because cultures are evolving and adapting to each other while competing to maintain dominance in relation to one another, there exists a state of steady tension and a potential for conflict.

Culture is remarkably diverse. Cultures can be alike in general ways, but no two societies have the same norms and values. Members of every society tend to use their culture's norms as the standards for judging other cultures, that is, to hold a view of things in which one's own group is the center of everything and all others are rated with reference to it. The practice of certain aboriginal people of leaving old people behind to die may seem cruel and inhumane to us, but they no doubt would view our habit of placing our elderly in nursing homes involuntarily as equally cruel and barbarous. Everyone to some extent has a group-centered perspective or is what anthropologists call ethnocentric, though few of us generally recognize it. It is important to understand this concept because it is the basis for establishing group differences, which then supports the processes of marginalization and discrimination. Understanding how this is done is our next task, therefore, we move from the general to the specific components of culture.

Culture

Social scientists define culture as all the values, norms, knowledge, behavior patterns, and artifacts that are transmitted from one generation to the next and form a way of life of a people. "Culture consists of patterns, explicit and implicit, of and for behavior acquired and transmitted by symbols, constituting the distinctive achievement of human groups. . . . Culture systems may, on the one hand, be considered as products of action, on the other as conditioning elements of further action" (Kroeber & Kluckholm, 1963, p. 357). Culture and society are interdependent. Society is held together by culture; the objects of culture are put to use by society. Culture exists because people are able to share their creations and pass knowledge from one generation to the next. The physical objects we produce and pass down are our material culture. Examples of material culture in our society include hospitals, social service agencies, retirement villages, and personal computers. Our more abstract creations, such as ideas, rules, and patterns of communication, are nonmaterial culture. Our discussion of culture begins with an examination of two of its most important nonmaterial aspects, norms and values (Smith & Preston, 1982).

Norms

All cultures share certain features. Two basic characteristics of every society's nonmaterial culture are its norms and values. Norms are the shared expectations and rules, both spoken and understood, that guide human behavior in life situations. Most of our actions are influenced by norms, which, among other things, tell us how to greet one another, how to conduct a social conversation, what clothing to wear, what foods to eat, and how to respond to illness and pain. Often norms are internalized to such an extent that we obey them without even being aware of doing so. Internalized norms become part of our very being. Norms are effective in motivating behavior and are enforced by rewards and punishments known as sanctions. When our actions fulfill shared expectations, we generally are rewarded (positive sanctions); failure to meet such expectations results in punishment (negative sanctions). As a culture's norms vary widely in importance, so does the severity of the sanctions applied to enforce them.

People from different cultures or those who are beginning to adapt to the dominant U.S. culture complain about the confusion, the difficulty of not understanding the rules or not being able to do what they would have done at home (original culture), which was regarded as appropriate (positive sanction). Eye contact is an example. Many cultures expect the individual to avert his or her eyes when interacting with individuals with greater authority, yet this is interpreted as inattention or lack of interest in U.S. social interaction. The reaction of the dominant culture is to use a negative sanction, a label, which the individual will carry without ever knowing the alleged violation or inappropriate behavior.

Folkways are those norms violated most often and are likely to involve the least intense feelings. The conventional rules of everyday life that we follow almost automatically, such as styles of dress, manners, speech, and phrasing, are folkways. For example, we wear tank tops at play, not in the office, and we usually address our close associates by their first names, not as Ms. or Mr. The violation of a folkway does not evoke feelings of disgust or indignation. Mores are the strongest norms and comprise the basic moral judgments of a society. Mores are standards of behavior that arouse intense feelings and, when violated, carry extreme consequences. Our society's mores forbid child kidnapping, and we find it unacceptable to kill cats and dogs for food. Behavior is both dictated and prohibited by mores, which tell us, for example, to love our parents and family and not to kill other people. However, some mores are held dearer than others, and their violations are condemned more strongly. Thus we would probably be more outraged by a parent physically abusing a child than by someone who mistreated a pet. Still, both individuals would be violating our mores. Community conflict over differing mores is often apparent in the definition of child abuse and child discipline. In many cultures, slapping a child as discipline is the expected norm, but in U.S. child welfare and legal circles this is considered abuse.

Mores are not immutable. Though they usually change slowly, the change is sometimes dramatic. For example, while racism is still far from eliminated, racial equality has been promoted actively through legislation and the courts, and penalties for most forms of racial discrimination have been imposed. Wife beating is officially a major crime, but its practice is widespread. Society increasingly is exposed to messages of antiviolence and the role of social services designed to end abuse. Sexism characterizes male-female relations in the workplace. However, human resource departments throughout the country are developing policy, grievance procedures, and are sponsoring in-service training programs to counter sexist behavior.

Certain folkways or mores merit formalization as laws. A law is a norm that has been written by a political authority and includes designated punishments for when the law is violated, which officials have the power to enforce. Our laws stopping domestic violence or elder abuse are examples of folkways that have been made into laws. Other laws, such as those prohibiting murder and rape, are legalized mores. Many cultures (Native and Asian) do not rely on law to resolve problems but use natural mediators, people with recognized community or cultural status, to bring offending parties together and to work through their complaints.

It is important that you understand that norms do not apply equally to every individual and group, and the boundaries between the three classes of norms often overlap. For example, today divorced persons generally are subjected to little of the social ostracism they once encountered, but certain religious groups have strict rules about divorce. This is also true for cultures that recognize nonlegal binding of man and wife into what the dominant society views as common-law marriage. Many churches would judge this as living in sin. And though some norms are so strong as to be enacted into laws, our laws do not always reflect how seriously a given norm is taken by society. In the United States, for example, oral or anal sex between the same or opposite sexes is still prohibited by law (sodomy) and in some states brings harsh penalties. Social researchers observe that what we say in public about our sexual lives and what we actually do in private is quite different. Society can attempt to change its norms by enacting laws, but these efforts usually meet much less success than laws based on existing norms. The controversy over legalized abortion also is a case in point. Norms are not static. They are fluid, shifting guidelines for thinking and behavior.

Values

Smith and Preston (1982) tell us that through the norms that guide behavior in specific situations, a society's values are expressed. Values are abstract and general notions about the qualities that members of a society consider good, right, and desirable. Values are the very heart of a society, and all norms originate in some value or values. For example, in a society that values high levels of achievement, it no doubt will be the practice to grant considerable rewards to highly educated members or those who have made it to the top of their occupations. Let's summarize some of the more important U.S. values.

The most basic value in U.S. society is freedom. This value pervades our language and every aspect of life, as seen, for example, in freedom of speech, freedom of assembly, freedom of religion, and our free enterprise economy. Freedom traditionally has meant individuality to most Americans, that is, the absence of restrictions that limit our ability to live and speak as we choose, to provide for and be responsible mainly to ourselves. Yet even this cherished value can provoke controversy and sometimes conflict. What happens, for instance, if one person's (or group's) freedom limits the freedom of others? Individuality is not a universal notion. Many of the cultures in the United States, such as Asians and Latinos, place greater importance on the family and the community. The individual has a defined place in the family and community, and freedom would accrue to these units and not to the individual in his or her home culture. Schools, hospitals, and social agencies violate this value regularly and without thought undermine the authority of parents, relatives, and community leaders when offering professional assistance to students, patients, and clients from another culture.

Americans value equality almost as highly as they value freedom. The U.S. Constitution states that all persons were created equal. Our nation's founders stressed that this new nation would not be an aristocracy in which power and privilege were reserved for a select few. Yet, the ideal of equality has never been fully achieved in the nation's history. Today, this value is as important as ever and is the force driving the efforts of all those who actively seek to improve their position in U.S. society, such as racial and ethnic minorities, women, lesbians, and gays. Yet on an individual level our feelings about equality are often contradicted by the facts of life; our innate talents and personal circumstances are very unequal. Social policy to achieve equality is hotly debated, particularly as to whether this value should apply to ends (for example, equal distribution of income) or to means (the idea of equal opportunity). Sometimes Americans feel that government programs to achieve equality represent excessive intervention and compromise freedom, and these two values conflict (Smith & Preston, 1982, pp. 60–62).

Americans have valued achievement very highly, often using this value as the yardstick to measure personal worth. An individual's efforts are the most highly prized means to success. Everyone is seen as having an equal chance of raising a good family or succeeding in business. Those who fail can fault only themselves. In fact, business practices that lead to success often are exempt from moral and ethical sanctions. In recent years, however, the importance of this value has begun to diminish somewhat as more personal measures of individual worth have gained prominence.

Associated with achievement and success is hard work, a value that has been crucial to our nation's continued development. The early Puritan colonists, who believed that success earned through labor was a sign that an individual was destined for a high place in Heaven, exalted work to an almost sacred status. Throughout our nation's history, hard work has been viewed as almost guaranteeing one's climb up the ladder of success and one's share in America's affluence. Americans value work for many noneconomic reasons as well. In our culture, work is a source of identity and a way of demonstrating mastery and competence. But in today's world, the access to quality education, effective job training, successful employment, and advancement is related strongly to one's race, gender, and social class. The barriers to these necessary resources too often are insurmountable for the populations studied in this text.

Americans consider themselves a charitable people, ready and willing to aid the disadvantaged and oppressed. This value is a basic part of the Judeo-Christian ethic, which stresses good works. Yet many social scientists point out that our economic system, which is based on self-interest, fundamentally contradicts our sense of altruism, which stresses selflessness. The effect of this conflict is unending frustration for all those who try to uphold both of these major values. Individually we are ambivalent, while collectively we are, at best, a reluctant welfare state.

All aspects of nonmaterial culture are passed from one generation to the next primarily through written and oral exchange. Indeed, human language and human culture, in the broad sense of the terms, are intimately linked.

Language and Culture

Robbins (1997) and Cyrus (1997) tell us that culture is the system of adaptation that is unique to *Homo sapiens.* It is the means we humans have devised to meet the challenges of the natural environment and satisfy our human needs. Relatively small, weak, and physically defenseless, early humans depended for survival on their ability to learn and reason, and the products of their knowledge became the first culture. Our success as a species is thus due to culture, which reflects our biological heritage. The human brain is able to absorb, manipulate, and store a tremendous amount of information, particularly abstract information. And the human voice is capable of producing a wide variety of very precise sounds. These two factors enabled humans to develop language, through which individual stores of knowledge could be shared and expanded. The feature of human biology that has been most important in the development of culture is our ability to communicate through symbolic language.

Unlike other species, which communicate through automatic fixed responses, we are capable of symbolic language, through which we give meaning to experience. Through language we exchange abstractions, plan for the future, and even reflect on our own actions, perceiving ourselves through the eyes of another. Language packages our self-perceptions, experiences, ideas, knowledge, and attitudes about the world, and it enables us to transmit culture from one generation to the next. Each of us is born with the biological potential to learn any language. This potential becomes limited in infancy, when we begin to acquire the language spoken in our home, receiving rewards for imitating the sounds and articulations. As we develop language, we also learn the nonmaterial aspects of the culture in which our families and we live. But if language is the means by which culture is transmitted, to what extent is our language determined by our culture? Does language affect the way in which we perceive the world?

According to the linguistic relativity hypothesis, language is our camera on the world. Though we all are capable of expressing the same thoughts and conceiving similar ideas, the particular language we speak predisposes us to interpret life in specific ways. An example of linguistic relativity would be the Hopi, whose language does not distinguish among past, present, and future as most Western languages do; instead, time and space are categorized on the basis of what has been made available to the senses and what has not. This notion is not easy for speakers of English to understand; indeed, our language can express the notion only vaguely.

Peter Farb (1968) suggests that according to this hypothesis, the differences between languages are much more than mere obstacles to communication; they represent basic differences in the "world view" of the various peoples and in what they understand about their environment. The Eskimo can draw on an inventory of about twenty very precise words for the subtle differences in a snowfall. The best an English speaker can manage are distinctions between sticky snow, sleet, hail, and ice.

The Eskimo language distinguishes among types of snow because these are important elements of the Eskimos' culture. Similarly, our language describes numerous dwellings, such as split-level, ranch house, apartment, two-family, duplex, studio, and loft, because having one's own home is an important part of modern U.S. culture. Other languages do not name all the colors in the rainbow, and still others describe types of wood in ways that ours cannot—all for reasons unique to their culture. But just because our perceptions of the world vary, as these language differences indicate, does not mean we are prisoners of language. With practice we too can distinguish among the types of snow known to Eskimos, and they can learn the names of the various structures Americans consider their homes.

Language and culture are linked in the same inextricable fashion, as are culture and society. Language is the means by which a society makes use of, transmits, and changes elements of its culture; and culture makes language meaningful, enabling society to survive.

Cultures vary enormously. Every culture embodies its unique perceptions of the world and is characterized by particular practices supported by a set of special values. In our society, hard work is valued, and we accumulate private possessions; many of the Native American tribes share everything and labor is not required or enforced. We frown on marital infidelity and find it acceptable for spouses to be possessive and jealous, but traditionally Eskimo hospitality requires husbands to offer their wives to male guests, and both husband and wife become insulted if refused. Americans raise cattle for food, but in India cows are sacred and walk freely about city streets.

We have seen how the structures of the Eskimo language and English are tied to important aspects of their respective cultures. We say the relationship between language and culture is adaptive, because it functions to protect or ensure the survival of that society, the particular form of culture. Just as certain languages are adaptive for certain societies, so have the various cultural practices and beliefs served human needs. Culture, as we stated earlier, is the means we humans have devised to adapt to the natural environment. A culture can be understood fully only in the context of its natural environment, because societies have responded to nature's infinite variety of challenges in ways just as diverse.

All societies are challenged by the size of their population and their supportable resources. Because Eskimos do not enjoy an abundance of food, their population must remain small; hence in certain Eskimo tribes, old people are left out in the cold to die. For similar reasons, some Indian tribes kill female infants, and others restrict young men to homosexuality until they reach a certain age. The United States began to check its population growth as the economy slowed and moved toward a high-technology industrial base. Over the past several decades, the proportion of white-collar, service occupations has increased, while agricultural and manufacturing jobs have declined. Society has responded to these pressures in a variety of ways, with stiffer immigration laws and by favoring later marriages, after many of a woman's child-bearing years have passed. More opportunities are now available to single persons, sharply contrasting with the shrinking economic options for those who marry while still in their teens. Opposition to premarital sexuality has eased considerably, and both single and married people have ready access to birth control.

Cultural Change

Because we view culture as a means of meeting the environment's challenges, we can appreciate how and why cultures change. The balance of external forces is always shifting, thus change occurs constantly, though not evenly, in a culture. Cultural change is the product of many factors, the most important of which are cultural borrowing, or diffusion; discovery; invention; and historical events.

Cultural borrowing is the spread of material and nonmaterial culture from one society to another and occurs largely through trade. Diffusion probably accounts for the largest proportion of cultural change. Though we scarcely realize it, many features of our culture originated elsewhere: Much of American literature and philosophy stems from Western European thought, and the spices found in the typical American kitchen were used centuries ago only in the Far East. As well, some aspects of American culture have found their way into other societies. Discovery and invention both derive from our capacity for self-perception. Discovery is the sudden recognition that something already in existence can serve our purposes. Sometimes our perceptions lead us to attempt to perfect or refine the way we adapt to the environment. History is also an important facet of the environmental context in which cultural change occurs. The development of U.S. culture depended on the colonies' achieving independence from British rule; had England won the Revolutionary War, our system of government surely would be different today, and our ties with Europe would not be the same. But we must remember that just as culture is a product of history, people are the agents of history, which records our deliberate acts.

While we can point to examples and sources of change in a culture, cultures generally are rather conservative, or resistant to change. People take comfort in established practices and tend to shy away from the unfamiliar. Changes in beliefs and values most often follow changes in custom and practice; for example, multicultural schools and work sites have increased social interaction, dating, intermarriage and, to some degree, tolerance for difference.

Material determinism is the idea that a culture's material elements determine its values and beliefs, which in turn serve to maintain and perpetuate the material culture. Karl Marx proposed this theory as a rationale for the exploitative capitalism practiced by many industrial societies in the mid-nineteenth century, which engendered low self-esteem among workers, who passively accepted the prevailing notion that competition and free enterprise were virtuous and their societies' idealized vision of work. In a modern context, material determinism can offer an interesting analysis of how and why the position of women in our society has changed and can account for the shifts in attitude that have accompanied our changing practices.

The war effort during World War II required women to participate in the labor force; jobs were plentiful, and women both worked and managed plants involved in munitions development and construction. After the war, the U.S. economy entered a recession, thus unemployment became a problem for returning veterans who then were competing with women for jobs. As an effort to address this mounting cultural strain, "a woman's place is in the home" gradually became the prevailing cultural value. The postwar baby boom ensued, and throughout the 1950s women were viewed primarily as helpmates to their husbands and homemakers whose main function was to serve their children's every need. The economic boom of the 1960s was responsible for many changes in U.S. society. Federal money could now be spent for jobs programs, and equality of opportunity and "a piece of the pie" for all Americans became rallying cries. The impact of the changing character of U.S. industry also was beginning to be felt; growing numbers of professional jobs required more people to attain high levels of education. With more leisure time due to technological advancements, many women who previously were homemakers began returning to college, only a few years ahead of their daughters. Women's Liberation was the result of all these changes; its success as a mass movement too was owed in part to new communications technology. And though feminism at first evoked impassioned opposition, as had its predecessor, the civil rights movement, today there are fewer numbers who oppose equal rights for women (Smith & Preston, 1982, pp. 71–72).

Every culture has a number of elements known as cultural universals. But cultural universals are very general features. The ways in which different cultures meet the demands of their environments often involves overcoming common problems that have to do with our survival as a species. In order to ensure the survival of its members, every society has devised ways of acquiring, distributing, and preparing food; treating the sick; assigning names; ensuring security; relieving tension; raising children; celebrating courtship and marriage; and burying the dead, among others.

Societies must be able to counter threats to their survival; but the specific ways in which this is done, the norms that develop, and the values that support them certainly differ. The norms that surround eating, bathing, and styling of hair, for example—basic human needs that must be met by all societies—vary considerably from East to West. Ethnocentrism develops to reinforce social stability and promote loyalty and group solidarity. If you assume that your culture is superior, you are likely to be strongly nationalistic and, in times of conflict and crisis, will make tremendous sacrifices for the welfare of society as a whole. While ethnocentrism can promote internal stability, it also can block cooperation among societies and groups. On the international level, long-standing ethnocentrism often poses a barrier to world peace, as seen in the Arab-Israeli conflict. Within our own borders, ethnocentrism has hindered understanding among classes, ethnic and racial groups, and generations. Nor is an awareness of ethnocentrism always enough to achieve intergroup cooperation and understanding. Cultural relativism, the recognition that each culture is unique to its context and that the norms and values of no one culture can be used as standards for judging any other, is a notion that can help us transcend our ethnocentrism. Thus, social behavior can be properly understood only when viewed in its total cultural framework and can be judged only by the standards of right and wrong in the particular society. This is a valuable perspective if we hope for accurate perceptions of ways of life different from ours.

Anthropologists and sociologists tend to view cultures as complex entities exhibiting varying degrees of integration. When we say that a culture is integrated, we mean that its values, norms, beliefs, and practices somehow mesh and fit within an overall operating scheme that is essential to the culture's survival. Large, modern societies, which often are composed of many diverse groups, are much more poorly integrated than earlier, less industrialized societies. In modern societies, schemes of operation are evolving constantly, as different parts of the society are adapting to changes occurring elsewhere. But relatively less integration is adaptive for modern societies, as lack of integration enables them to absorb change more readily than homogeneous societies. Thus, the modern society may consequently be better able to survive.

A major challenge to integration and a primary source of cultural strain is the disparity between the norms and values people espouse and how they actually behave. For example, our dearly held notion of equality may conflict with other values, such as freedom from government interference, when we are led erroneously to believe that too much of our money is being used to redistribute income to the poor. Those norms and beliefs that a culture tends to cherish are its ideal culture; the actual behavior of a society's members is its real culture.

We reasonably conclude that we tend to see the world in the context of our own culture. How could it be otherwise? Our culture is what we know. But ethnocentrism can breed condescension, and we sometimes can feel our culture is superior to all others. The various populations studied in this text are examples of how groups have been set apart by the dominant culture; have been blocked in full participation in the benefits and resources of society; and have been oppressed by cultural arrangements unlike their own.

Subcultures

We have discussed culture as a system of thought and action common to a society. A society as complex as our own is composed of many different groups; not everyone in a society shares every element of the larger culture. Some groups may have a lifestyle, norms, or values that differ from those of the dominant culture. This culture within a culture is called a subculture. In our own society, we can see many examples of subcultures: Blacks, Latinos, Italians, the working class, and the residents of the South are only a few groups with distinct styles. There are racial, ethnic, social class, regional, political, occupational, and religious subcultures, whose ways of life differ considerably. Whereas a subculture contains different beliefs, values, and norms, a counterculture is a subculture at odds with the larger culture. The beliefs, values, and norms of a counterculture consciously oppose those of the dominant culture. The queer movement of the 1990s is a recent example of a counterculture; its members especially rejected the dominant culture's stress on gender conformity and the privilege afforded straight, white, Christian men (heterosexism).

While culture helps us to understand the person-in-environment in a broad sense, a discussion of social class, as is true for race and gender, gives our understanding of person-in-environment greater specificity.

Social Class

A primary construction in Western cultural thought is the belief that the superior should control the inferior. Western religious and philosophical thought is the ideological basis of all forms of oppression in the United States. Interaction based on differential power can be characterized by dominance-subordination or inequality and can be affected by a variety of statuses and roles assigned by society. One social arrangement based on dominance-subordination is social class.

Most Americans are more familiar with problems caused by race, gender, and sexual orientation than those based on socioeconomic class. (These will be discussed in detail in the following chapters.) Class as used here relates to relative wealth and access to power. Classism is a process wherein the wealthy are privileged and assigned high status, while the poor and the working class and their cultures are stigmatized and disadvantaged simply because of relative wealth. The economic elite benefit from classist values, and those on the bottom suffer obstacles. Because classism is less visible than racism or sexism, we make many wrong assumptions. One such assumption is that we live in a meritocracy, wherein we advance based on ability or achievement. This implies that we are in control of economic well-being and are responsible for our success or failure. This thinking becomes the justification for blaming the poor for their poverty. These are simplistic and erroneous notions that have become part of the traditional American ideology.

All societies struggle with the question of how to distribute their wealth and power. In some cases, the distribution is relatively egalitarian, and in others it is dramatically unequal. Some societies use age or ancestry to apportion privilege. U.S. society places a priority on social class, gender, and racial categories, which are socially constructed. Rothenberg (1995) reminds us that class, gender, and race differences have been carefully forged as hierarchy. This means, as an example, that in the United States women are not described merely as different than men but also that difference is understood to leave them deficient. The same is true for race and class or other forms of social difference. People of color are not described merely as different from white people but also that difference is understood as deviance from an acceptable norm, even pathology. It becomes a way of rationalizing racism, sexism, classism, and other forms of oppression. Much of this nation's social policy and social welfare system reflect this thinking without it being consciously thought through. Because U.S. society is hierarchical, for many of us it does not reflect the nation's constitutional vision that we are created equal, that we are endowed by the Creator with certain unalienable rights: life, liberty, and the pursuit of happiness.

Sociologists use social class as descriptive and analytic tools. Commonly, class is employed to describe social stratification: a hierarchy of prestige rankings where individuals in society are located on a ladder according to the amount of money they earn, the level of education they completed, the prestige of their occupation, or the prestige conferred on them by others in the community. This ladder is divided into classes: upper upper, lower upper, upper middle, lower middle, and lower lower.

Used as an analytic tool, social classes are defined as a structure of association or social roles in the economy and in the workplace. The capitalist economy is divided into a number of roles, each with a set of responsibilities, privileges, duties, and obligations. Longres (1995) offers an example: Owners put up the capital for the business or service, define what the product or service will be, and decide how the work will be done. They are the ultimate authority on who will be hired, how much will be paid in wages, and who will be fired. Managers follow the direction of the owners and put the plans for service and production into operation; they are likely to do the actual hiring and firing. Thus the owners and managers are regarded as two different strata within the same social class. Workers offer their mental and physical skills to the managers and owners in return for wages. Workers also may be considered as different strata in the same class, such as white-collar workers, skilled workers, and semiskilled workers (p. 75).

Class, according to this definition, is a position a person occupies within a hierarchy. The essential element is domination and subordination. Social class is more than a description of prestige rankings. It is a tool for analyzing role or class conflict. Contemporary thinking about class suggests even greater complexity. In reality, however, social class position is still determined primarily by occupation, income, and education.

Power is a core component of social class; it exists on various levels: individual, interpersonal, institutional, and societal. Heller (1985), Wrong (1980), and Pinderhughes (1989) all define power as the capacity to produce desired effects on others; perceived mastery over self and others; the capacity to influence the forces that affect one's life. Social work clients, who are unable to meet their basic need for food, shelter, and clothing, or acquire goods and services, have little mastery over self and others. Power is the access to social and economic resources, which is correlated with social class.

Class is seldom talked about in the United States. Nor do we talk about class privilege, class oppression, or the class structure of society. Mantsios (1995) suggests that Americans shrink from using words that classify people along economic lines: "working-class," "upper-class," or "ruling class." While all social classes avoid class-laden vocabulary, they do use an array of other identifiers in their social presentation, for example, race, ethnic group, or locality. Workers are more apt to identify with their employer, their industry, or occupational group rather than with the working class. Americans are, however, "keenly aware of class differences . . . but . . . class is not in the domain of public discourse. Class is not discussed or debated in public because class identity has been stripped from popular culture" (p. 131). One exception is the self-reference of middle class. This general category is designed to gloss over differences and to avoid any suggestion of conflict or exploitation. Another exception is the occasional use of the polarities: the wealthy or the poor. Culturally, wealth and poverty are seen as natural and inevitable, one status to be avoided and the other to be aspired to.

Mantsios (1995) notes that there are four myths commonly related to social class in the United States. First, we are fundamentally a classless society. Second, we are a middle-class nation. Third, we are all getting richer. Fourth, everyone has an equal chance to succeed (p. 132). The first myth implies that class is irrelevant and differences that do exist are insignificant. All are equal in the eyes of the law and basic needs are met regardless of economic standing. The reality, however, is that there is great variation in economic well-being. The wealthiest 20% of our society holds 79% of the total wealth. There are 17,000 millionaires in the United States, while more than 15% of the population live below the federal poverty line ($14,335 for a family of four). One quarter of all children under the age of six live in poverty, while the income gap between the rich and poor is one of the largest in the industrialized world. If we were to translate this into social class categories, the upper class (rich) would constitute about 5% of the population. They would be employed in upper-level, white-collar executive and professional occupations that carry a good deal of prestige and allow for creativity and autonomy. The influence that this class has over government decisions and policy results in part from the reality that they are likely to be well informed, to associate with other powerful people, or to have their interests represented by legal counsel or interest group advocates.

The middle class constitutes about 50% of the population. Most have white-collar occupations with secure health care and fringe benefits. Many families, while dependent on their salaries, have assets derived from savings, investments, and home ownership. Middle-class people tend to have high rates of political participation and are vocal about their political position.

The working class comprises 35% of the population. Most have blue-collar positions in work settings more often unpleasant and dangerous, marked by close supervision, petty work rules, and intense production pressures. There is little job security and higher unemployment rates among the working class. They are less likely to have savings and other assets as a buffer for hard times, thus they are apt to suffer from low self-esteem and high levels of family disruption. The working class are less likely to own their own homes, and spend more of their income on housing.

The poor constitute about 36.9 million, or 14.5%, of the population (Rothenberg, 1995, p. 117). Approximately 30% of this population is persistently poor. Only a small percentage of the poor are a relatively stable underclass. Although most of the families in poverty are white, African Americans and Latinos are disproportionately poor. Female-headed families are more likely to be poor than two-parent families. They are less likely to have completed high school, and earn less than the federal poverty line. They earn their hourly wages through low-paying, low-skill, dead-end jobs with few if any benefits. Often,

Temporary Assistance to Needy Families, Food Stamps, Medicaid, and housing subsidies supplement their wages because their wages are below a level necessary for basic subsistence. The poor appear to be least informed about political issues and have the lowest rate of association or political participation. Therefore, it is very difficult to argue that the United States is a classless society.

The second and third myths are countered with the U.S. Census Bureau economic data suggesting that the middle class holds a very small share of the nation's wealth. The level of inequality is increasing and downward social mobility is becoming a reality for more and more people. Mantsios (1995, p. 142) notes that the chances of becoming poor in America is 1 in 10 for white men and women, 1 in 3 for white female heads of household, 1 in 3 for Latino men and women, 1 in 2 for Latina heads of household, 1 in 3 for black men and women, and 1 in 2 for black female heads of household.

The fourth myth fails to recognize the enormous differences between the rich and the poor, in relation to material well-being, health, mental health, infant mortality, disease exposure, housing, diet, education, disabilities, and life expectancy. Social class standing has a significant impact on our chances for survival.

The U.S. Department of Labor, Bureau of Labor Statistics, and the U.S. Department of Commerce, Census Bureau, provide important wage analyses based on the 1990 decennial census and quarterly reports on salaries. The National Committee on Pay Equity (1995), drawing from this extensive source of data, reports that the U.S. labor force is occupationally segregated by race and sex. The wage gap is a major cause of economic inequality in the United States today. While the wage gap has fluctuated, it has not disappeared in the last several decades. The cause of the wage gap is discrimination.

Education and Social Class

Education is a major component of social class standing. Grades and test scores are typically used as indicators of school performance, as is the level of grade completion the indicator of educational attainment; both are correlated strongly with social class. "Socioeconomic background . . . operates independently of academic ability at every stage in the process of educational attainment" (Sewell, 1971, p. 795). Longitudinal educational data suggest that the level of inequity is staying the same or getting worse (DeLone, 1978; College Entrance Examination Board, 1993). Connell et al. (1991, 1994), in their discussion of the relationship between social class and education, emphasize the centrality of the labor market and the dependency on a wage (or wage substitute) as elements of working-class survival. Increasingly, the key division in the labor market has become that between credentialed and uncredentialed labor. This points to the importance of the educational system in shaping modern class relations. Formal schooling is the route to credentials, and as a considerable body of research shows, the educational system spits out the bulk of working-class students before they get advanced credentials. Sennett and Cobb (1973) spoke of the hidden injuries of class. The cultural exclusion is only one of the ways society erodes the self-confidence of working-class people. Disdainful treatment in hospitals, surveillance by welfare agencies, media hostility, and blocked promotional structures are all familiar experiences for them.

The damaging relationship between educational authority and working-class families has been well documented (Walker, 1989; Connell, 1994). Without the credentials, working-class people are dependent on a weakening labor market, which has moved away from well-paid skilled jobs to poorly paid service industry positions with few benefits.

People do not choose to be poor or working class; instead, they are limited and confined by the opportunities afforded or denied them by a social system. The U.S. class structure is a function of its economic system, capitalism. This system is based on private rather than public ownership and control of commercial enterprises. It relies on the class division between those who own and control and those who do not. Under capitalism, these enterprises are governed by the need to produce a profit for the owners, rather than fulfill collective needs.

Social Identity Development

Much of the literature on cultural minorities addresses the issue of identity development, the processes and stages an individual goes through in order to develop an identity. This developmental approach is individualistic, conceptualizing tasks as personal adjustments in a generally hostile environment. (See Berger, 1996; Cass, 1979; Coleman, 1981–82; Hetrick & Martin, 1987; Savin-Williams, 1988; and Troiden, 1989.) Cox and Gallois (1996), in an extensive review of homosexual identity formation, note that the majority of these theories propose stage models, where a person goes through a number of stages in the development of an identity. This is a self-labeling process utilizing primarily cognitive operations. While this approach is useful in countering psychopathological conceptions, it fails to examine larger social factors. A social psychological perspective, specifically social identity theory (Tajfel & Turner, 1986), where the psychological processes of the individual are explained with explicit reference to the broader social context, will orient this chapter. Tajfel and Turner focus on white identity development as contrasting and interacting with various stages of minority development.

Social identity theory (Hogg & Abrams, 1988) focuses on the social or group-based aspects of identity and how these interact with the social structure. Attention is given to the derivation of positive self-esteem. There are two underlying processes here. The first is self-categorization, from which we develop a number of social identities. Second is the process of social comparison, which aims at the enhancement of self-esteem.

Social Categorization

To simplify an extremely complex world, we categorize groups of stimuli. This appears to be automatic, done unconsciously, and is adaptive to our functioning, as it allows a degree of predictability. We do this with our physical and social worlds. We also categorize ourselves. Cox and Gallois (1996) point out "social identity refers to aspects of oneself which form the basis of shared group membership. Self-categorization is not merely an act of self-labeling, but an adoption over time of the normative behaviors, characteristics, and values associated with the particular group membership" (p. 11). Examples can be based on gender (I am woman or I am man), ethnicity (I am Puerto Rican or I am Latino), political ideology (I am a socialist or I am a Democrat), or membership in a club or association (NASW or CSWE), and the behaviors and values that go along with such memberships. A result of self-categorization is that us/them dichotomies are formed. "We are African American (and therefore have certain characteristics, norms, and behaviors), and they are Haitian (and therefore have characteristics, norms, and behaviors) that we view as being of lesser value."

Everyone has multiple social identities. A white, heterosexual male has multiple dominant status, which is unlikely to be a source of problems but in fact the source of high self-esteem. For those with multiple minority identities (such as female, black, Muslim, lesbian), the development of self-esteem may be more difficult, because of negative reactions to one of the group membership from people in the others.

Often, social identities are potentially in conflict with each other (e.g., gay and Republican). The norms and values of these two groups are incompatible, thus requiring some resolution of the identities by the individual. In situations where a particular social identity is salient, group membership norms and values are highly accessible, leading to interactions based on intergroup perceptions. Such interactions are characterized by viewing others and oneself primarily from the positions of the relevant group memberships, as opposed to individual people. Intergroup comparisons are minimized, while intergroup differences are maximized (Cox & Gallois, 1996, p. 12).

Besides social identity, individuals have a personal identity. Personal identity refers to those aspects, behaviors, traits, and values individuals see as characterizing themselves as distinct from other individuals. In situations where personal identity is important, individual characteristics, relationships, and values, rather than those based on group membership, are seen as salient, leading to interactions of an interpersonal nature. In this sense, each person views the other as an individual, not as a representative of a particular social group.

Social Comparison

Hogg and Abrams (1988) state that self-concept consists of two aspects: social identity, based on memberships in social groups and derived through a process of social self-categorization; and personal identity, based on unique aspects of oneself. We aspire to an identity in which both aspects are perceived positively, which will result in high self-esteem. Self-esteem is determined primarily through social comparison. Social self-esteem is derived by comparing the social groups one belongs to with other groups, while personal self-esteem is derived from comparison of the self with other individuals. We choose dimensions upon which we can compare favorably with others. We establish social hierarchies to maintain power and privilege, giving race a predominant position and thus internalizing white privilege whenever possible. African Americans, for example, may emphasize their strong Christian faith in their comparison with ethnic whites, claiming they are acting in accordance with God's will and are not lax as are others. In this social comparison, whether based on fact or not, African Americans not only see themselves as distinct from ethnic whites, but better than them. Personal identity is believed to develop in the same way, by making downward comparisons, often with others who have similar social characteristics (i.e., in-group members). An example of this would be members of the same church self-identifying as "I am blessed," "I am truly blessed," or "I am a living saint." This is an evaluative process.

The social attributes embodied in our social identity are extremely important because they carry different levels of power, prestige, and status. Heterosexual males compare more favorably to gay men and women.

Dominant groups are in the position of being able to control the social status quo. Social groups jostle for position in the society, with members of dominant groups attempting to maintain a status quo that is favorable to them and subordinate groups attempting to alter the status quo in some way, so as to get a more favorable outcome for themselves. Social identity theory is about groups in conflict.

Social categories, particularly ones based on race, sex, or sexual orientation, usually do not develop from experience alone. Many categories important to society are defined by society in general. We learned the content of these categories as stereotypes: What is a male or female, what is a black, a Jew, or a lesbian woman or gay man? These are often discussed in terms of the mores of our society. These categories become the source of competition between social groups for social benefits, tangible or psychological in nature, such as the status for the social group.

Because of the inequalities in the power relations between groups, developing positive distinctiveness, as opposed to negative distinctiveness, is relatively easier for dominant groups than subordinate groups. The enhancement and maintenance of identity by subordinate groups is therefore problematic. We will see this in Chapter 4, where we discuss the internalization of oppression and the self-fulfilling prophecy.

Social work, as is true for any profession, must be pragmatic about its theory base. It needs knowledge for use in its assessment and interventions. The preceding discussion of culture, social class, and social identity development serves as a conceptual foundation for the following classification system.

Person-in-Environment Classification System

Karls and Wandrei (1994) tell us that in social work a client and his or her environment are regarded as interacting, each influencing and shaping the other. In their PIE system of problem classification, the worker's attention focuses on social role problems wherein mindfulness is given to interpersonal transaction that affects social functioning. This will be discussed to some degree later in the chapter and again in Chapter 4. The environment problems discussed here are the factors outside of the client that affect social functioning and well-being. The environment is seen as both the physical and the social context in which the client lives. "It is the sum total of the natural setting and the human-made circumstances outside of the person. The environment provides both resources and opportunities; it activates needs along with creating barriers to their fulfillment" (p. 23). Warren (1963) identified five environmental subsystems, which create a climate of social well-being for members of the community:

1. *Economic/Basic Needs System* includes social institutions and social agencies that provide food, shelter, employment, funds, and transportation.
2. *Educational and Training System* includes social institutions that transmit knowledge and skills, educate people about the values of society, and serve in the development of skills that are needed to maintain the society.
3. *Judicial and Legal System* includes social institutions and social agencies that control the social behavior of people.

4. *Health, Safety, and Social Services System* includes social institutions and social agencies that provide for health, including mental health, safety, and social services.
5. *Voluntary Association System* includes religious organizations and community social support groups that facilitate social and spiritual growth and development.

The authors added to Warren's five subsystems a sixth, *Affectional Support System*. This is a system of friendships and acquaintances that constitutes a person's individual social support system. Problems arise when these subsystems or institutions are unable to meet the needs of their members. It is important, therefore, to identify the problems in those institutions and social systems, because they clearly impinge on the social functioning problems presented by social work clients.

Each of the Environment Systems lists three to four problems, such as the lack of resource; the inadequacy of the resource; or barriers resulting from regulation, danger, or issues beyond the client's control. Under Food/Nutrition, four levels of systems problems are listed: lack of food 5101.XX, inadequate supply 5102.XX, documented malnutrition 5103.XX, and other problems 5104.XX. Each subsystems problem in the Environmental Systems is coded in the same fashion.

Specific attention is given here to a problem that is listed under each category: discrimination:

System	Discrimination Code
Economic/Basic Needs	5600.XX
Education and Training	6200.XX
Judicial and Legal	7200.XX
Health, Safety, and Social Services	8400.XX
Voluntary Association	9300.XX
Affectional Support	10200.XX

Under each of these categories, discrimination can be further codified:

Subcategory	Code
Age	01.XX
Ethnicity, color, or language	02.XX
Religion	03.XX
Sex	04.XX
Sexual orientation	05.XX
Lifestyle	06.XX
Noncitizen	07.XX
Veteran status	08.XX
Dependency status	09.XX
Disability	10.XX
Marital status	11.XX
Other	12.XX

After identification, each problem is assessed from the standpoint of severity: (1) no problem, (2) low severity, (3) moderate severity, (4) high severity, (5) very high severity, or

(6) catastrophic. The problem is then evaluated in terms of duration: (1) more than five years, (2) one to five years, (3) six months to one year, (4) one to six months, (5) two weeks to one month, or (6) less than two weeks. The social worker can then assess the client's coping skills: (1) outstanding, (2) above average, (3) adequate, (4) somewhat inadequate, (5) inadequate, or (6) no coping skills. The Severity, Coping, and Duration Indexes are used to amplify the assessment of the client's social functioning as recorded on Factors I and II. The Severity Index indicates the degree of change or transition experienced by the client. The Duration Index measures the recency and duration of the problem. The Coping Index gauges the internal resources available to the client for addressing the identified problems. The practitioner should use these indexes to complete the description of the client's social functioning and environmental problems and to provide an indication of whether social work intervention is required. Again, remember that each system lists discrimination as a potential problem. This is an anticipated life experience for each population discussed in this text. The level of severity and duration may vary considerably from person to person and at different points in the life cycle. The coping styles, the cultural resources, and barriers vary within and among each minority population.

Conclusion

The worker's use of a classification system that directs attention to both social role functioning and environmental problems affords easy introduction of culturally diverse content. This clarity during the assessment phase allows for greater specificity in selecting interventions, which are culturally sensitive, social class oriented, and more apt to be perceived as realistic by the client. Assessment and intervention based on the client's reality is affirmative practice on either an interpersonal or a social action level. Affirmative practice will be discussed in greater detail in Chapter 16.

References

Cass, V. C. (1979). Homosexuality identity formation: A theoretical model. *Journal of Homosexuality 4*(3): 219–35.

Coleman, E. (1981–82). Development stages of the coming out process. In Paul, Weinrich, Gonsiorck, & Hotredt (Eds.). *Homosexuality* (49–58). Beverly Hills, CA: Sage.

College Entrance Examination Board. (1993). College-bound seniors: 1993 profile of SAT and Achievement Test takers, Princeton, NJ: Author.

Connell, R. W. (1994, Summer). Poverty and education. *Harvard Education Review, 64*(2), 125–149.

Connell, R. W., Dowsett, G. W., Rodden, P., Davis, M. D., Watson, L., & Baxter, D. (1991). Social class, gay men, and AIDS prevention. *Australian Journal of Public Health, 15*(3), 178–189.

Cox, S., & Gallois, C. (1996). Gay and lesbian identity development: A social identity perspective. *Journal of Homosexuality, 30*(4), 1–30.

Cyrus, V. (Ed.). (1997). *Experiencing race, class, and gender in the United States* (2nd ed.). Mountain View, CA: Mayfield.

DeLone, R. (1978). *Small futures*. New York: Harcourt Brace Jovanovich.

Farb, P. (1968). Man at the mercy of his language. In *Man's rise to civilization as shown by the Indians of North America from primeval times to the coming of the industrial state.* New York: Dutton.

Heller, D. (1985). *Power in psychotherapeutic practice.* New York: Human Services Press.

Hetrick, E. S., & Martin, A. D. (1987). Developmental issues and their resolution for gay and lesbian adolescents. *Journal of Homosexuality 14*(1–2): 25–42.

Hogg, M. A., & Abrams, D. (1988). *Social identification*. London: Routledge.

Karls, J. M., & Wandrei, K. E. (1994). *Person-in-Environment System: The PIE classification system for social functioning problems*. Washington, DC: NASW.

Kroeber, A. L., & Kluckholm, C. (1963). *Culture*. New York: Vintage.

Longres, J. F. (1995). *Human behavior in the social environment* (2nd ed.). Itasca, IL: F. E. Peacock.

Mantsios, G. (1995). Class in America: Myths and realities. In P. S. Rothenberg (Ed.), *Race, class, and gender in the United States: An integrated study* (3rd ed., pp. 131–143). New York: St. Martin's Press.

National Committee on Pay Equity/The Wage Gap. (1995). The wage gap: Myths and facts. In P. S. Rothenberg (Ed.) *Race, class, and gender in the United States: An integrated study* (3rd ed.), pp. 144–151. New York: St. Martin's Press.

Pinderhughes, E. (1989). *Understanding race, ethnicity, and power*. New York: Free Press.

Robbins, R. H. (1997). *Cultural anthropology: A problem-based approach* (2nd ed.). Itasca, IL: F. E. Peacock.

Rothenberg, P. S. (Ed.). (1995). *Race, class, and gender in the United States: An integrated study* (3rd ed.). New York: St. Martin's Press.

Savin-Williams, R.C. (1994). Verbal and physical abuse as stressors in the lives of lesbian, gay male and bisexual youths: Associated with school problems, running away, substance abuse, prostitution, suicide. *Journal of Consulting and Clinical Psychology 62*(2): 261–69.

Sennet, R., & Cobb, J. (1973). *The hidden injuries of class*. New York: Vintage Books.

Sewell, W. H. (1971). Inequality of opportunity for higher education. *American Sociological Review, 36*(5), 793–809.

Smith, R. W., & Preston, F. W. (1982). *Sociology: An introduction* (2nd ed.). New York: St. Martin's Press.

Tajfel, H., & Turner, J. C. (1986). The social identity theory of intergroup behavior. In S. Worchel & W. G. Austin (Eds.), *Psychology of intergroup relations* (pp. 7–24). Chicago: Nelson-Hall.

Troiden, R. R. (1989). The formation of homosexual identities. *Journal of Homosexuality 17*(1–2): 43–73.

Walker, L. (1989). *Australian maid*. Ph.D. thesis, Sociology, Macquarie University.

Warren, R. (1963). *The community in America*. Chicago: Rand McNally.

Wrong, D. (1980). *Power: Its forms, bases, and uses*. New York: Harper & Row.

3

Ethnic Identity Development

Elizabeth Rodriguez-Keyes

The way in which traditional psychological theory addresses identity formation and ethnic identity development is explored in this chapter. This section reviews how ego psychology and object relations theories inform the understanding of the psychological issues for individuals who (im)migrate. There are many gaps in these traditional psychological theories. Therefore, the most recent literature on identity formation and ethnic identity development is used to explore and critique the traditional theories in order to better understand the process by which minorities negotiate acculturation. This is important because minorities represent 30% of the total U.S. population, that is, 97.25 million people residing in the United States. Latino minority groups represent 12% of the total U.S. population; with approximately 32.8 million people, this is the fastest-growing ethnic group (U.S. Census, 2000).

Traditional Psychological Theories

Erik Erikson and Ego Psychology

The concept of identity formation has received a great deal of attention in the psychoanalytic literature, with the greatest influence attributed to Erikson (Marcia, 1980, 1993). Erikson (1968) proposed an eight-stage developmental theory, which emphasizes the mastery of autonomy and individuation as the central task and views identity formation as a lifelong process. Therefore, this review of identity formation begins with a brief discussion on adolescent development according to Erikson.

Adolescence has been seen as a normal developmental period during which great biological as well as psychological changes take place. According to Erikson (1980) an individual goes through a normative crisis (i.e., a normal phase of increased conflict) during adolescence (identity vs. role confusion), the resolution of which is the formation of "an assured sense of inner continuity and social sameness which will bridge what he was as a child and what he is about to become" (p. 120).

Erikson stated that the end of childhood could be marked by the onset of puberty in combination with the acquisition of a set of skills and tools which aid the adolescent in the establishment of a sense of being and purpose in their world (1968). "Each successive stage and crisis has a special relation to one of the basic elements of society" and is a crucial period of vulnerability and growth (p. 250). He also believed that:

> The adolescent process, however, is conclusively complete only when the individual has subordinated his childhood identifications to a new kind of identification, achieved in absorbing sociability and in competitive apprenticeship with and among his age-mates . . . choices and decisions, with increasing immediacy, lead to a more final self-definition, to irreversible role pattern, and thus to communicate "for life." (1980, p. 119)

The rapid physiological change that young individuals undergo causes an increasing concern as they compare how they appear to others with how they view themselves. In fact, the identity crisis at this stage is the most climactic period in the process of human development, when adolescents face the challenge of understanding themselves and their place in society, coupled with recognizing different identities in different social contexts or groups, such as those based on gender, age, class, and ethnic group.

According to Erikson (1980), identity formation occurs for the most part on an unconscious level, with a conscious element working simultaneously. On an unconscious level, the collective identifications formed in childhood resynthesize with the psychological vicissitudes of the ego. "The sense of ego identity, then, is when the accrued confidence that the inner sameness and continuity prepared in the past are matched by the sameness and continuity of one's meaning for others" (1968, p. 261). The conscious element, on the other hand, is represented on both an internal and external level. Thus, the internal representation of identity is the sum of the roles that the adolescent perceives himself or herself as having in addition to his or her personality traits, while the external representation of identity is how others perceive his or her roles and personality traits.

Another influential contributor to the study of adolescence and psychoanalysis in recent years is Peter Blos (Adelson & Doehrman, 1980). Blos (1975) viewed adolescence "in its totality, as the second individuation process" (p. 157), with the first individuation process having occurred around the end of the third year of life. His theoretical framework is based on Mahler's concept of childhood separation-individuation. Mahler and her associates (1975) posited a process which occurs during the first three years of life, culminating in what was termed "psychological birth," or the first experience of a sense of separate self. The final stage of this developmental process of individuation involves the internalization of the mother object and the establishment of mental representation of the self as separate from objects. According to Blos (1975), adolescence is essentially concerned with relinquishing the parents as love objects and with finding parent substitutes or new love objects in order to form an individuated sense of self. Josselson (1987) states that Blos' concept of successful individuation resembled Erikson's view of identity, but she criticized Blos' requirement that adolescents must replace the parents as important love objects. She asserted that "separation-individuation in adolescence requires a revision of relationships with parents, a revision that nevertheless preserves connection" (Josselson, 1987, p. 19).

According to Josselson (1987), "identity is the stable, consistent and reliable sense of who one is and what one stands for in the world. . . . It is a way of preserving the continuity of the self, of linking the past and the present" (p. 10). Erikson (1980) spoke of identity at the end of adolescence as including all significant identifications of childhood, but superordinate to any single identification, and altering "them in order to make a unique and a reasonably coherent whole of them" (p. 121). Within a psychological, sociological, and anthropological framework, Weinreich (1988) defined a person's identity as "the totality of one's self-construal, in how one construes oneself in the present expresses the continuity between how one construes oneself as one was in the past and how one construes oneself as one aspires to be in the future" (p. 154). Marcia (1980) defined identity as a "self-structure, an internal, self-constructed, dynamic organization of drives, ability, belief, and individual history" (p. 159).

Each of these definitions involves a sense of self that is reasonably coherent and is linked to the past, and from which the individual can move toward the future (Weinreich, 1988). Identity formation "arises from the selective reputation and mutual assimilation of childhood identifications, and their absorption in a new configuration" (Erikson, 1980, p. 122). According to Erikson, it is a lifelong developmental process, which becomes a major developmental task of adolescence. The process is gradual and to a great extent unconscious (Josselson, 1980; Marcia, 1980, 1993). The conscious work of the ego around identity formation is largely reserved for late adolescence, when choice and action matter the most. Unsuccessful identity formation leads to identity diffusion, which is manifested in the inability to make commitments in areas such as a choice of career (Erikson, 1980).

Marcia (1980, 1993) operationalized Erikson's theoretical ideas about identity. He proposed four identity statuses, which reflect the ways in which a late adolescent might deal with the identity development: identity achievement, foreclosure, identity diffusion, and moratorium. Each status is defined by the presence or absence of crisis (a decision-making period) and commitment (the extent of personal investment) with regard to the areas of occupation and ideology. Individuals are categorized into each status according to the following definitions:

- *Identity Achievement:* those individuals who have experienced a decision-making process and are pursuing self-chosen occupation and ideological goals.
- *Foreclosures:* persons who are also committed to occupational ideological position, but these have been parentally chosen rather than self-chosen. They show little or no evidence of "crisis."
- *Identity Diffusion:* young people who have no set occupational or ideological direction, regardless of whether or not they may have experienced a decision-making period.
- *Moratoriums:* those young people who are currently struggling with occupational and/or ideological issues; they are in an identity crisis (Marcia, 1980, p. 161).

This model for identity research has become the dominant one in studies of identity formation (Josselson, 1987). Marcia (1993) reviewed empirical studies conducted on identity formation in adolescence. He divided them into four general areas: individual personality characteristics, patterns of interactions with others, developmental antecedents and consequences, and identity development in women. Studies of women's identity development were reported separately because the same variables had been rarely studied with both males and females, and because the findings were sufficiently different and problematic enough to warrant a separate discussion. Based on this review, he concluded that a new approach was needed for the study of women's identity development, which would go beyond occupational and ideological choices and would account for what appears to be the most important issue for adolescent girls, namely "the establishment and maintenance of interpersonal relationships" (Marcia, 1980, p. 179; 1993).

Early attempts at validating Marcia's model of identity formation with women subjects were unsuccessful (Josselson, 1973, 1987). Although researchers were able to demonstrate that men within each of the identity statuses behaved consistently and differently on independent measures of anxiety, authoritarianism, and cooperation, no such consistency was found for female subjects. As stated above, the focus on decision making related to careers and ideology (politics and religion) did not appear to coincide with what the salient identity-forming issues are for women. As a result, researchers extended the model to include decisions regarding interpersonal relationships, specifically regarding premarital behavior. Using the extended interview instrument with female populations yielded discrete and consistent status categories (Josselson, 1973, 1987).

Josselson (1973) studied 48 college seniors to determine what developmental and psychodynamic factors would influence the path a woman would take through the identity stage. The women were given the extended identity-status interview. Twelve subjects in each identity status were then interviewed by a clinical psychologist using a semistructured format that focused on biographical information, important developmental influences, areas of conflict and their management, history of significant relationships, descriptions of and attitudes toward family members, early memories, dreams, and recurrent fantasies.

Analysis of these interview data resulted in a composite description of the developmental path for women in each of these statuses. Based on these descriptions, Josselson concluded that identity formation and the individuation-separation process, as conceptualized by Mahler et al. (1975), were closely intertwined. Josselson saw Foreclosure women as not having gone through a process of individuation. The closeness of the family was of great importance to them. Identity Achievement women, by definition, have experienced crisis and have made commitments. Unlike Foreclosures, they are capable of seeing their parents as different from themselves. They have chosen ways in which they want to be like their parents and ways in which they want to be different. Moratoriums are psychodynamically more homogeneous than the other identity-status groups. They are straddling between two "major and distinct sets of ego organization, unable to opt for one side or another" (Josselson, 1973, p. 34). In essence, they are unable to commit to remaining a child or to become an adult.

Rosenthal (1987) added that the adolescent's cultural background and cultural development also need to be taken into consideration as contributing factors, such as how knowledgeable the adolescent is about his or her culture and how well his or her cultural traditions, rituals, and belief are supported. Erikson (1968) also suggested that when adolescents form cliques, or "in-groups" and "out-groups," they do so as a defense against identity confusion:

> Adolescents not only help one another temporarily through much discomfort by forming cliques and by stereotyping themselves, their ideals, and their enemies; they also perversely test each other's capacity to pledge fidelity. (p. 262)

Erikson (1980) considered identity formation to neither begin nor end with adolescence. Rather, he proposed that it is a lifelong task in human development: as people change their perceptions of themselves to take on a new role, and as others' perceptions of them change accordingly, identity formation continues throughout adulthood.

Erikson's (1980) psychosocial concept of identity linked the individual with community values, norms, and social roles, all of which are central in the understanding of ethnic and racial identity in a multicultural perspective. Berzoff (1996) stated that Erikson was the first psychoanalyst to articulate the interaction between the person and her or his environment, as he was also the first to consider the influence of culture and society on identity formation.

It is clear that the contributions of Erikson (1963, 1980), Blos (1975), Marcia (1980, 1993), Josselson (1973, 1987), and Weinreich (1988) to the understanding of adolescent development and early adulthood help explain issues of identity, self-image, roles, and relationships. However, ethnic identity also needs further consideration as a significant factor in the development of young adults. The formation of ethnic identity may be thought of as a process similar to ego-identity formation; it takes place over time, as one explores and makes decisions about the role of ethnicity in one's life. Some form of ethnic identification is often included in the models of acculturation (Szapocznik & Kurtines, 1980; Casas & Casas, 1994). The ethnic identity literature will be further discussed in the following sections.

Margaret Mahler and Object Relations

It is documented in the literature that there are psychological aspects to the process of acculturation, although few studies have been conducted in this area. One study conducted by Domenech-Ristorucci (1988) contended that there is a relationship between the degree of acculturation and the process of separation-individuation, as set forth by Mahler and her colleagues (1975). Domenech-Ristorucci discussed the correlation between the emotional separation from the mother country that occurs during acculturation as being akin to the separation from one's biological mother (1989). Mahler's theory of separation and individuation is a theory of psychological birth, which influences the autistic and symbiotic phases and the subsequent subphases of differentiation, practicing, rapprochement, and object constancy. These will be discussed further in the following.

- *Autistic phase* (birth to twelve weeks): The autistic phase is a time when the newborn lacks the capacity to be aware of, much less to relate to, external objects; his or her experience is limited to the maintenance or disruption of physiological homeostasis.
- *Symbiotic phase* (three to four weeks): A physiological maturational crisis occurs in which the infant shows increased sensitivity to external stimulation. This enhanced responsiveness brings with it a dim awareness of the mother as an external object.
- *Differentiation* (four months to ten months): This period is marked by the infant's beginning separation from the symbiotic unity. A growing interest in the world outside of the primary caregiver is stimulated by the abilities to roll, crawl, and eventually stand.
- *Practicing* (ten months to 24 months): This phase coincides with increased locomotion and ever-increasing bodily skills. The baby is now able to move some distance away from his mother, although the mother is still treated as a kind of "home base," to be returned to for what Mahler (1974) called "emotional fueling." The child's interest at this stage spills over from the mother to the inanimate objects of the world. Interest in the mother, and in her continuous availability for refueling, still takes precedence over interest in the world of things.
- *Rapprochement* (usually fifteen to eighteen months): This phase is probably the most complicated of the phases for both caregiver and child. This is the time when the child has opposing needs, between the need to cling and be close as well as the need to be separate and independently exploring the world. During this phase the child realizes that he or she is a very small person in a very big world. This realization brings with it a loss of the previously enjoyed ideal sense of self and the reappearance of a kind of separation anxiety occurs. (Greenberg & Mitchell, 1983, p. 274)

Throughout the separation-individuation process, the infant is constantly adjusting to the newly negotiated boundaries between himself or herself and the mother. To say that someone is truly individuated means that the person is able to maintain the representation of the absent object (mother). The love object will not be rejected or exchanged if it is no longer satisfying, and the love object is longed for and not rejected in its absence (Domenech-Ristorucci, 1988). Similarly, to say that someone is truly acculturated means that through negotiation, the individual has reached a comfortable compromise between differing cultural norms so that the traditional cultural (love object) is not rejected; rather, aspects of it are maintained and internalized even in its absence.

One's mother country and one's biological mother are crucial during acculturation and separation-individuation, respectively. An individual undergoing a process of acculturation is constantly negotiating between cultural norms and values from both the traditional and host cultures in order to attain a cultural identity. An infant undergoing separation-individuation is constantly negotiating developmental pressures in order to attain a sense of separateness and individual identity. In both processes one alters preexisting norms and, during these processes, emotional and psychological separation occur, resulting in a more defined and differentiated identity. Domenech-Ristorucci (1988) pointed out that the similarity between these two processes is not coincidental; rather, acculturation actually re-elicits the issues inherent in the psychological process of separation-individuation.

One's first relationship is with one's mother and is, at best, a very complex relationship. Resolution of the issues of separation-individuation can depend on an infinite number of circumstances, most of which depend on the relative availability of an average expectable environment. Berry's definition of culture indicates that culture is transmitted through members of society (1997). Because an infant's first relationship is with his or her mother, we can say that, just as the mother is critical in the infant's individuation process, she is critical in the process of acculturation because she transmits both psychological and cultural information to the infant. The immigrant mother communicates information to her children about her degree of acculturation as well.

The development of a sense of identity is an underlying factor both in acculturation and in separation-individuation. The relationship can be described in the following manner: A woman is raised on the mainland in a home with first-generation Puerto Rican parents. One can assume a certain degree of traditional cultural norms, but the second-generation Puerto Rican woman is also exposed to American cultural norms. She needs to negotiate this cultural frontier, which is what occurs during the process of acculturation. However, by definition, when an individual undergoes acculturation, a certain differentiation occurs, which implies separations. It appears that the process of acculturation actually elicits one's earlier separation and differentiation experience, which occurred during infancy while undergoing separation-individuation.

During acculturation, a person may struggle with feeling torn between differing cultural expectations. A person may experience conflicts associated with the potential separation process. These re-evoke earlier conflicts from the entire progression through separation-individuation, but highlighted in the rapprochement subphase when a child struggles with his or her desire to both reject and cling to his or her mother.

As one is developing a cultural identity (that is, a bicultural identity) a certain degree of adaptation can be assumed. This process revives developmental issues of late rapprochement and the development of object constancy. A compromise between the two cultural identities might be reached in a bicultural second-generation Puerto Rican woman. Motherland/mother can be internalized and kept constant without there being a constant threat of cultural/psychological loss, as in the solidifying of the process of object constancy.

Acculturation can be viewed as a phenomenon during which psychological processes are re-elicited and reworked to a certain degree. Acculturation then involves psychological separation, not unlike other situations in life in which separation is involved.

Review of the Contemporary Literature

Ethnic Identity Literature

Having explored the foundation of traditional psychoanalytic theory relevant to identity formation, it is equally important to lay a similar foundation of contemporary theory around the concepts of race, ethnicity, and cultural identity and how they relate to Puerto Rican women. The concept of race is often the first term used to discuss and define ethnicity; the two terms are often interchangeable in the literature (Bentacourt & Lopez, 1993). The term *race* is used to imply a set of physical or psychological characteristics that distinguishes group members (Bentacourt & Lopez, 1993). Race as a biological, genetic entity has not found extensive scientific support. Skin color, perhaps the first feature to be associated with race, exists along a continuum and shows great variability within and between "races." In the United States, phenotype has not historically been used to distinguish racial groups but rather descent, as indicated, for example, by the one-drop rule for individuals of African ancestry (Beutler, Brown, Crothers, Booker, & Seabrook, 1996). The legacy of race has achieved institutionalized status and continues to be reinforced by such institutions in the use of the preferred term *ethnicity*. The U.S. government, as well as psychological researchers, often requires individuals to select from a confusing set of options that define race, ethnicity, and national origin, including the categories of Caucasian, European American, African American, Hispanic, Latino, Asian/Asian American, and Native American (Beutler et al., 1996). The category Hispanic (inclusive of ancestry from Mexico, Central America, South America, Spanish-speaking countries of the Caribbean, and the U.S. territory of Puerto Rico) includes national origin from all countries having Colonial Spanish historical influence, but is not applicable in affirmative-action policies aimed to benefit Spaniards, the original Hispanics (Beutler et al., 1996). Despite its institutionalization, the term *race* seems to have undergone a paradigmatic shift within the social sciences toward *ethnicity*, a term that is indicative of cultural and socialization processes, rather than mere biology.

One issue of debate within the psychological literature concerns whether race and ethnicity are separable constructs. Helms and Talleyrand (1997) proposed that the terms *race* and *ethnicity* be treated as separate constructs, maintaining that individuals are treated by society based on their biological characteristics. Phenotypic characteristics such as skin color and facial features are fixed and immediately observable, whereas many ethnic and cultural characteristics (such as values, language, and clothing) are mutable and are therefore not taken into account. This distinction results in positive or negative treatment by society, as seen in racial socialization, that is virtually independent of the actual ethnic culture in which an individual is socialized (Helms & Talleyrand, 1997).

To denote race as a construct of socialization, Helms (1997) advocated the use of the terms *socio-race,* to signify the processes of racial socialization at the interpersonal or societal level, and *psycho-race,* to represent "intrapsychic dynamics assumed to result from racial socialization" at the level of the individual. The implication is that the term *ethnicity* should be used and measured when referring to cultural characteristics and that the terms *socio-race* or *psycho-race* be used when speaking of the process and psychological impact of racial socialization on individuals.

By contrast, Phinney (1996) and Alvidrez, Miranda, and Azocar (1996) offered definitions and conceptualizations of "ethnicity" which subsume the concept of race. In addition, the authors sought to promote knowledge about the way in which psychological processes are influenced by ethnic factors. Obtaining this knowledge serves to establish relations between particular ethnic variables and psychological outcomes, enabling practitioners to begin to make predictions about how cultural competence might be optimized with particular individuals.

Acknowledging numerous aspects of ethnicity, Phinney (1996) proposed three primary aspects believed to account for its psychological importance: ethnicity as minority status, ethnicity as culture, and ethnicity as identity. Ethnicity as minority status carries with it two principal implications. First, minority status denotes less power and is often accompanied by prejudice and discrimination, which have long been implicated as influences in personality formation (Gaines & Reed, 1995). Second, ethnicity may correspond to racial stereotypes that not only influence the way other people view ethnic group members, but can also become internalized within ethnic individuals themselves. Phinney (1996) summarized that the psychological influence of minority status will vary along several dimensions, including history of the ethnic-group society, current status in society, and individual experiences with prejudice, as well as a person's response to stereotypes and discriminations.

Ethnicity as identity involves the strength of identification with an individual's ethnic group. More specifically, ethnic identity denotes the "enduring fundamental aspect of the self that includes a sense of membership in an ethnic group and the attitudes and feelings associated with that membership" (Phinney, 1990). The concept of ethnic identity is viewed as a developmental process made up of many components: self-labeling, sense of belonging, positive evaluation of ethnic group, preference for group, ethnic interest and knowledge, and involvement in activities associated with the group (Phinney, 1990). In the delineation of what defines culture, Guarnaccia and Rodriguez (1996) also included "culture as ethnic identity," although their conceptualization of ethnic identity was restricted to self-identification.

Ethnicity as culture refers to the cultural characteristics of a group, such as typical norms, values, attitudes, and behaviors, which are specific to a common culture and are transmitted across generations. This aspect of ethnicity nicely subsumes the remaining components of the definition of culture offered by Guarnaccia and Rodriguez (1996), including language, events, celebrations, material signs, shared values, and views of mental illness. Phinney (1996) described a common approach found in both anthropology and cross-cultural psychology that attempts to identify specific cultural variables that distinguish ethnic groups by "peeling off layers of culture." The implication is that if culturally specific attributes/characteristics/values are measured and linked to particular psychological outcomes, culturally competent guidelines and practices for specific ethnic groups can be facilitated (Guarnaccia & Rodriguez, 1996).

Alvidrez et al. (1996) also addressed the issue of identifying the pathways from ethnicity to outcome. Five important variables were delineated which may serve in interpreting and explaining ethnic differences: minority status, socioeconomic status, acculturation, immigration history, and cultural factors. Compared to Phinney's tripartite definition of ethnicity, Alvidrez et al. did not explicitly state that the above variable actually defined ethnicity. However, the overlap is apparent between their concepts of minority status and cultural factors and Phinney's concepts of ethnicity as minority status and ethnicity as culture, respectively.

In conceptualizing and defining ethnicity, both Phinney and Alvidrez et al. offered at least one important piece that the other omitted in attempting to explain the pathway from ethnicity to psychological outcome. Helms and Talleyrand (1997) emphasized the conceptualization of race as a social construction that impacts the individual through the process of racial socialization and that should be distinguished from ethnic/cultural socialization. Consequently, these processes and, consequently, race and ethnicity seem to be inherently intertwined and reciprocal, especially for those individuals who experience both forms of socialization simultaneously.

Models of Ethnic Identity

The study of ethnic identity brings the concept of ethnicity from a nomothetic to an ideographic level by emphasizing the way individuals understand their own ethnicity. In the broadest sense, one's ethnic identity denotes attitudes about one's ethnicity. However, similar to the concepts of ethnicity and race, there are varied definitions and conceptualizations of ethnic identity, and, in fact, research on ethnic identity often fails to explicitly define the term (Phinney, 1996).

Several models of ethnic-identity development have been offered, including the social cognitive model (Knight, Bernal, Garza, & Cota, 1993), the crisis and resolution model (Ruiz, 1990), and the three-stage model (Phinney, 1989, 1990, 1996). Phinney (1990) and Casas and Pytluk (1995) reviewed the ethnic-identity literature and identified theoretical contributions from social-identity theory, social-learning theory, cognitive-developmental theory, and ego-identity models. Social-identity theory contributes to the models of ethnic identity at the most basic level. The theory asserts that people need a strong sense of identification with a group in order to develop a sense of well-being. Individuals of the minority group may potentially develop a negative social identity and seek to improve their status in various ways (Phinney, 1990). A relationship between ethnic identity and self-esteem has been documented in the literature (Phinney, 1991; Phinney, Cantu, & Kurtz, 1997; Phinney, Chavira, & Williamson, 1992; Phinney & Devich-Navarro, 1997).

Social-Cognitive Model of Ethnic Identity

The social-cognitive model (Knight et al., 1993) has theoretical underpinnings of social-learning and cognitive-developmental theories. This model is unique in that it takes into account two parallel but related processes in ethnic-identity formation: enculturation and acculturation. Enculturation is defined as the psychological process of ethnic-identity development in individuals. More specifically, it is defined as a dynamic and continuously developing socialization process wherein individuals learn via observation or specific instruction the numerous "cultural and psychological qualities" that are essential for functioning as a member of a particular group (Berry, 1997; Casas & Pytluk, 1995). By contrast, acculturation represents the process of socialization into an ethnic group other than one's own, while being influenced by the various factors involved in enculturation (Casas & Pytluk, 1995). The social-cognitive model seems to view the process of acculturation (racial socialization) and enculturation (ethnic socialization) as partners in the development of ethnic identity in the same way that Phinney (1996) viewed minority status and culture as components of ethnicity.

The social-cognitive model (Knight et al., 1993) promotes three clusters of variables that form ethnic identity in a complex interaction. The socialization content affects the developing self-concept, which determines behavior based on socialization values. The fifth level, cognitive development, which dictates the individual's ability to understand and incorporate social information gleaned from enculturation and acculturative experiences, restricts the four variables.

Bernal et al. (1993) provided a more explicit description of this developmental process in children. The process begins with children's acquisition of information about their ethnicity and group membership based on learning experiences within their social world of family, school, friends, community, and the dominant society. As children mature cognitively, they accumulate information and are able to integrate increasingly more complex social experiences related to their ethnicity. Social comparisons and awareness of society's often stereotypic attitudes toward their ethnic group are generally inevitable and may potentially affect self-descriptions and self-evaluations of competencies in life domains such as social development and academic or other achievements. A Hispanic child might initially adopt the Hispanic values taught by his family and community including, for example, familismo, respeto, cultural fatalism, religiosity, and the importance of connecting physical and emotional well-being. With increasing cognitive ability, this child may begin to assimilate the negative and stereotypic information provided by the dominant society with respect to his or her ethnic group. This process creates internal conflict for a child who is beginning to "own" his Hispanic ethnic identity and may potentially influence psychological well-being (Casas & Pytluk, 1995).

Bernal and his colleagues (1993) also offered three components of ethnic identity that are reflective of "stages" in the developmental process: self-identification (self-categorization), ethnic constancy (permanency of ethnic characteristics), and ethnic knowledge, including an understanding of relevant ethnic, cultural behaviors, values, feelings, and preferences surrounding one's ethnicity.

Crisis-and-Resolution Model of Ethnic Identity

The final two theories of ethnic identity formation, Ruiz's (1990) crisis-and-resolution model and Phinney's (1989, 1990, 1996) three-stage model have theoretical roots in ego-identity development. As summarized by Cuellar, Nyberg, and Maldonado (1997), ethnic identity is a component of the larger process of identity development and involves decision making with respect to the values, beliefs, and goals composing one's self-definition. The crisis-and-resolution model holds three premises at its foundation:

A. "The pressure to assimilate (adopt behaviors and values of the majority culture) can be psychologically stressful;
B. "Marginality (absence of feelings of belonging to any group) correlates with psychological maladjustment;
C. "Ethnic pride in one's ethnic identity is related to greater freedom of choice in the acculturation process." (Cuellar, Nyberg, & Maldonado, 1997, p. 127)

There are also five stages of ethnic-identity development in the crisis-and-resolution model, which focuses on ethnic-identity conflict, interventions, and resolutions. The first stage, the casual period, involves receiving messages from all individuals in a person's environment that either affirm or denigrate the family's ethnicity. The cognitive stage implicates faulty beliefs about ethnicity, including the association between ethnic-group membership and poverty/prejudice, as well as the belief that assimilation is the only way to achieve success. These first two stages relate to the initial assumptions in that they are likely to incite some level of psychological stress. The consequence stage is a period of ethnic identity "fragmentation" in which ethnic identity "conflicts" intensify, leading to the avoidance of ethnic self-image. This, presumably, results in marginality and intensified psychological distress, the foundation defined as Premise A. The working-through stage is brought about by a realization that an ethnic identity apart from one's true ethnicity is not a viable option and must be resolved by a "reclaiming" of the fragments of one's ethnicity, leading to the improved psychological well-being implied in Premise B. The successful resolution denotes greater self-acceptance, self-esteem, and recognition of ethnicity as a positive resource. Ethnic pride results in greater freedom of choice (Premise C), allowing for the development of a satisfying identity that is congruent with all parts of self (Ruiz, 1990).

The crisis-and-resolution model (Ruiz, 1990) was developed based on clinical practice with Hispanic clients to describe the process of development, transformation, and resolution of ethnic-identity conflicts. Casas and Pytluk (1995) speculated that at the casual stage, immigrant Hispanic families may "pressure" the adoption of Hispanic cultural values in their children, who are more rapidly undergoing the acculturation process and are exposed to the negative ethnic associations characteristic of the cognitive stage. Simultaneous pressure from traditional parents and dominant society may result in conflict between parent and child in the midst of the already difficult consequence stage, in which the Hispanic individual is experiencing a fragmentation of his or her ethnic identity. The working-through stage is characterized as common in Hispanic clients who present for counseling (Casas & Pytluk, 1995).

Three-Stage Model of Ethnic Identity

In developing her three-stage model, Phinney viewed ethnic-identity development as a dynamic process achieved over a period of time, requiring extensive self-examination and decision making similar to ego-identity development (1989). Consequently, a developmental theory of ethnic identity was proposed by Phinney (1989) in which ethnic-identity formation follows a process similar to that proposed by Erikson (1980) and Marcia's (1980) theory of ego-identity formation. Adolescents and adults who have not been exposed to ethnic-identity issues characterize the first stage, unexamined ethnic identity. During this stage, adolescents show a lack of interest in issues of ethnicity (similar to Marcia's "diffuse" identity), adopt a premature preference for the dominant culture, or remain tied to ethnic attitudes of parents without consideration of ethnic issues. This process is similar to the "moratorium" process that Marcia discussed, during which individuals immerse themselves in their own cultural practices (1980). The second stage involves the ethnic-identity search (similar to moratorium) during which individuals immerse themselves in their own cultural practices. They emerge in the third stage, having achieved ethnic identity, with a deeper understanding of and confidence in their ethnicity.

The components of ethnic identity most widely studied in the literature were also identified for inclusion in this model: self-identification, sense of belonging, attitudes toward one's ethnic group, and ethnic involvement (Phinney, 1990). Self-identification refers to the ethnic label individuals choose for themselves, a concept especially important for individuals of mixed-ethnic heritage. Understanding which parts of their heritage are acknowledged is relevant to a complete understanding of their ethnic identity. Although a difficult concept to operationalize, an individual's sense of belonging to the self-identified group is also important in a comprehensive understanding of ethnic identity. A positive or negative attitude toward one's ethnic group may be viewed as acceptance or rejection of one's ethnic identity, respectively. Finally, involvements in cultural and social practices of the identified ethnic group are the most common measures of ethnic identity. Indicators include language usage and preference, friendships, structured ethnic social groups, religious affiliation and practice, cultural traditions and activities, and political ideology and participation (Phinney, 1990).

Each of the three models of ethnic identity (social-cognitive, crisis-resolution, and three-stage) makes a unique contribution to a more complete understanding of the process of ethnic-identity formation. For example, the social-cognitive model asserts that the process of ethnic-identity formation involves enculturation, but also cannot be separated from the process of acculturation. This model acknowledges the conflict between ownership of Hispanic ethnic values and negative messages about Hispanic ethnicity received from the dominant society. In addition, the model is congruent with cognitive-developmental theory by maintaining that ethnic-identity formation is restricted by cognitive limitations within the maturational process. The crisis-resolution model provides an explicit set of testable premises as well as specific stages characterized by potentially measurable attitudinal and behavioral indicators. The first stage of the three-stage model allows for the existence of several possible paths to achieved ethnic identity and for the possibility that some individuals may proceed through the process without a great deal of conflict.

Conclusion

Despite the valuable insights in each model of ethnic-identity development, the theoretical models of the process of ethnic identity seem somewhat simplistic and overgeneralized. Certain questions arise pertaining to the universality of the models. What are the ethnic and racial socialization factors of the social-cognitive model that influence the developing self-concept and resulting behaviors? Does everyone reach achieved ethnic identity as described in the three-stage model only by immersion in cultural practice? To find empirical answers to these questions, ethnic identity must be further quantified and measured. However, while scholars debate these points, practitioners will use these models of stages of development as indicators for coping and adaptation. Workers need knowledge for use, and these stage frameworks help focus the assessment and intervention processes, providing clarification, insight, and support.

References

Adelson, J., & Doehrman, M. J. (1980). The psychodynamic approach to adolescence. In J. Adelson (Ed.), *Handbook of adolescent psychology* (pp. 99–116). New York: John Wiley.

Alvidrez, J., Miranda, J., & Azocar, F. (1996). Demystifying the concept of ethnicity for psychotherapy researchers. *Journal of Consulting and Clinical Psychology, 64*(5), 903–908.

Bentacourt, H., & Lopez, S. R. (1993). The study of culture, ethnicity, and race in American psychology. *American Psychologist, 48*(6), 629–637.

Bernal, M. E., Knight, G. P., Ocampo, K. A., Garza, C. A., & Cota, M. K. (1993). Development of Mexican American identity. In M. E. Bernal & G. P. Knight (Eds.), *Ethnic identity: Formation and transmission among Hispanics and other minorities.* Albany: State University of New York Press.

Berry, J. W. (1997). Immigration, acculturation, adaptation. *Applied Psychology: An International Review, 46*(1), 5–34.

Berzoff, J. (1996). Psychosocial ego development: The theory of Erik Erikson (pp. 103–126). In J. Berzoff, L. M. Flanagan, & Hertz, P. (Eds.), *Inside out and outside in.* New Jersey: Jason Aronson Inc.

Beutler, L. E., Brown, M. T., Crothers, L., Booker, K., & Seabrook, M. K. (1996). The dilemma of factitious demographic distinctions in psychological research. *Journal of Counseling and Clinical Psychology, 64,* 892–902.

Blos, P. (1975). The second individuation process of adolescence. In A. H. Esman (Ed.), *The psychology of adolescence* (pp. 156–176). New York: International Universities Press.

Casas, J. M., & Pytluk, S. D. (1995). Hispanic identity development. In J. G. Ponterro, J. M. Casas, L. A. Suzuki, & C. M. Alexandre (Eds.), *Handbook of multicultural counseling.* Thousand Oaks, CA: Sage Publications.

Cuellar, I., Nyberg, B., Maldonado, R. E., & Roberts, R. E. (1997). Ethnic identity and acculturation in young adult Mexican-origin population. *Journal of Community Psychology, 25*(6), 535–549.

Domenech-Ristorucci, D. D. (1988). Relationship between separation-individuation and aspects of acculturation in second-generation Puerto Rican women. *Dissertation Abstracts International, 50,* 2149B.

Erikson, E. H. (1968). *Identity, youth and crisis.* New York: W.W. Norton.

Erikson, E. H. (1980). *Identity and the life cycle.* New York: W.W. Norton.

Gaines, S., Jr., & Reed, E. (1995). Prejudice from Allport to DuBois. *American Psychologist, 50,* 96–103.

Garcia-Preto, N. (1998). Latinas in the United States: Bridging two worlds. In M. McGoldrick (Ed.), *Revisioning family therapy* (pp. 330–44).

Greenberg, J., & Mitchell, (1983). Margaret Mahler. *Object relations in psychoanalytic theory* (pp. 270–303). Cambridge, MA: Harvard University Press, 1983.

Guarnaccia, P. J., & Rodriguez, O. (1996). Concepts of culture and their role in the development of culturally competent mental health services. *Hispanic Journal of Behavioral Sciences, 18*(4), 419–443.

Helms; J. (1990). An overview of Black racial identity. In J. Helms (Ed.), *Black and white racial identity: Theory, research, and practice* (pp. 9–32). Westport, CT: Greenwood Press.

Helms, J. E., & Talleyrand, R. M. (1997). Race is not ethnicity. *American Psychologist, 52,* 1246–1247.

Josselson, R. (1973). Psychodynamic aspects of identity formation in college women. *Journal of Youth and adolescence, 2*(1), 3–52.

Josselson, R. (1987). *Finding herself: Pathways to identity development in women.* San Francisco: Jossey-Bass.

Knight, G. P., Bernal, M. E., Garza, C. A., & Cota, M. K. (1993). A social cognitive model of the development of ethnic identity and ethnically based behaviors. In M. E. Bernal & G. P. Knight (Eds.), *Ethnicity identity: Formation and transmission among Hispanics and other minorities.* Albany: State University of New York Press.

Mahler, M. S., Pine, F., & Berman, S. (1975). *The psychological birth of the human infant.* New York: Basic Books.

Marcia, J. E. (1980). Identity in adolescence. In J. Adelson (Ed.), *Handbook of adolescent psychology* (pp. 159–187). New York: Widely.

Marcia, J. E., Matteson, D. R., Orlofsky, J. L., Waterman, A. S., & Archer, S. L. (1993). *Ego identity.* New York: Springer-Verlag.

Phinney, J. S. (1989). Stages of ethnic identity in minority group adolescents. *Journal of Early Adolescence, 9,* 34–49.

Phinney, J. S. (1991). Ethnic identity and self esteem: A review and integration. *Hispanic Journal of Behavioral Sciences, 13*(2), 193–208.

Phinney, J. S. (1990). Ethnic identity in adolescents and adults: A review of research. *Psychological Bulletin, 100*(3), 499–514.

Phinney, J. S. (1991). Ethnic identity and self-esteem: A review and integration. *Hispanic Journal of Behavioral Sciences, 23*(2), 193–208.

Phinney, J. S. (1992). The multigroup Ethnic Identity Measure: A new scale for use with diverse groups. *Journal of Adolescence Research, 7*(2), 156–176.

Phinney, J. S. (1996). Understanding ethnic diversity: The role of ethnic identity. *American Behavioral Scientist, 42*(2), 143–152.

Phinney, J. S., Cantu, C. L., & Kurtz, D. A. (1997). Ethnic and American identity as predictors of self-esteem among African American, Latino, and White adolescents. *Journal of Youth and Adolescence, 9*, 34–49.

Phinney, J. S., Chavira, V., & Williamson, L. (1992). Acculturation attitudes and self-esteem among high school and college students. *Youth & Society, 23*(3), 299–312.

Phinney, J. S., & Devich-Navarro, M. (1997). Variations in bicultural identification among African American and Mexican American adolescents. *Journal of Research on Adolescence, 7*(1), 3–32.

Rosenthal, D. A. (1987). Ethnic identity development in adolescents. In J. S. Phinney & M. J. Rotheran (Eds.), *Children's ethnic socialization: Pluralism and development* (pp. 156–179). Newbury Park, CA: Sage Publications.

Ruiz, A. S. (1990). Ethnic identity: Crisis and resolution. *Journal of Multicultural Counseling and Development, 18*, 29–40.

Steele, C. M., & Aronson, J. (1995). Stereotypes threat and the intellectual test performance of African Americans. *Journal of Personality and Social Psychology 69*(5): 797–811.

U.S. Census Bureau. (2000). *The Hispanic population in the United States.* U.S. Department of Commerce.

Weinreich, P. (1988). The operationalization of ethnic identity. In J. W. Berry & R. C. Annis (Eds.), *Ethnic psychology: Research and practice with immigrants, refugees, native peoples, ethnic groups, and sojourners* (pp. 149–168). Berwyn, PA: Swets North American.

Zavala-Martines, I. (1994). Quien soy? Who am I? Identity issues for Puerto Rican adolescents. In E. Salett & D. Koslow (Eds.), *Race ethnicity and self* (pp. 89–116). Washington: NMCI Publications.

4

Dynamics of Oppression and Discrimination

George A. Appleby

Oppression will be analyzed as a by-product of socially constructed notions of power, privilege, control, and hierarchies of difference. Each notion is explicit in the institutional arrangements of racism, sexism, ethnocentrism, ableism, heterocentrism, classism, xenophobia, and religious bigotry. Oppression will be defined and its common elements of institutional power, economic control, violence and invisibility, and distortion will be discussed. Diversity will be analyzed from the perspective of assimilation, melting pot, and multicultural theories. Stigma and stigma management will be discussed as the result of discrimination based on social stratification, prejudice, and stereotyping of social constructed characteristics such as race, ethnicity, gender, and social class.

This discussion will become the foundation for our investigation of social psychological theories related to individual and group identity development, which, in turn, will help to explain the differences in individual and group attitudes, values, and behaviors. Identity development will help clarify variations in intergroup mobility, resiliency, and conflict, as well as bridge our understanding of such core ideas as hierarchies of oppression, oppressed and oppressor roles, internalized oppression, resistance to oppression, and, finally, multiple oppressions.

These ideas will be integrated into the person-in-environment (PIE) system presented throughout the text. Specifically, some of the macro, or sociological/anthropological, processes will help you formulate an appropriate assessment based on Factor II (Environmental Problems), while the micro, or social psychological, processes will add to assessment skills related to Factor I (Problems in Social Role Functioning).

Oppression and Power

A primary construction in Western cultural thought is the belief that the superior should control the inferior. Western religious and philosophical thought is the ideological basis of all forms of oppression in the United States. Interactions based on differential power can be characterized by dominance-subordination or inequality and can be affected by a variety of statuses and roles assigned by society.

Pellegrini (1992) in her study of gender inequality points out that oppression is all about power: the power to enforce a particular worldview; the power to deny equal access to housing, employment opportunities, and health care; the power alternately to define and/or to efface difference; the power to maim, physically, mentally, and emotionally; and, most importantly, the power to set the very terms of power. Racism, classism, sexism, ableism, and heterosexism together form a system of institutionalized domination. Being oppressed means the absence of choices. Power thus defines the initial point of contact between the oppressed and the oppressor.

Pharr (1988) broadens the analysis of oppression, focusing specifically on lesbian, gay, and bisexual people by pointing out that homophobia is a weapon of sexism. She suggests that the following are elements of all oppression: the imposition of normative behavior supported by institutional and economic power; disincentives for nonconforming, including the threat and use of violence for those who do not conform; social definition as "other"; invisibility of the "outsiders"; distortion and stereotyping; blaming the victim; internalized oppression; and the isolation or assimilation with tokenism of the "outsider." Most gay and lesbian scholars who view power and oppression from a social psychological or sociopolitical framework reference each of these elements of oppression (DeCecco & Shively, 1984; D'Emilio, 1983; Herek & Berrill, 1992; Humphries, 1972).

The discussion of power and oppression reminds the practitioner that social institutions have been developed by the dominant group to meet its needs and to maintain its power. When assessing the problems related to the six environmental systems, the worker must not assume that the client's access and use of these systems is consistent with his or her needs or appreciative of his or her strengths or barriers. As an example, when assessing Economic/Basic Needs System, ethnic foods may be unavailable in the local market or more costly than a client's budget allows. The lack of availability of ethnic food may be a barrier to maintaining ethnic practices, such as religious traditions, which may in turn be interpreted as not following one's parental/family duty. The client may experience this socially as isolation or psychologically as shame and alienation. There may be few multifamily homes in the area close to a client's employment, thus making it difficult to maintain a connection with his extended family and arrive at his job on time. The market owner or the employer may discriminate against the client in either scenario because he or she is viewed as less valued and not deserving of consideration or accommodation.

While oppression based on race, or ethnicity, or class, or gender, or age, or sexual orientation, or other social factors is each unique, all groups share life experiences with other oppressed people, in that power or the lack thereof is central to their social reality. Access to power and the individual's place within the social hierarchy of rank and authority are contingent upon the above social factors.

The converse of power, powerlessness, is the inability to exert such influence. Cyrus (1997, pp. 156–159) suggests that people who have power under any system find it beneficial to retain that system and to maintain the status quo. The interests and needs of the less powerful groups are not relevant to their goals. In any system, social arrangements operate to marginalize—that is, to confine to the edges of society—and subordinate the less powerful. This is often accomplished by stereotyping. Others project a set of assumptions and beliefs about the physical, behavioral, and psychological characteristics onto these groups. While stereotypes are a convenient filter and may seem harmless, it is hardly a benign process and provides the basis for prejudice. When prejudice is acted on, it is defined as discrimination, behavior that disadvantages one group in relation to another group and maintains and perpetuates conditions of inequality. "Discrimination includes those policies, procedures, decisions, habits, and acts that overlook, ignore, or subjugate members of certain groups or that enable one group of people to maintain control over another group. . . . Such discrimination creates obstacles and barriers for its targets and provides unfair privileges for its beneficiaries" (p. 159).

New immigrants and Native Americans often find that public schools lack culturally relevant education that supports their community and family norms. Religious holidays are not recognized or taboo subjects are discussed without family consideration.

Powerlessness is painful, and people defend against feeling powerless by doing whatever is necessary to bring them a sense of power. The stereotype of overly aggressive, cynical verbal behavior, commonly associated with many minorities, is an example of trying to redefine the interaction between people with unequal power. It both mocks and rejects the norms of the more powerful and serves to render them outsiders.

Basch (1975, p. 513) states, "The feeling of controlling one's destiny to some reasonable extent is the essential psychological component of all aspects of life." A sense of power is critical to one's mental health. Power is manifest in the individual's sense of mastery or competence. Coping with submission to power is the earliest formative experience, be it in the family, in the group, or in the adaptation to social roles. John Hodge (1975) stresses that the family in our society, both traditionally and legally, reflects the dualist values of hierarchy and coercive authoritarian control, which are exemplified in the parent-child and husband-wife relationships. As hooks (1984, p. 36) notes:

> It is in this form of the family where most children first learn the meaning and practice of hierarchical, authoritarian rule. Here is where they learn to accept group oppression against themselves as non-adults, and where they learn to accept male supremacy and the group oppression of women. Here is where they learn that it is the male's role to work in the community and control the economic life of the family and to mete out the physical and financial punishments and rewards, and the female's role to provide the emotional warmth associated with motherhood while under the economic rule of the male. Here is where the relationship of superordination subordination, of superior-inferior, or master-slave is first learned and accepted as "natural."

Power and privilege relationships are played out within a complex web of gender role expectation, performance, and violation. The dynamics of sexism provide valuable insights into our understanding of the power relationships implicit in heterosexism. In her text, *Feminist Theory: From the Margin to the Center,* bell hooks (1984) notes that unlike other forms of oppression, most people witness and/or experience the practice of sexist domination (a primary oppression) in family settings. We tend to witness and/or experience racism, ableism, or classism as we encounter the larger society, the world outside home. Heterosexism and negative religious attitudes, however, like sexism, are often first experienced within the home. Sexism is then defined as the subordination of an individual woman or group of women and the assumption of the superiority of an individual man or group of men based solely on sex.

Sexual Oppression

In our society, sexist oppression perverts and distorts the positive function of family. Family exists as a space wherein we are socialized from birth to accept and support forms of oppression. In his discussion of the cultural basis of domination, John Hodge emphasizes the role of the family: "The traditional western family, with its authoritarian male rule and its authoritarian adult rule, is the major training ground which initially conditions us to accept group oppression as the natural order" (hooks, 1984, p. 36). Power struggles, coercive authoritarian rule, and even brutal assertion of domination may shape family life for many so that it is often the setting of intense suffering and pain. According to Hodge (1975), the domination usually present within the family—of children by adults, and female by male—are forms of group oppression that are easily translated into the "rightful" group oppression of other people defined by "race" (racism), by nationality (colonialism), by "religion," or by "other means" [sexual orientation (homophobia and heterosexism)]. Thus, politically, the white supremacist, patriarchal state relies on the family to indoctrinate its members with values supportive of hierarchical control and coercive authority. However, it is still important to affirm the primacy of family life because family ties are the only sustained support system for so many exploited and oppressed people. Practice designed to rid family life of the abusive dimension created by sexist and/or heterosexist oppression without devaluing it should be a goal of interpersonal or clinical social work intervention.

Herek (1990) argues that ideologies related to sexuality and gender hold this system of hierarchical roles together. The ideology of gender, a system of beliefs, values, and customs concerning masculinity and femininity, is the context in which the individual defines his or her gender identity:

> For a little girl there are now dolls to play with and take care of, pretty clothes to try on, shiny black patent-leather shoes, and as a special reward she may help mommy with housework and stir the batter in the big white bowl. No one ever really tells her to be "domestic" or "esthetic" or "maternal" but she's learning. A little boy, meanwhile, is learning other things. Balls and bats have miraculously appeared to play with, realistic toy pistols, and trains, blocks, and marbles. The shoes he finds in his closet are sturdy enough to take a lot of wear, and just right for running. One day there is an old tire hanging by a rope from a tree in the back yard, just right for swinging. No one ever tells him to be "active" or "aggressive" or "competitive" but somehow, he's learning. (Blumenfeld & Raymond, 1993, p. 23)

This gender ideology is a socially constructed and learned process wherein many meanings are attached to the self as male or female. Heterosexuality is equated with "normal" masculinity and "normal" femininity, whereas homosexuality is equated with violating norms of gender (Herek, 1992, pp. 89–104). Acceptable sexual roles and desires are gender- and sexually prescribed, while role violations are stigmatized as deviant, abnormal, inherently sick, or dangerous. This can be seen in extremist and violent reactions to gay men who violate gender role expectations or who reject by default their "god-given" male privilege. In the recent past there have been a significant number of brutal murders of lesbians, African American men, and gay white men, which received national attention. Confusion is sometimes increased with the gender role nonconformity of growing numbers of straight men and women as well as with the greater visibility of norm-violating lesbians, gay men, and bisexuals.

This dynamic has all the ingredients of violence, too often experienced by minorities who are visible. Greater visibility appears to be interpreted as a challenge to white, heterosexual male privilege. Even in the absence of violence, these attitudes and prescriptive beliefs affect all minorities who must then process this hostility in developing their own identities, fashion their own responses to gender roles or social expectation, and navigate in a world of blatant discrimination. Discrimination, in terms of access to and respectful service by the health, safety, and social services, has been a concern of minority advocates in recent years. Health and human service professionals, who know little of the family and religious norms of an ethnic group or their cultural traditions dealing with health problems or psychological stress, are not prepared to intervene effectively. When they see no need to understand and modify procedures accordingly, they maintain the status quo, the hierarchy of difference, and do psychological violence to the integrity of the ethnic client.

Gender role conformity and nonconformity must also be evaluated within the context of different cultural expectations. What constitutes appropriate male or female role behavior is not always the same within or across cultures. Cultural cues may be sufficiently different so as to result in a misinterpretation of behaviors, especially related to gender role performance. These cues may be misinterpreted and labeled as deviant (lesbian/gay), as when diverse and culturally defined gender roles of macho men, androgynous men and women, passive men, and assertive women come in contact with dominant stereotypes. These diverse gender roles will be discussed in more detail in Chapter 10.

Rubin (1984, pp. 280–281) observes that acceptable sexuality should be heterosexual, marital, monogamous, reproductive, and noncommercial. It should be coupled, relational, within the same generation, and occur at home. It should not involve pornography, fetish objects, sex toys, or roles other than male and female. Gay and lesbian sexuality overtly and heterosexuality covertly violate many of these rules.

In any discussion of institutional oppression, the interrelatedness of power, gender role socialization, family, and religion must be recognized. Religion is a system of beliefs, values, and customs that forms the basis for group members' shared perception of social reality. It involves a worldview that is shared by its members, such as valuing patriarchy—male privilege, with its system of roles, relationships, and approved behaviors. One major function of religion is to support the social order. While the family teaches us the preferred gender roles along with the expected behaviors, religion teaches us to value these roles as good, necessary, appropriate, and legitimate. These religious and cultural lessons are well learned and serve as the foundation for much of sexism and homophobia.

Racial Oppression

Gender roles and sexism have been seen as social constructs, a classification based on social values. This is also true of race and racism, which are not simply black and white issues. Racism is the subordination of any person or group because of skin color or other distinctive physical characteristics. Racism, like sexism, is reflected in both individual and institutional acts, decisions, habits, procedures, and policies that neglect, overlook, exploit, subjugate, or maintain the subordination of the individual or the group. At some point in time, many different peoples have been considered racial groups and each subjected to racist treatment: the Irish, Jews, Italians, Poles, Latinos, Native Americans, Asian Americans, and African Americans. The hierarchy of difference and the social processes identified with sexism are in operation in the development and maintenance of racism. It is important that each client is asked about racism from the standpoint of his or her experience. Workers may be surprised at the distinctions groups make that may or may not be racist but may be barriers to their access and use of environmental systems. While overt racism has been the focus of social policy for some time, institutional racism, residual racial inequities that survive as indirect institutional subordination, has been given increased attention in recent years. This type of racism is the process of making decisions based on skill level, residential location, income, or education, all factors that are considered racially neutral. These outcomes appear to be the result of barriers set by both racism and classism, which may result in continued inequities associated with race alone.

Discrimination

The experience of discrimination often includes harassment, violence, and the social tendency to blame the victim for somehow being responsible for what is done to him or her.

It is necessary in the PIE assessment to look not only for evidence of system problems but also for the severity and duration of this and other problems. Blatant discrimination in one area, such as employment, over a long period of time, may become a major factor if combined with mild and periodic discrimination by landlords, teachers, lawyers, and doctors, over the short run. This cumulative experience with discrimination may spill over and manifest in a psychological hurtful relationship in the Affectional Support System or in an over-the-top, angry response when talking with a child's teacher.

Cyrus (1997) notes that power and privilege are unevenly distributed, and members of the dominant group tend to use their power to confirm and maintain the legitimacy of their privilege and to enforce the subordination of members of other groups. To survive socially, these groups develop strategies to cope with their subordination. This is more complicated, in that our society is organized in such a way as to make hierarchy based on difference appear natural and inevitable. Throughout our early socialization in families, churches, schools, and reference groups, we are taught to define others and ourselves in this way and to accept this kind of classification as natural. Quite apart from accepting the myth or ideology of difference, we come to believe that there should be differences in the first place. An example of this can be seen in Altman's (1982) analysis of why gay men are so hated by so many straight men. He concludes that gays challenge the conventional roles governing a person's sex, as well as the female and male roles in society. The assertion of a gay (and lesbian) identity is interpreted as an unacceptable difference by the dominant group, which, in turn, raises doubt related to the apparent naturalness of gender roles.

When looking at all oppressed groups, we see that each is predicated on the notion of difference constructed as deviance or deficiency. While value is placed on some differences, others will be devalued, thus a social hierarchy is established. Once this happens, it is possible to divide wealth, opportunity, and justice unequally without appearing to be unfair. The social construction of race, class, gender, and sexuality is different, where being white, male, Christian, European-American, heterosexual, physically and mentally able, and prosperous is the norm, and therefore the basis of privilege. Anyone who does not have these characteristics is understood to be less able or less worthy. The sense of privilege has been reinforced and perpetuated by both intentional and unintentional discrimination (Rothenberg, 1995). This hierarchy of difference and privilege is interrelated and reinforcing, each having significant influence on the social and psychological experience of marginalized people. When the marginalized individual or group internalizes this thinking, the process is complete and insidious. The worker in her assessment of a culturally diverse client's presenting problem must consider the client's description of the problem from the perspective of possible stigma internalization.

This discussion would be rejected by most Americans who believe they are not prejudiced (Vedantan, 2005). Over one million independent studies using the Implicit Association Test designed to examine which words and concepts are strongly paired in people's minds have been employed across a wide range of population groups. Harvard psychologist Mahzarin Banaji invited people via the Internet to take this test anonymously on the Harvard website. She found that 88% of white people had a pro-white or anti-black implicit bias; almost 83% of heterosexuals showed an implicit bias for heterosexual people over gays and lesbians; and two-thirds of non-Arab non-Muslims displayed biases against Arab Muslims. We use mental shortcuts—stereotypes—which require less effort to manage our complicated social environments. To take the Implicit Association Test, go to http://implicit.harvard.edu.

Diversity

Concepts such as hierarchies of difference and experience with oppression are helpful in understanding the social reality of marginalized people. However, the practitioner still needs to explore how these various subgroups interact with one another and how they fit into the overall U.S. culture. Three popular theories offer an explanation of the impact of different immigrant cultures on one another, and on the American way of life. The assimilation theory assumes that all new arrivals to the United States become absorbed into the dominant culture. According to this theory, Protestants from England created a society that reflected their home culture, and that new immigrants, those enslaved and transported here, or those who were here but lost power and autonomy, were forced to disregard their own cultural traditions and to adopt the values and norms of an Anglo culture. The assumption is that assimilation is necessary to survive here.

A second theory rejects the notion of British or European superiority and describes the United States as a melting pot. This theory emphasizes the blending of all heritages to create a culture that is uniquely American. The assumption is that no group is able to make its values dominant. Everyone is equally American.

Current theory suggests that the United States is multicultural, a combination of many subsocieties. "Each group retains some of its customs and traditions, that these are accepted as valid and valuable, and that all groups coexist" (Cyrus, 1997, p. 4). Each theory has a kernel of truth. However, we are not all assimilated, and some groups with specific values dominate U.S. culture while others are marginalized, devalued, or repressed. Multiculturalism has come under attack because of its supposed devaluation or destruction of traditional values. It is believed that ethnic, racial, gender, and sexual orientation perspectives distort American traditions. Some claim that supporters of diversity demand that everyone be politically correct. These critics argue a single perspective, the traditional one, while multiculturalism values diversity, the usefulness of examining cultural ideas from multiple perspectives, including the traditional one. This process will enrich our lives, broaden our society, and increase our understanding of the world.

The political reaction to each of these theories falls along a continuum. Some people are reactionary, opposing any change; some are radical, they support extreme change; in between are conservatives who want to maintain the status quo; and others are liberal, who favor reform. Cyrus (1997) reminds us that each position reflects a different response to the traditional ideology of U.S. culture. She defines ideology as a system of assumptions, theories, and beliefs characterizing a particular group or culture; the system supports or questions political, social, and economic arrangements. There are three tenets of traditional American culture; each has been challenged throughout our history, but the combination remains the national ideology.

The first tenet is Eurocentricity, the assumption of the supremacy of European Americans and their values and traditions. Judeo-Christian monotheism, Protestant work ethic, and scientific rationality are examples of subsets of this tenet. The conflict that these pose for some of the cultures found in our society is enormous.

A second principle is patriarchy, a hierarchical system of social organization in which structures of power, value, and culture are male-dominated. In this system, men are the natural heads of households, presidential candidates, corporate executives, college presidents, and so on. Women are seen as men's subordinates, playing supportive roles. This principle has been under serious attack over the last thirty years.

A third principle of American ideology is the belief in capitalism, the economic system of private ownership of property and free enterprise, with its accompanying importance of profits and competition, inequitable distribution of resources (income and wealth), economic recessions and depressions, and poverty. Our culture's emphasis on individualism and personal responsibility as components of capitalism stands in sharp contrast to the cultural values of cooperation, mutual responsibility, collective ownership, or sacredness of resources characteristic of many ethnic cultures living in the United States.

These ideological principles have left us a heritage of divisiveness and inequity. These tenets have been used to rationalize prejudice and negative attitudes about certain groups, and to justify discrimination, the actions that flow from those prejudices. Eurocentric prejudice and discrimination results in racism, ethnocentrism, and xenophobia, that is, the subordination of certain groups based on their origins and physical characteristics. Patriarchal values lead to sexism; heterocentrism; the subordination of women, gay men and lesbians, bisexuals and transgender people; and the assumption of the superiority of men solely on the basis of sex. Classism, which results from capitalism, fosters stigmatizing the poor and the working class and the devaluation of those less able. In this culture, high status is assigned to the affluent and their culture solely based on their relative wealth. The worker must always tune into her own assumptions and examine these as barriers to a thorough assessment of the client's social role and environmental functioning concerns. A PIE assessment that fails to consider the type of cultural adaptation the client has made is less than thorough. A culturally competent evaluation of the client's perception of the severity and duration of the problem, as well as his or her coping skills, will result in an effective problem-solving process.

Identity

The concepts of race and ethnicity are not easily distinguished from one another. Ethnicity is defined as membership in a subgroup within an environment dominated by another culture. The ethnic subgroups may be categorized by such traits as language, culture, customs, religion, traditions, physical characteristics, or ancestral origin. Race is defined as any group of people united or classified together on the basis of common history, nationality, or geographical distribution. Most scientists identify race solely in terms of physical characteristics, such as skin color, hair, or facial attributes. These characteristics are not as discrete as it would seem. Contemporary social science theory assumes that race is less of a scientific actuality than a social construct, a classification based on social values. Social scientists refer to this as social assignment rather than singularly as genetic composition. Racial and ethnic identity are considered fixed and unalterable, but, in fact, they are fluid and quite subjective. An assessment that does not attempt to clarify what the client thinks about her race and ethnicity or the worker's race and ethnicity will miss invaluable information and possibly the best direction in the intervention.

It is important to realize that many of us have multiple identities, which assume different levels of importance at different points in time. Most of us have acquired multicultural skills and strategies for accommodating identities that conflict or place demands on us at different points in our lives. These identities are modified via assimilation, those activities by which minority groups, either influenced by the dominant group overtly or covertly, abandon the unique features of their former cultures and adapt to the values and norms of European American culture or the Anglo-Protestant ethic. Society is made up of numerous subgroups, and every subgroup has been transformed by the influences of the dominant group. However, even if many features of the origin culture are lost or altered, members may continue to identify with the cultural group. Many European Americans such as Poles, Italians, Greeks, and Slavs are associated with the working class and are thus marginalized, unappreciated, and derided despite their many contributions. While some may struggle with their ethnic identity because of discrimination, others find that ethnic identity is not necessarily problematic but a source of connection, pride, and support. What cultural or group identities a client draws from or what skills are available to him can best be understood through the building of his narrative, personal story, which has been guided by ethnic-sensitive communication.

In U.S. culture, gender is the most remarkable feature of one's identity. It shapes our attitudes, our behavior, our experiences, and our beliefs about others and ourselves. Gender is so central to our perception of social reality that we often are not even conscious of how it shapes our behavior and social interactions (Cyrus, 1997, p. 64). Through socialization, we come to know the traditional definitions of masculinity and femininity. A man should be strong and mechanically oriented, ambitious and assertive, in control of his emotions, knowledgeable about the world, and a good provider. A woman should be passive and domestic, nurturing and dependent, emotional, preoccupied with her appearance, and maternal. These supposedly unalterable gender characteristics affect the physical and psychological aspects of one's life, as well as occupational choices and interpersonal relations.

Scientists will continue to debate the nature/nurture mix of gendered behavior, specifically its genetic etiology. Social scientists, on the other hand, see strong evidence of the central importance that culture plays in creating gender roles, which are only one kind of role we learn. We acquire our appropriate gender roles through socialization, a process by which we are taught those roles, social expectations, and the rewards and punishments that require us to conform. These are embedded in every aspect of culture. The treatment of infants and children, language, educational systems, religion, mass media, laws, medical and mental health institutions, occupational environments, and intimate relationships all teach appropriate gender behavior. Social science has helped us to understand how adults, as well as children, make assumptions about gender and then reinforce traditional expectations. We also learn how language teaches us about the ideas of male superiority and female inferiority. Heterocentrism is another process that limits our choices based on gender, in that it is an assumption that only heterosexual relationships and interests are acceptable. We see stereotypic behavior reinforced by notions of masculine supremacy and privilege, while violations of gender expectations result in stigma, anger, and violence. These gender expectations, in this society, are too often white, middle-class, white-collar, and heterosexual values. These values then become the standard by which minority groups evaluate themselves, by which the dominant group evaluates them, and, too often, by which social workers and other human service professionals assess their clients and design what they think are appropriate interpersonal interventions.

Stigma and Stigma Management

Oppression is an institutional process that is experienced personally as stigma, stress, guilt, and shame. Stigma significantly influences identity development. It is stigma that results in internalized oppression, which every minority person must learn to manage in the process of developing a healthy identity. It is the social, economic, political, and psychological consequences of stigma that the social worker may be called on to help reduce, extricate, or relieve. The concept of stigma comes out of labeling theory. This theory may be especially useful for social work practice because it unambiguously distinguishes between behaviors commonly believed to be stereotypic and the feelings of being stigmatized that arise as a particular reaction to them.

Erving Goffman (1963) talks about the nature of self-presentation and the role of stigma in interpersonal relations. People with stigmas are thought to be not quite human. The standards the stigmatized person incorporates from the wider society equip her to be acutely aware of what others see as her failing, inevitably causing her to agree that she does indeed fall short of what she really ought to be. Shame is one common consequence of a stigmatized person's failure to meet a specific set of standards, rules, and goals. Another is what Meyer (1995) terms "minority stress," or the conflict that arises with the social environment when the person does not fit the dominant values (p. 39).

Stigma represents for Goffman (1963) a spoiled identity, the idea that somehow one is imperfect in regard to the standards of the society in which one lives. It is a "mark or characteristic that distinguishes a person as being deviant, flawed, limited, spoiled or generally undesirable. The deviating characteristics of the person are sufficient reason for the occurrence of the stigma" (Lewis, 1992, p. 194). Stigma relates the self to others' views and, although the feelings of being stigmatized may occur in the absence of other people, the feelings associated with it come about through the stigmatized person's interactions with other people, or through his anticipation of interaction with other people. Thus stigmatization is an interpersonal process. Stigmas represent a violation of what is considered normal. The very idea of stigma implies that social value and worth reside not in the spoiled individual but in the societal value system as reflected in its standards, rules, and goals. Thus a stigmatized person has an expectation of rejection and vigilance about prejudice (Meyer, 1995).

As a result of continued exposure to prejudice and stigmatization, devalued individuals become members of a minority group, a segment of the population that suffers unjustified negative acts by the rest of society. These acts may range from mild discrimination to scapegoating.

While there are important differences between the two groups, there are many similarities in the development of a gay, lesbian, or bisexual identity with the development of racial or ethnic identity. Comparable stages in identity development have been found. The primary task for each involves the transformation of a negative, stigmatized identity into a positive, affirming one. However, a racial or ethnic identity is an ascribed status that is recognized and acknowledged from birth, while sexual identity is an achieved status that is generally not discovered until adolescence or adulthood (Garnets & Kimmel, 1993). Another way in which the groups differ is that persons of color, for the most part, are taught strategies by their families to manage their stigmatized identity. The families of gay men and lesbians cannot teach skills they don't have; on the contrary, these parents are often the initiators of gay and lesbian stigma and discrimination.

Effects of Stigmatization

People who have been stigmatized respond in a great variety of ways. Allport (1958) terms these "traits due to victimization" or "persecution produced traits." Some of these traits can be quite constructive and creative, while others can be rather unpleasant or destructive:

> Every form of ego defense may be found among members of every persecuted group. Some will handle their minority-group membership easily, with surprisingly little evidence in their personalities that this membership is of any concern to them. Others will show a mixture of desirable and undesirable compensations. Some will be so rebellious that they will develop many ugly defenses. (Allport, 1958, p. 140)

Allport enumerates the varieties of negative responses to stigmatization including: (1) obsessive concern resulting in feelings of deep anxiety, suspicion, and insecurity; (2) denial (from both oneself and others) of actual membership in the minority group; (3) social withdrawal and passivity; (4) clowning, being the court jester in an effort to be accepted by the dominant group; (5) slyness and cunning—oftentimes for mere survival; (6) identification with the dominant group, a sign of self-hate; (7) aggression against and directing blame to one's own group; (8) redirecting prejudice and discrimination against other minorities; (9) excessive neuroticism; (10) internalizing and acting out the negative social definitions and stereotypes, creating a self-fulfilling prophecy; and (11) excessive striving for status to compensate for the feelings of inferiority. Blumenfeld and Raymond (1993) emphasize that many of these more undesirable characteristics often are attributed to the minority as intrinsic but are in reality defenses to discrimination. Unfortunately, when these responses occur, they often lead to reinforcement of negative stereotypes and beliefs. When culturally diverse or oppressed clients interact with any of the six environmental systems, their behaviors and attitudes often are misinterpreted as psychologically inappropriate, possibly representing psychiatric qualities, and not as a cultural adaptation to the loss of power, control, or privilege.

The negative effects of stigmatization on some groups, such as gay, lesbian, and bisexual people, have been known for some time, especially the connection between stigmatization and psychosocial dysfunction (Meyer, 1995). Stigmatized individuals have been characterized as having disrupted emotional, cognitive, and behavioral response systems, likely to be caused in part by their feelings of shame and in part by their efforts to cope with prejudice. The stigma felt by the individual is profound, resulting in emotions as diverse as anger, sadness, humiliation, shame, and embarrassment. Lewis (1992) draws a major distinction between shame and guilt or regret. With shame the entire self is "no good," as captured in the expression "I am a bad person." Goffman's definition of stigma as a spoiled identity makes clear that a stigma constitutes a global attribution about the self as no good. In this case, a spoiled identity reflects a whole self made bad by minority status. The adjustment difficulties associated with stigma follow from the idea that the stigma defines the individual. The very act of stigmatization is shame inducing. It is not surprising to find in the discussion of stigma associated feelings of low self-esteem, depression, and acting-out behaviors: "Stigmas speak to the idea of difference and how difference shames us and those we know" (p. 207).

Christopher Bagley (*Advocate*, 11/12/96), a professor of social work at the University of Calgary, in his study of 750 youth (eighteen to twenty-seven years old) found a profoundly negative response to stigmatization in the fact that young gay and bisexual males are nearly fourteen times more at risk of suicide than their heterosexual contemporaries. These rates are far greater than the conventional wisdom that gay youth are at three times greater risk of suicide than their straight counterparts.

The negative impact of stigma is quite broad: It not only affects those who are stigmatized, but those associated with the person so too are spoiled. Goffman called this phenomenon "courtesy stigma." Thus stigmas are contagious; they impact on members of the family, friends, and even those who help stigmatized persons, such as social workers and other mental health professionals. For example, the parents of someone with a stigma are then stigmatized and may suffer a similar fate as their stigmatized disabled daughter or son. We see the impact of stigmatization when parents are informed that their child is physically or mentally disabled: First, they express shock and disbelief that their child is imperfect, lacking in "moral strength or physical or mental health." Second, they experience anger and rage. Third, sadness replaces the anger. Finally, the parents enter the coping stage; that is, they learn to cope with their shame and embarrassment over having such a child. The shame at having such a child can last a lifetime and can lead to many family difficulties, including a high rate of marital discord and divorce as each parent seeks to blame the other for the stigmatized child. It can become the family secret, it can be tolerated, or it can be mourned as a loss. However, some parents may resist the negative social construction of their child's marginalized status and accept it in the fullest sense. Some become active in support groups or advocacy organizations, such as Association of Retarded Citizens or National Association of Mental Illness. This may be the most positive adjustment for the parents.

It is important to remember, however, that "stigmatized individuals are not merely passive victims but are frequently able actively to protect and buffer their self-esteem from prejudice and discrimination" (Crocker & Major, 1989, p. 624). Blumenfeld and Raymond (1993) note some positive outcomes of stigmatization for gay and lesbian people: (1) strengthening of ties with fellow minority-group members, which deMonteflores (1986) calls "ghettoization"; (2) sympathy with and support for other minorities; (3) enhanced striving and assertiveness; and (4) challenging the status quo so as to bring about progressive social change, which deMonteflores (1986) calls "confrontation." In fact, members of stigmatized groups often have much higher levels of self-esteem than might be predicted based on the prejudice and discrimination that they face (Crocker & Major, 1989). There are several self-protective strategies that have been described which help increase self-esteem, such as identifying the prejudice directed against them for what it is and explaining experiences of rejection and perceived differences between themselves and others in the nonstigmatized group on that basis. Members of the stigmatized group may also reframe their own characteristics as positive and selectively devalue those of the dominant culture, what deMonteflores (1986) terms "specialization," that is, making oneself special as a consequence of the stigma. These strategies all tend to strengthen bonds among members of the stigmatized group (Crocker & Major, 1989). Browning, Reynolds, and

Dworkin (1991) in discussing generational differences with regard to handling stigma describe how the term *queer* has become a badge of pride, a signature of generational difference, a marker of a more freewheeling, combative social style. This process has been described extensively by scholars in relation to the use of the title black versus negro or Hispanic versus Latino.

Concealment, or "passing," is one possible way to cope with stigma. Those who are invisible, in that they do not fit the stereotype, may pass, that is, can allow or encourage others to believe that they are normal, while those who do meet the stereotyped expectations become visible. An individual may come to recognize his or her homosexual orientation without realistic models of what this means. The reaction may be "I'm the only person in the world like this" or "I'm not like them, thank God." Parents and other family members and friends are also likely to avoid or deny disclosure when their loved one does not fit the stereotype. Passing also implies what deMonteflores (1986) calls "assimilation," or learning the ways of the dominant group. Thus a minority person may have in-depth knowledge of both the dominant culture and the culture of the stigmatized subgroup, leading some to suggest that all minority people may be considered bicultural (Lukes & Land, 1990). It is possible to misunderstand behavior as constituting passing in the case of Native Americans or Asian Americans and racial identity. Neither group considers themselves people of color nor accepts the notion of white racial supremacy, thus they remain uninvolved in the debate related to race.

The process of consciously hiding requires lying and often omitting some personal information. This strategy of deception distorts almost all relationships and creates an increasing sense of isolation. A major aspect of passing, or concealment, is the ever-present need to self-monitor (Martin & Hetrick, 1988; Morrow, 1993).

Hammersmith (1988) suggests that there is a range of responses to stigmatization. These include stereotypic interpretation of behavior; social rejection, distancing, and discrimination; passing and altered self-concept; development of special subcultures; and "secondary deviation." The individual, his or her family, and often friends are confronted daily with stereotyping and social rejection. The images are all negative. By the time one reaches adulthood, the association (not necessarily conscious) between the minority status and the stereotype is formed. The peer groups, the mass media, and cultural tradition perpetuate these dehumanizing stereotypes. The individual may feel pressure or desire to establish distance from his negative status. Too few people, then, are socially and emotionally prepared to deal with this issue when it arises.

Rejection is another consequence of stigma, which produces distancing between those with the stigma and those without. The final means of coping with stigma is that of self-fulfilling prophecy or secondary deviance. This means that features of the stereotype may be embraced in protest or defiance or for lack of support for more normative styles of life. In deMonteflores's (1986) terms, this strategy combines elements of confrontation and specialization.

The PIE system was designed with an understanding of the complexity of these negative environmental dynamics, in that Factor II: Environmental Problem is given prominence in this classification system. The authors specifically listed discrimination as a potential problem for clients in each of the environmental systems. They identify a range of possibilities: age discrimination (mandatory retirement at age 65), ethnicity, color or language discrimination (African Americans are not able to move into Greenwich, CT), religious discrimination (Hindus required to work on a sacred day), sexual orientation (gay men and lesbians refused adoptions), lifestyle (landlords will not rent to people with pets), noncitizen status (schools will not enroll children of undocumented workers), veterans status (employers are biased against veterans of Kosovo war), dependency status (landlords will not rent to people receiving TANF), disability (there are no elevators to the second floor), marital status (married women not able to advance to supervisory levels), and other types of discrimination (landlords will not rent to parents of young children) (Karls & Wandrei, 1994).

While all clients may experience an inadequate level of available resources in any given environmental system or lack the necessary coping skills for a given problem, clients whose race, ethnicity, gender, social class, sexual orientation, age, ability, or immigrant or religious status are marginal may be blocked from access to a resource or full use of a resource because of their status. They are targets of discrimination.

The client's perception of the severity and duration of the problem are important qualifiers. The worker, in either case, not necessitating intervention, might not perceive the discrimination as disruptive, or it may be seen as nondisruptive by the client but disruptive by the social worker. The discrimination might be disruptive to the client's functioning but the distress is not judged as impairing general functioning, or the client is in a clear state of distress, either of which requires intervention. The discrimination is such that it requires changes in key or multiple areas of social role functioning (internalized racism) or in the environment (hate crimes), or sudden and negative changes out of the individual's control with devastating implications for adjustment (quarantine of people with AIDS or acute psychiatric disorders). These might require immediate and direct intervention.

Conclusion

Change in disempowering social arrangements is one of the goals of social work. As we develop an appreciation for the type, severity, and duration of stress on minority communities and the cultural barriers to their full participation in social institutions, we come to realize the importance of social change as a goal of contemporary practice. If, when assessing an environmental system, we identify a lack of resources or an inadequacy in resources, we are professionally required to initiate a process that will organize clients to develop their own capacity to find new resources, challenge service providers to use their own resources in a more appropriate fashion, or advocate for change on a legislative or administrative policy level. These interventions may or may not be driven by us, but we are obligated to initiate such action. Discrimination requires more than helping a client put up with this assault; the worker may help all affected clients organize or challenge the personal action or the de facto or de jure policy through advocacy, service evaluation, and policy or program change. Most community institutions, including social services agencies, have not engaged in this type of analysis or may not be committed to the organizational change necessary to accommodate the needs of marginalized people. Community education, organizing and development, case and class advocacy, social action, and policy and organizational change are transformative professional activities directed at social institutions. While these modalities are in less favor today, they continue to be among the most effective ways to promote social change. The experience of minority clients offers evidence that these modalities should be in great demand. Students and practitioners are encouraged to use the vast resources of the Internet. One site designed specifically for social workers is www.nyu.edu/socialwork/ip/.

References

Advocate. (November 12, 1996). Viewpoint: Christopher Bagley Study (p. 44). Author.

Allport, G. (1958). *The nature of prejudice.* Garden City, NY: Doubleday.

Altman, D. (1982). *The homosexualization of America.* Boston: Beacon Press.

Bagley, C., 1996. View point. *Advocate* (November–December): 44.

Basch, M. (1975). Toward a theory that encompasses depression: A revision of existing casual hypotheses in psychoanalysis. In J. Anthony & T. Benedek (Eds.), *Depression and human existence.* Boston: Brown.

Blumenfeld, W. J., & Raymond, D. (1993). *Looking at gay and lesbian life.* Boston: Beacon Press.

Browning, C., Reynolds, A. L., & Dworkin, S. H. (1991). Affirmative psychotherapy for lesbian women. *Counseling Psychologist 9*(2), 177–196.

Crocker, J., & Major, B. (1989). Social stigma and self-esteem: The self-protective properties of stigma. *Psychological Review, 96*(4), 603–630.

Cyrus, V. (1997). *Experiencing race, class, and gender in the United States* (2nd ed.). Mountain View, CA: Mayfield.

DeCecco, J., & Shively, M. G. (1984). From sexual identities to sexual relationships? A contextual shift. *Journal of Homosexuality, 9*(2/3), 1–26.

D'Emilio, J. (1983). *Sexual politics, sexual communities: The making of a homosexual minority in the United States, 1940–1970.* Chicago: University of Chicago Press.

deMonteflores, C. (1986). Notes on the management of difference. In T. Stein & C. Cohen (Eds.), *Psychotherapy with lesbians and gay men* (pp. 73–101). New York: Plenum Press.

Garnets, L. D., & Kimmel, D. C. (Eds.). (1993). *Psychological perspectives on lesbian & gay male experiences.* New York: Columbia University Press.

Goffman, I. (1963). *Stigma: Notes on the management of spoiled identity.* Garden City, NJ: Prentice-Hall.

Hammersmith, S. K. (1988). A sociological approach to counseling homosexual clients and their families. In E. Coleman (Ed.), *Integrated identity for gay men and lesbians: Psychotherapeutic approaches for emotional well-being* (pp. 174–179). New York: Harrington Park Press.

Herek, G. (1990). The context of anti-gay violence: Notes on cultural and psychological heterosexism. *Journal of Interpersonal Violence, 5,* 316–333.

Herek, G. (1992). The social context of hate crimes: Notes on cultural heterosexism. In G. Herek & K. Berrill (Eds.), *Hate crimes: Confronting violence against lesbians and gay men* (pp. 89–104). Newbury Park, CA: Sage.

Herek, G., & Berrill, K. (1992). *Hate crimes: Confronting violence against lesbians and gay men.* Newbury Park, CA: Sage.

Hodge, J. (1975). *Cultural bases of racism and group oppression.* New York: Time Readers Press.

hooks, b. (1984). *Feminist theory: From the margin to the center.* Boston: South End Press.

Humphries, L. (1972). *Out of the closets: The sociology of homosexual liberation.* Englewood Cliffs, NJ: Prentice-Hall.

Karls, J. M., & Wandrei, K. E. (1994). *PIE manual: Person-in-environment system: The PIE classification system for social functioning problems.* Washington, DC: NASW.

Lecca, P. J., Quervalu, I., Nunes, J. V., & Gonzales, H. F. (1998). *Cultural competency in health, social, and human services.* New York: Garland.

Leigh, J. W. (1998). *Communicating for cultural competence.* Boston: Allyn & Bacon.

Lewis, M. (1992). *Shame: The exposed self.* New York: Free Press.

Lukes, C. A., & Land, H. (1990). Biculturality and homosexuality. *Social Work, 35*(2), 155–161.

Martin, A. D., & Hetrick, E. S. (1988). The stigmatization of the gay and lesbian adolescent. *Journal of Homosexuality, 15*(1/2), 163–182.

Meyer, C. (1993). *Assessment in social work practice*. New York: Columbia University Press.

Meyer, I. H. (1995). Minority stress and mental health in gay men. *Journal of Health and Social Behavior, 36*, 38–56.

Morrow, D. F. (1993). Social work with gay and lesbian adolescents. *Social Work, 38*(6), 655–660.

Pellegrini, A. (1992). S(h)ifting the terms of hetero/sexism: Gender, power, homophobias. In W. J. Blumenfeld (Ed.), *Homophobia: How we all pay the price* (pp. 39–56). Boston: Beacon Press.

Pharr, S. (1988). *Homophobia: A weapon of sexism*. Little Rock, AR: Chardon Press.

Rothenberg, P. S. (1995). *Race, class, and gender in the United States: An integrated study* (3rd ed.) New York: St. Martin's Press.

Rubin, G. G. (1984). Thinking sex: Notes for a radical theory of the politics of sexuality. In C. S. Vance (Ed.), *Pleasure and danger: Exploring female sexuality* (pp. 267–319). Boston: Routledge & Kegan Paul.

Vedantan, S. (January 23, 2005). See no bias. *Washington Post,* W12.

Warren, R. (1963). *The community in America*. Chicago: Rand McNally.

5

Racism: African Americans and Caribbean Islanders

Julia Hamilton

This chapter is designed to prepare social workers and other health and human services professionals to better assess the impact of racism that people of color experience in their daily living and to become more aware of their own racist attitudes toward their clients. Factors I and II of the person-in-environment system will be used to introduce the discussion of relevant theories of practice.

Race is a concept that must be understood intellectually as well as emotionally. Defining race and racism can bring contextual clarity to people's confused perceptions, painful feelings, and problem behaviors. *Race* is a biological term classifying people who have the same physical characteristics. Its meaning is ambiguous, although in people's minds it is understood as a measure of difference referring to culture. Race in this country has come to take on a meaning that refers to differences between people based on color.

Racism is often equated with prejudice, which is the act of prejudging and expecting certain behavior from specific individuals. But the distinction between prejudice and racism is an important one. Racism raises to the level of social structure the tendency to use superiority as a solution to the discomfort about difference. The belief of superiority of whites and the inferiority of people of color, based on racial differences, is legitimized by societal arrangements. These arrangements limit the access to power, and then blame people of color for their failures that result from the lack of power. Although these arrangements may exclude some persons who are white, people of color are affected in far greater proportions based on color (Hopps, 1982, p. 3).

Defining Racism and Race

Racism is defined as the belief that objective or alleged differences between racial groups are justification for asserting the superiority of one racial group over another. Two types of racism exist. There is individual racism and institutional racism. Individual racism is an action performed by one person or a group that produces a racial abuse, for example, verbal or physical mistreatment. Frequently, this type of racism is intentional. There are several explanations for a negative response to difference. One centers on the fact that difference carries an implication of comparison and thus inequality, because we seem unable to view different forms as meaning merely not the same as. It seems we must place a value on any perceived differences and see them in terms of better than or less than, evolving inferences of both power and negativity.

Influenced by the dominant white, Eurocentric, middle-class, Protestant culture, Americans value competition, winning, and limited tolerance for individuals who do not respond in this fashion. The use of comparisons, ranking, and stratifying does not encourage respect for uniqueness or difference except in the sense of being the best. Americans signify power and encourage bias based on ethnocentrism. The perception that one's own group is better than others, and that the values of the group carry the meaning of better than, creates bias.

Being different increases a sense of aloneness, isolation, and abandonment—a sense of nonconnection to others—and threatens the sense of psychological wholeness and intactness that people need. While stereotypes can play a key role in relationships between persons who are culturally different, through social processes they also become critical factors in emphasizing the existence of differences, which, in turn, determine ethnic minority/majority status. Stratification is institutionalized into social structure. As a result, expectations generated by the dominant group about tasks and functions appropriate for the subordinate group have a profound effect on the conditions of the subordinates as well as those who are dominant.

Power thus becomes a central dynamic in the process of stratification, the personal and social consequences of which have been discussed in Chapters 1 and 2. Racism is the institutionalization of stratification and has operated in the United States to influence the realities of life changes and lifestyles of people of color. Institutional racism is defined as a system of structural arrangements that allow access to social resources based on beliefs in the superiority of one racial group and the inferiority of the other. Thus power becomes a primary factor in the cultural process.

Unlike individual racism, institutional racism is an action performed by one person or a group that produces racial abuse, for example, verbal or physical mistreatment. Frequently, this type of racism is institutional. One might argue, for instance, that individual racism occurs when a white customer, seeking information, approaches a group of five store employees and addresses the only white member, assuming that this individual is better informed than the others.

Unlike individual racism, institutional racism is not an immediate action but part of racist behavior patterns resulting from erroneous dominant cultural assumptions. Specifically, institutional racism involves discriminatory racial practices built into such prominent structures as the political, economic, and educational systems as well as other social institutions. Institutional racism is distinctly sociological, emphasizing social structures and establishing norms guiding people's behavior. Institutional racism is the prime factor in maintaining racism.

In social work, the person and his environment are regarded as interacting, so as to influence and shape one another. In the social role of the client, attention is given to interpersonal transactions that affect social functioning. The environmental problems outside of the client also affect social functioning and well-being. The environment is seen as both physical and social. The PIE system focuses our attention on the many subsystems in the community (macro system) that impact people of color. Discrimination, a major problem in the environment (Factor II), is often based on ethnicity, color, or language, which in turn creates problems in social role functioning for people of color (Factor I). As an example, the police have reported increased violent harassment of blacks and Hispanics in the community. Sexual orientation discrimination impacts people of color's social status more than that of white Americans.

Race and Developmental Process

Race over time has acquired a social meaning in which these biological differences via the mechanism of stereotyping have become markers for status assignment within the social system. The status assignment based on skin color has evolved into complex social structures that promote a poor differentiation between whites and various people of color.

This status assignment is an act of power and is a form of institutional racism, which affects the life opportunities, lifestyle, and quality of life for both whites and people of color. Although many forms of status assignment that result in exclusion and discrimination exist in this country, none is so deeply rooted consistently in actuality as that based on color (Hopps, 1982).

People with some sensitivity to the societal dynamics that sustain racism feel immobilized when it becomes an issue in the helping encounter. While blacks, Puerto Ricans, and other racial and ethnic groups are forced by racial oppression to be aware of themselves as members of racial groups, whites are generally unaware of their whiteness (Adams & Schlesinger, 1988, p. 25).

Spencer and Markstrom-Adams (1990) remind us that, according to Erikson, identity development is a major developmental task for which a stage is set during childhood and then played out during adolescence. These authors suggest that the complexity of identity development increase as a function of color, behavioral distinctions, language differences, and physical features is long-standing. Although frequently not addressed, stereotypes are generalizations about people based on such characteristics as those previously listed. A negative stereotype is similar in many respects to stigma, in that both terms refer to negative generalizations about people. This presents often unreasonable challenges in developing social competence necessary for successful social role functioning.

In order to acknowledge this complexity, the authors believe that "new conceptual frameworks shaped by models of normal developmental processes are needed (i.e., as opposed to deviance and deficit dependent formulations). New conceptual paradigms are necessary because racial and ethnic groups have heretofore been examined through pathology driven models" (Spencer & Markstrom-Adams, 1990, p. 4).

Traditional developmental theories often ignore the interplay of external societal factors with internal cognitive factors. For example, traditional developmental approaches often assume that experiments showing children of color's preference for white dolls when shown black and white dolls reflect low self-esteem or a negative individual identity rather than a societal bias toward color and whiteness. Such interpretations ignore contradictory findings from experiments that show African American children having extremely rich self-esteem. Their resilience is not captured in the earlier research. Traditional developmental models assume homogeneity among group members. It is assumed that all members of a particular group share all characteristics such as family forms, socioeconomic status, values, and even color. Variations are often as extensive among group members as between one group and another. This diversity must be recognized in attempts to understand the development of members of various people of color (Spencer & Markstrom-Adams, 1990, p. 290). For example, we must recognize that there is a wide variation among African American families: from single-parent female-headed to traditional nuclear to two-parent large extended and from low-income to middle-income to high-income families. Levels of coping and adaptation vary significantly. Similarly, it is important to recognize the wide cultural and language variety among Native Americans. This group includes all North American native people, including Indians, Alaska natives, Eskimos, and mixed bloods, each with a different history, cultural supports, and access to resources. Native Americans will be discussed in greater detail in Chapter 8.

The African American Community: A Socioeconomic Profile

Families of African heritage have come to the United States from many different countries for over four centuries. Although all immigrant groups have had acculturation problems, African Americans question whether the social, economic, and political hardships they encounter as a result of racial discrimination will ever render the American dream attainable for the larger group of African Americans in this country.

The African American group is very diverse in terms of geographic origin, age, acculturation, religious background, skin color, socioeconomic status, and strategies employed to cope with racism and discrimination. In today's American society, African Americans comprise about 12% of the population. Between 1940 and 1970, over 1.5 million African Americans migrated, most to the North and some to the West, and over 84% now live in urban areas. Racism and oppression continue to make it extremely difficult for African Americans to enter and remain in the economic mainstream. According to the U.S. Department of Labor, Bureau of Labor Statistics, from 1992 to 2000, the decline in jobless rates for African Americans was greater than those for Hispanics and whites. However, African Americans continue to be slightly more than twice as likely to be unemployed as whites. African American households earn less than the average; however, the share of Black households that earn between $25,000 and $74,999 (44.6%) is larger than the share that earns less then $25,000 (42.9%).

More African Americans than whites or members of other racial groups are homeless, incarcerated, or children in foster care or otherwise supervised by the child welfare system. It has been reported that in 1994, 44% (almost half) of the homeless population were African American. There is a high number of African Americans who are homeless; people who are homeless suffer from mental illness and disorders at disturbingly high rates. Socioeconomic status is linked closely to mental health, and poor mental health is more common among those who are impoverished than among those who are more affluent.

Educational Functioning and Achievement

Twenty-nine percent (29%) of African-American students, compared with 18% of white students, drop out of college after less than one year. African Americans on average may find themselves in a position where some educational and career opportunities are not accessible to them, and the cause may be factors such as socioeconomic status (not being able to pay for schooling), or even social pressures discouraging them from pursuing goals that are valued in the mainstream U.S. culture. Nevertheless, a record 79% of African Americans age 25 or older had completed at least high school—a rate double that in 1970. Marking another record, 17% (of which slightly more were women) had earned at least an undergraduate college degree—a rate triple that in 1970. Both statistics represent a 6% improvement from 1990.

African American Family Values and Patterns

Strong African American kinship bonds are traceable to Africa. African Americans share a heritage of ongoing traumatic and strong kinship bonds. Multicultural values revolve around collective structures; for example, the individual wishes of a family member are subordinate to the good of the family as a whole. The family unit is considered the most important transmitter of cultural values and traditions, and the value of the family is highly empha-sized. The African American family is the primary source of relationships and is expected to pay for educating, help with obtaining jobs, and assisting members of the family who are in trouble.

There are two major characteristics among African American people:

1. *Maintenance of Ethnic Identification and Solidarity:* A family socializes its members into ethnic culture through family lifestyles and activities. The family gathering and community celebrations of cultural holidays perpetuate ethnic awareness.

2. *Extended Family and Kinship Network:* Multicultural extended family and kinship networks function on the principles of interdependence, group connection, and reliance on others. Among African Americans there is an extensive reliance on kin-ship networks, which include blood relatives and close friends called "kinsmen." These networks arise from mutual needs for such things as financial aid, childcare, advice, and emotional support. Usually elderly grandparents take young African American children into their households in informal adoption. Gibson (2002) reports on the experiences of 12 African American grandmothers who assumed the parental role for their grandchildren.

Gibson found six major themes in the lives of African American grandmothers:

1. *Tradition of kin keeping:* Where the grandmother herself had the experience of being cared for by extended family members or elders in the household when she was a child.

2. *Relationship with grandchildren:* Where there is involvement and investment of quality care in the grandchildren in terms of a close relationship, a parent-child rela-tionship, keeping grandchildren in the care of the family, deterring traumatization, becoming the primary caregiver, and contributing care to the future generation.

3. *Distrust of the foster care system:* There is opposition to the placement of their grandchildren in foster care (e.g., fearing abuse in the system, fearing loss of contact with grandchildren, feeling pressure to avoid the foster care system, fearing that reunification will not occur, and yet experiencing the need to contact and work with the foster care system despite the distrust).

4. *Grandmother as the grandchild's only resource:* When the grandmother is the only relative coming to the aid of the grandchild and accepts the role of the primary care-giver.

5. *A strong relationship with the Lord:* Where there is an active faith and belief in the Lord as a source of help and assistance.

6. *Conflict between grandmothers:* Refusal of the grandchild's other grandmother to assist with caregiving because of personality traits, unwillingness to change lifestyle, adversarial relationship between the families, or racial mixture of the child.

Social Workers' Role

Social work intervention has focused on problems in living based on a person-in-environment paradigm. Our historical mission has been to care and advocate for the disenfranchised and oppressed, those who are left behind and face an alien world and daily struggle.

Proposed Model for Activism

Morales (1981) described a form of activist practice that takes into consideration an awareness of racial, ethnic, and political factors in providing services to assist with social problems. Devore and Schlesinger (1981) remarked, "The interface between private troubles and public issues is an intrinsic aspect of most approaches to social work practice." Their model of ethnically sensitive practice calls for attention to both micro and macro issues and their consequences, including the results of racism, discrimination, and poverty.

Cultural Values and Coping with Racism

Despite the existence of pervasive racial discrimination and realistic barriers, African American children have succeeded against the odds for many generations. Their social-emotional environment represents a major factor contributing to their adaptive development.

African American families constitute an important buffer between the child and the outside environment (Boyd-Frankin, 1989; Comer, 1985). An important aspect of this role of the family as a buffer, not unlike that of the social worker, is to help the child understand the outside world's messages and distinguish between those messages that are true or false. Many parents face difficult challenges raising children in adverse circumstances, but African American parents face added stressors and special tasks. They must teach their children how to handle the special issues of a bicultural existence without losing a core sense of themselves. Trying to function in and between two often contradictory cultures can produce conflicting developmental tasks and tensions (Baker, 1988; Pinderhughes, 1989). The pressure of racism and the effort by African American parents to minimize its damaging effects on their children are in fact a major stress not shared by their white counterparts.

An important set of strategies for coping with racism consists of introducing and sharing derivatives of African cultural values and practices. An African American child's preparation by parents and other social agents to understand and take pride in their culture can be a major source of resilience and coping, a racial consciousness that provides a necessary foundation for the coping strategies needed.

A number of variables are common to multicultural identity values. The most obvious distinguishing feature is skin color. All people of the earth have been classified according to the colors white, brown, black, yellow, and red. A "color" hierarchy has undermined ethnic identity. For example, White symbolizes innocence, purity and fairness; Black is associated with evil, darkness and dirt. Yellow conjures up cowardice, impurity and discoloration. Red is associated with rage. The derogatory tone of such idioms as "dirt black," "yellow belly," and "red skin" have caused them to become racial slurs, and they are still with us. Thus, these terms depreciate ethnic identity value.

Strengths of African American Women

Racism and oppression continue to cause great difficulties for African Americans to enter and remain in the economic mainstream. Cultural strengths are pride in culture, family, ethnic group identity, responsibility at an early age, religious values, the ability to set goals, hard work, honesty, coping with racism, and belief in education and God. The strengths of African American women derive from their personal, family, and community traits (Aquilar & Williams, 1993). Aquilar and Williams (1993) report that religious orientation and parental encouragement to pursue higher education had a more positive impact on African-American women than on Latino women, who completed their education after marriage, and who sacrificed to send brothers and sisters to college.

The women's personal strengths are persistence, determination, hard work, faith in God, assertiveness, the desire to help and to be role models for other women in their ethnic group, family support, and being achievement- or goal-oriented. Regarding racism, McGoldrick (1996) confesses: "I did not realize that I benefited from the effects of slavery and racism and do to this day. I am coming slowly and painfully to realize what it means that people who are 'white' carry around, in Peggy McIntosh's terms, a kind of 'invisible knapsack of privilege' containing special provisions, maps, passports and visas, blank check, and emergency gear (McIntosh, 1992). We cannot see it, but those who do not have one can."

Theories of Racism

Micro Level Theories of Racism

In *The Nature of Prejudice*, Gordon Allport (1954, pp. 307–310) suggested that prejudice is a three-stage learning process to which children in American culture are exposed. The following situation illustrates the first stage: Tanya, a six-year-old girl, comes running home and asks, "Mother, what is the name of the children I am supposed to hate?" In Allport's apt phrase, Tanya is "stumbling at the threshold of some abstraction" (Allport, 1954, p. 307). She identifies with her mother, seeks approval, and wishes to fuse her obedience to her mother with appropriate feelings toward her own social contacts. The child engaged in pregeneralized learning has accepted the information that a certain African American boy identity or a particular Native American woman identity is not to be trusted, but generalizations involving prejudice toward an entire racial or ethnic group still elude her. Language is the key to the development of racist thought. Listening to her mother, father, other adults, and older children express their prejudices toward different groups, Tanya will gradually be able to grasp which racial and ethnic groups are the culturally approved objects of prejudice. In Tanya's case, the second stage in learning prejudice begins with her mother's response to the question. Her mother might reply, "I told you not to play with black children. They are dirty; they have diseases; and they will hurt you. Now don't let me catch you talking or playing with them." Such a directive can initiate the period of total rejection. Promoted by parental order, children vigorously reject all members of a certain racial or ethnic group, in this case African Americans.

The third stage involves differentiation. Now the children have become more sophisticated, learning to make gracious exceptions when it seems appropriate. "Some of my best friends are Latinos, so how could I be prejudiced against Asians?" "The woman who took care of me when I was a child was Chinese and I loved her dearly." By about age fifteen, young people have become sophisticated enough to turn the racism faucet on and off at will. As part of the package, they have learned what Allport called "the peculiar double-talk appropriate to prejudice in a democracy," that is, speech in favor of individual rights and equality that simultaneously supports prejudice and discrimination (Allport, 1954, p. 310).

Another social psychological perspective is the frustration-aggression theory. Consider the following situation. An angry father scolds a five-year-old. The child in turn is angry and frustrated, then glances up at dad momentarily, wondering whether she might risk kicking him in the shins. But dad's towering height convinces her he is much too formidable, and so she takes a less satisfying but somewhat satisfying action. She slugs her innocent two-year-old brother. The frustration-aggression theory emphasizes that people blocked from achieving a goal are sometimes unable or unwilling to focus their frustration on the true source, and so they direct the aggression produced by frustration toward an accessible individual or group. The displacement of anger from the true source of frustration to this substitute, a so-called scapegoat, permits a release of tension called catharsis for racist individuals; scapegoating is often an emotionally charged process, quickly meeting their needs at a given time and place. While the frustration-aggression theory is a useful analytic tool, it could be refined. Sometimes frustration does not produce aggression, and thus it would be useful to determine when a frustrating situation produces an aggressive act and when it does not.

Macro Level Theory of Racism

Conflict theory contends that the struggle for power and wealth in society should be the central concern for understanding social interaction. However, many people are restricted or controlled by a limited number of powerful members of society, who impose their preferences, and such restrictions create or at least encourage conflict. According to the proponents of this theory, conflict produces change. The process of moving toward change is painful for the powerless.

Milton Gordon acknowledged conflict theory's perspective, admitting that groups with greater wealth and power are able to use those scarce resources to exploit groups that are less well situated (Gordon, 1978). This helps us to understand the inevitability of intergroup and intragroup stifle as people are forced to compete for basic resources and struggle to achieve upward social mobility.

Pluralism is a theory emphasizing that a dispersion of power exists in government and other social structures within U.S. society. Unlike assimilation theory, pluralism does not contend that all cultural differences will ultimately fade away. In fact, a proponent of the theory has argued that in modern times racial and ethnic identities have become stronger than in the past (Gordon, 1978). Whether assimilationist or pluralist, structural functional theories fail to address harsh realities of wealth and power inequalities. They simply assume that different racial and ethnic groups have essentially equal access to these scarce commodities, and that, therefore, they will have similar opportunities to receive the prized benefits of society. In contrast, conflict theories focus on issues of wealth and power and racial ethnic minorities' unequal access to these prized commodities.

One of the prominent conflict theories of racism is the caste analysis. A caste system is a socially legitimated arrangement of groups in which the hashing of the different groups is clearly designated, members' expected behavior is specified, and the movements of individuals from one group to another is prohibited. One feature of the caste system was the established set of beliefs subordinating blacks. Whites generally feel that people of color are inherently inferior. They also feel that people of color are a lower form of organism that is mentally deficient and emotionally underdeveloped.

In light of this dynamic, conflict theory helps to establish the frame of reference of social work because it puts a spotlight on domination and oppression, which might affect human behavior, and offers an explanation for those who are estranged and discouraged. Conflict theory directs the social worker to consider seriously his or her powerful relationships with clients.

In 1960 Oliver Cromwell Cox, an African American Marxist sociologist, analyzed the relationship between African Americans and whites. As a supporter of Marxist thought, Cox accepted Marx's claim that under capitalism modern societies would be divided into two basic classes. The ruling class depends on wealth and profits, while the working class depends on wages. Capitalism, Marx emphasized, was exploitative, paying workers barely enough to survive and forcing most of them to do assembly-line work. As a class they shared common grievances against the ruling class and the capitalist economic system. Organizing themselves into an army, workers would overthrow the ruling class and establish a new economic system, socialism, in which all citizens would own the means of producing wealth (Marx & Engels, 1960).

Cox also contended that as members of the working class, blacks and other people of color in capitalist society enforced all the limitations and problems imposed on white wage earners. In addition, they were racially exploited, designated inferior to whites, and denied many of the modest rights available to members of the white working class. Blacks experience double exploitation, which occurs for all people of color to some extent. Cox concluded that the core of the U.S. racial problem was that blacks wanted to assimilate by obtaining equitable opportunities in modern society, thus reducing greater exposure to disease, unemployment, poverty, and illiteracy. The white ruling class, however, opposed assimilation. Its members felt that it was to their advantage to keep blacks and other people of color economically, politically, and socially disprivileged. Whites used various techniques to keep people of color oppressed. Cox believed that lynching was the fundamental reliance of the white ruling class. Although the practice occurred more frequently in the South than in the North, he contended that support for what he called the "lynching attitude" existed among whites throughout the country (Cox, 1976). The dynamics presented here are similar to the elements of oppression discussed in Chapter 4.

Cox (1959) defined lynching as one group's use of mob action to kill a member of an oppressed group, thereby warning members of that oppressed group to accept an even more lowly status and to forsake any plans to rise above their subordinate position. For example, the violence in this country is a signification of lynching, which has more and more people of color killing each other, as well as white policemen killing people of color without any reason and by any means possible. He suggested that the extraordinary violence whites inflicted on blacks and people of color might have been necessary to overcome "possible inhibitions of conscience" occurring because people of color and white workers shared a common fight as exploited wage earners within industrial capitalism. He asserted that the only significant effect created by racism was that it prevented people of color and white workers from appreciating that under capitalism they shared common grievances. These shared grievances could have served as the basis for an organized interracial effort to overthrow the ruling class and capitalist system. Were Cox alive today, he might conclude that modern outbreaks of violence against racial ethnic minorities and people of color have produced a similar divisive effect.

Sidney Wilhelm is a modern proponent of a conflict theory of racism. Modern Marxist thinkers failed to recognize that racism exists independently of economic forces. According to Wilhelm, many theorists concluded that the destruction of capitalism would immediately eliminate any economic necessity for the continuation of racism (Wilhelm, 1983, p. 129). Currently, racism cuts across all social classes; blacks and other people of color who are spared oppressive economic conditions, nonetheless, are vulnerable to racism.

Some commentary on conflict theories of race relations seems appropriate. To begin, it should be emphasized that some of the observations about racism offered here are outdated, for instance, the southern caste system with associated lynching and other horrors has been largely dismantled. Nonetheless, we might consider the possibility that some oppressive social patterns described in this section are still applicable. While lynching no longer occurs, a similar process of terroristic intimidation, such as church burnings, continues the tradition of whites initiating violence against people of color.

Analyzing racism, some conflict theorists would include a third factor, gender. They have argued that poor women of color are most effectively understood if their three ethnic minority statuses are considered simultaneously. Several scholars have developed a unified theory of class, race, and gender, which considers diverse combinations of these three factors (Wilhelm, 1983). Many conflict theoretical analyses of American racism are compatible.

Internal colonialist theory emphasizes that whites have systematically controlled and exploited people of color and focuses on ethnic minorities' governance, restriction of movement, as well as supported cultural inferiority. The most articulate spokesperson during the Civil Rights era that capitalized the historical problem of racism as a psychosis was the irreverent Malcolm X. Previous leaders such as W. E. B. Du Bois and Booker T. Washington had many heated intellectual debates in the early part of the twentieth century on how to solve the problem of "people of color." Martin Luther King Jr. was fighting for the right to integrate public facilities and for blacks to have the right to become part of the economic mainstream. However, Malcolm X brought the race debate to the laps of urban blacks in a manner that threatened the political establishment unlike any other black leader. He discussed the issue of self-determination, or assimilation, and became the predecessor of the black power movement. The strategy was to reconstruct the mind-set of psychological slavery and create a truly self-sufficient nation that would protect itself from self-destruction. His premise was that as long as people of color are in bed with white supremacists, you would never escape their poisonous lies. He brilliantly used the press in a way to reach blacks, whites, and other people of color nationwide. Unfortunately, the media's portrayal of him as a black supremacist overshadowed his insightful ideas for the psychological reconstruction of people of color with its great emphasis on men of color.

The disadvantage of skin color, the fact that the dominant society prefers white to non-whites, is one that blacks and Latinos shared with the Japanese, the Chinese, and others. However, while Asians experienced harsh discriminatory treatment in the communities in which they were concentrated, some went on to prosper in their adopted land, thus suggesting that skin color alone was not an insuperable obstacle. Liebow (1967) argues that the greater success enjoyed by Asians may well be explained largely by the different context of their contact with whites.

Perceptions of Whites

Whites' perceptions of people of color reflect ambivalence and contradiction. People of color have been seen as basically incompetent, but supercompetent if they achieve; acceptable as nurturers and caring figures but not as equals; as angry when they appear arrogant (as whites are not); and as frightening when they appear competent, act assertively, or demonstrate ability to cope with racism without being demoralized. This list of conflicting reactions to people of color further identifies the ambivalence one group expressed: revulsion versus adoration; distaste versus wanting to get help from them; fear because they are destructive and dangerous versus pain over their despair.

Ordervay (1973) describes his psychoanalysis of a white social worker who had been working intensively with blacks to help them organize self-help programs. The social worker became increasingly fatigued because he felt too keenly the tragedy of black-white hostilities between friends in both groups and because both black and white militants constantly played on his loyalties, sympathies, guilt, and anxieties. He found himself viewed by some whites as a traitor and by some blacks as suspicious and dangerous.

The Changing Meaning of Race

The increasingly dominant perspective in the social sciences views race as socially constructed through political, legal, economic, and scientific institutions (Omi & Winant, 1994). From this perspective, "race can be understood as the historically contingent social systems of meaning that attach to elements of morphology and ancestry" (Lopez, 1976, p. 14). Thus the meaning of race finds its origins in social practices and in a system of social relations that signify social conflict and group interest. It is not individuals who create racial categories but macro-level processes in social institutions. Despite the growing debate over the ontological status of race, the concept continues to play a fundamental role in structuring personal identities, social relations, and worldviews. A major component of the self-concept and identity of many individuals is race, a prism through which interpretation of experience and relationships to social institutions are understood. Especially in this country, where dividing people into races has been an obsession, race dominates our culture and consciousness, coloring passions and opinions (Hacker, 1992, p. ix). Morphology and ancestry have long served as markers of group memberships and identity.

Racial identity theory suggests that individuals may be expected to vary in the degrees to which they identify with their respective racial groups, a result of the combined influence of personality characteristics, reference group orientation, and ascribed identity (Cross, 1987; Helms, 1990). Personality characteristics include generic processes such as level of self-esteem, anxiety, and other affective qualities. Reference group orientation refers to the degree to which the perceived value system or worldview of one's ascribed racial group is utilized as a quill to one's own beliefs, thoughts, and behavior. The moaning theme symbolized an examination and reappraisal of many of the problems and concerns of the masses of black people. Even though this theme in spirituals basically dealt with the relationship of black people with God, it also mirrored earthly concerns. For example, some spirituals discussed recent codes to express the desire for earthly freedom. Although the moaning themes in the blues generally dealt with the relation of black people to one another and to the world, they also reflected Godly concerns, if only to express spiritual ambivalence, turmoil, and doubt (Martin & Martin, 1995, pp. 91–93).

A general mood reflected in the blues and the spirituals was that black people should not keep dwelling on their pain, wallow in self-pity, or, using modern terminology, adopt a victim psychology, once the spirituals and the blues created the mood in which pain could be reexamined. They moved from identifying the sufferings to depicting the process of healing through collective empathy, collective support, and hope (Martin & Martin, 1995, p. 94).

The Hidden Injuries of Race

White social work faculty and white students tend to think that because they are not personally involved in keeping blacks and other people of color down, somehow the race problem does not exist. As Pinderhughes (1989) observed, many of them feel that because they too are in pain, in conflict, and confused, their human problems are no different from those of people of color. McIntosh (1992) noted that when white people adopt the color-blind "we are all only human beings" approach, they are generally utterly unaware of the advantage that white skin color automatically confers on them. McIntosh wrote that white people generally take "white privileges" for granted and are carefully taught to remain oblivious to themselves (Pinderhughes, 1989).

The matter of color is still a salient issue in social work. Although a far cry from what it was, color still affects social workers in their work with clients. Davis and Proctor (1989) found that the following was true, even in contemporary society:

- Most white workers prefer to work with white clients; white workers "generally are not knowledgeable about people of color, their lifestyles and communities" (p. 3).
- White workers are likely to bring preconceived ideas and attitudes about people of color to their practice (p. 3).
- Many white workers "avoid direct discussion of race, especially with people of color, and minimize the salience of race in interpersonal relationships" (p. 14).
- Whites prefer not to discuss racial issues and feign blindness to their client's race, maintaining that they strive to treat people of color like "any other client" (p. 14).

Caribbean Societies

The focus of this section is the Jamaican, West Indian family. It will examine Jamaican culture that may influence social worker intervention.

Brief History of Jamaica

Jamaica was discovered by Christopher Columbus, in his role as emissary, on his second voyage in 1493. The natives of the island were Arawak Indians; Africans first arrived in Jamaica in 1509 and were alleged to have come from the Ashanti, Yoruba, Ibo, and Fante tribes. By the middle of the seventeenth century (1655) the British had conquered the Spanish and taken over the island. In addition to the Arawak Indian natives, the Spanish, the African slaves, and the British, there were communities of Hispanic Jews, French, Germans, Scots, Irish, East Indians, Chinese, and Syrians. With the exception of the Jews, the other groups were brought to the island to work as laborers, particularly after emancipation and the loss of slave labor.

Geographically, Jamaica is the third largest island in the West Indies (146 miles long by 50 miles wide), with a population of 2.4 million in 1990. It is one of the group of islands that are collectively called the British West Indies.

Migration

The migration of West Indians to the United States dates back to the early nineteenth century. In the 1850s there were only a few hundred West Indians immigrating to the United States each year. Recent statistics indicate that in the years 1981–1991 there were approximately one million immigrants in the United States from the entire Caribbean. The Jamaican immigrants numbered one-fourth of that total. The immigration was characterized by separation from the family, feelings of dislocation, and adjustment to urban settings and colder weather. Most Jamaicans live in New York and Florida when they come to the United States. Social workers employed in large metropolitan areas are likely to encounter Jamaicans as clients.

Jamaicans sometimes travel to the United States with other family members, relatives, and neighboring families. Several Jamaican families often share an apartment or house, with each family occupying a bedroom. When a family moves out, the remaining families do not necessarily move into the unoccupied room; to save money, the extra bedroom might be rented.

One of the most difficult things Jamaicans have to cope with is physical and psychological isolation. Visiting extended family members is relatively easy on the island, because the country is so small. In Jamaica people know their neighbors and are familiar with local shopkeepers, clergy, and teachers. In the United States, however, people who were accustomed to living in their own homes and spending time outdoors can find themselves living in cramped apartments far removed from the countryside.

In addition to the isolation from their families, Jamaicans experience racial discrimination, which adds to their difficulties. Although racism has always existed in various forms on the Caribbean Islands, it is perceived and experienced differently by Jamaicans than by American Blacks. Many Jamaicans find the cruelty and invidiousness of racism in the United States shocking. Jamaican Blacks do not have the historical background of Jim Crow segregation, lynching, anti–Civil Rights aggression, and other acts of violence that have been perpetrated against African Americans in the United States.

Jamaican and American Blacks

The relationship between Jamaican and American Blacks is often ambivalent because the levels and types of racism in the United States that have made it not only useful, but also necessary, for American Blacks and Jamaican immigrants to present a united front in order to make progress. Jamaicans have frequently been exemplified by white society as good and industrious Blacks, whereas American Blacks have been stereotyped as lazy, criminal, and willing to live on public assistance.

Color distinctions in Caribbean society also play a part in this uneasy alliance: The lighter-skinned you are, the closer you are to the European end of the color continuum, and the higher your status in Caribbean society. However, in the United States, color shading and the meanings assigned to them are overtly ignored, and people are classified as Black or White. American Blacks believe that no matter how hard black people work, their color will prevent them from being justly rewarded. For some, the frustration has resulted in "learned helplessness," and they view efforts to break the cycle of poverty as futile.

Jamaica is a society of gender-role paradoxes. On the surface, sex roles are traditional and stereotypical and not affected by class, race, or age. Domestic training is emphasized in the belief that confining a young girl to the house will keep her out of trouble. Despite the emphasis placed on propriety, there are many unplanned, out-of-wedlock pregnancies and a considerable number of extramarital affairs. A primary part of the definitions of womanhood and of femininity is connected in the minds of Jamaicans. With motherhood, the woman's duties revolve around child-rearing, and a married woman without children is regarded as deviant.

Behavior

In Jamaica, the members of the middle and elite class are predominantly Protestant. A minority is Roman Catholic. Members of the lower classes are strongly influenced by folk beliefs of African origins. According to Lowenthal (1972) the meaning and practice of religion has been one way to differentiate the social classes in Jamaica. Thus, among the working class, the practice of religion is differentiated by the inclusion of African rites and emotionality in the Christian service.

The Jamaican family finds it difficult to admit that there is a problem it cannot handle, whether physical or psychological. If family members do consult a mental health professional, they often do so for a child with problems that may have come up at school, or for a medical complaint, at the suggestion of a physician who was unable to find a physiological basis for a client's symptoms.

For many social workers the genogram is a major assessment tool. When interviewing Jamaicans, it is important that the therapist begin by explaining the genogram construction process. African Americans in the United States, regardless of nationality, may have an appropriate cultural paranoia given the level of racism inherent in many institutions. It is therefore the responsibility of the social worker to explain the connection between the type of information asked for and its utility in therapy. The social worker should be aware of the identified patients' use of family titles (aunts, uncles, and so on) to denote people who are not actually related by blood. Family titles are also used to obfuscate the paternity of children.

A child's inability to explain certain family relationships should not be taken as a sign of slowness, but instead as the possibility that a family secret should be explored. Once the family is referred, the social worker should have little trouble getting members to come in because Jamaicans take seriously the advice of professionals. However, the social worker must choose a time for an appointment that will not require the father or mother to miss work. Jamaicans take the adage "time is money" very seriously.

The strengths of Jamaican families lie in their being so close-knit, an attribute that can be helpful to a social worker. The tradition of the extended family has been an important resource for Jamaican families. Social workers working with Jamaican families should be open to their cultural and belief systems as well as be able to address critical issues that affect Jamaican families. What social workers of the dominant culture often refer to as enmeshment has been and still is adaptive, because it provides individuals with emotional and practical support during times of stress. Social workers working with Jamaican families will find their work to be rewarding because the individuals are truly motivated to learn and help one another.

History

The Caribbean was first discovered and explored by Christopher Columbus. It was named after the Carib, a warlike tribe of cannibalistic natives that inhabited some of the Lesser Antilles at the time of the European conquest. The West Indies, which forms the nucleus of the Caribbean region, consists of two main groups of islands: the Greater Antilles (Cuba, Jamaica, Hispaniola, and Puerto Rico) to the north, and the Lesser Antilles, which again are subdivided into the Windward and Leeward Islands, to the east. The Caribbean Sea is of major importance for international shipping to and from the Panama Canal and is known for its natural resources, including oil.

The major ethnic group of the region is called the East Indians. African and European people have maintained to varying degrees their ability to reconnect with their ancestral heritage. The Caribbean people have strived to maintain ties with their ancestral links while creating something entirely new and different. Arising during the period of slavery, Creole languages were a result of the forced migration of African peoples to work on the European-owned plantations throughout the region. Creole language, or Patois, is a combination of African syntax structure and European lexicon (words). It arose out of a need for the slaves to communicate in a language closer to their native African languages than to the language of their overseers. The ensuing combination of French and African produced the French Creole spoken with national variations in Haiti, Martinique, Guadeloupe, St. Lucia, Dominica, and French Guyana. In the Dutch-influenced islands the combination of Dutch, Portuguese, English, and African results in Papiamento, and in Jamaica, Patois.

The majority of people in the Caribbean have spoken these various Creoles for over two hundred years. Because historically Creole was spoken mainly by a group of people who had been denied educational opportunities, it became associated with the poor and laboring classes, and often families would forbid their children to learn or speak it, encouraging them instead to work.

Jamaica: Population and Natural Resources

Jamaica has a population of about 1,890,000 of whom 79% are Black, 17% are people of mixed races, and the remaining 4% are East Indians, Chinese, and Europeans. The growth of the population has been determined largely by the two dominant groups of Black and people of color, each of which has increased more than threefold in the course of the past hundred years.

The number of White people has remained much the same as it was a hundred years ago. The East Indians first emigrated to Jamaica in 1845 to work on the sugar estates as contract laborers and in 1881 they numbered 11,000. Jamaica's population of 1,890,000 is large for a mountainous island, with a density of 340 persons to the square mile, which is six times the population density of the United States. At the present rate of growth the population will double in 40 years, and there may be 10 million people on the island in 2100. A Jamaican male child born 70 years ago could expect, on average, to live for thirty-seven years; the baby boy today looks forward to a lifespan of fifty-six years on the average. People live everywhere except in the heart of the inaccessible Cockpit Country and on the highest mountain of the Blue Mountains.

A Way of Life

In Jamaica there are no second-class citizens. Every man is equal before the law. Every man over twenty-one has the right to vote, can hold any post in the government or industry, can enter any profession, and can send his child to any school. Out of the colonial past with its splendor and squalor, romance and brutality has grown a society with a way of life that explodes by its achievements the myth of racial superiority. A young West Indian describes his heritage as "Dark people ringing in my veins fair people singing in sweet strains and when I bow my head to pray I bow with blue eyes, dark hands, and red hair."

Culture can be defined as the body of a people's expressions, values, meanings, and artifacts. The Caribbean culture is essentially tropical—some say "carnival"—to the extent that there is rhythm, architecture, and food that reflects the influence of the climate. The major ethnic groups of the region, namely the East Indians, Africans, and European peoples, have maintained to varying degrees their ability to reconnect with their ancestral heritage.

Culturally the Caribbean embodies legacies of slavery. Still lingering is the economics of single crop cultivation, which maintains the means of production in the hands of the few privileged landowners. Sugar and banana are the primary resources of such economics, and many Jamaicans still labor seasonally to make a living.

The European legacies of the specific countries can be identified as follows: Haiti, the Dominican Republic, Cuba, and Puerto Rico show the influences of the French and Spanish colonists, while Jamaica and Trinidad and Tobago show British influences. These territories constitute the largest islands as well as populations. Haiti is singularly populated by the critical mass of Afro-Caribbeans in the region. Cuba has the greatest number of European descendants, in particular Spanish, in its population. Across the islands there is a continuum of cultural manifestations ranging from an overwhelming African presence in Haiti and Jamaica to an overarching Spanish influence and presence in Cuba, the Dominican Republic, and Puerto Rico.

Jamaica is the site of the greatest number of Afro-Caribbeans in the West Indies. To this extent the language, food, ideologies, and ethnicity of Jamaica are similar in character to many parts of Africa from which enslaved Africans were brought. Resistance for this reason is seen as a major motivating source of culture. Populations of isolated Africans still inhabit this island.

Trinidad and Tobago is chiefly known as the home of calypso music and for the creation of the steel drum. This nation state, along with Guyana, is populated by the greatest number of East Indians in the Caribbean.

Caribbean ideas of celebration, worship, and artistic expression have been transmitted to the world through Rastafarian philosophy, reggae music, jerk cooking, and the use of regional rums and spices, among other practices. The Creole languages are perhaps one of the more clearly identifiable cultural forms originating in the Caribbean.

Rastafarianism began in the inner cities and poor sections of Jamaica where life was hard and unemployment was high. Rastafarianism holds that Emperor Haile Selassie who was Ras Tafari is God, and that black people can find salvation by moving back to Ethiopia. This original theology has changed over the years, as there are now many Rastafarian groups with no clear doctrine. "Jah," a name that can be found in the King James version of the Bible, is what Rastafarians call God. Most Rastafarians (men and women) wear their hair in dreadlocks, and the men cultivate beards.

Even though the countries of the Caribbean share a common geographic space, their colonial experience is one of the most influential factors determining the type of governmental systems and the levels of democracy that exist. The political traditions of the Caribbean are varied and mirror those of the former and present colonizing powers. The region constitutes a representative sample of the main forms of democracy that exist in the world. The Caribbean, therefore, is a very diverse region of political traditions. The single most important explanation for this diversity is the variety of colonial history and related influences.

Assessment

In 1959 the works of Sigmund Freud, Erik Erikson, and Abraham Maslow were not meant to consider people of color, their problems, or their potential. I am not saying, however, that because their works were Eurocentric or elitist—or even racist to some extent—they cannot be applied in part to the experience and issues of people of color. As a black social worker, I have gained great insight from the work of Sigmund Freud, particularly in the area of the "object loss and mourning." Freud believed that object loss begins in early childhood experiences in a situation of the infant when it is presented with a stranger instead of its mother. He wrote that because the infant cannot "distinguish between temporary absence and permanent loss" (Freud, 1959, p. 169), she feels that every time she loses sight of the mother she will never see her again. The infant in this state not only experiences mourning over the feeling of lost objects but also internal mental pain as equivalent to physical pain. Black people, for example, have suffered the loss of millions of black lives over generations. I am speaking of the countless losses caused by slavery, migration, war, abject poverty, and racial terrorism, and the myriad ways contemporary U.S. society still finds to inflict loss on blacks and other people of color. Although black people have had trouble with Freudian psychology, my position is that just as the class issue cannot be fully understood without a study of the work of Karl Marx, the issue of race cannot be fully understood without examining the work of Sigmund Freud.

Marian Wright Edelman (1998), prominent child welfare advocate, held that we are still losing our children to the city streets and to societal neglect. "We are on the verge of losing two generations of black children and other people of color to drugs, violence, to early parenthood, poor health and education, unemployment, family disintegration, and to the spiritual and physical poverty that both breeds and is bred by them" (p. 15). Experts in modern society show that the problem of loss and separation is intertwined with many other serious social and psychological problems. Bell (1973), in his pioneer study of attachment and separation, held that people who have experienced object loss through a sequence of responses to protest, despair, and detachment have a difficult time making healthy attachments with others.

In order for social workers to advance the goal of cultural diversity noted in Chapter 1, they must practice from a theory that people of color are vulnerable; all people of color, regardless of social class standing, are highly susceptible to victimization by a society that places little value on true diversity. A theory of people of color's vulnerability must incorporate a concept of entrapment and a belief that U.S. society deliberately sets traps and loves to keep people of color subordinate. Experience suggests, however, that people of color must be versatile to avoid the planned pitfalls of an oppressive and racist society. It suggests that such factors as education, racial consciousness, political awareness, knowledge of black history, hope, and being reality-based tend to help people of color develop greater versatility in avoiding societal entrapment and oppressive barriers, as well as finding strategies for rising above oppression.

From my perspective, a careful study of the works of Freud, Erikson, and Maslow will show students how their theories apply or do not apply to the experience of people of color. For example, Erikson's epigenetic life cycle can be applied only after a thorough understanding of it and a thorough examination of experience of racism for people of color. If we take Erikson's first oral-sensory stage of trust versus mistrust, we learn from a careful reading that he himself stated that "Mothers in different cultures and classes and races must teach trusting in different ways, so it will fit their cultural version of the universe" (Evans, 1969, p. 15). His belief supports what the black experience has demonstrated over the millennium, that to learn distrust is just as important. We have previously discussed the psychology of cultural paranoia. Erikson stated that, "If you don't mind my registering a gripe when these stages are quoted, people often take away mistrust, doubt and shame and all of these not so nice, negative things and try to make an Eriksonian achievement scale out of it" (Evans, 1969, p. 10). According to the first stage, trust is achieved. Actually, a ratio of trust to mistrust is a basic social process, which is a critical factor in the development of self. "When we enter a situation, we must be able to differentiate how much we can trust and how much we must mistrust, and I use mistrust in the sense of a readiness for danger and an anticipation of discomfort" (p. 15).

Erikson made his most detailed and stringent comments against American racism when he said to Newton that because he (Erikson) was white, "I thrived on that system that exploited your people, trended in spite of being an immigrant, a former drop out, and a Freudian" (Erikson, 1969, p. 98). Erik Erikson said that white society has to project its own negative identity onto black people and that white America cannot find its own most adult identity (Erikson, 1969, p. 60) by denying it to others. Thus, humanistic psychology allows knowing through feelings and intuition and hearing the voices of one's ancestors, whereas other helping professions criticize such knowing as being subjective, mystical, unscientific, and even the symphonies of a crazed mind. Social workers need to assess their own culture and ethnic identity as they reach out to help their clients. The following assessment list can be useful in learning about your ethnic background.

Assessment Process for the Social Worker

- What is your ethnic background? What has it meant to belong to your ethnic group? How has it felt to belong to your ethnic group? What do you like about your ethnic identity? What do you dislike?
- Where did you grow up and what other ethnic groups were there in your community?
- What are the values of your ethnic group?
- How did your family see itself? As similar to or different from other ethnic groups?
- What was your first experience with feeling different?
- What are your earliest images of race or color? What information were you given about how to deal with racial issues?
- What are your feelings about being white or a person of color? To whites: How do you think people of color feel about their color identity? To people of color: How do you think whites feel about their color identity?
- Discuss your experiences as a person having or lacking power in relation to the following ethnic identity: racial identity within the family, class identity, sexual identity, and professional identity.
- What are your thoughts about racism and how it impacts the lives of people of color?
- What do you expect or plan to do as a social worker to stop racism in the United States? (Pinderhughes, 1989)

Case Study

The theories for practice presented in this chapter help us to clarify our focus when assessing Factors I and II of the PIE system in relation to people of color. This was done to give clearer direction to the social worker's assessment and intervention efforts. The following case study will help you to see how we might use Factors I and II when assessing a client of color with several presenting problems.

David is a ten-year-old Native American/black American male who was referred by his school to the social worker at the mental health clinic for an evaluation. His fourth-grade teacher complained of unmanageable behavior, including fighting with other children, disruptive noises, talking during class, angry outbursts, and uncooperative behavior. He seemed to have trouble concentrating on assigned tasks, and his schoolwork had rapidly deteriorated during the past three months. He showed no motivation or interest in improving his performance.

David's parents also reported a change in his behavior in the past several months. He seemed more easily frustrated at home, displayed more temper tantrums, and fought continually with his siblings. When he wasn't being angry he tended to seclude himself in his room and remain uncommunicative or wander off for long periods of time, often coming home late into the evening. David also stole money and small items from siblings and evidenced persistent lying.

David lives with his parents, his grandmother, his aunt, two older sisters, and one younger brother. His parents relocated to an urban area from a primarily rural district two years ago, and his grandmother and aunt migrated last year and immediately moved in with the family. David's parents and his aunt work in skilled labor positions while his grandmother stays home with the children. In contrast to David, his siblings are described as "model children." They are good students, well liked among peers, easily managed, and well behaved and respected at home. They have been a source of pride to their parents, but David has been disappointing and frustrating. According to David's mother, his developmental history is normal—developmental milestones have been attained within the expected time period and no unusual illnesses or problems occurred during his early years. Prior to this year David had been an average student and well behaved and obedient at home.

Referral Issues

Several questions arise regarding David's referral. First, although it is clear that the referral came from David's school, it is not clear who referred him. Did a school counselor evaluate David's behavior? If so, valuable information might be available from this liaison. Second, the level of family involvement should be assessed. How supportive is David's family to the referral? Are they willing to participate in therapy or work on a behavioral problem with David? Third, was the referral an attempt to avoid serious dysfunctional and adjustment problems, or was David's referral because he can longer function in the classroom? Fourth, the social worker should ascertain the ethnic composition of the school and the class and solicit information about classroom structure and management that might be relevant.

Information about previous attempts to resolve the problem is crucial, particularly any previous therapeutic experiences. In addition, the degree of involvement of his extended family in these interventions should be documented. David has recently relocated to an urban area; information regarding the amount of contact with the reservation and potential tribal resources would be helpful, and if other interventions have been tried some measure of their effectiveness is crucial.

The teacher's chief complaints—disruptive, deterioration in academic work, concentration problems, and attention-seeking behavior—are symptoms one sees in many children diagnosed as having attention deficit disorder (ADD) with hyperactivity. Has this child been tested before? If yes, were there any signs of attention deficit or any indication of learning disabilities?

We would recommend a complete neuropsychological evaluation aimed at assessing the child's learning impairments. Previous tests and school reports should shed light on this question. If there has been a sudden change within the past three months, a detailed evaluation and neurological exam for the presence of tumors or other neurological deficits are strongly recommended. The nature of the disruptive noises and angry outbursts should be investigated in relation to the presence of a neurological condition. Finally, a history of the family's attempts to seek help for David's problem behaviors should be obtained. You should assess the family's experiences with formal mainstream services and helpers within the black community. Given the frequent dissatisfaction and distrust among blacks regarding their experiences with formal services and predominantly white institutions and schools, it would be important to assess this family's particular experiences and attitudes. This may provide useful information regarding their attitudes toward the present referral.

Referral information for this case indicated that although David's parents had noticed a change in his behavior, they did not seek services themselves prior to the school referral. This is not surprising given their cultural background and should not be interpreted as a sign of defensiveness or resistance to therapy. However, because David has been referred to the social worker at the mental health clinic by the school, it is possible that his parents will experience a sense of shame and embarrassment about his Native American culture. This culture emphasizes the belief that an individual's behavior reflects upon his entire family, and so David's parents might feel that the referral indicates their own failure to raise their son properly. It is important to explore the significance of the referral to the parents and to David himself. It is also important to know how David and his parents conceptualize the referral problem itself. Many Native Americans/blacks feel that difficulties can be overcome through hard work and dedication, and David's parents may view his problem behavior as something that he could change on his own if he tried hard enough.

Assessment of previous intervention strategies should also explore the potential role of the extended family. Because David's grandmother lives with him, it is quite possible that she, being the eldest family member, has a great deal of influence over the children.

Assessment Issues

The selection of specific assessment strategies is difficult to make on the basis of the available information. We assume that David's move from a rural reservation environment two years before and the recent arrival of members of the extended family have created some cultural dissonance for David. Initially, the social worker should assess the level of acculturation among various members of David's family and the level of cultural congruity between David's family and the new community in which they live. David may be trying to maintain a cultural identity in direct conflict with his family or his community. Without knowing more about the surrounding circumstances, it is difficult to formulate a diagnosis based on David's information. There may be extenuating circumstances where such acting out may be adaptive, for example, a very angry, hostile school environment or a prejudiced teacher. Misbehavior is not adaptive in a Native American home, however, where children are expected to be socially responsible, kind, honest, and to respect an extension of the reputation and pride of the central family. Have there been any recent changes in the patterns within the family system to which David may be reacting? Also, does David exhibit any behavior indicative of physical or sexual abuse? A family system approach that includes the extended family members who interact with David is recommended. Once a diagnostic evaluation is completed, treatment alternatives can be considered for David. If ADD is diagnosed, the primary intervention is an appropriate school placement and an individualized educational plan plus the possibility of stimulant medication on a trial basis.

Finally, the social worker should pay close attention to both verbal and nonverbal messages from David and his family. Because many Native American/black families' arguments are unspoken, the social worker must recognize that the dynamics of family interaction during and thereafter may not be over.

PIE Assessment of David

Factor I: Social Role Problems	*Code*
1. Familial Roles: Child	13

Type: Responsibility (parent expectations); (school expectations dependency   30
    anticipated)
Severity: High severity (school failure and behavior problems in school)
Duration: (one to six months)   4
Coping: Inadequate coping skills: (having difficulty solving problems and   5
    concentration in school)
Recommended interventions: Interventions are contingent upon a neuropsychological
    evaluation aimed at assessing the child's learning impairments. Possibly family
    therapy/ supporting of the family's attempts to seek help; bio-psychosocial evaluation
    in order to sort out David's cognitive and affective behavior; role play in order to sort
    out role identity in the family; and cultural role expectations will be advised.

Factor II: Problems in the Environment

1. Affectional Support System (support system struggling to meet affectional needs)   10102

    Discrimination: Color and culture   56
    Severity: Very high (impacts social role function and the environment)   5
    Recommended intervention: Consultation with client and with family because
        client and family become the most affective support system over the long term.

2. Education and Training Systems: (barriers to existing educational/training services,
    also absence of support services needed to access educational opportunities)   6104, 6105

    Severity: Will increase without appropriate educational support and mental health   5
    Duration: Resources are available and need to be accessed   4
    Recommended intervention: Mental health services as well as educational
        intervention should be provided, consisting of social supports and services
        for the child and family.

Factor III: Mental Health

DSM-IV

Axis I: Depression/Conduct Disorder
Axis IV: Parent/Child Problems (parenting)

Conclusion

The dominant American ideology assumes that society is an open and competitive place where an individual's status depends on talent and motivation, not inherited position. To compete, everyone must have access to education free of the fetters of family background or ascriptive factors like gender and race. To use a current metaphor: If life is a game, the playing field must be level, if life is a race, the starting line must be in the same place for everyone. For the playing field to be level, many believe education is crucial, giving individuals the wherewithal to compete in the allegedly meritocratic system. Thus equality of opportunity hinges on equality of educational opportunity.

References

Adams, A., & Schlesinger, S. (1988). Group approach to training ethnic sensitive practitioners. In C. Jacobs & D. Bowes (Eds.) *Ethnicity and race: Critical concepts in social work.* Washington DC: NASW.

Allport, G. W. (1954). *The nature of prejudice.* Cambridge, MA: Addison-Wesley.

Aquilar, M. H., & Williams, L. P. (1993). Factors contributing to the success and achievements of ethnic minority women. *Afflia, 8,* 410–424.

Baker, A. M. (1988). The psychological import of intrigue on Palestinian children in the West Bank and Gaza. *American Journal of Orthopsychiatry,* 496–505.

Balswick, J. O., & Balswick, J. K. (1995). Gender relations and marital power. In B. B. Imgoldsby & S. Smith (Eds.) *Families in multicultural perspective* (pp. 297–315). New York: Guilford.

Bell, D. A. (1973). *Racism and the American law.* Boston: Little, Brown.

Boyd-Frankin, N. (1989). *Black families in therapy: A multi-systemic approach.* New York: Guilford Press.

Chestang, L. (1989). *Character development in a hostile environment.* Chicago: University of Chicago Press.

Comer, J. (1985). *Black child care.* New York: Simon & Schuster Publishers.

Cox, O. C. (1959). *Caste, class and race: A study in social dynamics.* New York: Monthly Review Press.

Cox, O. C. (1976). *Race relations: Elements and social dynamics.* Detroit, MI: Wayne State University Press.

Cox, O.C. (Ed.) (1998). *Empowerment in social work practice: A sourcebook* (pp. 204–219). Pacific Grove, CA: Brooks/Cole.

Cross, W. E. (1987). *Shades of black: Diversity in African American identity.* Philadelphia: Temple University Press.

Davis, L. E., & Proctor, E. K. (1989). *Race, gender & class: Guidelines for practice with individuals, families and groups.* Englewood Cliffs, NJ: Prentice-Hall.

Devore, W., & Schlesinger, E. G. (1981). *Ethnic-sensitive social work practice.* St. Louis: Mosby.

Edelman, M. W. (1998). *The state of America's children yearbook.* Washington, DC: Children's Defense Fund.

Erikson, E. H. (1969). *Identity and the life cycle, selected papers.* Psychological Issues Series, edited by Stuart Hauser. Madison, CT: International Universities Press.

Evans, R. I. (1969). *Dialogue with Erik Erikson.* New York: E. P. Dutton.

Freud, S. (1959). Totem and taboo. In J. Strachey (Ed.), *The standard edition of the complete psychological works of Sigmund Freud.* Vol. 13: 1913-1914, 1–114.

Gibson, C. (2002). Being real: The student-teacher relationship and African-American male delinquency. New York: LFB Scholarly Publications.

Gordon, M. M. (1978). *Human nature, class & ethnicity.* New York: Oxford University Press.

Hacker, A. (1992). *Two nations: Black and white, separate, hostile, unequal.* New York: Scribner's.

Helms, J. (1990). *Black and white racial identity: Theory, research and practice.* New York: Greenwood Press.

Hopps, J. (1982, June). Oppression based on color (editorial). *Social Work, 27* (1), 3–5.

Liebow, E. (1967). *Talley's corner.* Boston: Little, Brown.

Lopez, F. (1976). *The Bell Systems non-management personnel selection strategy* (pp. 226–227). Cambridge, MA: MIT Press.

Martin, E. P., & Martin, J. M. (1995). *Social work and the black experience* (pp. 94–105). Washington, DC: NASW.

Marx, K., & Engels, F. (1960). Manifesto of the Communist party. In L. Fowler (Ed.), *Basic writing on politics and philosophy.* Garden City, NY: Anchor Books (originally published 1848).

McGoldrick, M., Giordano, J., & Pearce, J. (1996). *Ethnicity and family therapy.* New York: Guilford.

McIntosh, P. (1992). White privilege and male privilege: A personal account of coming to see correspondence through work in women's studies. In M. L. Anderson & P. H. Collins (Eds.), *Race, class, and gender: An anthology.* Belmont, CA: Wadsworth.

Morales, A. T., & B. W. Sheafor (Eds.). 1992. *Social work: A profession of many faces.* 6th Ed. Boston: Allyn & Bacon.

Omi, M., & Winant, H. (1994). *Racial information in the United States: From the 1960's to the 1990's.* New York: Routledge.

Ordervay, J. (1973). Some consequences of racism for whites. In W. B. Brown & B. Kramer (Eds.), *Racism and mental health*. Pittsburgh, PA: University of Pittsburgh Press.

Pinderhughes, E. (1989). *Understanding race, ethnicity and power: Key to efficacy in clinical practice*. New York: Free Press.

Rodriguez, C. (1996). *A critique of the race debate in the U.S. Latino community*. Columbia, MD: Cumaron Publishing.

Spencer, M. B., & Markstrom-Adams, C. (1990, April). Identity processes among racial and ethnic minority children in America. *Child Development, 61*(2), 290–310.

Sue, D. W. (1981). *Counseling the culturally different: Theory and practice*. New York: Wiley.

Thompson, R. (1989). *Theories of ethnicity: A critical appraisal*. Westport, CT: Greenwood Press.

U.S. Census Bureau. (2001). National Population Estimates. http://www.census.gov/popest/estimates.php

Wilhelm, S. M. (1983). *Black in a white society*. Cambridge, MA: Schenkman.

6

Women and Sexist Oppression

Barbara Worden

From birth we are considered either male or female and are treated accordingly. Everything in our lives is based on our gender identity. From babyhood and childhood our names, our clothes, our friends, our sports involvement, our family roles, and the importance of our education are often decided on the basis of our gender. As working adults, our pay scales, our professions, our work environments, even the public bathrooms we are allowed to use are affected by whether we are considered male or female. All human languages make a distinction between sex groups, and all societies use sex categorization as a basis for assigning people to different adult roles (Stockard & Johnson, 1992). Mimi Abramovitz (1996) asserts that gender, like race and class, structures the organization of social life, and gendered divisions often support the status quo. Because gender roles are assigned and enacted within our own family, gender is the most basic and perhaps the most pervasive category of diversity.

Writing about women and oppression is a complicated task because the philosophical topic is generally broad. At the same time, the condition of oppression and subordination affects women of all colors and social classes, and the feelings generated from this condition are personal to individual women. These feelings and conditions vary among women of similar social class and race and may vary greatly among women of different social classes and races.

When examining scientific research on the differences between men and women, a review of the literature shows that in meta-analysis studies on gender differences in cognitive abilities (Hyde, 1981), personality traits (Cohn, 1991), and social behavior (Aries, 1996), gender differences accounted for typically less than 5% of the variance. This means that there were greater differences within each gender than between them. Therefore, men differed more from other men and women from other women than men and women differed from each other. Some theorists and writers postulate that gender itself is a social construction and as such there are no universal truths about the nature of gender or gender identity. Social constructionism views people as active participants in perceiving and making sense of their surrounding environments. In this perspective, there are no universal truths about *innate* differences between men and women—but what exists, instead, are beliefs about gender differences, which are socially constructed, consensually held, and reinforced. These beliefs become our definitions of reality. Because of the consensual nature of these beliefs, the ability to define reality for a culture is inherent in those who are in the majority and those who hold the most power in the dominant society. These constructed beliefs then serve to maintain the status quo, particularly of those in the culture's power hierarchy (Worden & Worden, 1998).

Chapter 4 analyzes oppression of all marginalized groups as a by-product of these socially constructed notions of power and hierarchies of difference. Hierarchies of domination are experienced simultaneously and differently by different types of women. Therefore, there is no *single* generic gender oppression.

If gender is a social construct, then can all women be victims of oppression? Linnea GlenMaye (1998) argues that although women as a group are fragmented in a number of ways, women as a whole are united in two fundamental ways: (1) we are a distinct and separate biological sex, and (2) as members of this sex we share both the bodily experience of femaleness and the social condition imposed on us by virtue of our sex (p. 30). For this chapter, to unify these disparate, yet similar experiences is a task of articulating an interconnected web of theoretical constructs and frameworks while highlighting gendered and individual experiences. As no one theory or position can speak for all perspectives, this chapter does not represent or illustrate the oppression of all types and classes of women. It attempts to provide a broad framework of types of oppression that constrain women and a way of thinking about empowerment that can help release our clients and ourselves from various oppressive forces.

Other chapters in this book have defined the ecological and strengths perspective and the notion of a development of multiple selves or social identities. These social identities are used in the process of assimilation into the dominant group to avoid stigmatization. This chapter will not duplicate an explanation of these concepts but will seek to illustrate their use when working with women. Because gender is the earliest and the most basic unit of diversity, all women must develop a multitude of social identities to negotiate their way through various social roles.

There are many levels and lenses through which we can dissect and examine these identities. We shall begin our examination on a micro level of analysis by looking at a case study from the PIE framework. We flesh out our thinking in a mezzo level of analysis by looking at the broader conditions of gendered oppression in various contexts that affect women's lives. Our macro level of analysis takes a general look at knowledge construction and dominant versus subgroup positions and how this affects the contexts by which we acquire and verify knowledge. By adopting this approach, students who are interested in seeking further reading in any of the areas are clearly pointed in the desired direction.

As in other chapters, this chapter will analyze the following case study utilizing the PIE classification system for problems in social functioning (Factors I and II). We will frame the interventions from an empowerment perspective. This perspective enables practitioners to carry a dual focus: (1) to investigate and acknowledge the often oppressive reality of marginalized clients in our society and thereby give credence to the effects of internalized oppression and (2) to help clients discover their own strengths and potentials to mitigate the effects of that internalization process. The empowerment approach assumes that oppression is a structurally based phenomenon that affects both individuals and communities. It makes connections between social and economic justice and individual pain and suffering, and adopts the ecological perspective (Lee, 1996). A third focus can be added for our purposes, which is to explore the various social identities women use to fulfill their social roles.

Case Study

Jean is a twenty-seven-year-old half Korean and half American Caucasian woman. She is married to Tom, an American Caucasian, and the mother of three children: Brent, age six; Sarah, age four; and Tommy, age two. She recently sought counseling from a crisis service for battered women. Jean is depressed and withdrawn. She has a very small frame and reports that she has lost ten pounds in the past month. This weight loss, coupled with her flat affect, makes her appear quite ill. She denies any suicidal ideation, although she says that she doesn't know how she will continue to take care of her children and Tom's sick mother.

Jean's husband, Tom, is given to bouts of heavy drinking and questionable drug use. He has violent episodes in which he alternately verbally and physically abuses her. He likes to bring his friends home after a drinking binge and make her serve them breakfast. He verbally abuses her in their presence, adding to her humiliation. During these episodes he calls her sexual names and tells her he wants to send her back to Korea and keep the children here.

Jean and Tom met and married seven years ago when he was in the army and stationed in Korea. They moved to the United States and settled near his family. Jean wanted to come to the United States to escape a suffocating family in Korea and to find a better life. When they were first married, Tom was kind and loving. Although he liked to go drinking with his friends, he always came home at night, worked hard as a computer technician, and brought home his paycheck. The marriage was good after they had Brent. By the time Sarah was born, Tom was staying out later and later and coming home and passing out. At this time, his company had their first downsizing. Although Tom's job was saved, several of his friends lost their jobs. Rumors circulate that another big layoff is coming. Jean knows Tom is scared he will lose his job.

After Tommy was born, the marriage was marked by increasing arguments over money and Tom's drinking and suspected drug involvement. Tom began some minor drug dealing to make extra money. He swears he doesn't use anything himself.

Jean reports to the counselor that the verbal and physical abuse is escalating and she often can't sleep because she lies awake with fear. Jean sleeps with Sarah on the nights when Tom is angry and drunk. Jean asks the counselor what she is doing wrong to make Tom behave this way toward her.

She has a high-school diploma but little work experience. Tom went to computer school using the funds from his Army G.I. Bill. Jean always wanted to go to college, but worked during the first year of their marriage so Tom could get his degree. The children came quickly and there was no time for her to go to school. Now, when she and Tom discuss it, he tells her she isn't smart enough and it's not his place to watch the children. Her place is at home. Tom's mother is very sick and Jean makes daily visits to her mother-in-law's home. She feels it is her duty to care for her husband's mother. Tom's family often criticizes her mothering and lets her know that they wanted Tom to marry a Caucasian American.

Jean feels very bad about herself, her mothering, and her place in the family. She blames herself for Tom's drinking and possible drug involvement. She thinks she is causing him to abuse her. She has no family in this part of the country and feels that she doesn't fit with the Korean community and isn't really an American. She had one Korean friend whom she met at church, and with whom she discussed spiritual concerns. That friend recently moved away and Jean doesn't feel comfortable discussing her beliefs with others. Therefore she has no one with whom to discuss her problems and feels culturally isolated. She feels completely dependent on Tom, who is getting more and more angry and drunk. In addition, he is missing so much time at work that his job is now in danger.

The PIE Classification System for Problems in Social Functioning

PIE is not a diagnostic system, but a tool for collecting and ordering relevant assessment information for the purpose of planning effective interventions. It creates uniform statements of social role: environmental, mental, and physical health problems and client strengths. Social workers use four dimensions to describe their clients: (1) social functioning problems concerning their social role, (2) environmental problems concerning (possibly oppressive) social systems, (3) mental health problems, and (4) physical health problems (Karls & Wandrei, 1994). This chapter examines Factors I and II, which are unique to social work practice because they focus on the person/environment interaction.

The social role problem areas in Factor I are grouped into four major categories: (1) family roles, (2) other interpersonal roles, (3) occupational roles, and (4) special life situation roles (Karls & Wandrei, 1994). Two issues are important to remember when doing a PIE assessment. First, the categories are delineated by the social worker's perception of the role problems, not the client's perception. Second, the social role functioning problems and type are descriptive of the client's difficulty and not the other person(s) in the relationship(s). Therefore, the following assessment is of *Jean,* the person seeking assistance. Although Tom is having many difficulties, he will not be assessed unless he seeks services.

Utilizing the PIE classification, Jean's Factor I assessment reveals problems in functioning in three social roles: Family (spouse) 1280.524, other family role (daughter-in-law)

PIE Assessment of Jean

Factor I: Social Role Problem Identification	*Code*
1. Familial Roles: Spouse (1280.524)	12 = spouse role
	80 = mixed type
	30 = responsibility
	40 = dependency
	50 = loss
	70 = victimization
	5 = severity: very high
	2 = duration: one to five years
	4 = coping skills: somewhat inadequate
Daughter-in-law (1530.344)	15 = other family roles
	30 = responsibility type
	3 = severity: moderate
	4 = duration: one to six months
	4 = coping skills: somewhat inadequate
Immigrant—Legal (4650.314)	46 = legal immigrant
	50 = loss type
	3 = severity: moderate
	1 = duration: more than five years
	4 = coping skills: somewhat inadequate
Factor II: Environmental Problem Identification	
(10102.524)	101 = affectional support
	2 = discrimination
	5 = severity: very high
	2 = duration: one to five years
	4 = coping skills: somewhat inadequate

1530.344, and an immigrant role (legal) 4650.314. Jean's spousal role is classified as a mixed type because she exhibits pieces of responsibility (30), dependency (40), loss (50), and victimization (70). Although Jean is mixed race and technically part American, she is exhibiting problems of immigrants who lose their culture and native support system when they move to a foreign country. Factor II assessment reveals that Jean interacts minimally with environmental systems outside the family. Therefore, we note Jean's problems in the Affectional Support System 10102.524. Note that Jean's coping index is listed as 4, which equates to somewhat inadequate coping skills. This classification is relevant because, although we can accurately assess the degree of severity of Jean's social problems, we cannot determine the strength of her coping skills because her oppression is so pervasive. She has survived intact and continues to mother her children and serve her husband and his family. However, she presents with severe weight loss, sleeplessness, and diminished ability to function. Until environmental interventions assure some degree of safety and security for Jean and her children, we will not be able to accurately assess her ego strengths and coping ability. Therefore, this category itself is somewhat arbitrary and will change as the assessment and interventions progress. The PIE Assessment of Jean breaks down the coding to help you understand the elements of the PIE classification system for this case.

The Empowerment Framework

The empowerment approach to social work practice marries the concepts of individual problems and social and economic justice. Therefore, it is very effective when working with populations who are marginalized by mainstream U.S. society. Lee (1994) suggests using a "fifocal," or five levels of foci, when working with women or other oppressed groups:

- A historical view of oppression, including knowledge of related social policy
- An ecological perspective, including adaptive functioning capacities and stress reactions; acknowledgement of unequal power arrangements and internalized oppression
- An ethnoclass perspective, which acknowledges the effects of sexism, racism, and classism
- A feminist perspective, which highlights the particular oppression of women
- A critical perspective, analyzing the link between individual pain and strategies for social change

Institutionalized, systemic, and interpersonal sexism interact to dominate women by both structural and psychological means. When women seek agency services to further their own well-being and safety, workers must be aware of the dimensions of oppression under which these women struggle. The PIE factors help us to outline these dimensions and therefore allow us to question the veracity of Jean's level of coping. As we more clearly understand her perception of these pressures and her role obligations, we will draw a more accurate picture of Jean herself.

This means that not only must the worker observe the old social work dictum of "starting where the client is," and understand her view of her own personal oppressions, but the worker must also understand how culturally reinforced gender stratification, sexism, and, to a degree, racism, have placed direct and indirect obstacles in the way of her growth. We will examine this sexism and gender stratification following the case analysis.

Within the empowerment framework, the worker and the client share relational power, with the client being the resource for change and the worker being the facilitator. Roles and responsibilities are mutual and shared, but the potential to release power resides in the client, not the worker (Lee, 1996). There are three interlocking levels of this process: (1) the personal, which is a development of a more positive and potent sense of self—self-esteem, self-direction, and competence; (2) the interpersonal, which critically examines one's relationships and the immediate surrounding environment and the use of these relationships to increase one's problem-solving potential; and (3) the environmental, which gathers personal and collective resources and strategies and self-help efforts to reach the stated goals (Gutierrez, Parsons, & Cox, 1998; Lee, 1996). Because of the focus on all three levels, both the strengths perspective (Saleebey, 1997) and the Life Model of Social Work Practice (Germain & Gitterman, 1980, 1996) are compatible with the empowerment framework.

In this approach to practice, the worker begins with the client's self-defined problem focus and promotes more reflection and problem solving on the person: environment transactions, including the client's role in them. In this reflection process, the experience and effects of oppressive conditions and possible solutions are considered (Lee, 1996). Also, within this process is the identification of social identities and expected social roles.

If we approach Jean's case from the empowerment perspective, we can see many levels of gender and racial discrimination. In addition, her cultural expectations of her familial roles add to her inability to consider solutions to her debilitating situation. Although Jean has been living in the United States for seven years, she is very culturally bound. Her Korean ancestry dictates her prescriptions of her social roles as wife, mother, and daughter-in-law. She is duty-bound to care for her husband and his family. We see this in her first decision to forgo her own education so Tom could attend computer school. This decision, although it is congruent with her familial role as dutiful wife, increases her dependence on her husband and decreases her involvement in the broader social/economic environment. She, therefore, minimizes her own social identity to emphasize her role as supportive wife. As the children arrive, her family roles multiply and intensify, and her contact with social supports further decreases. She does not complain about this further loss of self and immersion in the family. Indeed, it is congruent with her identity. When her mother-in-law falls ill, her duties to her husband's family increase, and she is again culturally bound to serve in this capacity. Jean does not report being overwhelmed by these obligations. However, as Tom's behavior becomes more irresponsible and abusive, Jean increasingly blames herself. She has little input from outside the family system, and this system itself is further oppressing her. Jean has little, if any, sense of her own self or her needs. Her primary concern is safety for herself and her children.

We see in this example that Jean is victimized by her husband and his family, and is further ostracized because she is Korean in a Caucasian family. In addition, she is cut off from her culture, her church, and her cohort group of Korean women. Therefore, her coping skills are further diminished. Poor women of color add the crushing oppressive influences of poverty, gender, and race. If Jean and Tom separate, Jean may be further oppressed as she is plunged into poverty. She has few occupational skills, having sacrificed her education so that

Tom could attend computer school. She would be dependent on his providing child support, a shaky prospect indeed. These influences then have more of a systemic and pervasive impact on the victims of oppression.

Bartky (1990) speaks of a psychological oppression, which mirrors Fanon's "psychic alienation." This form of oppression is one way the dominant culture sends messages of inferiority to those who occupy inferior or marginal status. Because Jean sought services from a crisis shelter, the first intervention concerns her very real safety issues. Addressing the environmental concerns, a safety plan and possible shelter stay must be discussed. Once this is in place, counseling can center around examining her interpersonal relationships and developing a stronger sense of self and personal identity, which is different from the social role as Tom's obedient wife. As we begin to contemplate this task, we bump into our first structural and systemic encounter with sexism and gendered oppression.

Male Models of Structured Reality

Current trends in the mental health movement had their roots in Freudian psychology. Freud's view of gender differences strongly reflects a historical-sociological context. Freud gave short shrift to female development, as an analog to male development has long been a feminist criticism of psychoanalytic theory. Feminist scholars who have been writing for the past two decades are currently challenging the veracity of this model, based not only on drive theory but also on the centrality of the male experience. These scholars and students of the psychology of women distinguish themselves by debating two broad issues in the body of psychological literature: (1) the valuation of the male phallus as a developmental concern for both sexes, challenging the assumption that anatomy is destiny; and (2) the inequality (political, social, intellectual, and emotional) of the feminine gender role (Worden & Worden, 1998). To this debate, we can add the value of female development as a relational, not a separate, being. Miller (1986), Chodorow (1978), Gilligan (1982), and Lerner (1988) are the voices of these scholars now challenging the existing conceptualizations of women's moral and psychological development. (For a general discussion of their contributions, see Worden and Worden, Chapter 3, "Differences in Experience.")

In traditional Western psychological theories of development, the self has long been viewed as the primary unit of study. However, the notion of a self does not appear to fit women's experience (Miller, 1991). The self has often been separated from its surrounding environment and studied as a separate entity. It is seen as developing through a complex series of processes leading to a sense of psychological separation from others. From this, there follows a quest for power over others and power over natural forces, including one's own body (Miller, 1991, p. 25).

The mature self is predicated on greater separation of self from others. The goal is not to develop a greater capacity for connection or interdependent, mutually satisfying relationships. The self is seen as autonomous and independent, gaining mastery over internal impulses, while striving to satisfy personal needs and desires. In this model, feminine gender development is seen as inferior to and lesser than male identity development. These models are important to our study because they tell us what should happen in human development. It has also been assumed that what is "normal development" for men is "normal development" for women.

Currently, several changes have evolved in the developmental literature. First, modern psychoanalytic theorists have broadened their conceptualization of feminine gender identity. There is a growing belief that young females become aware of and value their inherent femininity, rather than envy their lack of male genitalia. Second, ego psychologists have also broadened the developmental lens to weigh the familial and cultural influences on the developing ego and sense of self. Thus gender and personality development are not merely a consequence of innate and narcissistic biological drives but of interactions of biological drives and the surrounding environment.

Prominent feminist scholars have been developing a more current notion of the self. In the literature, it has been called by several similar terms: "interacting sense of self" (Miller, 1991), "self-in relation" (Jordan & Surrey, 1986), and "relational-self" (Jordan, 1997). A salient feature of this sense of self is an emphasis on the necessary and nurturing value of being in relation with others. One's sense of self-esteem and effectiveness is enhanced by relating to and tending to the interactions with others (Miller, 1991). In this paradigm, it is not because of relationships that women are oppressed or victimized, but because of the nature of those relationships. We can see with Jean that she is at the center of a complicated web of relationships to which she feels both obligated and very attached. It is the nature of these relationships that helps shape her sense of identity and sense of self. When working with Jean on her Factor I social roles, particularly her spousal role (1280.524), it is important to tease out which elements of this role she fulfills through role obligation and which elements give her a greater sense of her own self. For a short but thorough summation of the development of psychoanalytic thought and feminine development, see Chehrazi (1987). For a short summation of various feminist paradigms, see Worden and Worden (1998).

Let's take this male model of structured reality and place it within its broader framework to help explain the situation many of our clients face as they find their way through our system of mental health.

Madness as a Feminist Construct

Institutional and structural sexism is inherent in the history of mental illness, its definitions of madness, and its treatment of the mentally ill. When studying madness or its opposite, mental health, we must consider how, in a cultural context, notions of gender influence the definition and treatment of mental illness.

Showalter (1985) in her feminist history of psychiatry and madness analyzes in depth the English culture and its definitions of female madness. However, her historical assertions can be applied to U.S. cultural trends as we trace the development of psychiatric thought and theories and their effect on women. Showalter sees madness as the way of the desperate for communicating their powerlessness.

When discussing the history of mental illness, historians have considered social class, rather than gender, as the determining variable in diagnosis and treatment options. Historically, the wealthy and upper social classes have had different options for treating and housing their mentally ill family members. In Victorian times, upper-class patients were treated in private asylums or resided as guests on large estates. Often their families could keep them in the home, assisted by a staff of servants. Lower-class patients went to public facilities and were warehoused, starved, and beaten. These families, in Victorian times, had no means to keep them safe.

In contemporary U.S. society, the wealthy still have the option for private pay treatment. Middle and lower classes are bound by the limited treatment options of managed care, short stay hospitalizations and abbreviated treatment. Those without insurance may inhabit the population of the homeless mentally ill, a large and growing population in today's world.

Two early ideological shifts are important to the study of women, as the dialectic of reason and unreason became gender-related and was linked to both the definition of madness and social reform. The first is the significant shift on the lens of madness—from defining lunatics as brutes or ferocious animals (e.g., the wild male who needs confinement) to lunatics as sick human beings (the delicate, poetic mad woman who needs pity and kindly care). The victimized woman became a kind of cult figure for the Romantics (Showalter, 1985, p. 8).

The second ideological shift is that several types of feminine maladies were seen as rooted in the nature of femininity and female sexuality. These suppositions led to assumptions concerning feminine irrationality that could be subjected to and tamed by masculine rationality. These cultural images emphasized feminine vulnerability and dependence on masculine goodwill and protection. Women and madwomen alike were the victims of eighteenth- and nineteenth-century parental restrictions and male oppression. This image of women as victims in need of protection is reinforced in our current public policy laws of *femme coveture* (see section on family policy).

Showalter (1985) parallels images of nineteenth-century English culture and psychiatry through the historical phases, starting with psychiatric Victorianism (1830–1870), in which asylums (inpatient facilities) were designed to contain feminine irrationality and provide paternalistic therapeutic techniques to bring the feminine nature into rational, masculine control.

Following the Victorian era, psychiatric Darwinism (1870–1920) emerged, which viewed insanity as the product of organic defect, poor genes, and an evil environment. The lunatic was a degenerate, akin to today's socially defined undeserving poor. Darwinian therapists began to dictate proper feminine behavior for women of all social classes. In part, this psychiatric evolution was in response to the developing women's movement. At that time, middle-class women were beginning to organize on behalf of higher education, the right to work, and to gain political rights. The psychiatric diagnoses of the times were filled with female nervous disorders based on hysteria and various eating disorders. The classic female disorder, hysteria, became the focal point for the next evolution, psychiatric modernism (1920–1980). This phase saw the emergence of psychoanalysis and the diagnosis of female hysterics.

In each of these periods, the prevailing attitudes were shaped by the macro influences of their current cultural context and social thought and the micro influences of individual male physicians who pioneered psychiatric theory building and shaping the social role of psychiatrists.

During the previous psychiatric evolutions, the essential gender and power imbalances that saw femininity and madness as synonyms were not addressed. Currently, we see the development of another evolution in the work of feminist theorists and feminist therapy movements. In this evolution, the cultural connections between femininity and madness are directly challenged and reformulated. In addition, as we have outlined, the very notions of the development of a sense of self and the importance of relationships and a nurturing environment are introduced into the developmental literature.

Therefore, when working with Jean, the worker must carefully assess Jean's awareness of her own sense of self—how strong is this sense and how is it tied to her successful role performance? For example, is Jean's sense of self stronger when she advocates for her children? Is she seeking mothering and connection with her ill mother-in-law? How oppressive was her Korean family of origin? What was she fleeing in her home country? What are the elements of "the better life" she sought in the United States? From her perspective, has she found it? What is missing? What would have to change for these missing pieces to be provided? How oppressive does she view her environment to be? What are *her* expectations of her family members and potential support systems? How are these expectations and sense of self culturally and class bound?

Here is where the worker and Jean must struggle to balance an emerging sense of empowerment by increasing consciousness of external oppression and a potential decrease in her sense of self because of her mounting disconnection with familiar role expectations.

Macro-Analysis: Feminist Epistemologies and the Nature of Knowledge Making

For us to understand the multiple frameworks for women and oppression, we must turn to the theoretical roots of the various definitions of oppression and subordination and understand the philosophical nature of varieties of oppression.

Several theoretical strains have evolved in explaining the oppression or subordination of women throughout the past two centuries. In the mid-nineteenth century, early feminists utilized general theoretical constructs concerning domination and inequality that were not connected to gender. By the mid-twentieth century, debates raged between those feminists who utilized traditional theoretical models and those who proposed newer, more radical ways of thinking (Jagger & Rothenberg, 1993).

These conditions are rooted in the epistemological argument concerning the nature of reality and construction of theory. It is not the purpose of this chapter to articulate the nuances in arguments concerning theory construction. Therefore, this topic is treated with general brevity, and additional references are provided for the student interested in philosophical and phenomenological issues.

One camp, the logical positivists, assumes the dominant group position and argues that reality is both universal and objective and can be measured and explained through scientific inquiry (traditional theory construction). This camp believes that objective truth exists and can be observed and measured. The observer is separate from the observed phenomenon, measurements are constructed, data is analyzed, and truth is found. This truth can then be extrapolated to the general population of phenomenon studied and be declared universal in its application. Using this line of reasoning, we would declare that gender differences are innate and infuse the population as a whole.

Many of these knowledge makers deny the political and social context of their frameworks and claim objective scientific truth. This is the nature of traditional scientific inquiry, often referred to in feminist literature as white, male western European scientific methodology. When factors are discovered, they are considered to be scientific, rational, and universally true. These findings are then incorporated into the popular culture and adopted into the prevailing value system as benchmarks of reality. They are then incorporated as part of the cultural symbolism of the day. When one approaches the meanings of cultural symbolism in this way, one sees that male dominance is passed from one generation and one culture to another through shared knowledge bases and shared symbols of that knowledge. These symbols then define and edit our world for us into a framework that is masculine in its nature and its terms.

The other camp, subjective relativists, argues not only about how the data is gathered but also about the way in which that knowledge is interpreted. Advocates of this camp take the position that objectivity is what those in power agree upon. Some theorists highlight different points of reference; for example, feminists emphasize gender bias, others racial or class bias. But the general consensus is that truth (and reason) is a cultural convention framed by the selected use of cultural and social power. Truth is, therefore, relative and often masks specific social interests. These social interests usually serve those dominant groups, which hold societal power: for example, males, politicians, and the socially and culturally elite and powerful business interests. (For an excellent discussion of these issues, see Loraine Code's chapter "Taking Subjectivity into Account," in Alcoff & Potter, 1993.)

Feminist theorists (one subgroup of subjective relativists) offer critiques of concepts and theoretical frameworks that deny or do not recognize oppressive social or structural forces. Feminist analyses in many disciplines highlight both the context and the status of the knowledge makers in that discipline. They are suspicious about a general or a universal truth, and instead highlight (1) the politics of the knowledge makers, (2) the impact of social status on knowledge making, and (3) the effect of disparate power relations (Alcoff & Potter, 1993). Cognitive authority is usually associated with a cluster of variables involving race, class, culture, age, gender, and sexuality (Alcoff & Potter, 1993, p. 3). Therefore, we can conclude that *all* epistemologies are bordered by some text or context and are then political.

Feminist epistemologies articulate their politics and recognize a complex, multilayered existence of oppressive forces, which affect all women of all races in all countries. Feminist consciousness then becomes a consciousness of impartial victimization. This is not to say that all feminists think of all women as helpless victims, but feminist thinkers are aware of alien and hostile forces outside of oneself that affect all women by enforcing an oppressive system of sex-role differentiation (Bartky, 1990).

However, the groundwork for any feminist theory is laid from two empirically valid sources: (1) the personal experience of individual women, and (2) the intersubjective agreement among women concerning the conditions under which they live. The purpose of this knowledge gathering is to understand how power differentials between men and women exist and are maintained and to understand the oppression of women and how it relates to other forms of oppression. Through these channels change is possible.

Feminist thinkers place at the center of theory construction the tenet that we, as women, are the most authoritative perceivers of our own reality. However, there are great differences between both populations of women and individual women. Our commonality is that we are *women,* but we are different from each other racially, ethnically, religiously, sexually, and in our social class, and often, national identification. No one story exists for all those gendered as *women.*

A basic assumption is that the oppression of individual women is connected through systematic oppression and subordination, rather than through individual misfortune or dysfunction (not blaming the victim). Women's oppression is part of the way the world is structured. This structure is called patriarchy and has a historical, material, and psychological base. This is why feminists believe that all women, no matter how privileged, are affected by oppression, because all women are subjected to the hierarchical ranking of their gender. This ranking is called gender or sexual stratification, which perpetuates dominance of the male gender. For some feminists, the term *patriarchy* is symbolized by men, for some it is the political system, for others it is our societal structure itself.

Patriarchy is often loosely used to describe any structure or system in which men traditionally have more power or access to power than women. Different schools of feminist thinking deconstruct the patriarchical power structures at different points. Three theoretical traditions are common among feminist scholarly writings. Liberal feminists focus on issues of rights and justice and how they equally or unequally apply to both genders. Socialist feminists focus on social relations and institutions' preservation of male dominance. Marxist feminists focus on how societal arrangements promote both capitalism and gender inequality (Stockard & Johnson, 1992; Zerbe Enns, 1997). (For an excellent discussion of the restrictions of theory construction, see Frye [1993, pp. 103–111], and for a discussion of theoretical frameworks, see "Why Theory," in Jaggar and Rothenberg [1993, pp. 75–79] and "Subjects, Power and Knowledge" by Helen Longino in Alcoff and Potter [1993].)

There remains some degree of distrust of any theoretical framework among contemporary feminist thinkers. Many contemporary groups of women, including racial, ethnic, and sexual minorities, proclaim that both traditional and feminist theories fail to account for their experiences and continue to marginalize them.

Young and Dickerson (1994) argue that the notion of sexism cannot be delineated from the effects of racism, classism, and the reality of national identities. In his essay on sex and race, Chafe (1998) sees that sexism and racism are intertwined in at least three methods of social control exercised by the dominant culture to keep both women and African Americans "in their place." He sees (1) physical intimidation and threats of violence against both groups. The traditional notion that women need a male protector speaks to the assumption that women are not capable of taking care of themselves. (2) Domination of the economic status of both African Americans and women by the white, dominant, masculine hierarchies of power. When women must please their mates, sexually and through other services, honest communication and mutuality are impossible. In addition, when women work, pay inequality and the positions designated as "women's work," along with sexual harassment, keep equality in the workplace as a distant goal. (3) The aspirations and goals of both women and minorities are limited. When women challenge the status quo, or protest their designated role, they are often labeled angry feminists, unsexed, or saboteurs of family values (pp. 476–482).

Some black feminist theorists understand race, class, and gender as simultaneous forces. They conceptualize the oppression of women not as additive (e.g., race + class + gender), but as multiplicative forces (e.g., race × class × gender), which are institutionally embedded in the context of racial and class order (Brewer, 1993). We can see all these areas of social control in operation when we consider Jean, our case example. In addition, her cultural heritage encourages her to be submissive and adopt a caretaking role in her husband's family. As a social worker works with Jean to build and restore her own sense of self, Jean may experience a great sense of loss by discarding these roles. Social supports and environmental interventions may help to ameliorate these losses, but we can expect a split between her proscribed Factor I social roles and her emerging sense of self.

If the worker and Jean do not acknowledge this split and help Jean negotiate her way through this sense of loss, progress and change may be limited. Jean may tend to reduce her fight against her oppressive roles to mitigate her empty feelings. Here is when the worker and Jean must be clear and consistent concerning her choices and her emerging sense of independence. Sometimes the increased feelings of independence that accompany a stronger sense of self are too threatening and symbolize too much disconnection from loved ones and familiar patterns. This change must be acknowledged and worked through by both Jean and the worker.

When studying the social science literature on gender and racial inequities, one finds a variety of terms to describe conditions of oppression and discrimination. Gender discrimination tends to focus on individuals (women of all races) and their unequal access to resources and opportunities. Gender stratification implies a more institutional and systematic web of sexual inequality. *Sexism* is a term used as a parallel to racism, although the sources of sexism and racism are different (Stockard & Johnson, 1992). (For a more thorough discussion of these terms and their uses, see "Gender Inequality in Cultural Symbolism and Interpersonal Relations" in Stockard and Johnson [1992].)

Given these perspectives and frameworks for weighting the various "isms," we could struggle endlessly with knowledge construction and definitional issues and still not reach agreement concerning the labels for and types of gendered oppression and discrimination. Therefore, we will leave this issue and hopefully have given you some thoughts and questions to further explore. We move now to a mezzo level of analysis, examining the various forms of oppression that all women experience in various degrees.

What Do We Mean by the Oppression of Women?

To be conscious of external oppressive forces is the beginning of a sense of empowerment. Bartky (1990) states, "feminist consciousness is a consciousness of victimization" (p. 15). This consciousness is a divided consciousness in two ways. First, it is an awareness of unjust treatment of women by the surrounding environment that enforces an often stifling and oppressive system of sex-role differentiation. Victimization is impartial, and occurs on a macro, societal level. The damage is done to each one of us personally and is felt at a familial and individual level. Understanding this sense of victimhood raises one's level of consciousness, and, through this increased awareness, one can begin to release energy and begin a journey of personal growth. Second, women of different colors and classes are privileged in ways that are uneven. Caucasian women are often privileged in socioeconomic status, earning potential, and educational levels. Finally, women of color suffer both the oppression of gender and race.

Stereotyping.   Extreme stereotyping of both women and people of color depicts them as childlike, often dependent, more intuitive than rational, and less capable of scientific achievement. White women are often seen as comparatively frigid, and women of color as lustful and overly sexed. Stereotyping furthers oppression in three ways: (1) Rigid female stereotypes lead to rigid female roles. (2) When women are viewed as a global stereotype, it is impossible to attend to and recognize an individual woman's needs. (3) When we believe the stereotype about ourselves, it is impossible to tend to and seek recognition and validation of our own needs. Self-direction and autonomous decision making become difficult. Add to these economic and political obstacles in the environment, and any effort to make our own way becomes monumental. The greater and the more public the effort, the more the traditional concepts of femininity are denied.

Lacking a culture of our own, we adopt the culture of our men and therefore subscribe to a truncated definition of the self, which either conforms to cultural stereotyping or sets parts of us struggling against each other. This is true for Jean, who leads her life through rigid cultural and gender role stereotypes. Her (1) lack of education, (2) economic dependence, (3) cultural proscriptions, and (4) lack of cultural and social supports inhibit her from articulating and meeting her own needs.

Linnea GlenMaye (1998) describes three general conditions that all women share as a result of being subject to psychological and structural gender oppression: (1) profound alienation from the self, (2) the double-bind of either meeting one's own needs or serving the needs of others, and (3) institutional and structural sexism (p. 31).

The following section will highlight various forms of structural sexism and gender bias that affect all women in a variety of ways.

Women and Work

Women have always worked. McBride Stetson (1997) asserts that the United States has differing social policies concerning gender and the work ethic. For men, particularly upper- and middle-class professional men, work can be valuable. It can enhance their sense of self-esteem and develop their intellect and skill. Thus men may work to develop themselves, to contribute to society, and to achieve maturity and independence. Society holds that women work when the traditional arrangement of male breadwinner/female homemaker fails. This assumption is based on the notion that paid work has a different place in women's lives and is in conflict with their primary roles as mothers. When married women do work, their work has a different meaning than when married men work. Their income is often considered secondary, or supplemental to the real family wages. This assumption completely ignores the plight of poor and minority women who are often forced to work for wages below the poverty line.

In the United States, more than twelve million women work full time in jobs that pay wages below the poverty line, and many more women than men are part of the working poor. In 1995, on average, women earned only 71.4 cents for each dollar that a man earned. The wage gap, which is predicated on gender segregation, still hovers around 30%. This has not varied much since it was first measured in 1961, when it stood at 40% (Rothenberg, 1998). Despite gains in women's workforce participation at all levels, gender segregation, as represented by the 30% difference in pay scales, is still a problem in the United States.

This chapter will not analyze various workplace policy initiatives but will leave this topic with the assertion that gender segregation and unequal work status continues to discriminate against women at all levels of the workforce—from the welfare to workfare programs to the highest rungs of the corporate ladder. These facts lend credence to the notion that all women are affected by oppression.

Family Policy, Welfare, and Gender Roles

One consistent area of gender bias is demonstrated in the underlying principles of family and welfare policies. As we enter a new millennium, there is little consensus concerning family values or family life in the United States. Each state and region is culturally and ethnically diverse, with various degrees of acculturation of their indigenous ethnic groups. Women's attitudes about their familial roles are in turmoil, especially as more and more families need at least two incomes to survive. As the frequency of divorce and single parenthood increases, women struggle to reconcile their work and family roles.

However, as policy debates rage onward, in private, most women live in traditional family structures and carry the lion's share of both homemaking and work responsibilities.

As family law has developed, so have three successive theories of gender role relationships in marriage: As industrial capitalism was on the rise late in the eighteenth and early nineteenth centuries, a shift in women's roles took place, and it was reflected in family policy. In the nineteenth century, a unity of husband and wife was dominant. At marriage, a woman's separate status *(femme sole)* disappeared, and she became the legal responsibility of her husband. She forsook all her property, wages, and right to contracts. The husband was responsible for her acts, and he could restrain her and correct her behavior. This coverture (or a *femme coverte,* or covered woman) reinforced patriarchal family structures. These laws were enacted to protect women, although they also hobbled them.

In the industrial age, women stayed within the home and men went out to work. But women were no longer allowed to be economically productive. Women were seen as the weaker sex, and our subordination to men became grounded in our economic dependence. This ethic is often called the "cult of domesticity" or the "cult of true womanhood" (Abramowitz, 1996, p. 38). This form of coverture protected primarily wealthy middle-class white women. This structurally cemented that wealthy white women were perceived differently from poor women and women of color, who were often denied the "rights of womanhood." They could not embrace the social definition of the good wife and mother because they were forced by poverty and poor wages to work long hours outside the home. They faced exploitation on the job and dangerous working conditions. "This notion of separate gender spheres placed poor and immigrant women and women of color in a double bind at home and reinforced their subordinate status in the market. Separate spheres, which recognized and sustained the household labor that white women performed for their families, offered no such support to non-white women" (Abramowitz, 1996, pp. 38–39). However, this protection can be seen as a form of social control. If a woman cannot earn a living wage, then she must depend on a man, marriage, and family life as a rational source of financial support.

By the early 1900s through the 1960s, a separate but equal legal status was dominant. In this view, marriage is an equal partnership in which each spouse makes a different, but equal contribution.

As more and more women entered the workforce, a third theory of marital gender roles emerged: marriage as a shared equal partnership. This view depended on an overlapping of duties, rather than duties assigned according to gender.

This chapter will not debate the divorce and parental rights advances, which feminists challenge as oppressive to women. Our aim is to give a broad view of the status of women within marriage and those women who live on the brink of poverty without benefit of a marital partner. This ideology of women's roles is deeply encoded in social welfare policy. Conforming to the ideology of women's roles has been used to distinguish among women as deserving or undeserving of aid since colonial times (Abramovitz, 1996).

Feminization of Poverty

Closely tied to gender roles and economic status is a term that emerged in the national consciousness in the 1970s and remains true in the 2000s. The feminization of poverty posits that women are poor because of the effect of their traditional gender roles on their ability to accumulate economic resources. The traditional coverture (*femme coverte* or covered woman) common-law marriage contract reinforces patriarchal structure and is reinforced by many social and economic institutions. This preferred family form fosters the woman's economic dependency in the family. If she is divorced, a teen mother, or over age sixty-five, she is likely to be living in poverty. Women earn less than men for the same work, their share of national income is less, and income is stratified by both ethnicity and gender with African American and Hispanic/Latina women at the bottom—women's job status is lower than men's. If married, they earn less than their husbands. If single and the head of a family, their family income is lower than that of comparable families headed by men (McBride Stetson, 1997, p. 333).

The 1980s and 1990s marked the end of the post-WWII expansion of the U.S. welfare state, which was based on the 1935 establishment of Social Security. All entitlement programs were retrenched or eliminated, and the role of the federal government in social welfare programs has decreased and continues to decline. This strategy, launched in the early 1980s, was designed to redistribute income upwards, shrink social welfare programs, cheapen the cost of labor, and weaken the political influence of popular movements (Abramowitz, 1996; pp. 349–350).

While business leaders and economists pushed to lower the cost of production, the market began to downsize corporations, export production to low-wage countries, and depress fair market wages of the working U.S. population. This trend, which penalizes working women of all races and income levels, continues and appears to be heating up. More and more companies are laying off minimum-wage and middle-management personnel. The global economy allows products and services to be cheaply made in third world countries. Income is being distributed upward, with the middle and lower classes at, or near, poverty level. Job security is a luxury of the past.

Another social trend that greatly affects the lives of women in all economic strata is the myriad changes in the family structure. First, the marriage rate is declining, and the number of single mothers is on the rise. In addition, the divorce rate is rising, leaving an increasing number of divorced women to manage their homes and families—while reeling from the effects of a family breakup. They are then forced into a gender-segregated labor market where women are often in marginalized contingency jobs with little financial security.

Government policies are also to blame for the feminization of poverty. Insufficient alimony, child support, and nonenforcement of support orders along with small retraining allowances (those funds given to women when they divorce to allow for education and training) keep women from earning a living wage.

Many politicians and citizens refuse to recognize any policy issues in the plight of women and poverty and discrimination. They cite personal failures, cultural factors, ethnic characteristics, and failure to perform the traditional feminine roles as reasons women and their families are poor. The conservative approach argues that welfare encourages dependency. They believe that when the government provides support, it is rewarding laziness, family breakup, and illegitimate pregnancy. The underlying assumption is that the poor are morally deficient and choose welfare and the "easy life of government dependency" over good jobs, with good pay and childcare. Current welfare reform is attempting to restore the patriarchal family structure. This attempt, begun in the 1970s and 1980s and symbolized by the Republicans' "Contract with America," attempts to modify the marital, childbearing, childrearing, and work choices of AFCD mothers (Abramovitz, 1996, p. 355). It continued with the agenda of the FSA (Family Support Act) to shrink the federal government's involvement with the welfare state.

We saw in 1994 both Clinton's "Work and Responsibility Act," which made welfare both transitional and temporary, and the Republicans' "Contract with America," which dropped all education and training programs while tightening time and monetary limits on workfare programs. By November 1995, the Department of Health and Human Services was granting states permission to experiment with time limits and workfare programs. There was no parallel incentive for businesses to hire, train, or provide childcare benefits to women who were trying to work their way off the welfare roles.

Researchers found that OBRA (Omnibus Budget Reconciliation Act of 1981) forced women to use soup kitchens, live in inadequate housing, and stay in unsafe, often violent relationships. Many women and their children were impoverished or forced to the brink of impoverishment (Congressional Budget Office, 1987). In addition, these changes in welfare and workfare were flooding the labor market with low-wage workers and depressing their wages by more than 10%. At times their wages were below the federal minimum wage (Congressional Budget Office, 1987; Mishel & Schmitt, 1995).

In addition, the Republicans, determined to hold onto rigid, patriarchal family structures, took aim at illegitimacy as a social problem, claiming that welfare and single mothers were our nation's biggest social problem. Historically, single mothers were widowed (a socially acceptable category), but more recently single mothers have never been married. This poses a great threat to patriarchal structures. The subsequent welfare reforms effectively punished single mothers in at least three different ways. (1) The FAMILY CAP, or child exclusion act, denied AFDC to children born while their mothers are receiving aid and to unmarried teen mothers and their children. (2) If mothers refused to (or couldn't) identify the child's father, their benefits could be withheld. (3) States received extra federal funds for reducing their nonmarital birth rates without increasing the number of abortions (McBride Stetson, 1997, pp. 363–64).

These government efforts are attempts to control poor women's reproductive choices, and, when enforced as a condition of aid, they take advantage of women's weak financial situation. They magnify the effects of sexism on an already disempowered population. Further, these punitive and coercive efforts fly in the face of statistics, which show that welfare mothers do not have more children than nonwelfare mothers and do not have more children to receive more money. In addition, most women on welfare receive benefits for an average of two years and do not remain as long-term cases (U.S. Dept. of Health, 1995).

To meet the needs of this population and combat the effects of racism and sexism on a micro level, positive outreach, parenting classes, job training, and adequate childcare arrangements must be provided. Businesses and workplaces need incentives to hire, train, and provide benefits for this population as they attempt to work their way off welfare and into a productive societal role.

Conclusion

This chapter has attempted to highlight the broad areas in which women face a series of oppressive social policies and role expectations. Our case study highlights these oppressive forces at an individual level. We can see that Jean's Factor I role problems are a result of cultural and social role expectations and a poor fit within her extended family. She believes she is a victim and has no way out of this debilitating situation. Should she and Tom separate, she will face further discrimination in the policies of the workplace and Temporary Assistance for Needy Families (TANF).

Because Jean's Factor II problems begin with her affectional support system (see PIE assessment chart), her experiences of environmental problems begin with the familial system. Here we see both gender and racial discrimination of a severe nature. Because Jean has little formal education and may face these discriminations in the judicial system as well as the workplace and possible social service systems, she will need strong advocates to negotiate this uphill battle.

Any social work interventions must first examine and then intervene in the surrounding social systems to (1) ensure that Jean does not decrease her emerging sense of self and (2) work toward a more adaptive fit between Jean and each of the systems with which she engages on her journey to independence for herself and her children.

Helpful Websites

www.feminist.org/
The Feminist Majority and the Feminist Majority Foundation: This foundation seeks to eliminate forms of discrimination across the globe. This site offers links to other pages

covering global feminism projects, feminist leadership, campus projects, abortion rights, and other topics of concern.

www.beingjane.com
This page attempts to redefine feminism as the empowerment of women of all cultures to bridge the gap between the early pioneers of feminist ideology and future generations.

www.columbia.edu/cu/irwg/
This page gives access to the Columbia University Institute for Research on Women and Gender. It lists up-to-date undergraduate and graduate programs and provides links to a guide for Women's Studies on the Internet.

www.advancingwomen.com
This site offers an academic, refereed electronic journal on women and leadership, which had its debut in March 2000. The website is called *Advancing Women*.

www.nyu.edu/socialwork/wwwrsw
This site is an excellent general guide to social workers on a variety of subjects.

www.psychology.org
This page lists other websites and resources for psychological theory and research. It has no gender-specific topics, but the easy-to-read hierarchical structure can point you in the right direction for useful information or further research.

References

Abramovitz, M. (1996). *Regulating the lives of women*. Boston: South End Press.

Alcoff, L., & Potter, E. (1993). *Feminist epistemologies*. New York: Routledge.

Amott, T., & Matthaei, J. (1991). *Race, gender and work: A multicultural perspective*. Boston: South End Press.

Aries, E. (1996). *Men and women in interaction: Reconsidering the differences*. New York: Oxford University Press.

Bartky, S. L. (1990). *Femininity and domination*. New York: Routledge.

Brewer, R. (1994). Race, class, gender and U.S. state welfare policy: The nexus of inequality for African American families. In G. Young & B. J. Dickerson (Eds.), *Color, class and country: Experiences of gender*. London: Zed Books, Ltd.

Brewer, R. M. (1993). Theorizing race, class and gender: The new scholarship of black feminist intellectuals and black women's labor. In S. M. James & A. P. A. Busiz (Eds.), *Theorizing black feminisms: The visionary pragmatism of black women*. New York: Routledge.

Chafe, W. (1998). Sex and race: The analogy of social control. In P. S. Rothenberg (Ed.), *Race, class, and gender in the United States* (4th ed.). New York: St. Martin's Press.

Chehrazi, S. (1987). Female psychology: A review. In M. R. Walsh, *The psychology of women: Ongoing debates*. New Haven, CT: Yale University Press.

Chodorow, N. (1978). *The reproduction of mothering*. Berkeley, CA: University of California Press.

Code, L. (1993). Taking subjectivity into account. In L. Alcoff & E. Potter, *Feminist epistemologies*. New York: Routledge.

Cohn, L. D. (1991). Sex differences in the course of personality development: A meta analysis. *Psychological Bulletin, 109*, 252–266.

Congressional Budget Office. (1987). *Work related programs for welfare recipients.* Washington, DC: U.S. Government Printing Office.

Frye, M. (1993). The possibility of feminist theory. In A. M. Jaggar & P. S. Rothenberg (Eds.), *Feminist frameworks.* New York: McGraw-Hill.

Germain, C. B., & Gitterman, A. (1980). *The life model of social work practice.* New York: Columbia University Press.

Germain, C. B., & Gitterman, A. (1996). *The life model of social work practice: Advanced theory and practice.* New York: McGraw-Hill.

Gilligan, C. (1982). *In a different voice: Psychological theory and women's development.* Cambridge, MA: Harvard University Press.

GlenMaye, L. (1998). Empowerment of women. In L. M. Gutierrez, R. J. Parsons, & E. O. Cox (Eds.), *Empowerment in social work practice* (pp. 29–51). Pacific Grove, CA: Brooks/Cole.

Gutierrez, L. M., Parsons, R. J., & Cox, E. O. (Eds.). (1998). *Empowerment in social work practice: A sourcebook.* Pacific Grove, CA: Brooks/Cole.

Haraway, D. (1985, 1990). Manifesto for cyborgs. In K. Hansen & I. Philipson (Eds.), *Women, class and the feminist imagination* (pp. 580–617). Philadelphia: Temple University Press.

Harding, S. (1991). *Whose science? Whose knowledge?* Ithaca, NY: Cornell University Press.

Hyde, J. S. (1981). How large are cognitive gender differences? A meta-analysis using w and d. *American Psychologist, 36*, 892–901.

Jagger, A. M., & Rothenberg, P. S. (Eds.). (1993). *Feminist frameworks.* New York: McGraw-Hill.

James, S. M., & Busia, A. P. A. (1993). *Theorizing black feminisms: The visionary pragmatism of black women.* New York: Routledge.

Jordan, J. (1997). Relational development: Therapeutic implications of empathy and shame. In J. Jordan (Ed.), *Women's growth in diversity: More writings from the stone center.* New York: Guilford Press.

Jordan, J., & Surrey, J. (1986). The self in relation: Empathy and the mother-daughter relationship. In T. Bernay & D. Cantor, *The psychology of today's woman: New psychoanalytic visions.* New York: Analytic Press.

Jordan, J. V. (1997). A relational perspective for understanding women's development. In J. V. Jordan (Ed.), *Women's growth in diversity: More writings from the stone center.* New York: Guilford Press.

Karls, J. M., & Wandrei, K. E. (1994). *Person-in-environment system.* Washington, DC: NASW.

Lee, J. A. B. (1994). The empowerment approach to social work practice. New York: Columbia University Press.

Lee, J. A. B. (1996). The empowerment approach to social work practice. In Francis J. Turner (Ed.), *Social work treatment interlocking theoretical approaches* (4th ed., pp. 219–249). New York: Free Press/Simon & Schuster.

Lerner, H. G. (1988). *Women in therapy.* New York: Harper & Row.

McBride Stetson, D. (1997). *Women's rights in the U.S.A. Policy debates and gender roles* (2nd ed.). New York: Garland.

Miller, J. B. (1986). *Toward a new psychology of women* (2nd ed.). Boston: Beacon Press.

Miller, J. B. (1991). The development of women's sense of self. In A. G. Caplan et al., *Women's growth in connection: Writings from the Stone Center.* New York: Guilford Press.

Minnich, E. K. (1990). *Transforming knowledge.* Philadelphia: Temple University Press.

Mishel, L. R., & Schmitt, J. (1995). *Cutting wages by cutting welfare: The impact of reform on the low-wage labor market.* Washington, DC: The Economic Policy Institute.

Mohanty, C. T. (1991). Introduction: Cartographics of struggle. In C. T. Mohanty, A. Russo, & L. Torres (Eds.), *Third world women and the politics of feminism* (pp. 1–47). Bloomington, IN: University of Indiana Press.

Rothenberg, P. (Ed.). (1998). *Race, class and gender in the United States: An integrated study.* New York: St. Martin's Press.

Saleebey, D. (Ed.). (1997). *The strengths perspective in social work practice* (2nd ed.). New York: Addison-Wesley Longman.

Showalter, E. (1985). *The female malady.* New York: Pantheon Books.

Spelman, E. V. (1988). *Inessential woman: Problems of exclusion in feminist thought.* Boston: Beacon Press.

Stockard, J., & Johnson, M. M. (1992). *Sex and gender in society* (2nd ed.). New York: Simon & Schuster.

U.S. Department of Health and Human Services. (1995, September). *Report to Congress on out-of-wedlock childbearing*. West Hyattsville, MD: Author.

Worden, M., & Worden, B. (1998). *The gender dance in couples therapy*. Pacific Grove, CA: Brooks/Cole.

Young, G., & Dickerson, B. J. (1994). *Color, class and country: Experiences of gender*. London: Zed Books.

Zerbe Enns, C. (1997). *Feminist theories and feminist psychotherapies*. Binghamton, NY: Harrington Park Press.

A Multidiversity Perspective on Latinos

Issues of Oppression and Social Functioning

Edgar Colon

The Latino population in the United States is a diverse community whose sociopolitical history is characterized by political struggle and economic and educational accomplishment. It is a U.S. community of considerable diversity of cultural, racial, ethnic, and national origin. It is a community on the forefront of significant demographic change and sociopolitical growth in the twenty-first century.

Recently, the United States Census reported that approximately 31 million Latinos reside in the country (U.S. Bureau of the Census, 2001). As a consequence of their young age upon immigration into the country and their high fertility rate, the Latino population is a rapidly growing and youthful Spanish-speaking community. The Latino population is on average eight years younger than African Americans, and fully one-third of all North American Latinos are under the age of 15 (Bean, Chapa, Berg, & Sowards, 1994). The image of Latinos as a predominantly rural, farm-oriented people is prevalent in many Western states, but on the East coast, urban residence for Latinos is the norm. In fact, nearly 85% of all Latinos live in urban areas (2001). The Latino population is an aggregation of several subgroups: Mexicans, Central and South Americans, Puerto Ricans, Cubans, and Dominicans.

At present, Mexican Americans are the largest group among Latinos. The second largest group is made up of people from Central and South America. The Puerto Rican subgroup is the third largest group. Cubans make up one of the smallest population groups at approximately 6% of all Latinos. Dominicans are also a rapidly growing Latino subgroup, making up approximately 2% of the Latino population, at more than two million people.

Historically, the Latino community has resisted melting into the American melting pot. Recently arrived Latinos have been intent on maintaining their language, cultural values, and other group-specific characteristics. Gonzalez-Wippler (1982) and Ortiz (1995), for example, point out that Latino political refugees who come to the United States tend to continue fighting to preserve their distinctive cultural identity.

Moreover, Latino subgroup communities do this in a way unique to their individual and collective needs (Keefe, 1992). Consequently, it is difficult to speak of Latinos as a consolidated population. The situation is one of a group in formation whose boundaries and self-definitions are in a state of flux (Massey & Denton, 1992).

The purpose of this chapter is to explore the major cultural dimensions that must be considered in social work assessment and intervention planning with Latinos. The person-in-environment classification system is used to frame the discussion on social work practice assessment and intervention planning. The chapter begins with a sociodemographic profile on the primary Latino subgroups (in relation to present size) in the United States, followed by an overview of Latino culture and values. Lastly, we present a section which describes assessment and intervention issues utilizing the PIE classification system functional areas of social, health, and mental health, with relevant practice implications and two illustrative case studies.

Hispanic versus Latino Terms

The cultural and sociopolitical differences among Hispanic and Latino groups are considerable and so too is their geographical distribution within the United States. Yet despite these differences, the terms *Hispanic* and *Latino* have united many Spanish-speaking groups in common political causes (Tienda, 1988; Hayes-Bautista, Hurtado, Valdez, & Hernandez, 1992).

In the Latino population, culture represents a way of life that binds Latinos together through their language, values, beliefs, and practices that are considered appropriate and desirable. It guides and influences their thinking and shapes their behavior in their social environment (Green, 1999). Moreover, it is important to recognize the nature of intragroup cultural, political, and social heterogeneity and its influences on this population (Lee, 1996; Lum, 1999). In some contexts, this heterogeneity is perhaps best reflected in the broad range of self-referents used by Spanish-speaking persons (Padilla, 1999).

Hispanic is not a term coined by the people it identifies. Its general familiarity is the result of a decision by the U.S. government's Office of the Management and Budget in 1978. This decision was made to help census takers who needed a term for whites (and others) who claimed some degree of Spanish language and/or cultural affiliation. The 1978 Federal Register defined the Hispanic as a person of Mexican, Puerto Rican, Cuban, Central or South American, or other Spanish language or culture or origin, regardless of race. Hayes-Bautista (1978) notes that the term *Latino* is one coined by the people it is meant to identify. Moreover, for the Latino person the use of this term provides the advantage of a linguistic association and a geographic referent (Marin, 1993).

Viewed from this perspective, *Latino* would appear to be the more historically and sociopolitically accurate term to describe and identify populations of Caribbean and Latin American origin living in the United States. The term *Latino* will be used throughout the chapter to refer to members of the Latino population.

The sociodemographic characteristics of the U.S. Latino population makes a compelling argument for the development of social work practice approaches that consider the diversity of historical experience and present-day reality faced by U.S. Latinos.

These Latino population characteristics must be viewed within a broad social, political, and economic context that recognizes the influence of immigration and acculturation, race, class, and environment as well as forms the basis for the interaction of all people. The following section describes several of these characteristics.

Sociodemographic Profile

First, it is important to underscore the fact that the Latino population is not a unitary ethnic group. On the contrary, this population is quite heterogeneous, composed of subgroups that vary by national origin, racial stock, generation status in the United States, and socioeconomic level. Second, it is also important to note that the racial and ethnic diversity within this population is both rich and complex in regards to issues of racial and ethnic self-identification.

The following are several brief descriptions of important factors that should be considered when attempting to understand the heterogeneous nature of the contemporary U.S. Latino population.

Racial and Ethnic Identity

Racial identity as exhibited among the Latino population truly reflects the rainbow spectrum of physical characteristics and racial makeup. Given this reality, the inner dynamics of ethnic identity for many Latinos may lead to ambivalent identification with ethnic group membership (Kleinman, 1978). Moreover, inner conflicts in ethnic identity may ultimately find expression in some form of overt behavior. In relation to negative self-identification, aspects of the ethnic self may be actively rejected or disowned.

Gregory (1978) describes the denial, avoidance, and attempt at escape among people of color as "passing." He points out that it may include changing one's appearance so as not to look ethnic, name changing, moving to nonethnic neighborhoods, and dating and marrying outside of the ethnic group. Positive aspects of ethnic identity lead to enhanced feelings of self-efficacy and personal worth. Closely linked to issues of racial and ethnic identification among Latinos is their present poverty and social status in the United States. The following reports relevant sociodemographic census data.

Poverty and Social Status

About 30% of Puerto Rican families live below the poverty level, are lower in educational attainment (median number of school years completed, 12.0), and experience high unemployment (9.1%). Females head approximately 40% of all Puerto Rican families. In contrast to Mexican Americans and Puerto Ricans, Cubans are, on average, older (median age 41.4 years). However, like the other major Latino subgroups, Cubans are, on average, relatively less prosperous (median family income, $26,858) but have a lower rate of unemployment than the other two groups (6.1%). One of the primary reasons suggested by labor studies for the present Latino poverty and social status is the present level of participation in the U.S. labor force (Aponte, 1993).

Labor Force Participation

Contrary to the popular opinion that Latinos are all agricultural workers, approximately 85% of Hispanics live in large urban centers. However, a significant number of Latinos hold semiskilled or low-skill positions. Compared with the U.S. white population, Mexican Americans are young (median age 23.6 versus 33.2), generally less well off financially (median family income, $21,325 versus $33,142), and uneducated (median number of school years completed for individuals aged 25 and over, 10.8 versus 12.7), and they suffer from a higher rate of unemployment (8.5% versus 5.2%). Puerto Ricans are also young (median age, 26.8 years) and quite poor (median family income, $18,932). Clearly, in order to fully understand the sociodemographic profile of Latinos in this country, one must understand the complex nature of Latino immigration to the United States (Paulino, 1994; Torres & Bonilla, 1993).

Latino Immigration

The diversity that exists among Latino groups is underscored by the history of Latino immigration to the United States. Knowledge of the history of Mexicans, Puerto Ricans, Cubans, and other Latino groups will enable evaluators working with these groups to gain insight into their economic and social status. Because of its geographic location, California is the port of entry for most immigrants from Latin America. The largest concentration of these newcomers consists of Mexicans and Central Americans (Hayes-Bautista, 1978).

The diversity that exists among Latino groups in the United States is underscored by the history of Latino immigration to the United States. The following sections briefly describe the important factors relative to the recent Latino subgroups immigrating to the United States.

Mexicans.   At the end of the Mexican Revolution in 1919, Mexicans moved north of the Rio Grande in pursuit of political freedom and jobs. Today, many Mexicans come to the United States to escape abject poverty and political unrest and to improve their standard of living. Totaling 13.4 million people, Mexicans represent 63% of the Latino population in the United States and thus constitute the largest Latino subgroup. California, Arizona, New Mexico, and Texas are home to 80% of Mexicans.

The significant increase in the immigration of young, male Mexicans to the United States, especially those without INS documents, has resulted in the expression by some non-Latino citizens of hostile, violent, and discriminatory behaviors. During the 1990s, a San Diego newspaper reported that these behaviors and oppressive attitudes fostered such a high degree of xenophobia that two young men decided to "hunt down" Mexicans. These individuals were brought to trial for shooting and killing someone they assumed to be an undocumented Latino. In a related case, five San Diego teens were charged as adults for the murder of a sixty-year-old Mexican legal resident during a brutal attack against Mexican farmworkers in a work encampment (Moran, 2002).

Puerto Ricans.   Although Puerto Ricans have been migrating to the United States since the nineteenth century, it was not until 1925 that Puerto Rican *colonias* (colonies) appeared in New York City; the oldest and largest of these settlements is El Barrio in East Harlem. After World War II, migration escalated.

Puerto Ricans migrated to the United States for political and economic opportunity. Several economic and political antecedents precipitated the massive migration after World War II. As a result of U.S. trade and economic policies in the 1940s, which were termed Operation Bootstrap, the island's economy became increasingly geared to industrialization and away from agriculture. This shift created an unemployed labor pool that could not be absorbed on the island. So in effect Puerto Ricans were pushed from their homeland to seek jobs in the United States.

In 1957 a labor shortage in secondary labor markets (e.g., hotels, the garment industry, and domestic work) in the Northeast caused the federal government to recruit Puerto Rican laborers; as a result, the largest influx of Puerto Ricans ever (more than 52,000) arrived in the United States (Rodriguez, 1989). This amounted to almost one third of the island's population, and represented women as well as men.

Over the next decade, the demand for industrial jobs declined. As a result, the standard of living for Puerto Ricans in the United States deteriorated during the 1970s and the 1980s. Given these factors, it appears that Puerto Ricans, despite their U.S. citizenship, have suffered intensely the ravages of poverty.

According to the United States Census 2003 General Population Demographic Profile, Puerto Ricans comprise 1.310% of the total United States population of 282,909,885.

Cubans.   Unlike most foreign influxes into the United States, modern-day Cuban immigration came in waves. During the first wave, which took place throughout the early 1900s, an estimated 79,000 Cubans of all economic and social classes settled in the United States, primarily in Florida.

The second wave began when Fidel Castro came into power in 1959. By 1973, some 273,000 Cubans, mainly from the business and professional classes, had sought exile. In 1980, the third wave of Cuban immigrants began to arrive—an estimated 118,000 people, many of whom had initially sought asylum in the Peruvian Embassy and had consequently left the island by boat from the Port of Mariel. This wave reflected a mix of social and educational classes.

With only 1.1 million people of Cuban descent, Cubans represent the smallest major Latino population living in the United States. Although the vast majority of them (59%) live in Florida, many live in New Jersey (10%), New York (10%), and California (8%) (U.S. Bureau of the Census, 1991).

Central and South Americans.   During the 1980s and 1990s Latino arrivals have been from Central American countries, particularly El Salvador and Nicaragua. According to the 1989 Census Bureau Report, three million people from Central and South America now live in the United States.

Leslie and Leitch (1989) report that most of these immigrants are fleeing from political violence, war, and poverty in their homelands. Moreover, unlike other groups that came before them for similar reasons (e.g., Vietnamese and Cubans), many of these new immigrants are denied legally recognized refugee status. The recent immigration laws have excluded many of these individuals from receiving the support services and aid granted to other refugee groups. Presently, this Latino subgroup primarily resides in the Northeast metropolitan areas.

Dominicans.   Since the late 1980s, the number of Dominicans arriving in the United States has increased as the economic situation in the Dominican Republic has worsened. In 1993, an estimated 800,000 Dominicans lived in New York City (Novas, 1994). In general, the Dominicans who have immigrated to the United States have been of lower socioeconomic status. Most Dominicans have settled in New York and New Jersey, and, as of 1991, 70% of Latino small businesses in New York City were owned by Dominicans (Novas, 1994; Grasmuck & Pessar, 1996).

Latino cultural practices have served as protective factors for the Latino population (Carillo, 1988). Shared traditions and values have kept Latinos together as an ongoing, distinctive community despite devastating poverty, high unemployment, decrepit housing, and poor health status. The following section describes the important cultural practices that have helped the Latino community remain resilient and strong.

Latino Normative and Cultural Values

Latino Racial and Class Identity

Latino race and ethnicity is an equally important concept in the ecological perspective with multiple definitions and relevance to service providers. Ethnicity also represents a sense of peoplehood, a psychological and social identity involving commonality and loyalty to race, religion, nationality, and ancestry (Devore & Schlesinger, 1981; Pinderhughes, 1989; Zuniga, 2001). It refers to the degree to which an entire ethnic group is distinct in relation to their cultural values, norms, and social patterns. Culture and ethnicity thus serve as insulating forces in the nurturing environment for Latinos. They insulate Latinos from social and cultural affronts from the broader society.

In the nurturing environment, which may include their *communidad* and *familia,* Latinos experience a high measure of personal competence and social adaptability. They also experience high levels of relatedness—a desirable level of social interaction and involvement with family and friends that are commonly absent outside the community. Latinos experience a sense of belonging, purpose, and *orgullo y dignidad* (pride and dignity) in the *communidad* and draw their strength from the important values of respect, dignity, and personal relationships and support from the *familia*.

Respect, Dignity, and Personalism

The values that guide Latino culture influence the nature of interactions not only with individuals but also with the larger society (Garcia & Marotta, 1997). The value of *personalismo,* which means the trust and support that is established with others by developing warm, friendly, and personal relationships, influences social interactions. Latinos tend to favor and respond better to a congenial, personal manner than to an impersonal interest in their problems. Because Latinos relate more effectively to people than to institutions, they object to and do not respond well to formal, impersonal structures and environments (Solomon, 1983).

Respeto and *dignidad* are other important values in Latino culture. While people everywhere enjoy and expect respect from others, the language and symmetry of respect vary from one cultural group to another. The value of respect often characterizes the nature of social interaction between Latinos and professionals. Latinos respond better to these social interactions, particularly in the workplace, after a brief social conversation has occurred before the formal, more businesslike discussion. The interaction may consist of simply asking the individual how he or she is feeling today. The type of initial interaction sets the emotional climate for the beginning of a more relaxed and warm set of future interactions.

Two other distinctive interpersonal values mentioned by Marin and Marin (1990) relate sensibilities to space, time, and relationships. Latinos tend to view space, time, and relationships as more contact-oriented than whites, comfortably standing close to one another and with body touch. Relationships are expected to be both expressive and instrumental. Individualism is valued in the sense that the uniqueness and specialness of persons are in what they do and their relationships with others (Green, 1999).

Help-Seeking Behaviors

The values and norms of mutual help that are the folkways of Latino families contrast with the values of the professions and therefore organizational systems, such as "impartiality, rationality, empirical knowledge, and ethics committed to the dignity of the individual and public welfare" (Solomon, 1983, p. 331; Drachman & Ryan, 1991; Giordano & Giordano, 1977).

Lenrow (1978) has noted that in providing services to oppressed minority communities, professional norms have not been sources of criticism from those communities; criticisms have been about bureaucratic organization and processes, economic self-interest, emphasis on technique, and defensiveness about using sources outside the profession.

Latinos are goal-directed and purposeful, seeking relatedness to significant others through social, emotional, and cultural exchanges, and constantly striving for competence and self-confidence in their judgments, decisions, and relationships (Green, 1999). Key concepts such as transactions, goodness of fit, relatedness, and competence are significant in this perspective. However, none may be as relevant as the concepts of family and personal relationships.

Latino Family

The Latino family tends toward an extended family structure (Garcia-Preto, 1990). This tends to be patriarchal with great power and responsibility going to the male head of household. Further, the family is viewed as the focal point of mutual aid in the Latino community, based on the cultural norm of *personalismo* and that nonfamilial organizations are not generally trusted.

Because of the centrality of the family in Latino community life and the adhesion of generations under the concept of *pater familias* (male domination), decisions about the behavior of an individual in the family are usually the result of a group process overseen by the men (Garcia-Preto, 1990). The Latino family differs from the Anglo norm of autonomy by emphasizing interdependency and mutual help and support in time of need (Solomon, 1983).

In the Latino culture, *la familia* and interdependence among its members are highly valued. Latino families have strong ties to each other and have maintained many of the qualities of the extended family system (Vega, 1990). Latinos depend more on the family for services, emotional support, and advice than they do professionals (Matthiasson, 1974; Martineau, 1977). Latinos often consult other family members and the *compadre* (best man) on matters of health. In addition to parents and siblings, the traditional Latino family may include aunts; uncles; cousins; close family friends, who are often referred to as honorary aunts and uncles; and *padrinos* (godparents).

Gender Roles

Gender roles in Latino cultures are rigidly defined. The code of male honor, well known as machismo, defines a man as the provider, protector, and head of household. The Latino male represents the family within the community. He is expected to ensure the family honor and therefore enforce community standards of respectability.

In relation to this role, there is a prevalent association with drinking, fighting, and sexuality; however, these are not essential features, although they figure prominently in folklore and stereotypes (Green, 1999). De La Cancela and Martinez (1983) suggests that it is more appropriate to view the man exhibiting the machismo role as a man with honor, dignity, and pride, all expressions in the orderly hierarchical relationships of the traditional Latino family.

The female gender role is often viewed in Latino culture, particularly Puerto Rican culture, in the traditional context of *marianismo* (a Catholic veneration of the qualities of the Blessed Virgin Mary). Women are seen as spiritually more sensitive than men, and part of that spirituality and, therefore, spiritual superiority over Latino men, involves a martyr complex. The martyr complex requires women to be willing to take on suffering and sacrifice for the good of the husband and the children. That willingness is the mark of a good mother, a highly valued role. In relation to the Latino spouse, these traditional sexual codes of behavior seem to condone oppression of one group (female) by another (male); however, these relationships are complex, and power relationships between the sexes are not straightforward (Ghali, 1977). A supportive network important to the Latino culture is the *compadrazgo* and *padrino* (coparent) family system.

Family Support System

Along with material, moral, and spiritual responsibilities of the godparents toward the godchild, functioning as a form of indigenous social security, *compadrazgo* binds the godparents and the godchild's parents into a pattern of mutual respect and help. Puerto Ricans in this system constitute a network of ritual kinship, as serious and important as that of natural kinship, around a person or a group (Fitzpatrick, 1976).

Padrinos take seriously their coparenting responsibilities and have special obligations (e.g., encouraging religious practice and providing discipline). When children experience economic, health, or other problems, someone in the extended Latino family system will embrace these children and, if necessary, raise them as their own. These children are lovingly called *hijos de crianza* (raised sons and daughters; Ghali, 1977; Molina, 1983).

Lastly, other factors, such as social supports/networks, hope, or a sense of coherence may intervene in significant ways. Age, gender, sexual orientation, race, social class, spirituality/religion, ethnicity, abilities, lifestyle and culture, health status, experience, attitudes, vulnerabilities, and other personality features will affect whether an event, status, or process will be experienced as stressful. The ecological perspective is uniquely suited for practice with Latinos. It provides a contextual framework for understanding how Latinos interact throughout the life cycle within a biopsychosocial, cultural, and spiritual context.

A PIE Perspective of Working with Issues of Oppression and Social Functioning

The Council on Social Work Education and the National Association of Social Workers promote the education of social workers who in their practice meet the requirements of a pluralistic society and who are able to practice in organizations that serve vulnerable populations. One such population is the Latinos. Moreover, in addressing the social needs of the Latino population, social workers are expected to demonstrate ethical responsibility that requires their application of culturally competent skills.

Contemporary social work views human needs and problems as generated by the transactions between people and their environments. The goal of social work practice is to enhance and restore the psychosocial functioning of persons, or to change the oppressive or destructive social conditions that negatively affect the interaction between persons and their environments.

The ecological model of practice recognizes that transactions between the individual and the environment are products of all these domains and levels and are thus complex, and disruption of the usual adaptive balance or goodness of fit often results in stress. This approach to practice emphasizes the adaptive, evolutionary view of human beings in constant interaction with all elements of their environment.

Within a diversity and strength perspective, as the Latino community rapidly increases in both number and political power, human service organizations are being challenged to increase services to Latinos. Therefore, a greater need has also emerged for the development of evaluation approaches that take into consideration the cultural values and community norms held by Latinos. It is also evident that the Latino community has unique social problems that must be addressed in a culturally sensitive manner.

Failure to recognize Latino clients' strengths would be partially due to the societal norm of cultural blindness, or the melting pot ethos (Solomon, 1983). Effective practitioners act on the social work commitment to respect human diversity by placing all clients in their own cultural context and to draw on a strengths perspective.

This perspective reflects the integration of theories of human development and behavior across the life cycle, emphasizing the reciprocal interaction that occurs between individuals and their environment and the influence that culture and ethnicity have on Latinos across the macro, mezzo, and micro levels.

Two factors contribute to the evaluator's capacity to build and sustain the familial and community security: (1) sensitivity to the traditional values of *respeto* and *personalismo* (Abad, Ramos, & Boyce, 1974) and (2) the evaluator's readiness to act as an advocate in relation to access and service needs.

It is assumed that all clients possess untapped reserves of mental, physical, and emotional resources that can be called on to help them develop, grow, and overcome their problems. The client's perception of his or her life problem, as well as the worker's understanding of the perception, must be seen as complex and variable. All people do not necessarily experience particular events or processes in the same way as either negative or positive.

Assessing for Social Functioning Problems

Latino cultural interactions serve as protective factors for the group. Shared traditions and values have kept Latinos together as an ongoing, distinctive community despite devastating poverty, high unemployment, decrepit housing, and poor health status. The Latino culture continues to provide for living and common foundations for viewing the world.

Researchers have also found that it serves as a health-enhancing variable; that is, Latinos who remain close to their cultural traditions experience better health outcomes (Darabi & Ortiz, 1987; Scribner & Dwyer, 1989). Zambrana (1987) reports that among Mexican women, immigrants practice better nutrition and have fewer premarital births, lower rates of smoking and alcohol use, and higher regard for parental roles than those Latinas that have lived longer in this country.

The task ahead is to better understand the life transitions, environmental pressures, and the interpersonal processes that are unique to the Latino community. While this general model of intervention moves us in the proper direction, it becomes more complicated in the specifics.

It is important that the process of social work assessment and intervention planning in relation to the recently arrived Latino immigrant include an assessment of the level of acculturative stress being experienced by individuals and the family. Solomon (1983) suggests that social workers assess for internal and external factors that either increase or decrease the subjective experience of stress and, as a result, mediate the risk of stress-related diseases. The external factors that can be assessed include current individual and family social and economic conditions. External factors might include individual temperament, problem-solving skills, sense of internal control, and self-esteem.

Assessing for Mental Health Problems

Immigration and Acculturation.   The most common and problematic consequence of acculturation for the Latino immigrant is the breakdown of traditional cultural and family norms. Carrillo (1988) notes that for Latino immigrants, acculturation may take the form of challenges to traditional beliefs about male authority and supremacy, role expectations for men, and standards of conduct for women. Given these challenges, Carrillo points out that a number of problems can emerge in relation to the Latino immigrant's ability to accept, conform to, or adhere to new standards of conduct. Moreover, Solomon (1983) adds that it is during periods of individual cultural adaptation that acculturative stress is most pronounced. He also suggests that individual and family inability to handle this stress can result in individual and family withdrawal and isolation.

Carillo (1988) suggests that the impact of acculturation on Latinos recently first arrived in the United States can be assessed by studying the types of material loss they have experienced. He argues that the significance of cultural material involves values, beliefs, and norms that are essential to the cultural paradigm or worldview of the person. Moreover, when cultural values of this magnitude are lost or become less central, acculturation has reached a significant point, and one might wonder what remains of the individual's cultural attachment.

In sum, among Latinos ethnic identity formation results from the integration of various personal experiences of acculturation one has received as a member of U.S. society along with the messages that have been communicated and internalized about ethnicity by family members and significant others. Based on the outcome of this internalization process, the Latino person's ethnic identification may be positive, negative, or ambivalent. The internalization of this sense of ethnic self may lead to a movement toward either greater or lessened commitment to intragroup, intergroup, and individual values.

Assessing for Health Problems

Latino health beliefs and behaviors are also important to understanding the sociodemographic issues that confront the social work practitioner working in Latino communities. These beliefs have a very pervasive influence on the decision-making process engaged in by many members of Latino communities.

Health, Illness, and Belief Systems.   The strength of Latino health beliefs and behaviors varies by degree of acculturation, educational attainment, and socioeconomic status.

The Latinos' personal commitment to traditional folk medicine beliefs and folk healers does not inhibit the acceptance of modern medical practices (Nall & Spielberg, 1967).

Latino health-related beliefs take a holistic view of health and illness. Good health means that a person is behaving according to his or her own conscience, God's mandate, and the norms and customs of the church, family, and local community (Gregory, 1978). Latino health beliefs and knowledge derive from a combination of sources: medieval Spanish traditions, indigenous Indian magical health beliefs, elements of Western health traditions, and biomedical knowledge (Saunders, 1954).

Although folk healers are not unique to Latinos, they play an important role in the physical and mental health culture. Religious beliefs play a central role in the work of the folk healer. The folk healer provides a mechanism through which language and symbols are used to explain disease and illness, seek treatment, and identify options for prevention. Latino folk practitioners use a holistic approach to health and mental health assessment and treatment. They use a variety of treatment methods, including *sobos* (massages), *yerbas* (herbs), and *limpiadas, barridas,* and *banos* (spiritual cleansing practices).

Clark (1959) and Snow (1974) conducted early research that found that Latinos often practice folk medicine and use patent medicines to treat common illness. The remedies used for the treatment of these illnesses were bought at *botanicas* (an herb and religious articles grocery store) found in a neighborhood with a significant concentration of Latinos and that sells the herbs and religious articles folk healers may prescribe.

Trotter (1981) reported that 21% of the Latino population in the southwestern United States reported using herbs and other home remedies to treat episodes of illness compared with 12% of the total population. Research data also reveal that 33% of the U.S. Latino population believed illness can be treated more effectively with home remedies than with prescribed medicine, compared with only 24% of the total U.S. population (Chesney, Thompson, Guevara, Vela, & Schottstaedt, 1980).

The role of folk illnesses among Latino groups reflects sets of physical and personal symptoms that are believed to result from natural and supernatural events (Le Vine & Padilla, 1980). These symptoms may influence help-seeking behaviors and compliance among Latinos. Although the approach may vary among Latino subgroups, Samora (1961) argues that Mexican, Puerto Rican, and Cuban folk healers all believe that illness is either caused by an intentional act of God or other supernatural forces, by the exercise of the will of others through the *mal de ojo* (evil eye), *prueba de manda* (test), or the power of *envidia* (envy).

Many of the disease categories used by Latinos suggest the notion of a disturbance in the balance between one's physical and social well-being. A manifestation of this notion is the beliefs implicit in the Hot-Cold theory (Gregory, 1978; Harwood, 1971). This theory is derived from the Mediterranean influence in Latin America and the Hippocratic ideas concerning bodily humors associated with fire, earth, water, and air. In essence, this theory suggests that Latino individuals may view good health as a condition of balance among these four humors. Folk illnesses often described in studies of Latino communities include the following maladies:

Mal de Ojo (Evil Eye).   The notion of the *mal de ojo* is perceived as resulting from a dangerous imbalance in social relationships. The reported symptoms are usually high fever, headaches, and sleeplessness. Green (1999) reports that the eyes of another person are the agent for the initiation of the condition. For example, a *mal de ojo* may occur when an adult who is jealous of the parent admires a child or when a woman has been exposed to danger by a glance from a man. The remedy for this ailment is based on removing the unnatural power that one individual may hold over another by praying, gently rubbing the body with a whole egg, or engaging in any practice that drains off the threatening power of the relationship (Green, 1999; Trotter, 1981).

Empacho (Stomach Upset). The *empacho* may occur when a person is psychologically stressed during or right after eating (Green, 1999). The reported symptoms are a severe feeling of fullness and stomach pains. The remedy for this ailment is often discussion with family members and friends to lessen the stressful response.

Ataque de Nervios (Bad Nerves or Nerve Attack). The *ataque de nervios* is a culturally appropriate way of strong emotional expression when confronted with stressful life events such as a funeral, an accident, or a visit to an emergency room. The emotional expression is an outlet for dealing with strong feelings of grief, anger, and personal discomfort (De La Cancela & Martinez, 1983). The reported symptoms include shouting, swearing, and striking out at others, falling down into seemingly an unconscious state, and possibly convulsions. The remedies are the provision of fixed attention and emotional support and, at times, praying over the person. The condition rarely requires medical attention.

Susto (Fright). The *susto* is an ailment closely associated with the *ataque de nervios* in regards to the level of emotional stress. However, the *susto* is viewed as the result of daily life stresses that are validated with the family and community. Thus social validation facilitates individual recovery within a social support network (O'Neill, 1976).

In examining Latino folk beliefs and views toward illness, it is evident that groups play a prominent role. Delgado (1982) has conducted extensive group studies. One such study explored the role of *espiritismo* (spiritualism) among Puerto Ricans. Delgado found that *espiritismo* is an important component of social group behavior among Latino subgroups.

In sum, the practice of spiritualism provides a mechanism for Latinos, particularly Puerto Ricans, to engage in important group membership emotional-spiritual support activities (Kosa & Zola, 1975; Garrison, 1977; Harwood, 1971; Comas-Diaz, 1981). *Espiritismo* is defined as the belief that good and evil spirits which influence human behavior surround the visible world. It is essential that social workers appreciate the value of *espiritismo* as a therapeutic tool for engaging in assessment and intervention work with Latinos.

Case Study 1

A recently arrived family from El Salvador has been experiencing many problems with finding work for the father and assisting the two children, ages six and ten, with adjusting to school. The stressors that the father has been feeling have caused him to increase his use of alcohol from once a week to every day. As a result of his increased drinking, the mother and the father are now actively quarreling on a daily basis. The children are very stressed by this behavior, as they are unaccustomed to it.

Factor I: Problems in Social Functioning

1. *Familial Roles:* The social worker must work with the family, taking into account the important role of the family in Latino culture. The family must be helped to draw on its strengths as a family system. The role of religion would also be an important avenue to explore when assessing for the impact of problems in social functioning on the family. It is also of critical importance that the role of male pride (machismo) is taken into consideration when working with this family.

2. *Other Interpersonal Roles:* The Latino family is a gregarious and religious system. Therefore, it is important for the social worker to assess for the roles of extended family members and individuals in friendship groups who might be called on to help the family address its problems. The identification and engagement of natural support systems is also of value when working with Latino families.

3. *Occupational Roles:* The ability to work is important to the Latino family; therefore, it is important for the social worker to discuss the issue of work and the reality of feelings surrounding unemployment, especially for the father.

4. *Special Real-Life Situation Roles:* For this Latino family, the reality of their status as recent arrivals to the United States is critical to understanding their social reality. Therefore, it is important to discuss the feelings associated with this social situation and to address them in a sensitive manner.

Factor II: Problems in the Environment

Economic/Basic Need Problems

1. *Food/Nutrition:* Given the stresses that this Salvadoran family is experiencing with their status as new arrivals, the issue of obtaining adequate food has become an important one. The father finds himself less able to provide the nutritional needs of the family as the pressures of the workplace increase.

2. *Shelter:* For this family, the issue of adequate shelter has yet to become a problem as they are paying the rent on time. However, as life pressures increase, it is likely that the ability of the family to meet its monthly rental will be seriously challenged.

3. *Employment:* As was indicated in the general description of this family's life circumstances, the father has experienced many problems finding and keeping adequate employment. Therefore, this area will continue to affect the emotional health of the family system.

4. *Economic Resources:* The economic resources of this family are seriously threatened as the family finds itself unable to meet basic needs of food and shelter.

5. *Transportation:* The issue of transportation is an ongoing difficulty for this family as it attempts to find inexpensive means of getting family members to school and to work.

6. *Discrimination:* The issue of discrimination is a daily reality for this immigrant family in a hostile environment.

Case Study 2

This case vignette illustrates the adaptation issues faced by a recently arrived Dominican family that arrived in the United States during the "Marielito" immigration wave.

I came to the United States to seek better educational and employment opportunities. My family includes myself and others. I am 23 years old. My wife is 22 years old. We have a four-year-old son. My family and I came to live with relatives in a predominantly Dominican community in Brooklyn, New York. The first four years of our life in New York City were difficult for all of us. I had to take a low-skilled, low-paying painting apprentice job in an area construction site. My wife did not work as we felt that she should be watching over our son as he was reaching a difficult age in his development. During our fifth year in the United States, out of despair and desperation, I began to associate with a group of Dominican men who were using intravenous heroin. As I became more hopeless about my life and that of my family in the United States, I also began to use drugs. I could not believe what I was doing. I was very ashamed of myself. Sadly, by the second year of my now heavy use of heroin, I began to feel ill. The shock for my family and me was that an area physician diagnosed me with AIDS. I and my family have reacted to the diagnosis with secrecy and great shame. As a proud family, we refuse to seek help from the government.

Factor I: Problems in Social Functioning

Given the complex and unique response of this family to helping systems in the United States, the social work practitioner must ensure that he or she engages in a culturally sensitive approach to intervention planning. The intervention plan must consider the unique behaviors, emotions, and culturally congruent coping strategies of this family. It is important to assess for the severity and extent of psychological and emotional stress affecting each family member. The goal of assessment and treatment is to help the family, within a culturally sensitive framework, to overcome and ultimately manage the distress and despair associated with the father's illness.

Factor II: Problems in the Environment

This Dominican immigrant family has unique needs and varying attitudes toward seeking help from human service professionals (Georges, 1990). Therefore, the social worker practitioner engaged in working with this family must individuate the assessment and intervention planning process to account for the unique needs of each family member.

The social work practitioner must ensure that he or she engages in a culturally competent approach to intervention planning. The intervention plan must consider the unique behaviors, emotions, and culturally congruent coping strategies of this family. It is important to assess for the severity and extent of psychological and emotional stress affecting each family member.

Conclusion

It is clear that in the twenty-first century Latino communities are emerging as highly complex social collectives. Ethnicity, nationality, levels of acculturation, generation, socioeconomic status, race, legality of residence, and language differences can characterize them, to name the obvious differences. These characteristics influence the way in which assessment and intervention planning can be effectively provided, while incorporating Latino norms and values.

The concept of culture is too often viewed as a static phenomenon. This view of culture suggests that the unique characteristics of an ethnic group are unchanging. Moreover, a static view of culture leads to labels and other symbols of cultural belonging as fixed and not altered by the changing reality of group development. Green (1999) proposes a view of culture and thus ethnic identity that focuses on the transactional nature of culture and is therefore most appropriate for understanding the Latino cultural experience. This view involves actively attending to the ways in which cultural symbols and group processes of ethnic identity development are maintained through interaction with the environment.

In order to truly appreciate the complexity and the nature of the inter- and intragroup diversity among Latino subgroups, it is critical that Latino culture is viewed as continually being modified through the constant interaction of a group with its environment, including other ethnic groups and the social structures that influence the development of Latino subgroups. Consistent with the ecological perspective that the necessary fit of the individual and the family environment is assured when resources, such as food, shelter, and clothing, are supplied at the appropriate time in the appropriate way, this transactional view posits that culture serves as a mediator in the individual and group interaction. This mediator therefore functions as a marker for differentiation and as a coping response to stratification.

The knowledge, values, and skills proposed in this framework only serve as a foundation for cultural intervention with Latinos. Indeed, cultural competent practice is a personal and professional matter, one that requires each professional to embrace the concept of cultural diversity and to develop a framework that reflects his or her level of experience, comfort, and familiarity. In this framework, the ecological perspective is suggested as one approach that is considered uniquely suited for practice with Latinos.

Lastly, the principles and skill approaches in this chapter suggest a starting point. They do not propose an end in itself but a guide for a cultural learning process. They raise issues of relevance, application, principles, and alternatives. This chapter proposes continuous learning, a commitment to valuing diversity in its many forms and structures. As culturally competent practice evolves in the profession, practitioners will respond with new and creative approaches to social work practice, a renewed awareness and sensitivity, and a firm commitment to valuing diversity.

References

Abad, V., Ramos, J., & Boyce, E. (1974). A model for delivery of mental health services to Spanish speaking minorities. *American Journal of Orthopsychiatry, 44*(4), 584–595.

Aponte. R. (1993). Hispanic families in poverty: Diversity, context, and interpretation. *Families in Society: The Journal of Contemporary Human Services, 36,* 527–537.

Bean, F., Chapa, J., Berg, R., & Sowards, K. (1994). Educational and sociodemographic incorporation among Hispanic immigrants in the United States. In B. Edmonston & J. S. Passel (Eds.), *Immigration and ethnicity: The integration of America's newest arrivals* (pp. 114–129). Washington, DC: Urban Institute Press.

Carrillo, J. E. (1988). *AIDS and the Latino community. Centro de Estudios Puertorriquenos.* New York: Hunter College Bulletin.

Chesney, A., Thompson B., Guevara, A., Vela, A., & Schottstaedt, M. (1980). Mexican American folk medicine; implications for the family physician. *Journal of Family Practice, 11,* 567–574.

Clark, M. (1959). *Health in the Mexican American culture.* Berkeley, CA: University of California Press.

Comas-Diaz, L. (1981). Puerto Rican espiritismo and psychotherapy. *American Journal of Orthopsychiatry, 4*(4), 636–645.

Darabi, K. F., & Ortiz, V. (1987). Childbearing among Latino women in the United States. *American Journal of Public Health, 77*, 25–28.

De La Cancela, V., & Martinez, I. Z. (1983). An analysis of culturalism in Latino mental health. *Hispanic Journal of Behavioral Sciences, 5*, 251–254.

De La Cancela, V., & McDowell, A. (1992). AIDS: Health care intervention models for communities of color. *Journal of Multicultural Social Work, 2*, 107–109.

Delgado, M. (1982). Cultural consultation: Implications for Hispanic mental health services in the United States. *International Journal of Intercultural Relations, 6*, 227–250.

Devore, W., & Schlesinger, E. G. (1981). *Ethnic sensitive social work practice*. St. Louis: C. V. Mosby.

Drachman, D., & Ryan, A. S. (1991). Immigrants and refugees. In A. Gitterman (Ed.). *Handbook of social work practice with vulnerable populations* (pp. 618–646). New York: Columbia University Press.

Fitzpatrick, J. P. (1976). The Puerto Rican family. In R. W. Haberstein & C. H. Mindel (Eds.), *Ethnic families in America: Patterns and variations* (pp. 192–217). New York: Elsevier.

Garcia, J., & Marotta, S. (1997). Characterization of the Latino population. In J. Garcia & M. C. Zea (Eds.), *Psychological interventions and research with Latino populations* (pp. 1–14). Boston, MA: Allyn & Bacon.

Garcia-Preto, N. (1990). Hispanic mothers. In Ethnicity and mothers (special issue), *Journal of Feminist Family Therapy, 2*(2), 1–65.

Garrison, V. (1977). Doctor, espiritista, or psychiatrist? Health seeking behavior in a Puerto Rican neighborhood in New York City. *Medical Anthropology, 1*(2), 65–188.

Georges, E. (1990). *The making of a transnational community: Migration development and cultural change in the Dominican Republic*. New York: Columbia University Press.

Ghali, S. B. (1977). Culture sensitivity and the Puerto Rican client. *Social Casework, 58*, 459–468.

Giordano, J., & Giordano, G. P. (1977). *The ethno-cultural factor in mental health*. New York: Institute on Pluralism and Group Identity.

Gonzalez, J. (1978). Language factors affecting treatment of schizophrenics. *Psychiatry Annals, 8*, 68–70.

Gonzalez-Wippler, M. (1982) *Santeria experience*. Bronx, NY: Original Publications.

Grasmuck, S., & Pessar, P. (1996). Dominicans in the United States: First and second generation settlement, 1960–1990. In S. Pedraza & R. G. Rumbaut (Eds.), *Origins and destinies: Immigration, race, and ethnicity in America* (pp. 280–292). Belmont, CA: Wadsworth.

Green, J. W. (1999). *Cultural awareness in the human services*. Englewood Cliffs, NJ: Prentice-Hall.

Gregory, D. (1978). Transcultural medicine: Treating Hispanic patients. *Behavioral Medicine, 5*, 22–29.

Harwood, A. (1971). The hot-cold theory of disease. *Journal of the American Medical Association, 216*, 1153–1158.

Hayes-Bautista, D. (1978). Chicano patients and medical practitioners: A sociology of knowledge, paradigms of lay professional interaction. *Medical Anthropology, 2*, 47–62.

Hayes-Bautista, D., Hurtado, A., Valdez, R., & Hernandez, A. (1992). *No longer a minority: Latinos and social policy in California*. Los Angeles: UCLA Chicano Studies Research Center.

Keefe, S. E. (1992). Ethnic identity: The domain of perceptions and attachments to ethnic groups and cultures. *Human Organization, 51*, 35–43.

Kleinman, F. (1978). Culture, illness and care: Clinical lessons from anthropologic and cross-cultural research. *Annals of Internal Medicine, 88*, 251–258.

Kosa, J., & Zola, I. K. (1975). *Poverty and health: A sociological analysis*. Cambridge, MA: Harvard University Press.

Lee, M.-Y. (1996). A constructivist approach to help seeking process of clients: A response to cultural diversity. *Journal of Clinical Social Work, 24*, 187–202.

Lenrow, P. (1978). Dilemmas of professional helping: Continuities and discontinuities with folk healing roles. In L. Wispe (Ed.), Altruism, sympathy, and helping: Psychological and sociological principles. *Hispanic Journal of Behavioral Sciences, 4*, 315–329.

Leslie, L., & Leitch, M. L. (1989). A demographic profile of recent immigrants: Clinical and service implications. *Hispanic Journal of Behavioral Sciences, 4*, 315–329.

Le Vine, P. S., & Padilla, A. M. (1980). *Crossing cultures in therapy: Pluralistic counseling for the Hispanic.* Monterey, CA: Brooks/Cole.

Lum, D. (1999). *Culturally competent practice: A framework for growth and action.* Pacific Grove, CA: Brooks-Cole.

Marin, B. V., & Marin, G. (1990). Effects of acculturation on knowledge of AIDS and HIV among Hispanics. *Journal of Hispanic Behavioral Sciences, 12*(2), 110–121.

Marin, G. (1993). Defining culturally appropriate community interventions: Hispanics as a case study. *Journal of Community Psychology, 21,* 149–1612.

Martineau, W. (1977). Informal social ties among urban black Americans: Some new data and review of the problem. *Journal of Black Studies, 8,* 83–160.

Massey, D. S., & Denton, N. A. (1992). Racial identity and spatial assimilation of Mexican Americans in the United States. *Social Science Research, 22,* 1–27.

Matthiasson, C. (1974). Coping in a new environment: Mexican American in Milwaukee, Wisconsin. *Urban Anthropology, 3,* 422–436.

Molina, C. (1983). Family health promotion: Conceptual framework for "La Salud" and "El Bienestar" in Latino communities. In S. Andrade (Ed.), *Latino families in the United States* (pp. 35–44). New York: Planned Parenthood Federation of America.

Moran, G. (2002, June 27). Migrant attackers to be sentenced. *San Diego Union-Tribune,* B1, B9.

Nall, F., & Spielberg, I. (1967). Social and cultural factors in the responses of Mexican-Americans to medical treatment. *Journal of Health and Social Behavior, 8,* 299–308.

Novas, H. (1994). *Everything you need to know about Latino history.* New York: Plume/Penguin Press.

O'Neill, C. W. (1976). An investigation of reported fright as a factor in the etiology of susto, "magical fright." *Ethos, 3,* 41–63.

Ortiz, V. (1995). The diversity of Latino families. In R. Zambrana (Ed.), *Understanding Latino families: Scholarship, policy, and practice* (pp. 18–30). Thousand Oaks, CA: Sage.

Padilla, Y. (1999). Immigrant policy: Issues for social work practice. In P. L. Ewalt, E. M. Freeman, A. E. Fortune, D. L. Poole, & S. Witkin (Eds.), *Multicultural issues in social work: Practice and research* (pp. 589–604). Washington, DC: NASW.

Paulino, A. (1994). Dominicans in the United States: Implications for practice and policies in the human services. *Journal of Multicultural Social Work, 3*(2).

Pinderhughes, E. (1989). *Understanding race, ethnicity, and power: The key to efficacy in clinical practice.* New York: Free Press.

Rodriguez, C. E. (1989). *Puerto Ricans: Born in the U.S.A.* Winchester, MA: Unwin Hyman.

Samora, J. (1961). Concerns of health and disease among Spanish Americans. *American Catholic Sociological Review, 22,* 314–323.

Saunders, L. (1954). *Cultural differences and medical care: The case of the Spanish speaking people in the Southwest.* New York: Russell Sage Foundation.

Scribner, R., & Dwyer, J. H. (1989). Acculturation and low birth weight among Latinos in the Hispanic HANES. *American Journal of Public Health, 79,* 1263–1267.

Snow, L. (1974). Folk medical beliefs and their implications for care of patients: A review based on studies among black Americans. *Annals of Internal Medicine, 81,* 82–96.

Solomon, B. B. (1983). Value issues in working with minority clients. In *Ethnocultural issues in social work practice: Manual of reading 1991–1993.* Needham Heights, MA: Ginn.

Tienda, M. (1988). Familism and structural assimilation of Mexican immigrants in the United States. *International Migration Review, 81,* 383–408.

Torres, A., & Bonilla, F. (1993). Decline within decline: The New York perspective. In R. Morales & F. Bonilla (Eds.), *Latinos in a changing U.S. economy: Comparative perspectives on growing inequality* (pp. 85–108). Newbury Park, CA: Sage.

Trotter, R. T. (1981). Folk remedies as indicators of common illnesses: Examples from the United States-Mexican border. *Journal of Ethnopharmacology, 4,* 207–221.

U.S. Bureau of the Census. (2001). *The Hispanic population in the United States; March, 2001.* Washington, DC: Government Printing Office.

U.S. Bureau of the Census. (2003). *American community survey, multi-year profile.* Washington, DC: Government Printing Office.

Vega, W. A. (1990). Hispanic families in the 1980s—A decade of research. *Journal of Marriage and the Family, 52,* 1015–1024.

Zambrana, R. E. (1987). Ethnic differences in the substance use patterns of low-income patterns of low-income pregnant women. *Family Community Health, 13,* 1–11.

Zuniga, M. (2001). Working with Latino families: Ethical considerations. In R. Fong & S. Furuto (Eds.), *Culturally competent practice* (pp. 47–60). Boston: Allyn & Bacon.

8

Native Americans: Oppression and Social Work Practice

Jack Paul Gesino

The use of Aboriginal Theory in social work practice and its contribution to the healing methods of Native Americans and other ethnic groups has recently been proposed (Nabigon & Mawhiney, 1996). However, social work intervention with Native Americans remains limited. The profession of social work may be insensitive to the spiritual and structural needs of Native Americans. Voss, Douville, Little Soldier, and Twiss (1999) note that social work literature continues to view Native Americans as a social problem group and "fails to recognize the unique contributions that American Indian tribal and shamanic-based traditions of help and healing can make in shaping social work theory, practice, and social policy at a foundational level" (p. 228).

Insensitivity to Native peoples' ways of life commenced with Columbus's visit to America and can be seen in America's ongoing attempts at genocide of Indian cultures. Native Americans are one of the most oppressed groups in the United States. Removal from their land, false or broken treaties, relocation to reservations and boarding schools, and the outlawing of spiritual traditions like the Ghost Dance are a few of the many instances in which Native Americans experienced attempts to deprive them of their culture. Historically, many Native Americans have been forced from their lands of origin, uprooted repeatedly, and grouped together with other native tribes who were hostile to each other (Marks, 1998, p. xvii).

Native Americans have been dispossessed, experiencing painful dislocations and "impoverished existences under the near control of representatives of the United States government and culture" (Marks, 1998, p. xvii). To avoid the possibility that they may apply intervention models that are inconsistent with the cultural traditions that support Native Americans' own health behaviors, social workers must acquire a more thorough understanding of the history of racism toward Native Americans and of their cultural, political, and extended family networks, and, importantly, their spiritual traditions (Red Horse, 1978).

History of Racism

Native Americans continue to experience much discrimination in a variety of social contexts. Joe Starita (1995), in recounting Guy Dull Knife's experience with discrimination, provides one example of society's approach to Native people over fifty years ago.

> In his youth, he, like many Pine Ridge Lakota, had ventured no farther than the border towns, and the early impressions had never left. He remembered the dirty looks, the waiting for whites to enter first, the standing in line, others cutting in front of them, the occasional cursing, clerks tailing him up and down the aisles and the signs that said *NO DOGS OR INDIANS ALLOWED*. (p. 326)

The situation today has not dramatically improved. Russell Means (1995), a noted Native American activist, recalls in his autobiography numerous experiences with discrimination. He described one situation where "[t]hree elderly white ladies looked me up and down as though I were a statue. It was an infuriating, hateful, racist moment. . . . In that humiliating moment, I came to realize how white people look upon us: We're not real human beings, we don't exist, we have no cares, no rights, no sensibilities. We're tourist attractions" (p. 111).

The discrimination experienced by Native Americans is the result of the long history of European cultural racism and colonialism toward Native Americans (Williams, 1996, p. 335). The General Allotment Act of 1887 began a program of cultural assimilation and ethnocide. "The Allotment Act sought to encourage the destruction of tribalism and the assimilation of Indians into white civilization by parceling out treaty-guaranteed reservation lands to individual tribal members and surplus tribal lands to non-Indians" (Williams, 1996, p. 335). Williams (1996) notes that Congress initiated a number of policies that perpetuated a "legacy of racism" toward Native Americans. For example, Congress legislatively terminated 109 Indian tribes and bands in the 1950s and 1960s.

The United States' most noted effort at ethnocide was the development of Indian Boarding Schools. The most well known school, the Industrial School at Carlisle, was established in 1879 at Carlisle, Pennsylvania. Carlisle's founder, Richard Henry Pratt's, stated goal was to "kill the Indian and save the man" (Child, 1996, p. 78). Native American children were separated from their families, tribes, and land. Their hair was cut, their language forbidden. Disease ravaged and killed many. The children were forbidden any identity with their cultural and familial traditions.

This attempt to eradicate the Native American cultural traditions was most flagrant in the area of their religious beliefs. Tinker (1996) states,

> The phenomena referred to by the term Native American religions . . . have been misunderstood, maligned, romanticized, and misappropriated. In almost every case the authoritative and definitive analysis of particular Native American non-Indians, and thus nonadherents, who lacked any lifelong experiential basis for their analysis, have written religious traditions. It seems that now, at the end of the twentieth century, deeply held Indian traditions and beliefs have been politicized—on the one hand by academic experts, and on the other hand by New Age aficionados who have mistakenly seen Indian spirituality as a new trade commodity. (p. 537)

The federal government's attempt to civilize Native Americans was a direct affront upon traditional Native American religions and their own health resources (Joe, 1996). In discussing the effects from their attempts in dealing with genocide, Weaver (1998) notes that generations of Native Americans have experienced considerable trauma, which has led to a state of "unresolved grief" (p. 206).

Maria Yellowhorse Braveheart Jordan in LaDuke (1998) states, "[t]his unresolved grief, a repercussion of the loss of lives, land and aspects of culture rendered by the European conquest on the Americas, is a significant psychological factor contributing to current Lakota social pathology" (p. 14).

Unfortunately, the social and health problems of Native Americans are seen as individual pathologies. Little attention is given to the institutional barriers and racism that contribute to these problems. Discriminatory and racist practices against Native people are so ingrained in U.S. society, few can see its ongoing effects. Vine DeLoria Jr. (1995) in his book *Red Earth, White Lies* provides an illustration of this invisible racist boundary.

> In recent years, we have seen a number of famous personalities in the field of sports, particularly sports broadcasting, fall into disgrace because of their racial remarks about other minorities—primarily African Americans and Jews. Thus, a Dodger executive is fired

because he casually stated that African Americans were not smart enough to work in the front office; Jimmy the Greek related on a national telecast that African Americans had large muscles with their hips apparently extending farther up the back than whites because slave owners had bred them for these characteristics. Both of these personalities were fired for the better image of the game. Marge Schott, owner of the Cincinnati Reds, in private conversation, made derogatory remarks about African Americans and Jews and received a year's suspension from baseball. Why are these remarks regarded as mortal sins even while derogatory symbols and names of American Indians spark the opposite effect and trigger intense chastisement of Indians when protested? (pp. 21–22)

The invisibility of racism and discrimination toward Native people contributes to intervention strategies that are directed toward changing individual pathology and not the environmental and institutional factors that led to the social and health problems they experience. This emphasis must change. Voss et al. (1999) make a similar call.

In their content analysis of social work articles published between 1980 and 1989, McMahon and Allen-Meares (1992) found 22 articles on Native Americans. The majority of these articles (86.4 percent) proposed individual interventions, whereas the remainder of the articles published proposed institutional change as the appropriate method of intervention. Considering the traditional Lakota emphasis on tribalism and shamanism in help and healing traditions, a question must be raised: To what extent does the repertoire of practice methodologies institutionalized in the dominant culture's social work theory and practice impose the cultural values of individualism and materialism (empiricism) on Lakota culture? (p. 230)

The history of and ongoing racism and discrimination experienced by Native Americans has considerable bearing on how Native people view themselves, their problems, and those who attempt to help. Weaver (1998) in her study of Native American social workers' perception of the knowledge, skills, and values necessary for culturally competent service provision to Native American clients found that the respondents felt that "[s]ocial workers must understand the atrocities of the indigenous holocaust in this country and the unresolved pain associated with it" (p. 221).

Present Day: Social and Health Problems

The 1990 census reports about 685,000 Native Americans living on reservations. There are 314 federally recognized tribes. Some 300 reservations, most administered by the federal government, are clustered and scattered through 33 states (Marks, 1998, p. xviii). There are roughly 2 million Native Americans living in the United States (U.S. Bureau of the Census, 1993).

Native Americans experience a disproportionate number of social and health problems in the United States. They are overrepresented in the child welfare system (Hogan & Siu, 1988; Wares, Wedel, Rosenthal, & Dobrec, 1994 in Weaver, 1999), suffer higher rates of certain health problems (May, 1988; Parker, 1994 in Weaver, 1999; Joe, 1996), and are among the poorest people in the United States (Little Eagle in Weaver, 1998). Social and health problems, including drug and alcohol abuse, violence, suicide, unemployment, child and elder abuse and neglect, and other behavioral problems, consistently plague large percentages of Native American groups (Weaver, 1998, p. 98). Native Americans are also more likely to be victims of violent crimes than any other racial group. They are victims of violent crimes at a rate more than twice the national average. The rate of violent crimes against Native American women is nearly 50% higher than that for black men (Kilborne, 1997).

Native people are not a homogeneous group. For this reason, there is a variation in the rates in which some tribes experience social and health problems. The knowledge that the extent of such problems affects each tribe differently extends our understanding of the corrosive effects of such social and health ills. For example, the Lakota-Sioux of South Dakota suffer disproportionately from a variety of social and health problems. Thirty-one percent of Native Americans die before their forty-fifth birthday (Voss, Douville, Little Soldier, & Twiss, 1999). Even though the overall adjusted death rate for Native Americans is 35% greater than the U.S. rate, the age-adjusted death rate for Native Americans in the Aberdeen area of South Dakota, which includes most of the Lakota-Sioux Indian reservations, exceeds 1,000 (Voss, Douville, Little Soldier, & Twiss, 1999, p. 229).

Alcoholism remains one of the most serious social and health problems facing Native Americans. Native people die from alcoholism at almost five times the overall rate for the nation (Levy, 1996). Seventy-five percent to eighty percent of Indian suicides involve the use of alcohol (Frederick, 1973 in Nofz, 1988); Native Americans twenty-five to thirty-four years of age have a terminal liver cirrhosis rate nearly fifteen times the national rate (Schinke, 1985 in Nofz, 1988; Joe, 1996); crimes related to alcohol and other drug use occur up to twenty times more often among Native Americans than among whites in the same geographic areas (May, 1982 in Nofz, 1988).

Again, the extent of the alcohol problem is best understood by examining how particular tribes may be affected. Levy (1996) notes that looking at the overall rates of alcoholism among Native Americans obscures the considerable differences in the cultural and environmental circumstances of each tribe. For example, during the 1980s, the average annual age-adjusted mortality rate from "selected alcohol-related" causes for twenty-one northern states was forty-five deaths per 100,000 population. By contrast, the eight mountain states where most reservations reside averaged sixty-six deaths, a rate nearly 50% higher (p. 18).

There are tribal differences in the patterns of drinking. Levy (1996) notes that the statistical data on drinking patterns fails to reflect the distinctiveness of the problem among Native cultures. He states, "Alcohol use and abuse is a heterogeneous phenomenon both among and within various tribes, and no global explanation, either racial or social appears to account for it" (Levy, 1996, p. 19). However, health service statistics indicate that alcohol-related death rates in the Aberdeen area of South Dakota where the Lakota-Sioux reservation resides are at 59.6 per 100,000 compared with 6.4 per 100,000 for all races, and 24.6 per 100,000 for all Indians. This makes the Aberdeen area alcohol-related death rate seven times the national average; almost three times that of Native people nationally (LaDuke, 1998, p. 14).

Mental Health

Suicide remains another major social and health problem among Native Americans. As with alcoholism, suicide rates vary among tribes. Some tribes report a suicide rate several times higher than the national average, with the rate among Native American teenagers ten times higher (Davenport & Davenport, 1987). Again, different tribes experience a disproportionate number of suicides. The suicide rate on one of the Lakota reservations in South Dakota is almost seven times that of the U.S. average, and generally is at least three times the suicide death rate of all non-Indians in the state of South Dakota (LaDuke, 1998, p. 14).

In addition, Native Americans experience the increasing presence of incurable chronic health problems. Poverty and acculturation have negatively impacted on the overall health practices of Native Americans and have contributed to many of their health conditions (Joe, 1996). Diabetes is endemic in some tribes, with some communities reporting a 60% to 70% incidence of non-insulin-dependent diabetes mellitus in the population over age forty-five (Joe, 1996, p. 240). Joe (1996) states, "The human cost of this disease is staggering, especially since significant numbers of those with NIDDM develop vascular complications that lead to cardiovascular diseases, blindness, amputation of limbs, or renal failure" (p. 240).

Poverty exerts a heavy price on the health of Native people. Rates of poverty vary among tribes and among age groups within tribes. In 1994, government statistics defined Shannon County, South Dakota, home of the Oglala Sioux, as the poorest in the country. The percent of the people living in poverty was four times the national average—63% versus 14%. The infant mortality rate was six times the national average (Starita, 1995, pp. 343–344).

If we look at elder Native Americans as a specific vulnerable group, we can understand the way poverty has impacted on Native Americans' health. Their housing frequently lacks plumbing or electricity (Chapleski, Lichtenberg, Dwyer, Youngblade, & Tsai, 1997; NICOA, 1981) and is often in extreme disrepair. Poverty is widespread, with more than 30% of American Indians age sixty and over living at or below 125% of the federal poverty level. On some reservations, more than half are below the official poverty level (Chapleski et al., 1997).

Native American elders are in worse health, have less access to health insurance, and experience higher mortality risks than white elders (Agree, 1998; John, 1991, 1995 cited in Chapleski et al., 1997, p. 590). Extant research has determined that Native Americans suffer from a higher rate of chronic ailments such as diabetes, liver and kidney disease, high blood pressure, emphysema, and gall bladder problems than do white populations (Agree, 1988; Chapleski et al., 1997; Edwards & Edwards, 1989; NICOA, 1981 as cited in Chapleski et al., 1997, p. 590).

One last health and social problem confronting Native Americans that should be mentioned is physical abuse and violence. The existence of abuse among Native people may be surprising to some given some of the basic tenets of Native culture including respect for elders, commitment to the welfare of tribal members, and the unique value of children (Carson, 1995 in Hudson & Armachain, 1998, p. 538). Hudson and Armachain (1998) in their survey of Native Americans found that in comparison to the other two racial/cultural groups, higher percentages of Native Americans (25.5%) reported having been abused at some time during their lives and having abused someone (8.1%) than did the Caucasians (18.0% and 6.7%) and African Americans (16.6% and 4.3%) (p. 542). These statistics underscore the high prevalence of health problems, substance abuse issues, and mental health concerns among Native Americans.

Family, Beliefs, and Rituals

As described earlier, Native Americans are not a homogeneous group. There are 314 legally recognized tribes each with their own distinct customs and cultural values. Considerable diversity characterizes Native American communities (Gross, 1995). To describe specific characteristics of tribal beliefs regarding family will not fully account for this diversity. Nonetheless, kinship ties are an important cultural aspect of Native people. In most tribes there is a strong belief and interaction pattern that emphasizes the primacy of the extended family and kinship ties. There is a strong value that acknowledges and demonstrates respect for one's family and kinship ties. The family is viewed as the most important means for human interaction (Ewalt & Mokuau, 1995).

Early descriptions of Native American family life provide a glimpse of the importance of the family in the late 1800s. Charles A. Eastman, a mixed-blood Sioux, in his book *The Soul of the Indian: An Interpretation* (1911) spoke eloquently of the family. He states, "There was no priest to assume responsibility for another's soul. That is, we believed the supreme duty of the parent" (p. 27). In recounting the role of the mother, Eastman (1911) notes

> The mother's spiritual influence counted for most. Her attitude and secret meditations must be such as to instill into the receptive soul of the unborn child the love of the "Great Mystery" and a sense of brotherhood with all creation. (p. 28)

Grandparents were and remain an important influence in the Native American family. Grandparents are seen as having the responsibility "of acquiring the youth with the national traditions and beliefs. It is reserved for them to repeat the time-hallowed tales with dignity and authority, so as to lead him into his inheritance in the stored-up wisdom and experience of the race. The old are dedicated to the service of the young, as their teachers and advisors, and the young in turn regard them with love and reverence" (Eastman, 1911, p. 34–35).

Children were (and to a similar extent still are) reared by learning through their own observations. Bentz (1996) tells us that adults teach Native American children by

> relying strongly on nonverbal cues rather than verbal directions; engaging the spiritual world in the child-rearing process by praying, chanting, and singing, as well as by conferring special names to give children guidance and power; educating children for their future roles by including them from infancy in all social, economic, and ritual activities; using stories to provide an understanding of the world and its relationships, both of those between individuals and that between man and nature; . . . teaching children their responsibilities to each member of their kinship group. (pp. 115–116)

In the Native American family, all members assume different roles of protector, initiator, and storyteller, to name a few. These and other roles vary among tribes depending on whether the tribe was a nomadic hunting and gathering society or a horticultural society. As such, tribes have different hierarchical social structures. However, in most tribes today all members are required to contribute to the family or clan according to their ability.

Values and Traditions

Today, many Native family traditions and values have been undermined by non-Native influences (Wilson, 1999). Notwithstanding, the basic values underlying kinship ties in Native American cultures remain (Bentz, 1996). One of the reasons for this stability of family values is the interconnectedness of these values with their world and religious beliefs. Bentz (1996) notes the Native American strong family values are intimately an "attitude [that] is a reflection of [their] religious orientation" (p. 116). Jerry Mander (1991) provides a good description of Native people's beliefs in his comparison of these beliefs with our current culture's technological beliefs.

Native people do not share our current culture's superiority to nature. The lifestyle of many tribal families, especially those of the Western Plains, fostered a deep attachment to the land.

> Over time . . . they began to derive meaning from the rivers, mountains and valleys, from a particular butte or stone formation, a different rock or tree and from the wide variety of wildlife that inhabited the lands. Gradually, the Lakota came to accept that each living thing, like them, was endowed with its own spirit. They believed that the trees and plants, the fish, birds and four-legged animals, all had the same right to live as they, and this knowledge was shared and passed down to the people, from one generation to the next. (Starita, 1995, p. 156)

Most Native Americans continue to engage the world through their strong beliefs and bonds with nature. They use ritual and ceremony to help cope with the difficult circumstances of their lives. Wilson (1999) notes,

> By following the prescribed instructions "the people" were able to secure the favor and assistance of powerful spiritual forces. But there was far more at stake here than simply gratifying immediate physical needs. Because everything in the universe was interrelated, and because "the people" were at the center of it, their rituals not only regulated their own relationship with the sacred and other living beings but also ensured that the whole natural order was properly maintained. (p. 25)

Voss et al. (1999) summarize Native American values of family and beliefs of nature when they state, "everything is intimately connected and related to everything else biologically, spiritually, and physically" (p. 231).

Spiritual Traditions of Native Americans

Considerable distrust of those offering help exists among Native Americans (Williams & Ellison, 1996). Much of the distrust is the result of the long history of racism, but also of the fact that those attempting to help Native Americans often discount Native American religious traditions and their role in the health care problems and practices of tribal groups (Joe, 1996). Williams and Ellison (1996) note, "Most American Indian cultures have a high degree of integration of religious and health beliefs; healing cannot be separated from culture or religion" (p. 148). Jerry Mander's discussion of the differences between technological peoples (Western society) and Native peoples increases our understanding of a number of subtleties. The economic, conceptual, and attitudinal differences are significant in a work-driven, success-oriented dominant society. There are diametrically different approaches to politics and power, sociocultural arrangements, relation to the environment, architecture, religion, and philosophy. Each of these cultural components has significant implications for functioning in a Eurocentric society.

The characteristics in each column of Table 8.1 form an internally consistent logic. Mander (1991) notes that when comparing politics, hierarchical power makes more sense for operating a large-scale technological society than would a consensual decision-making process, which is much too slow to keep pace with rapidly changing material cultural needs associated with the dominant culture.

TABLE 8.1

Technological Peoples	*Native Peoples*
Economics	
Concept of private property a basic value: includes resources, land, ability to buy and sell, and inheritance. Some state ownership. Corporate ownership predominates.	No private ownership of resources such as land, water, minerals, or plant life. No concept of selling land. No inheritance.
Goods produced mostly for sale, not for personal use.	Goods produced for use value.
Surplus production, profit motive essential. Sales techniques must create "need," hence advertising.	Subsistence goals: no profit motive, little surplus production.
Economic growth required, especially in capitalist societies, hence need for increased production, increased use of resources, expansion of production and market territories.	Steady-state economics: no concept of economic growth.
Currency system—abstract value.	Barter system—concrete value.
Competition (in capitalist countries), production for private gain. Reward according to task/wages.	Cooperative, collective production.
Average workday, 8–12 hours.	Average workday, 3–5 hours.
Nature viewed as "resource."	Nature viewed as "being"; humans seen as part of nature.
Politics and Power	
Hierarchical political forms.	Mostly nonhierarchical: "chiefs" have no coercive power.
Decisions generally made by executive power, majority rule, or dictatorship.	Decisions usually based on consensual process involving whole tribe.
Spectrum from representative democracy to autocratic rule.	Direct participatory democracy; rare examples of autocracy.

TABLE 8.1

Technological Peoples	*Native Peoples*
Politics and Power	
Operative political modes are communist, socialist, monarchist, capitalist, or fascist.	Recognizable operative political modes are anarchist, communist, or theocratic.
Centralization: most power concentrated in central authorities.	Decentralization: power resides mainly in community, among people. (Some exceptions include Incas and Aztecs.)
Laws are codified, written. Adversarial process. Anthropocentrism forms basis of law. Criminal cases judged by strangers (in U.S., western Europe, Soviet Union). No taboo.	Laws transmitted orally. No adversarial process. Laws interpreted for individual cases. "Natural law" used as basis. Criminal cases settled by groups of peers known to "criminal." Taboo.
Concept of "state."	Identity as "nation."
Sociocultural Arrangements and Demographics	
Large-scale societies; most societies have high population density.	Small-scale societies, all people acquainted; low population density.
Lineage mostly patrilineal.	Lineage mostly matrilineal, with some variation; family property rights run through female.
Nuclear two- or one-parent families; also "singles."	Extended families: generations, sometimes many families, live together.
Revere the young.	Revere the old.
History written in books, portrayed in television docudramas.	History transmitted in oral tradition, carried through memory.
Relation to Environment	
Living beyond nature's limits encouraged; natural terrain not considered a limitation; conquest of nature a celebrated value; alteration of nature desirable; anti-harmony; resources exploited.	Living within natural ecosystem encouraged; harmony with nature the norm; only mild alterations of nature for immediate needs: food, clothing, shelter; no permanent damage.
High-impact technology created to change environment. Mass-scale development: one-to-millions ratio in weaponry and other technologies.	Low-impact technology; one-to-one ratio even in weaponry.
Humans viewed as superior life form; Earth viewed as "dead."	Entire world viewed as alive: plants, animals, people, rocks. Humans not superior, but equal part of web of life. Reciprocal relationship with nonhuman life.

(continued)

TABLE 8.1 *(continued)*

Technological Peoples	*Native Peoples*
Architecture	
Construction materials transported from distant places.	Construction materials usually gathered locally.
Construction designed to survive individual human life.	Construction designed to eventually dissolve back into land (except for pyramids built by minority of Indians); materials biodegradable in one lifetime.
Space designed for separation and privacy.	Space designed for communal activity.
Hard-edged forms; earth covered with concrete.	Soft forms; earth not paved.
Religion and Philosophy	
Separation of spirituality from rest of life in most Western cultures (though not in some Muslim, Hindu, or Buddhist states); church and state separated; materialism is dominant philosophy in Western countries.	Spirituality integrated with all aspects of daily life.
Either monotheistic concept of single, male god, or atheistic.	Polytheistic concepts based on nature, male and female forces, animism.
Futuristic/linear concept of time; de-emphasis of past.	Integration of past and present.
The dead are regarded as gone.	The dead are regarded as present.
Individuals gain most information from media, schools, authority figures outside their immediate community or experience.	Individuals gain information from personal experiences.
Time measured by machines; schedules dictate when to do things.	Time measured by awareness according to observance of nature; time to do something is when time is right.
Saving and acquiring.	Sharing and giving.

Source: From *In the Absence of the Sacred: The Failure of Technology and the Survival of the Indian Nations* by Jerry Mander. Copyright 1991 by Jerry Mander. Reprinted with permission of Sierra Club Books.

Practice Implications

In order to understand ways of helping Native Americans, health care and social service professionals must learn some of the basic health beliefs and practices of Native Americans. In addition, they must become acquainted with the religious traditions of Native Americans, which are an inseparable part of their everyday living and are crucial to know if we are to be of some assistance.

The social structure and cultural traditions of Native Americans are "infused" with a spirituality that cannot be separated from other activities in which they participate. Many of their activities are accompanied by attention to religious detail. "In the Northwest, harvesting cedar bark would be accompanied by prayer and ceremony, just as killing a buffalo required ceremonial action and words dictated by the particularities of tribal nation, language, and culture" (Tinker, 1996, p. 539).

"The most distinctive aspect of Native American religious traditions is the extent to which they are wholly community based and have no real meaning outside the specific community in which the acts are regularly performed" (Tinker, 1996, p. 539).

This community exerts influence on the Native American family structure, which heavily influences individual behavior patterns because "family transactions occur within a community milieu" (Red Horse, 1978, p. 67). "The communitarian nature of Indian ceremonies represents a key distinction between Native American religious traditions and modern Euro-American New Age Spirituality, with its emphasis on radical individualism" (Tinker, 1996, p. 539).

In the Indian worldview, this community—this legitimate source of identity—is intimately linked to and derives directly from the significance of spatiality, of space and place. Joseph Epes Brown (1991) identifies "Primal" elements that are universal and fundamental to most Native American religious traditions. They include the following four elements:

1. Religion cannot be conceived as being separable from any other aspects of Native American culture.
2. Language must be understood to have special elements. For example, Brown (1991) states,

    [W]ords have a special potency or force that is integral to their specific sounds: What is named is therefore understood to be really present in the name in unitary manner, not as "symbol" with dualistic implications, as is generally the case with modern languages. An aspect of the sacred potency latent in words in primal tradition is the presiding understanding that words in their sounds are born in the breath of the being from whom they proceed, and since breath in these traditions is universally identified with the life principle, *words are thus* sacred *and must be used with care and responsibility.*

    Such quality of the spoken word is further enhanced by the understood close proximity of the source of breath, the lungs, with the heart which is associated with the being's spiritual center. (p. 3)

    As such, when Native Americans engaged in storytelling as a method of teaching certain values, the act of storytelling is not a symbolic act, it is not bound by time.
3. Native Americans' experience of time and process is not understood in the Western linear manner, but in terms of the "circle—that is cyclical and reciprocal" (Brown, 1991, p. 4).
4. "A presiding characteristic of primal people is a special quality and intensity of interrelationship with the forms and forces of their natural environment" (Brown, 1991, p. 4). There are no dichotomies such as animate or inanimate. "All such forms under creation are understood to be mysteriously interrelated. Everything is relative to every other being or thing. Thus, nothing exists in isolation" (Brown, 1991, p. 53). Weaver (1998) citing DeLoria and Lytle (1983) notes "a sense of connection to the land is a primary

factor in the psychological makeup of Indian people. As the land is alienated, social cohesion erodes. Connection to the land is intimately intertwined with native religion, values, culture, and lifestyle" (p. 208). Charles A. Eastman furnishes a clearer picture of the importance of Native American religious life and feeling for the land.

Whenever, in the course of the daily hunt, the red hunter comes upon a scene that is strikingly beautiful—a black thundercloud with the rainbow's glowing arch above the mountain; a white waterfall in the heart of a green gorge; a vast prairie tinged with the blood-red of sunset—he pauses for an instant in the attitude of worship. He sees no need for setting apart one day in seven as a holy day, since to him all days are God's. Every act of his life is, in a very real sense, a religious act. He recognizes the spirit in all creation, and believes that he draws from it spiritual power. His respect for the immortal part of the animal, his brother, often leads him so far as to lay out the body of his game in state and decorate the head with symbolic paint or feathers. (Eastman, 1911, p. 47)

Intervention

Social workers must learn about these spiritual beliefs if they are going to intervene on behalf of Native people. When treating such conditions and other ailments, Native Americans understand that interventions involve treating the whole person—mind, body, spirit, and emotions. Many Native peoples do not distinguish between mental or physical health, good or bad. Voss et al. (1999) note that for some tribes these elements coexist in each person. They state, "Mental and physical health are viewed as inseparable from spiritual and moral health . . . [as such] good mental or emotional health is related intimately to good spiritual, moral, and physical health" (p. 235). "Moreover, these interventions must extend beyond the individual because, according to Native beliefs, if certain health problems are left untreated, the unhealthy situation can affect family members and even the entire community. Thus many healing ceremonies treat the whole family or the whole community in an effort to restore balance and harmony in the group" (Joe, 1996, p. 238).

For most Native Americans, treatment involves reestablishing harmony and understanding the why of the illness. As such, most tribes seek the why of an illness either through natural or supernatural causes. In addition, the treatment will involve either natural or supernatural interventions.

Charles A. Eastman, recounting his observations of the Sioux's ceremonial rites, notes, "There is no doubt that the Indian held medicine close to spiritual things" (1911, p. 47).

Healing ceremonies involve creating a sense of harmony. This harmony is represented in the context of the Native American religious beliefs—the four cardinal directions, the four winds, or the four directions marking the medicine wheel. Many tribes use a variety of treatment modalities in treating individuals. "Most healers work in the patient's home, where healing ceremonies may be less public and involve primarily the patient and the patient's family. Depending on the tribe, the type of illness, and the type of intervention, some healing ceremonies may require a few minutes, while others require days; or a series of different ceremonies may be called for that extend over a period of one or two years.

While ministering to the sick is often considered a curative role, most healers in Indian communities view themselves guides or catalysts in the healing process. For example, "through prayers, songs, and other related activities, healers help create an appropriate curative environment" (Joe, 1996, p. 239).

The preceding material was provided in an effort to add to the knowledge base necessary for culturally competent practice with Native Americans (Weaver, 1998). The PIE system may help practitioners' assessment of Native American problems; however, one should use caution. As Weaver (1998) states,

> Whereas a variety of tools have been developed to assess cultural identity, the majority have not been normed with Native American clients. Many such assessment tools rely heavily on language usage as a primary indicator of attachment to culture. Although such measures may be appropriate for members of immigrant groups who made choices about language retention or adoption of English, these tools do not fit as well for Indian peoples who often lost language abilities, not through choice to assimilate but through assimilation policies that they were subjected to against their will. (p. 208)

The use of the PIE model must be consistent with the cultural care principles and practices outlined by Mercer (1996). "Cultural care can be defined as the learned and transmitted values and beliefs that enable people to maintain their well-being and health and to deal with illness, disability, and death" (Leininger, 1990; 1992 in Mercer, 1996, p. 186). Cultural care principles with Native Americans may include

- Communication: Listening, not interrupting; it may be rude to interrupt someone when they are speaking
- Clan, Family Associations: Family is the center of a client's social structure; to be without family support may be perceived to be a real measure of poverty
- Personal Space: The formation of a circle may be important
- Privacy (Mercer, 1996)

It must be remembered that any intervention with Native Americans is based on the need to "restore physical well-being to the body and harmony to the damaged social and spiritual relationships" (Williams & Ellison, 1996, p. 148). Social workers must understand the depth of Native American spiritual traditions. The spirit dimension is a powerful source of help for many Native peoples, and as Voss et al. (1999) note, "an often-neglected area in social work practice and human behavior literature" (p. 235). Voss et al. (1999) make it clear that "All social or health care services are first and foremost spiritual endeavors" (p. 239).

The PIE System and Native Americans

This author suggests that PIE Factor I: Social Role Problem Identification and the associated social role definitions and types of role problems is inconsistent with how Native Americans would perceive their health problems. In fact, the Factor I classification, which separates out social role problems from environmental factors, clashes with the belief that there are severe limitations of this "Cartesian dualism on our thinking and consequently on our treatment models and pedagogy" when applied to Native Americans (Voss et al., 1999,

p. 239). For example, Karls and Wandrei (1994), when describing the Dependency Role Type problem, state,

> If a person's dependency needs are not adequately met, the individual's role performance may be negatively affected. A correlate of dependence is independence. Independence is freedom from influence, control, or manipulation of others. It is the ability of a person to assume responsibility in directing his or her life. To be independent is to initiate behavior based on one's convictions and resources without being unduly influenced by others. (p. 19)

Juxtapose this with the following description of working with the Lakotas:

> Tribalism is a pervasive cultural attitude or interactional style that emphasizes the primacy of the extended family and kinship relations over individualism [which emphasizes the importance of individual identity]. To stand above one's family, extended family, or kinship community is not a good thing among traditional Lakotas. The notion of a separate, independent individual ego is foreign to the Lakota cosmology. (Voss et al., 1999, pp. 230–231)

By applying Factor I of PIE, the social worker may unsuspectedly "rigidly reinforce a kind of colonialism (promoting 'therapeutic progress') with the goal of 'civilizing' the Indian" (Voss et al., 1999, p. 233).

Notwithstanding, Factor II: Environment/Problems in the Environment may lend itself to a better description of the kinds of problems Native Americans are confronting and is also consistent with their cultural traditions. Karl and Wandrei (1994) note,

> The environmental problems that follow are the factors outside of the client that affect social functioning and well-being. The environment is seen as both the physical and social context in which a person lives. It is the sum total of the natural setting and the human-made circumstances outside of the person. The environment provides both resources and opportunities; it activates along with creating barriers to their fulfillment. (p. 23)

Comparing this description of Factor II with the knowledge that environmental influences, including the history and current racism toward Native Americans, the policies of the Indian Health Service and the Bureau of Indian Affairs, federal laws such as the Indian Child Welfare Act and the lack of true tribal sovereignty have contributed to the continued suffering and ongoing feelings of loss and effects of post-traumatic stress disorder (Weaver, 1999), one finds the Factor II classification system more consistent with Native American intervention ideology.

The following case illustrates the use of Factor II of PIE for assessing problems confronted by Native Americans.

Case Study

The following case is an excerpt from *The Dancing Healer* by Carl Hammerschlag (1988).

> Mary is a twenty-year-old unemployed, high school graduate Navajo Indian woman. She was referred to the community mental health social worker after being accused of stealing shoe

polish from a department store. Mary's behavior is described by police and family reports as consisting of angry outbursts and verbal challenges to fight. She dares anyone in authority to do something to her. She lives alone, is unemployed and on welfare. Mary was adopted at the age of three by a white family. Her father was found frozen to death after another night of heavy drinking. Her mother was also an alcoholic. Mary was one of twelve children. She was angry with her white mother for adopting her. She was angry with her Navajo mother for abandoning her. She had completely lost touch with her family on the reservation.

PIE Assessment of Mary

Using Factor I: Social Role Functioning, Mary's difficulties in social role functioning could be classified as Family Role Problem–Child Role. Mary could be described as having a problem with this role because she does not accept her adopted mother and by implication her adopted family's customs or the family's identity. The types of problems experienced by Mary in her role could be described as the Ambivalence Type and Isolation Type. With respect to the Ambivalence Type, you could say that Mary is experiencing a state of internal tension regarding her adopted mother, her birth mother, and people in authority. With regard to the Isolation Type classification, Mary's behavior appears to represent a feeling of being alone and apart from others in response to her belief that she is being treated differently. In addition, she has withdrawn from her adopted family and friends.

Karls and Wandrei (1994) make the point that the PIE classification for Social Role functioning tries to avoid defining social roles in a culture-specific context, and they urge social workers to take into account the specific cultural and societal role definitions influencing the client (p. 24). This instruction is an admission that the PIE classification of Social Role Problems is limited in clarifying some problems faced by certain culturally diverse groups of people. Defining Mary as having a problem with ambivalence and isolation in her family/child role locates the problem within Mary. Unsuspectedly, this negates most Native Americans' belief that revolves around an emphasis that includes a spirit-centered worldview. As such, Mary (and most Native people) sees "the entire universe imbued with and intimately related to spirits and spiritual forces that have real power to influence outcomes" or one's behavior (Voss et al., 1999, p. 230). Seen in this light, Mary's problem may be understood less as a problem in her role performance than as "soul loss" or a "dislocation of the spirit"; thus her problem involves and should be located in the larger spiritual world (Voss et al., 1999, p. 235).

There is one last objection to using the PIE classification of Factor I with Mary and with Native Americans in general. Many Native Americans continue to distrust the Western interpretation of their traditions and their health and social problems. To use the PIE classification of social role problems, which focuses on the individual and not on the large spiritual world of Native Americans, only reinforces this distrust. Social workers require a deeper appreciation of the nature of this distrust. Numerous Native American scholars (DeLoria, 1999; Weaver, 1999; Voss et al., 1999; Gross, 1995) believe that Western knowledge and science continues to exclude or cannot admit that "anything mysterious can exist or that any kind of behavior or experience can remain outside of its ability to explain" (DeLoria, 1999, p. 148).

Vine DeLoria, Jr. is perhaps the most outspoken Native American scholar regarding the distrust of Western knowledge and science. The following long excerpt is intended to provide the reader with a richer understanding of Native peoples' mistrust of imposed classification and/or knowledge of their lives and behavior.

> The revolt against social sciences is not simply a few Indian activists criticizing anthros and the suspicion with which Indians in science and engineering view theories in their fields. Rather the problem is the credibility and applicability of Western knowledge in the Indian context. The objections are easily understood. Western technology largely depletes resources or substitutes a mono-cultural approach to a complex natural system. We tend to hide this fact by talking about production rather than extraction but this linguistic acrobatics is not sufficient to escape Indian critique. Social science in the Western context describes human behavior in such restrictive terminology that it describes very little except the methodology acceptable to the present generation of academics and researchers. While an increasing number of Indian students are mastering the language and theoretical frameworks of western knowledge, there remains the feeling of incompleteness and inadequacy of what has been learned.
>
> More important, whatever information is obtained in higher education must, in the Indian context, have some direct bearing on human individual and communal experience. In contrast in the non-Indian context, the knowledge must simply provide a means of identification of the experience or phenomenon. It helps to deal with specific examples to illustrate the point. A Western observer faced with the question of how and why certain species of birds make their nests is liable to conclude that it is "instinct." And this identification of course tells us nothing whatsoever, but it does foreclose further inquiry because a question has been answered.
>
> In the Indian context the answer would involve a highly complicated description of the personality of the bird species, be it eagle, meadowlark, or sparrow, and the observed behavior of the bird would provide information on time of year, weather, absence or presence of related plants and animals, and perhaps even some indication of the age and experience of the particular bird. In this comparison Indian knowledge provides a predictive context in which certain prophetic statements can be made. Western science, for all its insistence on reproduction of behavior and test conditions and predictability of further activities, provides us with very little that is useful.
>
> Indian knowledge is designed to make statements that adequately describe the experience or phenomenon. That is to say, they include everything that is known about the experience even if no firm conclusions are reached. (DeLoria, 1999, p. 147)

In an effort not to add to the continued distrust held by Native Americans of Western science and knowledge, social workers should use considerable caution when using Factor I of PIE to describe the behavior of Native Americans.

Although seemingly a contradiction in spirit from the aforementioned objections to the PIE classification system, Factor II: Environmental Factors is most congruent with Native Americans' beliefs and with the underlying causative factors of their health and social problems. Karls and Wandrei (1994) describe the environment as consisting of the physical and social context in which a person lives. It includes the natural setting and the human-made circumstances outside the person. Factor II focuses on the external elements outside of the client that affect the client's social functioning and social well-being (p. 28).

Factor II's concern with the physical and natural setting provides a strong link for understanding the social and health problems of Native Americans and their beliefs, although, as DeLoria (1999) notes, "When we talk with non-Indians about nature, there is really nothing we can say in universal Western concepts that is going to make a lot of sense" (p. 224). Nonetheless, nature and their physical surroundings are intimately connected to Native Americans' behavior and relationships. There may be differences among tribes in response to the environment but there remains a strong tie for all tribes.

DeLoria (1999) provides a deeper understanding of this intimacy:

> The simple proposition that Indians love nature and embrace it does not tell you why different tribes manifest their relationship to the land in different ways. If you talk to tribal peoples in those particular lands, you will get a better insight into why their religion and their culture developed in certain ways. People in the woodland areas deal with dream analysis and with loss of "soul" because in an intimate relationship with a great deal of vegetation and life you are in danger of losing your psyche among all the other life forms. This is not articulated in a set of doctrines. But it is alive within a community of people so intimately related to the natural environment that the *natural environment shapes the very way they relate to each other and their conception of the world they live in.* (p. 224)

Factor II fits well with the above description of Native Americans' intimacy with their environment. It helps to guide the social worker toward intervening with those environmental systems that can assist Native Americans in finding resources and opportunities that contribute to their social functioning and social well-being. Importantly, Factor II addresses the issue of discrimination in each of the environmental systems. Discrimination remains a powerful ongoing experience for many Native Americans (Starita, 1995; Means, 1995).

Let's use Mary's case study to illustrate the utility of Factor II in addressing the social and health problems of Native Americans. Rather than having a problem in her social role functioning, Mary can be seen as experiencing obstacles in the following systems: Voluntary Association System and Affectional System. In regard to the Voluntary Association System, Mary had no opportunities outside of her adopted family to satisfy and meet the needs for social support and interaction, specifically a group that met her needs for an Indian identity. In terms of her Affectional Support System, Mary was without a network of social relationships. There was no one in her support system that could help her identify with her Native American beliefs or culture.

Hammerschlag (1988) continues the account of Mary, and you can see how attention to her Voluntary and Affectional Systems allowed for an intervention that was consistent with her cultural beliefs.

Mary was helped by a social worker to find her birth family. The family sponsored a traditional Navajo welcoming-home ceremony. The ritual of the ceremony helped to heal some of the suffering Mary had experienced for many years. The traditional Navajo ceremony held by Mary's family to welcome her back helped to restore Mary's balance—and theirs too. This was the way in which they could come together again, and Mary could become whole.

> The ceremony was held in a hogan. Mary was frightened that she would make mistakes and not be able to repeat exactly the words of the prayers. Her sister helped her learn her part in the ritual.

The medicine man knew every word for the entire ceremony in exactly the right order, each line with its appropriate melody. As he sang, he sprinkled multicolored sands on the ground with movements of his thumb and forefinger, creating what many believe to be the greatest folk art on this continent.

Mary stared at the sand painting in awe. It depicted a Navajo legend about a child who was lost to the tribe, but who returned in another form. The medicine man asked Mary to sit in the middle of the painting. Now she could actually mingle with the heroic figures and absorb their strength.

The medicine man tied feathers and spruce on Mary and placed stone and wooden fetishes, holy objects, on her. He twirled a wooden noisemaker and made a huge roar. Mary felt the breeze from this instrument as if it were blowing her old confused and angry self away. The medicine man gave her a pipe filled with sweet tobacco. He smoked it; she smoked it; and they blew clouds of tobacco smoke over themselves and toward the sky. For everyone, the atmosphere was charged with feeling.

This was how Mary's odyssey ended. She could like flush toilets, watch television, become well-educated, and still be Navajo. She could perceive the world as angry and hostile or as nurturing and sustaining. She had the choice. She could always connect with the things that really mattered. Mary now works among her Navajo people as a health professional.

When we met, Mary was filled with anger at her own exploitation, then anger at white people. She finally gave up the anger. All of what she was served to remind her not to close her eyes to other realities. By hearing all the voices within her, Mary made a new friend. Mary kept the parts of herself in alignment by remembering the words sung in her ceremony:

> Happily—may you walk with God—
> Happily—may you walk—
> Happily—may you feel light within—
> Happily—with feeling may you walk—
> Happily—may you walk with God.

All of us need to connect with authentic paths home. (pp. 44–45)

Conclusion

This chapter was intended to assist social workers in gaining a deeper appreciation of Native Americans and to help develop a sensitivity to their cultural identities and beliefs when trying to understand their social and health problems. Specifically, within applying the PIE classification system, social workers must use extreme caution in trying to categorize the behaviors of Native Americans. Although classification paradigms may fit Western scientific standards, they may shed little or no light on the true nature of Native peoples' troubles. Perhaps the best preparation social workers can have if they are truly going to help Native Americans is to remember what N. Scott Momaday (1997), a Native American writer, has to say about words:

Words are spoken with great care, and they are heard. They matter, and they must not be taken for granted; they must be taken seriously and they must be remembered. . . . By means of words can one quiet the raging weather, bring forth the harvest, ward off evil, rid the body of sickness and pain, subdue an enemy, capture the heart of a lover, live in the proper way, and venture beyond death. Indeed, there is nothing more powerful. When one ventures to speak, when he utters a prayer or tells a story, he is dealing with forces that are supernatural and irresistible. He assumes great risks and responsibilities. He is clear and deliberate in his mind and in his speech; he will be taken at his word. Even so, he knows that he stands the chance of speaking indirectly or inappropriately, or of being mistaken by his hearers, or of not being heard at all. To be careless in the presence of words, on the inside of language, is to violate a fundamental morality. But one does not necessarily speak in order to be heard. It is sometimes enough that one places one's voice on the silence, for that in itself is a whole and appropriate expression of the spirit. (pp. 15–16)

Social workers must learn not to take liberty with words, like classification systems, which can serve as a distraction and thus become blind to the sacred and the mysteries of Native peoples. Any classification system, if it is to improve assessment and intervention, must reflect the cultural reality of the group targeted for assistance. PIE may require further refinement to be helpful with Native Americans.

References

Agree, E. M. (1988). *Portrait of Native American elderly*. In Hearing before the Select Committee on Aging, House of Representatives (Comm. Pub. No. 100-645): Washington, DC: U.S. Government Printing Office.

Bentz, M. G. (1996). Child rearing. In F. E. Hoxie (Ed.), *Encyclopedia of North American Indians* (pp. 115–118). Boston: Houghton Mifflin.

Brown, Epes, J. (1991). *The spiritual legacy of the American Indian*. New York: Crossroad.

Carson, D. K. (1995). American Indian elder abuse: Risk and protective factors among the oldest Americans. *Journal of Elder Abuse and Neglect, 7*(1), 17–39.

Chapleski, E. E., Lichtenberg, P. A., Dwyer, J. W., Youngblade, L. M., & Tsai, F. (1997). Morbidity and comorbidity among Great Lakes American Indians: Predictors of functional abilities. *Gerontologist, 37*(5), 588–597.

Child, B. J. (1996). Boarding schools. In F. E. Hoxie (Ed.), *Encyclopedia of North American Indians* (pp. 78–80). Boston: Houghton Mifflin.

Davenport, J. A., & Davenport, J. (1987). Native American suicide: A Durkheimian analysis. *Social Casework, 68*(9), 533–539.

DeLoria, V. (1995). *Red earth, white lies*. New York: Scribner.

DeLoria, V. (1999). *Spirit and reason*. Golden, CO: Fulcrum Publishing.

DeLoria, V., & Lytle, C. M. (1983). *American Indians, American justice*. Austin: University of Texas Press.

Eastman, C. (1911). *The soul of the Indian: An interpretation*. Lincoln and London: University of Nebraska Press.

Edwards, W. S., & Edwards, B. (1989). *Questionnaires and data collection methods for the institutional population component* (National Medical Expenditure Survey Methods 1, DHHS Publication No. (PHS) 89-3440). Rockville, MD: National Center for Health Service Research and Health Care Technology Assessment.

Ewalt, P. L., & Mokuau, N. (1995). Self-determination from a Pacific perspective. *Social Work, 40*(2), 168–176.

Frederick, C. (1973). *Suicide, homicide and alcoholism among American Indians*. Rockville, MD: U.S. Department of Health, Education and Welfare, Publication #ADM 74-42.

Gross, E. R. (1995). Deconstructing politically correct practice literature: The American Indian case. *Social Work, 40*(2), 206–214.

Hammerschlag, C. A. (1988). *The dancing healer*. San Francisco: Harper.

Hogan, P. T., & Siu, S. (1988). Minority children and the child welfare system. *Social Work, 33,* 493–498.

Hudson, M. F., & Armachain, W. D. (1998). Elder abuse: Two Native American views. *Gerontologist, 38*(5), 538–548.

Joe, J. R. (1996). Health and healers. In F. E. Hoxie (Ed.), *Encyclopedia of North American Indians* (pp. 237–240). Boston: Houghton Mifflin.

John, R. (1991). The state of reason on American Indian elders' health, income security, and social support networks. In The Gerontological Society of America (Ed.), *Minority elders: Longevity, economics, and health*. Washington, DC: The Gerontological Society of America.

Karls, J. M., & Wandrei, K. E. (1994). *Person-in-environment system*. Washington, DC: NASW.

Kilborne, P. T. (1997). For the poorest Indians, casinos aren't enough. *New York Times,* 6/11, A-1–B-11.

LaDuke, W. (1998). Return of Buffalo nation. *Native Americans* (Winter), 10–21.

Leininger, M. M. (1990). Historic and epistemologic dimensions of care and caring with future directions. In J. Stevenson (Ed.), *American Academy of Nursing* (pp. 19–31). Kansas City, MO: American Nurses Association Press.

Levy, J. E. (1996). Alcoholism, Indian. In F. E. Hoxie (Ed.), *Encyclopedia of North American Indians* (pp. 16–19). Boston: Houghton Mifflin.

Mander, J. (1991). *In the absence of the sacred*. San Francisco: Sierra Club Books.

Marks, P. M. (1998). *In a barren land*. New York: William Morrow.

May, P. A. (1982). Contemporary crimes and the American Indian: A survey and analysis of the literature. *Plains Anthropologist, 27,* 225–238.

May, P. A. (1988). The health status of Indian children: Problems and prevention in early life. In S. P. Manson & N. G. Dinges (Eds.), Behavioral health issues among American Indians and Alaska Natives: Explorations on the frontiers of the biobehavioral sciences. *Journal of the National Center Monograph Series, 1*(1), 244–289.

Means, R. (1995). *Where white men fear to tread*. New York: St. Martin's Press.

Mercer, S. O. (1996). Navajo elderly people in a reservation nursing home: Admission predictors and culture care practices. *Social Work, 41*(2), 181–189.

Momaday, N. S. (1997). *The man made of words*. New York: St. Martin's Press.

Nabigon, H., & Mawhiney, A. (1996). Aboriginal theory: A Cree medicine wheel guide for healing first nations. In J. Turner (Ed.), *Social work treatment*. New York: Free Press.

National Indian Council on Aging (NICOA). (1981). *American Indian elderly: A national profile*. Albuquerque, NM: National Council on Aging.

Nofz, M. P. (1988). Alcohol abuse and culturally marginal American Indians. *Social Casework, 69*(2), 67–73.

Parker, J. G. (1994). The lived experience of Native Americans with diabetes within a transcultural nursing perspective. *Journal of Transcultural Nursing, 6*(1), 5–11.

Red Horse, J. (1978). Family behavior of urban American Indians. *Social Casework, 59,* 67–72.

Schinke, S. P. (1985). Preventing substance abuse with American Indian youth. *Social Casework, 66* (April), 213–219.

Starita, J. (1995). *The Dull Knifes of Pine Ridge*. New York: G. P. Putnam's Sons.

Tinker, G. E. (1996). Religion. In F. E. Hoxie (Ed.), *Encyclopedia of North American Indians* (pp. 537–541). Boston: Houghton Mifflin.

Voss, R. W., Douville, V., Little Soldier, A., & Twiss, G. (1999). Tribal and shamanic-based social work practice: A Lakota perspective. *Social Work, 44*(3), 228–242.

U.S. Bureau of the Census. (1993). *We the . . . first Americans*. Washington, DC: U.S. Printing Office.

Wares, D. M., Wedel, K. R., Rosenthal, J. A., & Dobrec, A. (1994). Indian child welfare: A multicultural challenge. *Journal of Multicultural Social Work, 3*(3), 1–15.

Weaver, H. N. (1998). Indigenous people in a multicultural society: Unique issues for human services. *Social Work, 43*(8), 203–211.

Weaver, H. N. (1999). Indigenous people and the social work profession: Defining culturally competent services. *Social Work, 44*(3), 217–227.

Williams, E. E., & Ellison, F. (1996). Culturally informed social work practice with American Indian clients: Guidelines for non-Indian social workers. *Social Work, 41,* 147–151.

Williams, R. A. (1996). Laws of Indian communities. In F. E. Hoxie (Ed.), *Encyclopedia of North American Indians* (pp. 334–337). Boston: Houghton Mifflin.

Wilson, J. (1999). *The earth shall weep.* New York: Atlantic Monthly Press.

9

Asian Americans: Ethnocentrism and Discrimination

Michie N. Hesselbrock and Cheryl Parks

Asian Americans are the fastest growing ethnic minority in the United States. Since 1990, the Asian and Pacific Islander population has grown at a rate of 4.5% per year. The number of Asian Americans was estimated to be 8.8 million in 1994, an increase of 1.5 million since the 1990 census. That number was expected to increase to 12.1 million by 2000 (U.S. Bureau of the Census, 1995). While the social work literature has long emphasized the importance of understanding the diversity of cultural factors affecting ethnic minorities for effective social work interventions, little is known about Asian Americans living in the United States. The presentation of problems, demeanors, and behavioral mannerisms by Asian clients is likely to be different from those manifested by mainstream Americans and may not be accurately perceived as a true reflection of clients' attitudes, values, and behaviors (Kim, 1995). Policy makers, agency administrators, and clinicians in social service agencies are not well prepared to work with Asian clients (Kim, 1995).

According to the 1990 census, Chinese represent the largest portion of Asian Americans in the United States (1.64 million). Filipinos represent the second largest group (1.41 million), followed by Japanese (847,000), Asian Indians (815,000), Koreans (799,000), and Vietnamese (615,000) (U.S. Bureau of the Census, 1995). While the first wave of Chinese, Japanese, and Korean immigrants established themselves in this country over several generations during the past hundred years, the greatest proportion of Asians currently living in the United States is foreign born, including 63% of Chinese, 80% of Koreans, and 64% of Filipinos (Castro, Proescholdbell, Albeita, & Rodriguez, 1999).

Historically, social work agencies have paid little attention to working with Asian Americans, and social service resources for Asians, typically, are available only in large metropolitan areas. Recently, however, social workers are paying more attention to the Asian cultural and social factors that may form the core of the Asian client's functioning. As a profession, social workers are increasingly learning the importance of understanding and accepting the cultural uniqueness of clients rather than assuming assimilation within the majority culture (Kim, 1995). In order to be effective, social workers need to utilize not only traditional interventions but also more culturally sensitive approaches to respond to Asian clients.

Understanding of the Asian clients' immigration history, culture, and belief systems is an essential ingredient of effective social work intervention. Of equal importance is knowledge and understanding of the family structures, attitudes about help seeking, and support systems available to Asian clients. Finally, it is also important to assess the degree to which individuals and families have integrated into the community.

Despite similarities in the geographic locations of their home countries, Asians living in the United States are very heterogeneous in terms of ethnicity, history, and culture and value systems. Often, generalizations about the behaviors and beliefs of one Asian culture cannot be applied to another. As mentioned earlier, immigration patterns and history vary across the different subgroups of Asians, and these differences may manifest in the clients' belief systems and behaviors. Without recognition of the diverse nature of Asian clients, the utility of social work services will be limited.

Immigration and Resettlement Patterns and Consequences

While the U.S. Bureau of the Census lists only ten major subgroups under the heading of Asian and Pacific Islanders, Asian Americans living in the United States comprise more than sixty separate ethnic/racial subgroups, each with their own language, culture, history, and immigration experience (Yen, 1992). Among Asians, Southeast Asian refugees, Filipinos, and Koreans are the fastest growing groups of new Americans. Adaptation of these immigrants and refugees in the new country varies depending on how recently they came to the United States, the circumstances of leaving their home countries, and differential resettlement processes after entering the United States. Unlike the majority of European immigrants, most Asian immigrants have had to learn both a completely new lifestyle as well as a language that is quite foreign to them. Many have had to contend, as well, with anti-Asian immigration policies that targeted different groups of Asians. These policies limited many from entering or bringing family members into the United States as well as limited the civil rights of those who were already residents.

While most social policies and services consider Asian to be a single ethnic identity, there is great diversity in the group identification, immigration history, and culture of the various members contained within Asians. The major groups of Asians in the United States are Chinese, Japanese, Filipino, Korean, Asian Indian, and Southeast Asian. Each ethnic group has brought its unique cultural heritage, experienced different immigration processes, and dealt with unique immigration policies in the United States. These differences are reflected in the process of adjustment, ethnic community development, and construction of social structures by and among the different Asian immigrant groups.

Chinese

While some historians indicate that Asians lived on the North American continent before the Common Era, the first documented immigration of Asian people to the United States began with the Chinese, who arrived in the mid-1800s during the California Gold Rush (Kumamoto, 1995). The majority of these Chinese immigrants came from southeastern coastal provinces. They were, for the most part, young men who were motivated to escape from the Tai-Ping Revolution of 1850 and poverty. Most intended to stay only temporarily, just long enough to accumulate money and return to China (Matsuoka & Ryujin, 1991). Chinese immigrants worked as field hands and as domestics; the Chinese laborer made a significant contribution to the completion of the transcontinental railroad system. Initially welcomed for their performance of many needed services, the Chinese were quickly considered to be a threat in the poor economy of the late nineteenth century. Operating under the perception that the Chinese were taking the limited employment opportunities available, many communities turned against them. It was not an uncommon occurrence for Chinese immigrants to be violently attacked and expelled from these communities (Matsuoka & Ryujin, 1991).

Chinese immigrants brought with them an opium smoking habit to the United States (Ray & Ksir, 1999). While opium smoking remained within Chinatowns in San Francisco and New York, the practice spread rapidly among gamblers and prostitutes (Ray & Ksir, 1999). The fashionable young men and women in San Francisco began visiting the opium smoking dens. The Chinese were blamed for corrupting the moral character of citizens. By 1875, opium smoking was considered widespread in the United States among all segments of society, and a city ordinance in San Francisco, and later in New York, forbade opium smoking (Kumamoto, 1995). In 1890, federal law restricted all but U.S. citizens from importing opium and manufacturing smoking opium in the United States (Ray & Ksir, 1999). As the Chinese were blamed for the widespread opium addiction among non-Chinese in San Francisco and New York, increased racial tensions led to the passage of the Chinese Exclusion Act in 1882, prohibiting Chinese immigration. Many Chinese men, who had planned to stay in the United States temporarily and left their families in China, were unable to bring their families to the United States after passage of this legislation. Many of these families, separated by the emigration of the husband or father, were never reunited (Matsuoka & Ryujin, 1991; Kim, 1995).

In order to protect each other from the violence against them, Chinese immigrants segregated themselves in tight-knit enclaves, isolated from the larger society (Ho, 1976). Arriving in the United States with many traditional social and economic practices from the old country, Chinese immigrants maintained their traditional ways of life within these enclaves. These communities of Chinese helped new immigrants to obtain employment, represented new immigrants in the larger society, and mediated disputes between and among members and the majority culture. The associations also helped to facilitate social and economic independence of new immigrants by providing venture capital and financial advice (Matsuoka & Ryujin, 1991).

Japanese

Japanese immigrants came to Hawaii and California around the turn of the century, during the Meiji restoration (which restored the Emperor's ruling power and transferred the country from a feudal system to a democratic society). The increase in social unrest and unemployment created by the Japanese government's efforts to industrialize an agrarian economy, as well as lack of farmland to support extended families, motivated many individuals to seek a better life elsewhere. Most of these immigrants settled on the West Coast in the United States and in Hawaii, where they were welcomed as farm workers. They also worked in mines, at lumber camps, in canning factories, and on the railroad. However, as the number of immigrants increased, anti-Japanese sentiment grew among U.S. workers. These anti-Asian sentiments were manifested through laws that limited immigration, restricted land ownership, disqualified eligibility for naturalized U.S. citizenship, and prohibited interracial marriages. Many communities could force expulsion of Japanese without fear of being charged legally (Ishisaka & Takagi, 1982; Matsuoka & Ryujin, 1991).

The first generation of Japanese immigrants *(Issei)* was creative and resourceful in overcoming the barriers imposed on them. The law prohibited noncitizens from owning property. It also prohibited the Japanese from becoming naturalized citizens. In order to get around the law, the *Issei* bought farmland in the names of their children, who were citizens by virtue of their birthright. In order to deal with the policies that blocked economic development by Japanese immigrants, the *Issei* developed their own lending institutions by pooling their money and loaning it to each other on a rotating basis. This system, operated on values of mutual trust and obligation, provided capital for many *Issei* business ventures and became the foundation for the development of the Japanese American community (Matsuoka & Ryujin, 1991). The community maintained the traditional cultural values and provided both social and economic support for its members.

The economic independence gained through the ingenuity and hard work of these Japanese immigrants was suddenly taken away with the onset of World War II. When war was declared against Japan, fearing that Japanese immigrants might be more loyal to Japan than to the United States, the government forced a mass evacuation of Japanese Americans from the West Coast, imposing a tremendous economic loss among them. Many lost their businesses and were moved out of their houses and farmland with few of their belongings. They were removed from the West Coast and kept in camps for the duration of the war. In order to survive the hardship, individuals and families held in the internment camps coalesced into a close-knit Japanese community characterized by strong mutual support. After the war, they had to start all over again. This relocation and incarceration of 110,000 Japanese Americans represents the most punitive social and psychological event in their immigration history (Matsuoka & Ryujin, 1991). Yet, despite these drastic anti-Japanese policies enacted by the government during the war, most Japanese men and women identified themselves as Americans, and many Japanese young men volunteered in the United States military services (Kitano, 1981).

Filipinos

The immigration of Filipinos also began in the early 1900s. However, the largest influx of these migrations occurred after 1924 when a gentlemen's agreement between the United States and Japan stopped the flow of Japanese immigrants into the country. In order to fill labor demands for seasonal farm workers and by canneries of the Pacific Northwest and Alaska, Filipinos were employed as laborers replacing Japanese workers as a source of cheap labor (Castro et al., 1999). The Philippines has a long history of being under the control of Spain and the United States. Since they were under U.S. rule at that time, the Filipino immigrants were granted some rights and privileges as residents of a U.S. colony, but they were kept in low-level service positions or as manual laborers. Filipinos were denied ownership rights to property and the right to vote (Matsuoka & Ryujin, 1991). The immigration of Filipinos decreased when the number of available white workers increased during the Depression (Melendy, 1976).

The second influx of Filipinos to the United States occurred after a 1965 revision of the immigration laws. The new immigrants were well-educated and highly skilled professionals, but their training and skills were not recognized by professional organizations in the United States. Being unable to utilize their skills and training, most found themselves underemployed (Ishisaka & Takagi, 1982).

In contrast to the Chinese and Japanese, Filipino immigrants did not emerge into their own ethnic community. This was due, at least in part, to the cultural and regional diversity of their homeland and the transient, seasonal nature of the early immigrants' work (Lott, 1976). Consequently, most immigrants did not have the same resources that the Japanese and Chinese immigrants enjoyed, such as protection, solidarity, mutual aid, and economic supports. Consequently, they had difficulty establishing a foothold in U.S. society (Lott, 1976; Matsuoka & Ryujin, 1991).

Koreans and Asian Indians

Koreans began to enter the United States around the turn of the century to escape from war, disease, and famine. Asian Indians also began immigrating to the United States as laborers around the turn of the century. They worked in the lumber industry in Washington and on farms in California. However, Asians were barred from entering the United States after

1924 when the legislature passed the National Origins Act. The number of immigrants from Asian countries virtually ceased until 1965 when immigration laws were once again changed.

Southeast Asians

The influx of refugees from Southeast Asia, including Vietnamese, Laotians, Hmong, Thais, and Cambodians, began after the fall of Saigon in 1975. These refugees left their homelands to escape both from the consequences of war and from poverty. In contrast to earlier Asian immigrants, who were mostly young men without their families, the Southeast Asians included men, women, and children. Whole families composed of people of all ages and representing a wide range of socioeconomic strata left their homelands together. Refugees evacuated from Vietnam were moved initially to refugee camps before being relocated to the United States and other countries. The refugees who came to the United States were first brought to military bases in California, Pennsylvania, Arkansas, and Florida. Under the refugee resettlement programs, they were scattered all over the country through "adoption" by host families and organizations (Hirayama, 1982). Since 1975, over 860,000 Southeast Asian refugees have resettled in the United States (Hirayama, Hirayama, & Cetingok, 1993). This relatively new and rapid influx of Southeast Asian refugees has presented serious challenges to the social work agencies that offer services to them. Despite high rates of depression and psychosomatic problems, these refugees, in general, do not seek mental health services because they have different perceptions of mental illness. Further, the mental health service systems are not equipped to serve them. Very few social workers are familiar with their culture, and social workers rarely speak their languages (Hirayama et al., 1993).

Southeast Asians who live in the United States also suffer from a lack of social supports in a community. This is partly due to the dispersion resettlement policy of the federal government. The transition to life in the United States is much easier for the immigrants and refugees who live in large metropolitan areas where the same ethnic minorities are concentrated. Many Asian immigrants and refugees in these urban locales maintain nonassimilation by living in a community composed of the same ethnic group. They are able to maintain a separate cultural cohesiveness, with traditional customs, values, languages, and ethnic organizations. Access to the ethnic community, its food, culture, and entertainment, is much easier for them, especially when contrasted to those living in rural communities or parts of the United States where there is a low concentration of ethnic minorities from the same country. The process of acculturation and assimilation for these people is much more difficult and traumatic (Hirayama & Hirayama, 1988).

Studies of Southeast Asian refugees consistently find higher rates of mental health problems than in the general population (Hirayama, 1982). Among the refugees, factors identified as at risk for mental health problems include separation from families and other support systems, greater dissimilarity between home and host countries, psychological trauma of wartime experience, and lowering of socioeconomic status due to underemployment. Further, because of the U.S. government policy to scatter these refugees across the country, many former refugees continue to be isolated from their native culture. Services to this group of Asians require additional time and effort to overcome language barriers as well as helping them to deal with the trauma associated with the experience of leaving their native land, living in refugee camps, and undergoing resettlement (Hirayama & Hirayama, 1988).

In summary, Asian clients may bring with them the consequences of different immigration and resettlement processes. Further, clients from different subgroups will have different resources. For example, social workers may have more access to ethnic community resources for Japanese and Chinese clients on the West Coast, while other ethnic groups may have few resources or lack ready access to their respective ethnic communities.

Norms, Beliefs, and Cultural Stereotypes

The lack of understanding about the complex nature of different Asian subgroups has played a major role in the creation and persistence of Asian stereotypes (Kim, 1995). Asian Americans have been considered a hardworking and quiet model minority on the one hand, while they were criticized for being exclusive of other ethnic minorities and not interested in assimilation to the larger society on the other (Kim, 1995). Asians are also considered to have few problems with juvenile delinquency, divorce, mental illness, alcohol and drug misuse, or poverty (Sue & McKinney, 1975). However, recent evidence suggests that a segment of Asian Americans tend to be underemployed and earn lower incomes. Kitano (1981) found that the median income of Chinese men in Los Angeles was lower as compared with Caucasian men in the same city. Similar findings about Asians are reported by others (Morales, 1981). While reports indicate that, among "old" Asians, a high proportion of Asians are college educated and earn the median household income or above, a disproportionately higher segment of Asians are also underemployed and living below the poverty level (Kim, 1995). Researchers have also found that drinking patterns vary within groups of Asian Americans. Among adolescents and college students, the rates of drinking and heavy drinking are lower for Asians than other ethnic groups. However, Japanese Americans have the highest rates of heavy drinking when compared with other Asian groups. Further, Southeast Asians are considered to be at high risk for heavy drinking (Makimoto, 1998).

Asians, as a whole, have been considered the model minority as they actively pursued upward mobility and avoided social confrontations and conflict with mainstream Euro-American society. Despite hardships, most Japanese Americans and Chinese Americans have achieved relatively high levels of education and economic independence (Castro et al., 1999). Many Japanese and Chinese, who are the second or third generations of these immigrants, tend to have relatively higher educational attainment, larger families, and higher than average family income (Bennett & Martin, 1997). This is in contrast to the "new Chinese," Koreans, Filipinos, and Vietnamese, who are relative newcomers to this country and who have not yet established themselves well economically or socially (Kitano, 1989). Consequently, attitudes and lifestyles of the foreign-born "old-country" Asian may be more closely associated with the new immigrant and may have little relevance for groups who have been here for several generations (Kitano, 1989).

While Asians as a whole earn higher than average incomes and report higher levels of education than other ethnic minority groups, the recent immigrants are generally poor, unskilled, and uneducated. The median income of Japanese Americans is much higher than that of Vietnamese Americans (Zane & Sasao, 1992). The former refugees have not recovered from the downward shift in their occupations. It is expected that the gap between the wealthy and the poor will increase (Yen, 1992). Variations in educational attainment also exist among Asian Americans. While the established Asian Americans achieved higher than average education, school dropout rates of Filipinos are much higher than those for white Americans (Zane & Sasao, 1992).

Lack of understanding of Asians among potential employers, stereotyping, philosophical differences about work ethic, and language all impose obstacles for immigrants to be competitive on the job market. After a few bad experiences with negative people, they may be afraid to deal with non-Asians socially. These difficulties may be risk factors for mental health and substance abuse problems (Amodeo & Jones, 1997).

Common Beliefs

While subgroups of Asians present unique histories, cultures, and languages, it is important that social workers also understand that commonalities within and between groups exist as well. Some commonalities in the traditional culture and norms that exist across subgroups provide a foundation to the expressed attitudes, values, and behaviors of different groups and generations. Those belief systems commonly identified in Asian culture across groups need to be understood.

One of the fundamental differences between Asian and U.S. cultures is that, while religious traditions vary among Chinese, Koreans, Japanese, Southeast Asians, and Indians, the cultural tradition of Asian people has been founded on non-Judeo-Christian beliefs. The major cultural traditions are founded mostly on Buddhism. Others include Confucianism, several branches of Buddhism, Taoism, and Confucianism (China), Hinduism (India), and Shintoism (Japan). These religions emphasize moderation and harmony with one's people and environment.

In contrast to the Anglo culture of individualism, assertiveness, individual achievement, and spontaneity, Asian cultures value responsibility to others, interdependence, restraint, moderation, and group achievement. Asian cultural traditions emphasize the importance and value of the family and community before the individual, while the Judeo-Christian tradition emphasizes individualism and independence of the person. In Asian culture, the identity of an individual person is considered to be integrated with and dependent on that of the family or community rather than apart from them. The values, attitudes, and behaviors of the individual are expected to be consistent with those of their own family or the community. Thus it is the community that defines the role of individual, and individuals are expected to perform their prescribed roles in harmony with their own surroundings.

The "old" Japanese and Chinese immigrants have maintained their own traditional extended families for several generations. Traditionally, the structure of the Asian family is patriarchal, with communication flowing vertically from the parents to children, and from the husband to the wife. Children are taught their obligation to the family, and individual family members' wishes are secondary to the good of the family as a whole (Kim, 1995). The traditional value of respect for one's ancestors and family traditions pretty well prescribes the role and function of individual family members. Family members are highly dependent on each other, and family values are characterized by respect for one's elders, one's ancestors, and family tradition. Usually women occupy a lower status in the traditional Asian family. Domestic violence against women is tolerated, and occurs frequently, but very few cases are reported to law enforcement (Kim, McLeod, & Shantzis, 1992). These family values and attitudes that define each member's identity are in stark contrast to U.S. values characterized by self-determination, independence, autonomy, and respect for the dignity and uniqueness of the individual (Chin, 1983; Kim, 1995). In social work agencies, a typical Asian client from a traditional family could be considered less autonomous and less independent while being perceived as obedient, cooperative, considerate, and polite (Kim, 1995).

Asian families value education of their children. The children's educational performance is considered to be a family matter, and it is given prominence and recognition in the Asian community. When a child does poorly in school, he or she must face parental disapproval, criticism, and disappointment. The feeling of shame may spread among relatives, as well. Consequently, any gap in parental expectations and the child's own achievement invites fear of failure and becomes a serious source of stress for children (Kim et al., 1992).

A conflict in the newly immigrated family may also develop out of the differential acculturation rate among family members. The children tend to learn the new language much more quickly and adopt the new culture much more readily than their parents. Their behavior also tends to be influenced by peers, not their parents. Children tend to be more individualistic rather than exhibiting consideration for or conformity to parental expectations. Because of poor language skills on the part of parents, children may assume some adult responsibility in the community, creating a role reversal for the family that could be in direct conflict with the traditional family structure.

Another problem that affects recent immigrants from Asia is downward social mobility. It is difficult to obtain employment that is consistent with a person's training and skills acquired in the old country. The lack of retraining opportunities also contributes toward the downward mobility of employment possibilities. Thus, the effects of downward social mobility are a further complication in the lives of adult immigrants who may suffer already from poor self-esteem resulting from family role reversals.

In addition to the added responsibility at home, children often encounter difficulties in public schools. They may have difficulty with language; parents may not be able to help with their homework. Also parents tend not to participate in children's school activities or organizational events (e.g., PTA, school open house, teacher-parent conferences, and so on) due to their own language problems. Hirayama (1985) studied seventy-four recent immigrant and refugee children who attended public schools in one southern city in the United States and found that one third of the students had poor adaptation to the schools. The factors associated with this poor adaptation included lack of help with homework, inability to complete homework, placement in a lower grade than the age-appropriate class, a perception of U.S. peers as mean, and being a recent arrival in the United States. Hirayama (1985) also found problems related to the lack of understanding about Asian students among teachers, counselors, and other students.

Asian children may appear to school counselors to be withdrawn while they may be, instead, just being quiet and polite until they learn to express themselves in the new school. Further, Asian children in school may face negative social attitudes conveyed by teachers, or rejection and teasing from other non-Asian peers in school. The parents may not contact the school because of their poor language skills and lack of familiarity with the school system.

This lack of contact and absence of parents from school activities could be misunderstood by the school officials as a lack of parental interest in their children's educational process.

Another characteristic of the Asian culture is a high degree of emphasis on reserved emotional expression and internalization of strong feelings. While the problem brought in by the individual family member is considered to be a reflection of the whole family system, the issues are not openly discussed among the family members. Maintaining peace and harmony among family members is one of the highest priorities in Asian families (Kim, 1995). Generally, self-control in the expression of emotions and feelings is emphasized and arguments or controversies are not encouraged. This characteristic of self-control among Asians could be perceived as nonassertive, suspicious, or introversive when contrasted with the Western cultural value placed on spontaneity and assertiveness (Chin, 1983). In a therapeutic relationship, Asian clients may not express their disagreements or negative reactions to social workers, even when they do not agree with them. Often, the lack of disagreement is mistakenly taken as the clients' agreement with the social worker.

Another belief system common among Asians is avoidance of shame. The socially unacceptable behavior of the individual is considered to be a family shame. Thus, avoiding family shame is also a means of controlling the individual family member. Rebellion, substance abuse, delinquent behavior, and poor school achievement by individuals are considered to be the failure of the whole family, thus bringing shame on the entire family (Kim, 1995). It therefore becomes important to take care of the family member's problems within the family system rather than seeking outside help. To share the negative information with outsiders could bring disgrace on the family name. This traditional attitude of Asians, that family matters should not be discussed outside the family, is one of the reasons for the underutilization of social services among Asians.

Implications for Social Work Practice

Kim et al. (1992) describes several cultural nuances that may influence therapeutic relationships. They include the following:

1. Children will not make eye contact with an adult because direct eye contact is considered disrespectful.
2. The expression of "yes" and "no" in Japanese and Korean languages mean the opposite of those expressions in English.
3. Some Asians express politeness through maintaining an agreeable demeanor. This demeanor should not be mistaken for acceptance or understanding of what the worker expects.
4. Asians tend to avoid physical contact (hugging, facial contact, and so on) in social interactions.
5. Some Asians do not feel comfortable receiving compliments.
6. Many Asians consider bringing children to a formal gathering acceptable.
7. Asians believe that parents have a right and responsibility to spank or physically punish children when they misbehave.
8. The exchange of small gifts is considered an important aspect of social interactions.

Knowledge of Asian culture could improve social work interventions in several ways. Kim (1995) makes several suggestions for utilizing Asian cultural characteristics to enhance social work practice. First, the emphasis on family and on the individual as part of the family could be a strength in the client's support system. By involving family members in dealing with the individual's problem, strong family ties may be related to better outcomes.

While it is important for a social worker to recognize the client's unique cultural background, the universal human needs of clients should also be recognized. Berg and Miller (1992) suggest the importance of the social worker's ability to balance the impact of culture on a client's worldview with how clients personally experience ethnic and cultural influences. The emphasis on shame in Asian culture makes Asian American clients amenable to finding solutions quickly. Asian American clients could restore their dignity and sense of competence by focusing on rapid resolution to problems that baffle and embarrass them (Berg & Miller, 1992).

Strategies need to be identified to overcome the underutilization of social services among Asians. Targeted public service announcements as well as other specific and targeted outreach programs could be effective (Kim, 1995). Similarly, community education programs could be an effective way to reach potential clients for early intervention and prevention of mental health problems.

Drawing on the tradition of the mutual help network in the Asian community may be an effective strategy to access resources and facilitate effective service delivery. Asian clients tend to have strong family ties and extended kinship networks that could serve as an important source of social support. However, it is also noted that the families can be a significant source of stress for the individual when intergenerational and family role conflicts exist among and between family members (Zane & Sasao, 1992). When working with a client, the individual client-worker relationship would be more effective than a group because Asian clients do not like to share their personal problems with nonfamily members. Open discussion in a group setting may not be an effective strategy because the sharing of personal information and exchange of opinions may contradict the Asian value of humility and modesty (Kim, 1995).

Case Study

Mr. Yee is a fifty-four-year-old male, a Vietnamese refugee who owns a small grocery store in an inner city in the Northeast. He worked as a clerk for the U.S. Army and was stationed in Saigon. Mr. Yee came to the United States on a massive airlift after the fall of Saigon. He and his family were brought into the refugee camp in Pennsylvania. A church in a small community outside of Hartford, Connecticut, sponsored him. He and his family met some Vietnamese families after moving into the small New England community, but no close relationships had developed with the Vietnamese in the area. He and his family have many contacts with various members of the church, but socialization with the church members is limited to Sundays when the family attends worship services. He commutes to Hartford from his suburban home every day.

Mr. Yee has been having problems with neighborhood youths coming to the store and shoplifting. He also has problems communicating with customers. His wife, who speaks better English than he, helps in the store. He has difficulty in managing a group of young people when several of them come into the store as a group.

Some of the neighborhood residents consider the Yees as taking advantage of them because Mr. Yee charges higher prices for almost all merchandise than in a supermarket. Some youths have left graffiti with racial slurs. The work at the store has been a source of stress for Mr. Yee for quite some time, and he began drinking every day after closing the store and continued to drink after returning home from the store in late evening.

In Vietnam, alcohol was used for ceremonial and social occasions, and drinking among men was encouraged. Men's intoxication was accepted as long as it did not interfere with going to work the next day. Culturally, a low opinion is held of a person dependent on alcohol. Mr. Yee was in a car accident, and the police officer detected alcohol on his breath. The blood alcohol level was .11, and, as the first offense, he was sent to the alcohol education program. This has been a very humiliating experience for Mr. Yee, who considers himself a law-abiding, hardworking citizen. While he was unable to understand the content of the lectures given at the alcohol education classes, he completed the classes, and he was recommended to receive outpatient treatment for his alcohol problems. He was quite embarrassed about the whole incident and was not about to follow the recommendation to seek help for an alcohol problem.

PIE Assessment of Mr. Yee

A PIE assessment would focus on his familial role as a spouse with mixed type problem related to his perceived loss of status with his wife and his dependency on her to communicate with customers, service providers, and neighbors. Isolation from traditional culture, specifically the norms and roles expected of him prior to arriving in the United States and the confusion related to expectations of him now, appear related to his drinking. The severity of the problem is high while the duration appears to be less than a year. His coping seems inadequate at present (1280.445).

Factor II of PIE directs our attention to the lack of culturally relevant education to help him adapt to this culture and to more appropriately use the services of the judicial and the mental health systems related to his alcoholism. While the duration of the problem is short, the severity appears high, in that he is not benefiting from these services because he does not fully understand the change process expected of him (6103.43; 8108.43). His limited involvement with religious, community, or affectional support groups (9101.43; 9201.42; 10101.43) does not bode well with his Factor I problems. Building a social support system to replace what he has left in Vietnam should begin while he addresses his alcoholism. The cultural differences in attitude toward intoxication must be understood before designing an intervention that might work with this client.

This case study should help you see that the meaning of the problem from the client's perspective, and therefore the activity the social worker initiates to address it, may be quite different than that which is appropriate in the dominant culture.

Conclusion

This chapter presented a broad view of Asian Americans. It was intended to assist social workers in developing greater theoretical depth when assessing client problems in social role functioning and selecting culturally sensitive interventions in family and community systems. You are cautioned to avoid generalization because Asian Americans are quite diverse in terms of migration history and acculturation patterns. The norms and cultural beliefs presented here should be used as a broad guide. The clinician should explore the meaning that a client and his or her community assigns to behavior or community experience.

References

Amodeo, M., & Jones, L. K. (1997). Viewing alcohol and other drug use cross culturally: A cultural framework for clinical practice. *Families in Society: The Journal of Contemporary Human Services, 78,* 240–254.

Amodeo, M., Robb, N., Peou, S., & Tran, H. (1996, September). Adapting mainstream substance-abuse interventions for Southeast Asian clients. *Families in Society: The Journal of Contemporary Human Services, 77,* 403–412.

Berg, I. K., & Miller, S. D. (1992). Working with Asian American clients: One person at a time. *Families in Society: The Journal of Contemporary Human Services, 73,* 356–363.

Castro, F. G., Proescholdbell, R. J., Albeita, L., & Rodriguez, D. (1999). Ethnic and cultural minority groups. In B. S. Mcrady & E. E. Epstein (Eds.), *Addictions: A comprehensive guidebook.* New York: Oxford University Press.

Chin, J. L. (1983). Diagnostic considerations in working with Asian Americans. *American Journal of Orthopsychiatry, 53,* 100–109.

Hirayama, K. K. (1982). Evaluating effects of the employment of Vietnamese refugee wives on their family roles and mental health. *California Sociologist, 5*(1), 96–110.

Hirayama, K. K. (1985). Asian children's adaptation to public schools. *Social Work in Education, 7,* 213–229.

Hirayama, K. K., & Hirayama, H. (1988). Stress, social supports, and adaptational patterns in Hmongs refugee families. *AMERASIA, 14*(1), 93–108.

Hirayama, K. K., Hirayama, H., & Cetingok, M. (1993). Mental health promotion for South East Asian refugees in the U.S.A. *International Social Work, 36,* 119–129.

Ho, M. K. (1976). Social work with Asian Americans. *Social Casework, 57,* 195–201.

Ishisaka, A. H., & Takagi, C. Y. (1982). Toward professional pluralism: The Pacific/Asian American case. *Journal of Education for Social Work, 17,* 44–49.

Kim, S., McLeod, J. H., & Shantzis, C. (1992). Cultural competence for evaluators working with Asian-American communities: Some practical consideration. In M. A. Orlandi (Ed.), *CSAP cultural competence series I. Cultural competence for evaluators* (pp. 203–260). Rockville, MD: U.S. Department of Health and Human Services, Alcohol, Drug Abuse and Mental Health Administration, Office of Substance Abuse Prevention.

Kim, Y. O. (1995). Cultural pluralism and Asian Americans: Culturally sensitive social work practice. *International Social Work, 38,* 69–78.

Kitano, H. H. (1989). Alcohol and the Asian American. In T. D. Watts & R. Wright (Eds.), *Alcoholism in minority populations.* Springfield, IL: Charles C. Thomas.

Kumamoto, F. H. (1995). Asian Americans. In J. Philleo & L. G. Epstein (Eds.), *Cultural competency for social workers: A guide for alcohol and other drug abuse prevention professionals working with ethnic, racial communities* (pp. 105–155). Washington, DC: U.S. Department of Health and Human Services, DHHS Publication #95-3075.

Leonard, C. A., & Cheung, Y. W. (1991). Selected references on topics related to ethnicity and adaptation. *The International Journal of the Addictions, 25,* 767–774.

Lott, J. T. (1976). Migration of mentality: The Philipino community. *Social Casework, 57*(3), 165–172.

Makimoto, K. (1998). Drinking patterns and drinking problems among Asian Americans and Pacific Islanders. *Alcohol Health and Research World, 22,* 270–275.

Matsouka, J. K., & Ryujin, D. H. (1991). Asian American immigrants: A comparison of the Chinese, Japanese, and Filipinos. *Journal of Sociology and Social Welfare, 18*(3), 123–133.

Melendy, H. H. (1976). Philipinos in the United States. In N. Hudley (Ed.), *The Asian American: The historical experience* (pp. 101–128). Santa Barbara: Clio Press.

Morales, A. (1981). Social work with third world people. *Social Work, 26,* 45–51.

Ray, O., & Ksir, C. (1999). *Drugs, society, and human behavior,* 8th ed. New York: WCB McGraw-Hill.

Sue, S., & McKinney, H. (1975). Asian Americans in the community mental health care system. *American Journal of Orthopsychiatry, 45,* 111–118.

U.S. Bureau of the Census. (1995). *Statistical briefs: The nation's Asian and Pacific Islander population–1994.* Washington, DC: Author.

Westermeyer, J. (1976). Cross-cultural studies of alcoholism in the clinical setting: Review and evaluation (pp. 359–377). In M. W. Everett, J. O. Waddell, & D. B. Heath (Eds.), *Cross-cultural approaches to the study of alcohol.* Chicago: Aldine.

Yen, S. (1992). Cultural competence for evaluators working with Asian/Pacific Island American communities: Some common themes and important implications. In M. A. Orlandi (Ed.), *CSAP cultural competence series I. Cultural competence for evaluators* (pp. 261–291). Rockville, MD: U.S. Department of Health and Human Services, Alcohol, Drug Abuse and Mental Health Administration, Office of Substance Abuse Prevention.

Zane, N., & Sasao, T. (1992). Research on drug abuse among Asian Pacific Americans. In J. E. Trimble, C. S. Bolek, & S. J. Niemcryk (Eds.), *Ethnic and multicultural drug abuse* (pp. 181–210). New York: Harrington Park Press.

10

Lesbian, Gay, Bisexual, and Transgender People Confront Heterocentrism, Heterosexism, and Homophobia

George A. Appleby

Human behavior surrounding sexuality, intimacy, affection, and identity is complex, and this complexity has to be acknowledged when dealing with sexual orientation. Even the words that are used to describe gay, lesbian, transgender, and bisexual identity are complicated and hotly debated. Many now reject, for example, the term *sexual preference,* once considered correct for describing gay, lesbian, or bisexual phenomena, because it seems to reduce a core identity or master status to a matter of taste, like whether one likes tacos or spring rolls. The term *sexual orientation,* which is the one used in this chapter, is now generally preferred because it seems to suggest something more fundamental to the person than just a casual choice among equally available alternatives. The other term used here, *sexual identity,* emphasizes self-labeling, although it has both social and psychological components. However, sexual orientation can be seen as more stable than sexual identity, which may change over a person's lifetime (Chung & Katayama, 1996). Just as gay, lesbian, and bisexual people must negotiate their social and psychological identity development in the context of a heterocentrist, homophobic, and heterosexist society, social work and other mental health professionals must develop their understanding of sexual orientation issues in a context that until recently viewed homosexuality as pathology in and of itself. It was only in 1973 that the American Psychiatric Association (APA), which sets the prevailing terms in the United States for classifying psychopathology through its *Diagnostic and Statistical Manual,* now in its fourth edition (APA, 1994), removed homosexuality from its list of psychiatric disorders. Thus anyone living with such identification or learning about mental health before that time had to deal with the prevailing psychiatric view of a homosexual sexual orientation as a mental illness. It is not surprising, therefore, that the remnants of that attitude are still commonly encountered in the professional context today, in professionals, in clients, in their families, and in the community (Appleby & Anastas, 1998).

The view of a gay, lesbian, or bisexual orientation as a form of psychopathology was gradually replaced by the idea that being lesbian or gay is a stable and fixed positive identity. Sexual orientation refers to a characteristic of an individual that describes the people he or she is drawn to for satisfying intimate affectional and sexual needs—people of the same gender, the opposite gender, or of both genders. We use the terms *lesbian* and *gay* in preference to *homosexual* to refer to men and women who are not heterosexual, or *straight.* In part, this is done because of the history of pathologizing attached to the term *homosexual.* In part, it is done because patterns of development and adaptation to a same-gender sexual orientation, like many other aspects of development, tend to differ somewhat between men and women. However, we sometimes use the term *homosexual* to refer to both genders together, especially to refer to specifically sexual phenomena. However, the term *homosexual* has been used in the past to refer only to males, so care must be taken in using the term not to render the experiences of women invisible (Garnets & Kimmel, 1993). However, the terms *gay* and *lesbian* are often used to refer to men and women who not only engage in same-gender sexual and/or affectional activities but who also adopt what is termed a homosexual lifestyle to some degree or other. Some object to this concept of lifestyle, too, because it may seem to trivialize what is a life by suggesting that it has elements of fashion to it. In fact, this discussion touches on the controversy about whether there is a gay or lesbian culture in the true sense of the term and about whether open participation in that culture is necessarily desirable for lesbians, gays, and bisexuals (Lukes & Land, 1990). This issue of culture was discussed in greater depth in Chapter 2.

The term *sexual identity,* which is increasingly emphasized in the literature, refers to self-labeling as lesbian, gay, or bisexual (Reiter, 1989). Because sexual behavior and self-labeling are often not consistent with each other, some have differentiated the concepts by noting that "identity changes [while] orientation endures" (Reiter, 1989, p. 138). Although sexual identity is usually experienced as psychological, or internal, it is also influenced by interpersonal, social, and cultural experience (Cox & Gallois, 1996).

While sexual orientation certainly involves sexuality, it is just as strongly related to affectional and social needs that are not just sexual. Gay, lesbian, or bisexual people who are not currently sexually active retain their basic sexual orientation, just as a heterosexual person does. In fact, viewing gay, lesbian, or bisexual people as overly sexualized or compulsively sexually active is one form that homophobia can take. Based on research findings and practice experience, we now know that sexual orientation is not just about sex and sexuality; it is about sexuality, emotionality, and social functioning. The development of a sexual identity represents the integration of all of these aspects of sexual orientation into a coherent whole, an authentic sense of self, with a self-label that is subjectively meaningful and manageable. Differences in sexual orientation are based on whether a person directs his or her sexual and intimate affectional feelings and behavior toward same-gender, opposite-gender, or both same- and opposite-gender others. Thus, some bisexual people explain their choice of love object as the result of finding specific personal qualities of the individuals they choose to relate intimately to as more important than the person's gender (Weinberg, Williams, & Pryor, 1994; Eliason & Raheim, 1996). This conceptual definition suggests that sexual orientation should be assessed on multiple dimensions (Chung & Katayama, 1996).

The definition of sexual orientation that we have so far given is primarily a psychological one; that is, it is mental, affective or emotional, and behavioral. It has nothing to do with appearance and identifiability, because there is a great range in how gay, lesbian, and bisexual people look, how they present themselves, and thus how identifiable they may be. In fact, the great majority of gay, lesbian, and bisexual people are not visible or identifiable as such. Nor is any visible gay, lesbian, or bisexual community or subculture available or attractive to all gay, lesbian, and bisexual people. In fact, the formerly pejorative term *queer* has been adopted by some gay, lesbian, and bisexual activists to indicate a specific identification with and participation in the visible gay, lesbian, and bisexual culture and political movement that flourishes in some large cities and to distinguish a cultural and/or political commitment from sexual orientation itself.

Rubin (1984, pp. 280–281) observes that acceptable sexuality should be heterosexual, marital, monogamous, reproductive, and noncommercial. It should be coupled, relational, within the same generation, and occur at home. It should not involve pornography, fetish objects, sex toys, or roles other than male and female. Gay, lesbian, bisexual, and transgender people violate many of these rules in most cultures.

Transgender people are the least studied and the most discriminated against of all sexual minorities. Cross dressing and gender blending have existed everywhere throughout human history. Despite anatomical differences between males and females, there is potential for considerable physiological and anatomical variation among individuals with the same sex organs and much overlap between the two genders. Bushong (1995) reminds us that one's gender is on a continuum with most people at either end of the female to male scale, but a significant minority are somewhere in between. There are those whose gender does not match their physiological gender. A term used to characterize such individuals is *gender dysphoria*. As is the case with same-gender sexual orientation, gender dysphoria is not pathological but a natural aberration that exists within the population. Estimates vary, ranging from 1% to 3% percent of the population. Gender norms depend strongly on the time, location, and the history of a culture (Bornstein, 1994; Wilchins, 1997).

Transgender people have varying sexual orientations ranging from heterosexual to bisexual to homosexual. They also have varying degrees of discomfort with their physiological gender of birth. Bullough, Bullough, and Elias (1997) report equal numbers of male-to-female and female-to-male transsexuals. Some transsexuals identify themselves at a very early age, well before puberty, while others emerge in their retirement years. There appears to be a surge in coming out during the mid-life years when there is a reevaluation of one's life. Generally speaking, transgender people fall into five primary groups:

Cross dresser (Transvestite): people who have a desire to dress and in general appear as members of the other gender. Most cross dressers are heterosexual men. Their sexual orientation has nothing to do with their cross dressing.

Transgenderist: people who avoid gender role extremes and tend to be androgynous. They often incorporate both female and male aspects into their appearance. They may live part of their lives as the other gender or a blend of both. They may live entirely in the other gender role but with no plans for genital surgery.

Transsexual: people whose gender identity most closely matches the other sex. These individuals often feel trapped in the body of their biological gender and long to rid themselves of their primary and secondary characteristics. They yearn to live as members of the other sex. Many make the transition through hormonal and surgical techniques. Most transsexuals are born and initially live as males. There are two subcategories: (1) primary—individuals who are intensely gender dysphoric usually at an early age (ages four to six); and (2) secondary—individuals who come to a full awareness of their condition in their twenties and thirties and may not act on their feelings until even later in life. Secondary transsexuals are likely to go through phases of cross dresser or transgenderist.

Androgyne: an individual that presents both or neither culturally constructed gender signifiers.

Intersex: a medical term used to identify a mixed sexual physiology; aspects of both male and female are present at birth (Transgender Education Network, 1999).

Mental health professionals have come to understand the need to help transgender people explore options other than socially assigned, rigid, bipolar gender roles. Some have come to view cross dressing and other ways of transgressing socially imposed gender limitations to be no less natural. It is the position of this text that the problems experienced by transgender people are more often the result of widespread social sanction and discrimination (Brown & Rounsley, 1996). For further information, check out the readings in the reference section and the resources on the Internet at www.thetaskforce.org/

Social work scholars and social scientists over the last three decades have observed that lesbians and gay men are as diverse as heterosexual men and women. Lesbians and gay men, however, more often share several psychosocial processes: identification and confrontation of sexual differences; socialization in the gay and lesbian communities; self-identification or coming out to self and others; sexual experimentation; development of a sexual identity; nurturance of sexual and intimate relationships; formation of families of choice, often coupling, separating, and coupling again, sometimes raising children, often supporting families-of-origin and friends; and lifelong contribution to professions and communities while under psychological and social duress (Sullivan & Jackson, 1999; Appleby & Anastas, 1998; Mallon, 1997; D'Augelli & Patterson, 1995; Herek & Berrill, 1992; Garnets & Kimmel, 1993; DeCecco, 1988; Berger & Kelly, 1986). Much of the social and psychological duress was presented in Chapters 2 and 4 and is shared with other devalued minority groups.

Homophobia, heterosexism, and heterocentrism are probably the most common environmental problems (Factor II of the PIE system) affecting lesbians, gay men, bisexuals, and transgender people. Practice experience and research warn that institutional discrimination and negative interpersonal attitudes result in problems related to acquiring and maintaining employment (530l, 5302, 5303) and shelter (5201, 5202, 5203), education and training (62XX), judicial and legal protections (72XX), access and appropriate services in the health, safety, and social services (84XX), and too often in religious and community life (93XX). These social forces, combined with sexism, racism, and classism, generate both institutional and psychosocial barriers to healthy development. These barriers plus the obstacles in finding a new positive identity and getting guidance and support from an invisible and often vilified community may affect social role functioning and well-being (Factor I of the PIE system). Lesbians and gay men, however, have demonstrated profound social, psychological, economic, and political resiliency throughout an almost universal history of rejection, violence, and oppression. Yet, in the course of the life cycle, some, understandably, will find need for social services. Because there is little documentation of the adaptation of bisexuals or transgender people, our knowledge is limited to primarily anecdotal information and untested assumptions about the shared experiences of all sexual minorities.

This chapter is designed to prepare social workers and other health and human services professionals to better assess the concerns, problems, and issues presented by gay, lesbian, bisexual, and transgender clients and then to more effectively intervene with the widest array of interpersonal and social change methods appropriate to the presenting problem. Ultimately, this is an effort to help professional clinicians to minimize the influences of heterosexism and homophobia in their practice, and over time, in the environments in which their clients function. The emphasis is on the knowledge, values, and skills needed for practice. Factors I and II of the PIE system will be used to guide the discussion of relevant theory for practice. Specifically, the task is to identify that knowledge most helpful in conducting a gay- or lesbian-sensitive assessment and a lesbian- or gay-affirming intervention.

It has been well documented historically that lesbians and gay men and any other sexual minority experience oppression at the behest of religion, popular culture, civil and criminal legal codes, psychiatry/psychology, and mass media (Storr, 1999; Appleby & Anastas, 1998; Mallon, 1998; Katz, 1976, 1995; Berube, 1990; Chauncey, 1994; D'Emilio, 1983). As targets of institutionalized discrimination, they continue to be at risk of stigmatization and violence. Therefore, it is understandable that gay and lesbian clients appear in the full range of social work agencies and programs. While most have the same needs as their nongay counterparts, the differences may be significant, in that sexual orientation may have an impact on the perception of the problem, how the problem is sustained in the social environment, the availability of formal and informal resources to help resolve the problem, the levels of personal coping, and how interventions are evaluated for effectiveness.

Much of the normative social and behavioral science knowledge that informs social work practice, policy, and research is relevant to our understanding of practice with sexually diverse clients. However, there are contextual differences that demand attention. Those theories that help us to understand the context of practice with sexual minorities are also the foundation of a theory for practice.

History

First, it is important to briefly review the gay and lesbian struggle in this country, so that we might put theory and practice within an appropriate context. There are numerous social histories of lesbian and gay communities (e.g., Tripp, 1975; Katz, 1976; Boswell, 1980, 1995; Berube, 1990; Cruikshank, 1992; D'Emilio, 1983; Faderman, 1991; Fitzgerald, 1986; Marcus, 1992; Herdt, 1992; Chauncey, 1994; Fellows, 1996), and, while interesting and informative, it is beyond the scope of this chapter to do anything other than summarize. Scholarship focusing on the historic and social development of the bisexual or the transgender is limited (Boenke, 1999; Bornstein, 1994; Bullough & Bullough, 1993; Bullough et al., 1997; Bushong, 1995; Klein, 1993; Weinberg, Williams, & Pryor, 1994; Israel & Tarver, 1997; Storr, 1999).

After a quarter century of bitter political struggle, by the 1970s, a growing sense of community was translated into the development of visible economic, social, and political institutions. Many lesbians and gay men migrated to a handful of large cities (New York, Boston, Philadelphia, Washington, D.C., Atlanta, Miami, Dallas, Chicago, Denver, Minneapolis, Phoenix, San Francisco, and Los Angeles) known to be more accepting of diversity (D'Augelli & Patterson, 1995). This migration resonates with what Carol Germain (1980, 1991) would refer to as an adaptive response to environmental pressures by either changing oneself, by changing the environment, or by migrating. Migrating appears to have been a common adaptation for many gay men and lesbians as they contemplated coming out, which is positively associated with effective coping. This effort to build a community is a major strength and a potential resource for clients.

The anti-gay backlash of the last half of the 1970s initiated by the new right served to mobilize newly recognized communities into political solidification. Virulent attacks by the religious right, such as the Moral Majority, the Christian Coalition, and the Family Research Council, activated greater collaboration between lesbians and gay men. These attacks forced many nonpolitical gays to join lesbian/gay groups, to reframe many of the faulty stereotypes, and to strengthen their identification with the gay/lesbian community. Many angry activists, at this point, began to critique the unresponsive community institutions for their lack of knowledge or concern for this marginalized population.

The AIDS epidemic was a dominant impetus to lesbian/gay community building. AIDS service organizations developed rapidly in most urban areas, usually with the money raised by and energy provided by the lesbian/gay community. However, it was the lack of national religious and political leadership, inadequate funding, and increased evidence of discrimination based on both sexual orientation and HIV status that led to greater militancy. Groups such as the AIDS Coalition to Unleash Power (ACT-UP), Treatment Action Group (TAG), and Queer Nation rejected progressive politics in favor of civil disobedience and self-assertion (Shilts, 1987; Kramer, 1989). These groups, along with lesbian and gay professionals, took the lead in challenging the lack of commitment of health and social services professionals and organizations in delivering adequate services and in removing barriers to these services, such as professional discrimination and bias, as well as regulations and procedures. Others became active in less militant groups, such as the National Gay and Lesbian Task Force, the Human Rights Campaign, the Lambda Legal Defense and Education Fund, the National Lesbian and Gay Health Association, and/or various professional associations. As the epidemic spread through all strata of American life, eroding the persistent stereotypes held about gay and lesbian life, and as social circumstances put them in a position to do so (i.e., loss of partners, friends, active discrimination and challenging the rights of surviving partners), more people openly acknowledged their sexual orientation.

Today, the most well known lesbian/gay communities exist in geographically bounded neighborhoods in several large cities and are characterized by high visibility, many formal and informal institutions, and considerable political clout. The many community organizations and activities in these neighborhoods serve as cultural centers, gathering places, and forums for the expression of lesbian/gay culture. They foster a powerful psychological sense of community and facilitate socialization into the many different niches of urban lesbian/gay life (Appleby & Anastas, 1998; D'Augelli & Patterson, 1995). By the mid-1990s, almost every moderate and large size city had, at least, some rudimentary lesbian and gay community (lesbian or gay bar) and thus the means to share culture and to address other needs and concerns.

As members of a stigmatized group, many gay and lesbian people simply welcome and seek out places, occasions, and activities where they can enjoy the company of others who are clearly identified in that context as lesbian or gay as well. In some areas, especially in large cities, a gay and lesbian community exists consisting of those gathering places such as restaurants, bars, coffee houses, bookstores, community centers, churches, and synagogues. There are businesses seeking a gay and/or lesbian clientele (travel, insurance, liquor companies, real estate agencies, hotels, resorts and guest houses, accountants, repair and redecorating services, computer support services, printing and publishing, florists, photographers, and pet care services). In the very largest cities, there are annual Gay and Lesbian Business and Consumer Expos, Gay Pride parades, and festivals. There are also social services, health, political, arts, and media organizations dedicated to engaging and serving the lesbian and gay populations. Because of the recent proliferation of organizations and services for the gay and lesbian community, a variety of institutions and mechanisms have developed to publicize and connect people with them. There is a gay and lesbian national hotline, which can be reached via e-mail at glnh@msn.com. Or use a search engine and enter such terms as *gay, lesbian, bisexual,* or *transgender* to find other resources. GAYNET is a national discussion and news network for gay, lesbian, and bisexual concerns. The social worker or client can subscribe via e-mail to majordomo@queernet.org or go directly to their site at www.queernet.org/. There are several other excellent nongovernmental resources for sexual minority related issues: www.hrc.org (Human Rights Campaign) and www.ngltf.org (National Gay and Lesbian Task Force) have many helpful practice links, www.gladd.org

(Anti-defamation league) has many useful lists and has an emphasis on advocacy, www.pridelinks.com/ lists diverse resource links, and www.gayorder.com has even more resource links. See the appendices in G. Appleby and J. Anastas (1998), *Not Just a Passing Phase: Social Work with Gay, Lesbian, and Bisexual People* (New York: Columbia University Press), for an extensive listing of Internet, advocacy, and organizational resources for sexual minorities. In addition, on a local level many cities have a lesbian/gay telephone switchboard or an information line for the purpose of identifying community resources, events, and activities. Some of these agencies double as a crisis line and a referral source for health, mental health, and legal services. Most bars, community centers, and other businesses, such as bookstores, distribute regional newspapers and have a community bulletin board.

A cursory review of several typical community resource directories shows that they include political groups (ACT-UP, Gay and Lesbian Democrats, Bi-Nation, Queer Nation, AIDS Action Council, Lambda Law Students Association, Lesbian Avengers, Log Cabin Gay Republicans, Radical Faeries, Anti-violence League, and an array of other legal and civil rights groups) and professional groups (Gay and Lesbian Insurance Workers, Business Guild, Gay Mental Health Professionals, Network of Gay, Lesbian, and Bisexual Educators, Gay [Police] Officers Action League, Gay and Lesbian Fire Fighters, Lambda Health Alliance, and Postal Employees Network). There are numerous support groups: adolescents infected/affected by HIV/AIDS, lesbians dealing with weight issues, African American men, AA, AL-ANON, and other twelve-step groups, bisexuals, cancer patients, family and friends of persons newly diagnosed with HIV, people of color, gay fathers, gay men, incest survivors, lesbians, lesbian parenting, co-parenting or wanting to parent, married men, older lesbians, Parents and Friends of Lesbians and Gays (PFLAG), spouses of lesbians and gays, post-op transsexuals, youth, and college students. There are social groups for nudists, lesbian and gay choruses, bikers, car enthusiasts, folk dancers, rail fans, jugglers, classical music, theater, gay Olympians, leather men, softball, golf, hiking, skiing, and other sports. Religious groups are listed for Christian Bible Study, Jews, Baptists, Catholics (Dignity), Unitarian Universalists, Ecumenical Catholics, Episcopalians (Integrity), Metropolitan Community Church (interdenominational), Congregational (United Church of Christ), Presbyterians, Methodists, witches' covens, and New Age variants. The range and number of organizations that focus on some aspect of spirituality are impressive and reflective of how some gay men and lesbians cope with social dissonance. There is a growing literature chronicling the spiritual gatekeeper role that homosexuals have played historically and continue to assume in contemporary culture (Evans, 1978; Halifax, 1979; McNaught, 1988; Clark, 1989, 1990; Barzan, 1995). It is important that the practitioner learn about these community resources and how to connect clients to these necessary social supports or services. Most of these resources can be accessed through your state's information and referral network, telephone directories, and the Internet. A referral would be appropriate whenever a client presents with problems related to Voluntary Association (9101 through 93xx) or Affectional Support Systems (10101 through 102XX).

During contemporary history, some lesbian and gay social workers organized nationally and locally. After several decades of political struggle, the NASW and the CSWE now have gay, lesbian, and bisexual national committees and commissions that have been granted monitoring, education, policy, and program consultation roles in relation to practice and education standards, equity issues within the profession, and a social action and civil rights agenda for the profession directed to reducing discrimination against lesbian, gay, and bisexual people. After years of organizing, a majority of the state chapters of NASW have developed standing committees or lesbian and gay networks for the purpose of support for lesbian and gay workers, education for the general membership, and social action to end discrimination and to increase social justice. Parallel to this development, almost every major academic or professional organization (e.g., the American Psychiatric Association, American Psychological Association, National Nursing Association, National Education Association, National Lesbian and Gay Health Association), as well as national bodies for accountants, architects, engineers, pharmacists, police, veterans, and university faculty in most disciplines, has advanced similar groups or caucuses. Many of these caucuses have begun formal dialogues with the intent of collaborating on issues of mutual concern, such as social workers and psychologists working together as advocates for lesbian and gay youth. The National Gay and Lesbian Task Force, the Human Rights Campaign, the Lambda Legal Defense and Education Fund, and the American Civil Liberties Union are the principal national civil rights organizations addressing themselves to lesbian and gay civil rights issues such as nondiscrimination, domestic partnership, marriage, foster and adoptive parenting, anti-violence, and property and custody rights both at the state and national level. Given this history of community and organizational growth, the social, political, and economic visibility and influence of the lesbian, bisexual, and gay minority will continue to grow.

Now that we have a general understanding of modern U.S. history as it relates to the strengths of gay, lesbian, and bisexual people, we can examine the institutional context of historical oppression.

Historical Oppression in Context

Despite the gay rights movement and some supportive legislation, homosexuality is largely hidden in U.S. society, and, when publicly recognized, it is often condemned or stigmatized. While American attitudes toward homosexuality have changed over the last twenty years, we are still a society that condemns homosexuality. In 1973, 73% of the general population thought homosexuality was wrong. This percentage dropped to 61% in 1996 (*Advocate*, 1996). However, according to a 1996 *Newsweek* poll, nearly 84% of Americans support equal employment rights for gay men and lesbians. The Human Rights Campaign, www.hrc.org, found that in 1994, 70% of the voting population did not realize that anti-gay job discrimination is still widespread and predominantly legal (Goldberg, 1996). Most Americans support equal treatment for gay and lesbian people even as gay people remain among the most disliked group of citizens in the nation. Data suggest that while moral censure of homosexuality is on the decline, the opposition to most specific cases of equal treatment has transformed into support. While Americans strongly disapprove of gay men and lesbians, their sense of fairness is violated by discrimination in the workplace. Over the last two decades, scholars have sought to explain this phenomenon of widespread disapproval of homosexuality and a slowly developing tolerance in some areas of life.

Heterocentrism, homophobia, and heterosexism are interrelated social forces that serve as the context of the psychosocial development of gay men and lesbians. These forces are major environmental pressures that impact on individual development and the potential for forming a healthy sexual identity, as well as on the ability to cope and to adapt to the social and psychological stressors associated with a stigmatized social status. These forces can become barriers to healthy adaptation, to managing life transitions, and to the mastery of the interpersonal processes necessary for optimal social functioning. They also affect the service systems that people turn to in times of crisis and need. Thus the first task is to understand these concepts and then to identify their manifestations in the lives of sexually diverse people, which can include the experiences of stigma, guilt, and shame. These experiences may dramatically affect social role functioning or interaction with environmental systems. Recall the thorough discussion of oppression in Chapter 4, and specifically the relatedness of discrimination, power, privilege, and control. Each of these concepts is a component of heterosexism and will have primary influence on individual and group identity development.

Definitions

In 1972, Weinberg first presented the concept of homophobia as society's fear, dislike, or hatred of gays, lesbians, and bisexuals—an attitude that often resulted in acts of discrimination. Homophobia, like all forms of oppression, is used to impose and reinforce control and mastery over others. Weinberg's use of the term *phobia* deliberately suggested that homophobia is irrational, fear-driven, and, at least for some people, a defensive maneuver to ward off something both feared and desired. Prior to this decade, negative attitudes toward homosexuality were not seen as a problem. Naming this negative attitude has been an extremely important step in defining it as a social problem. However, Weinberg's definition does not make distinctions among the various levels of feeling, understanding, or action.

In the last twenty years, the concept of homophobia has been studied and debated by numerous scholars (Neisen, 1990). Herek (1993), a most prolific student of homophobia, offers a necessary refinement of the earlier concept. He suggests that the focus be shifted to an analysis of societal behaviors and the impact this has on attitudes and beliefs. Homophobia is now understood as a result of heterosexism, "an ideological system that denies, denigrates, and stigmatizes any nonheterosexual form of behavior, identity, relationship, or community" (p. 89). Herek further notes that, like racism, sexism, and other ideologies of oppression, heterosexism is manifested both in societal customs and institutions and in individual attitudes and acts. Heterosexism and heterocentrism can be used interchangeably; however, the more contemporary term, *heterocentrism,* captures the primary essence of the concept, the centrality of heterosexuality, in the definition of sexual attitudes, beliefs, feelings, and behaviors, as well as roles, traditions, norms, and social institutions. This concept accommodates the sexual statuses of bisexual and transgender with greater ease. In institutions like religion and the legal system, it constitutes cultural heterosexism (heterocentrism); as manifested in individual attitudes, perceptions of reality, and behaviors, it constitutes psychological heterosexism. This definition of heterosexism also captures much of the meaning commonly associated with the term *homophobia.*

Homophobia, according to Blumenfeld, is "the fear and hatred of those who love and sexually desire those of the same sex" (1992, p. 283). Homophobia, which has its roots in sexism, is manifest in fear and hatred, which encourages damaging heterosexist acts.

Heterosexism is discrimination by neglect, omission, and/or distortion, whereas often its more active partner, homophobia, is discrimination and hurtful behavior by intent and design (Blumenfeld & Raymond, 1993). Homophobia and heterosexism, like other forms of oppression, are used to impose and reinforce control and mastery over others by a system of rewards and punishments at both systemic and interpersonal levels.

Homophobia is not really a phobia in the true psychiatric sense of the term. The phobic and defensive connotation discourages recognition that attitudes toward homosexuality can serve other nonpsychological functions, such as a vehicle for expressing cultural or religious values. New terms such as homo-ignorance, homonegativity, and homohatred are more inclusive and neutral and are also used at times in this text. However, heterosexism and homophobia are used as well, in part because they are the most widely known and well-researched ways of conceptualizing anti-gay and anti-lesbian prejudice.

The reader is cautioned, however, that while many of these terms may be used interchangeably, each implies a different level of cognitive and affective involvement. Homo-ignorance suggests a minimal level of discriminatory or prejudicial behavior and results often from the lack of knowledge or from the uncritical acceptance of cultural stereotypes or myths, such as the assumption that a gay man will only choose noncompetitive and nurturing jobs because of his supposed identification with female gender roles. The homo-ignorant individual, for example, may find it hard to believe that there are gay construction workers, athletes, engineers, lawyers, or ruthless businessmen. Prejudice of this kind suggests that increased and more accurate knowledge can reduce negative attitudes. Homonegativity implies moderately discriminatory attitudes and behavior resulting from nominally held beliefs that stigmatize gay, lesbian, and bisexual people. A homonegative individual may vote against extending the right of same-sex marriage because of a conservative religious conviction seemingly divorced from any appreciation for the civil rights implications and the privileges associated with the institution of marriage. Homohatred is the most active form of discrimination and prejudice stemming from strongly held religious beliefs and heterosexist convictions, which allows for no other religious or cultural possibility. An individual who joins a local Family Research Council and becomes passionately involved in a political campaign to block the board of education's adoption of an inclusive diversity curriculum because it includes mention of gay and lesbian youth suicide demonstrates homohatred.

The term *homophobia* fails to capture the personal and social reaction to all marginalized sexualities. You should maintain a more inclusive perspective (bisexual and transgender). Homophobia used in its broadest sense has many dimensions: the personal, that is, the personal belief system that gay people deserve to be pitied or hated because they are unable to control their perverted desires; and the interpersonal, wherein there is a transformation of the personal belief system into active bias or prejudice. This transformation, in turn, affects relationships. The personal and interpersonal levels of homophobia are damaging to the development of a positive self-identity, thus thwarting effective coping and social role functioning. Another level is the institutional. On this level, discrimination is systematic on the part of governments, businesses, and religious, educational, and professional organizations by promulgating laws, codes, or policies that enforce discrimination. This is conceptually related to cultural homophobia, sometimes referred to as collective or societal, and refers to the social norms or codes of behavior that, although not expressly written into law or policy, nonetheless work within a society to legitimize oppression. This level of homophobia results in attempts either to exclude images of sexual minorities from the media or from history or to represent these groups as immoral or deviant. Evidence of institutional heterosexism or cultural homophobia is extensive: widespread discrimination in all areas of life; negative and marginalizing attitudes of the general population and, specifically, the helping professions; increased incidence of gay and lesbian bashing; inordinate length of time to respond to AIDS; high rate of gay teen suicide; morbidization of gay and lesbian relationships; and the low number of states that provide civil rights protection. Both Factors I and II might be implicated here. While most lesbians and gay men develop effective defenses against noxious, non-nurturing environments by learning to redefine the self in an affirming way or to manage their stigma constructively, some will be overwhelmed by the lack of family and reference group support and the unfiltered hostility all around them, and fall back on psychologically numbing and dysfunctional adaptive behavior, such as addictions or a cycle of unsatisfying relationships.

In their exploration of gay and lesbian identity development in the context of homophobia, Appleby and Anastas (1992) note that cultural homophobia is manifested in a conspiracy to silence this minority by redefining the reality of gay and lesbian people, by denying the existence of their unique culture, their popular strength, and their efforts to define or label themselves. The dominant fear of overvisibility of gays and lesbians results in the creation of defined public spaces and negative symbolism or stereotyping.

The Roots of Oppression

A thorough discussion of the etiology of homophobia and heterosexism includes consideration of several divergent explanations. Social theories highlight the power of patriarchy in defining and maintaining gender roles and male privilege (Andersen, 1983), the devaluation of the self resulting from socialization, and the limiting nature and role of the family in gay and lesbian adaptation (Lynn, 1966). The social control function of psychiatry and the medicalization of social life should be appreciated (Altman, 1971, 1982; Bayer, 1987, 1989; Szasz, 1970). The current heterosexist, as well as racist, sexist, and classist, social order is largely understandable in terms of gender-assigned roles based on a system of male privilege. Much of this was discussed in greater detail in Chapters 1 and 2 as the conceptual framework for understanding oppressed and marginalized people, in general.

Gender Ideology

Sexuality is shaped by society as the enactment of social scripts: All human sexual behavior is social scripted behavior. The sources of sexual arousal are to be found in sociocultural definitions, and it is extremely difficult to conceive of any type of human sexual activity without this definitional aspect. It is not the physical aspects of sexuality but the social aspects that generate the arousal and organize the action.

The notion of gender as a social construction, while presented in Chapters 2 and 4, requires at least a brief review here because of its centrality to heterosexism (heterocentrism) and to the virulent power of homophobia in this society. Herek (1990) argues that ideologies related to sexuality and gender hold this system of hierarchical roles together. The ideology of gender, a system of beliefs, values, and customs concerning masculinity and femininity, is the context in which the individual defines his or her gender identity.

This gender ideology is a socially constructed and learned process wherein many meanings are attached to the self as male or female. Heterosexuality is equated with "normal" masculinity and "normal" femininity, whereas homosexuality is equated with violating norms of gender (Herek, 1992, pp. 89–104). Acceptable sexual roles and desires are gender and sexually prescribed, while role violations are stigmatized as deviant, abnormal, inherently sick, or dangerous. This can be seen in extremist and violent reactions to gay men who violate gender role expectations or who reject by default their "god-given" male privilege. Confusion is sometimes increased with the gender role nonconformity of growing numbers of straight men and women, as well as with the greater visibility of norm-violating lesbians, gay men, and bisexuals. Even in the absence of violence, hateful attitudes and prescriptive beliefs affect lesbians and gay men who must process this hostility in developing their own identities, fashion their own responses to gender roles, and navigate in a world of blatant heterosexuality and invisible homosexuality.

Gender role conformity and nonconformity must also be evaluated within the context of different cultural expectations. What constitutes appropriate male or female role behavior is not always the same within or across cultures. Cultural cues may be sufficiently different so as to result in a misinterpretation of behaviors, especially related to gender role performance. These cues may be misinterpreted and labeled as deviant (lesbian/gay), as when diverse and culturally defined gender roles of macho men, androgynous men and women, passive men, and assertive women come in contact with dominant stereotypes.

Heterosexual Privilege

So far, the emphasis has been primarily on negative attitudes toward sexual minorities. However, understanding heterocentrism also requires an appreciation of the systematic ways in which heterosexuality is supported. Blumenfeld (1992) offers an accessible synthesis of contemporary thinking related to homophobia and heterosexism, which is consistent with the previous discussion of the ideologies of gender and sexuality. He conceptualized heterosexism as a system of advantages bestowed on heterosexuals. It is the institutional response to homophobia that assumes that all people are or should be heterosexual and therefore excludes the needs, concerns, and life experience of those who are not. This is heterosexual privilege: the daily ways that make married persons comfortable or powerful, providing supports, assets, approvals, and regard to those who live or expect to live in heterosexual pairs.

The fact that you live under the same roof with someone of the opposite sex triggers all kinds of societal assumptions about your worth, politics, life, and values. It also triggers a host of unearned advantages and conferred dominance or power (McIntosh, 1988, pp. 16–17). This heterosexual privilege, supported by the ideologies of gender and sexuality, is the core of cultural heterosexism. It is like the air we breathe; it is so ubiquitous that it is hardly noticeable, especially to those who have it. However, those who do not participate in this privilege pay the price. Again, it must be emphasized that religion, law, psychiatry, and popular culture have played key roles in teaching and reinforcing a gender ideology, all significant contributors to heterosexism and lesbian and gay discrimination. This privilege goes unrecognized by heterosexuals but remains a constant source of stress for the sexually diverse as they attempt to bring visibility and legitimacy to their nonheterosexual intimate roles within an extended family, among nongay friends and neighbors, and among coworkers and service providers or professional colleagues. Heterosexual privilege is problematic in gay and lesbian social role functioning because it implies a loss of power, a degree of ambivalence, and a possibility of isolation because gay men and lesbians are judged as not playing by the "natural" rules. If there is little or no understanding of the paradox of this situation, it is possible that one's coping skills will be less than adequate.

Carol Tully (2001) identifies twenty-five commonly held gay/lesbian/bisexual/transgender (GLBT) myths and stereotypes in American culture. Those selected have no basis in fact and are based in institutional homophobia. Drawing from the research literature, she notes that reality alone contradicts many of these beliefs.

- Long-term relationships are uncommon among lesbians and gay men.
- Most gays and lesbians abuse alcohol and drugs.
- Children raised in gay or lesbian families are more likely to be gay or lesbian than children raised in non-gay homes.
- It is possible to identify lesbian and gay people by commonly held behavior and physical characteristics.
- Gay men and lesbians are more promiscuous than non-gays.
- Most pedophiles and child molesters are gay.
- Homosexuality is a mental illness.

Religion

In any discussion of homophobia or heterosexism, the interrelatedness of power, gender role socialization, family, and religion must be recognized. Religion is a system of beliefs, values, and customs that forms the basis for group members' shared perception of social reality. It involves a worldview that is shared by its members, which includes valuing patriarchy, male privilege, with its system of roles, relationships, and approved behaviors. One major function of religion is to support the social order. While the family teaches us the preferred gender roles along with the expected behaviors, religion teaches us to value these roles as good, necessary, appropriate, and legitimate. These religious and cultural lessons are well learned and serve as the foundation for much of homophobia and heterosexism.

A sizable portion of the U.S. public is admittedly, proudly, and sometimes militantly anti-homosexual, despite anti-discrimination legislation and the high visibility of lesbians and gay men as a growing political, economic, and cultural influence. The hatred for gay men and lesbians develops out of fear and self-righteousness. Religion has taught that gay people are inherently evil, and true believers are ever alert for the sins of their neighbors. Comstock (1991) identifies eight possible references to the disapproval of homosexuality in Judeo-Christian scripture: Genesis 19; Leviticus 18:22, 20:13; Romans 1:18–32; 1 Corinthians 6:9; 1 Timothy 1:10; Revelation 21:8, 22:15. Biblical scholars are far from agreeing on which refer definitely to homosexuality, but the consensus is that the two verses in Leviticus alone clearly indicate and prohibit homosexual relations, explicitly condemning male homosexuality and prescribing death for those practicing it. Specifically, because of the Judeo-Christian roots of the legal system and social policy in the United States, it is these references that have influenced and continue to buttress social policy and legal practice concerning lesbians and gay men. This relationship between religion and law is seen as a major dimension of Herek's notion of cultural heterosexism.

These biblical references suggest that the truly religious person (the biblical literalist) is not only justified in hating and denigrating homosexuals but also almost required to do so as an act of piety. Their self-righteousness justifies their attitudes and actions while insulating them from other points of view (Pierce, 1990). These teachings, however, also have a significant impact on gay, lesbian, and bisexual people themselves: "Coping may be particularly difficult for people of color, from cultures that totally reject homosexuality, or from fundamentalist or doctrinaire religious backgrounds that find scriptural reasons to define homosexuality as intrinsically sinful or evil" (Lloyd, 1992, p. 93).

Because most contemporary Christians do not believe in biblical inerrancy but interpret scriptures within a historical, cultural, and linguistic context, anti-gay and lesbian laws literally based on these biblical references are irrational. This religion-based hatred of homosexuality is ironic, in light of the finding that the words *homosexual, homosexuality,* and *sodomite* do not exist in classic Greek or Hebrew, nor do they appear in the Bible until 1946 (Maniaci & Rzeznik, 1993). These words are neither recorded before that time nor are they words that would have cultural meaning in that period of Hebrew and Greek history. Even without this most recent revelation, theologians and biblical scholars such as Boswell (1980) pointed to the contradictions in the text, as well as the selective attention to homosexual behavior and not other behavior equally vilified. He observed that "if prohibitions which restrain a disliked minority are upheld in their most literal sense as absolutely inviolable while comparable precepts affecting the majority are relaxed or reinterpreted, one must suspect something other than religious belief as the motivating cause of the oppression" (p. 7). Top scholars, such as New Testament professors L. William Countryman (1988) of Berkeley, Robin Scroggs (1983) of Union Theological Seminary, and Daniel A. Helminiak (1994), a well-respected theologian and Roman Catholic priest, join Boswell to show that those who perceive Bible passages as condemning homosexuality are being misled by faulty translation and poor interpretation. Each also points out that the Bible has been used to justify slavery, inquisition, apartheid, and the subjugation of women. The impact of these marginalizing religious beliefs and behaviors on the lives of gay, lesbian, and bisexual people should not be minimized. The power of socialization via the church and the family results in the widespread negative attitudes, a system of laws and civil policies that discriminate and punish, a national environment of physical and psychological violence too seldom addressed, and the historic inaction with regard to AIDS, lesbian health care, and youth suicide.

Psychiatry/Psychology

There are other social institutions that share responsibility for societal homophobia and heterosexism; these include medicine, psychology, and psychiatry. Each have played a social gatekeeping role, that is, taking what is thought to be immoral or unacceptable, at a given point in time, and labeling these then as dysfunctional, deviant, or a social problem. These professions continue to contribute to an aura of "scientific" legitimacy to the view that homosexuals are both mentally and physically deviant (DeCecco, 1988).

In attempting to provide an understanding of aberrant behavior, psychiatry assumed from the faltering religious tradition the function of protector of the social order, "substituting the concept of illness for that of sin" (Bayer, 1987, p. 10). In assuming that heterosexuality represented a medical norm to which they were obliged to help homosexuals conform, they unconsciously enforced the cultural hegemony of heterosexuality. While more psychiatrists today are apt to see mental illness as a social construction and that the profession reflects the values and demands of society, many, primarily those analytically trained, are unconvinced of the naturalness of homosexuality. A survey of clinical psychologists found that more than one in five practicing therapists still treat homosexuality as a mental illness, despite the fact that it is no longer classified as such; in addition, a full 45% of those surveyed did not consider such behavior unethical (Douglas, Kalman, & Kalman, 1985). However, in 2002 their updated survey noted that only 7.9% of psychology students held this belief. Thus the religious and professional validation of anti-homosexual prejudice reinforces the general view of homosexuals as undesirable and deviant persons in general society and, by extension, within the family as well. These complementary sources of anti-gay condemnation mean that authorities to which the individual or the family may turn for information on homosexuality are as likely as not to simply reinforce the family's misconceptions rather than encourage critical reflection on them (Strommen, 1990).

Law and Policy

Widespread legal and social discrimination against lesbians and gays remain the current political reality. Only eleven states—Wisconsin (1982), Massachusetts (1989), Hawaii (1990), New Jersey (1990), Connecticut (1991), Vermont (1991), California (1992), Minnesota (1992), Rhode Island (1995), New Hampshire (1997), and Nevada (1999)—have laws protecting lesbian, gay, and bisexual civil rights. Approximately 150 cities and counties nationwide have passed local same-sex rights ordinances (Vaid, 1995, pp. 8–9). Minnesota is the only state to extend human rights to transgender people, but stopped at covering Medicaid health insurance (Swan, 1997). This political situation is ironic, in that the United States boastfully presents itself as the leading democracy and an advocate of civil rights, while quietly most European and industrial nations have passed legislation to protect gay, lesbian, and bisexual people. Many of these same nations are in the process of legalizing same-sex marriage, while Scandinavia, Spain, and the Netherlands have granted legal recognition of same-sex marriage.

In 2005, however, Massachusetts became the first state to allow same-sex civil marriage. Vermont and Connecticut have legalized civil unions, while ten states and the District of Columbia recognize domestic partnerships. Hawaii, California, Oregon, and New Jersey have enacted a variation of these laws (NGLTF, 2005). The NGLTF and the Human Rights Campaign (HRC), two leading GLBT civil-rights organizations, have refocused their political attention to civil marriage, domestic partnership, and civil unions. Grassroots energy has been redirected to the state level to organize against the federal bill, Defense of Marriage Act, which defines this institution as the exclusive domain of heterosexuals, and to build constituencies in support of gay marriage. The NGLTF's analysis of the costs of discrimination, using Connecticut as an example, points out that same-sex couples are denied equal treatment under Social Security policy, federal tax law, immigration, inheritance, and health care protocols that allow married couples to protect their families, such as the Family and Medical Leave Act. Analysis clarifies that by allowing same-sex couples to marry, no one is harmed, and that couples and their children will access benefits and programs designed by the government to promote family stability and financial security (Dougherty, 2005).

In the United States, one civil right related to same-sex unions is presently under attack. More and more states are pursuing legislation to prevent the recognition of lesbian or gay marriage after Congress passed the Defense of Marriage Act (DOMA) in 1996. This is significant because this legal procedure, overtly tied to religious tradition, results in a valuable array of civil rights and privileges not available to those couples that do not or cannot marry. The bulk of U.S. law pertains to issues of property, inheritance, family relations, adoption, and access to health and social insurance. These are legal rights and privileges assured by marriage. *Advocate* (10/27/1998) argues that sodomy laws, the remnants of colonial law when "crimes against nature" were often punishable by death, have been seen as meaningless and rarely enforced in recent history, and are potential barriers. These same laws can be used to block the passage of equal rights and are impediments to success with custody cases or challenges to the military. Sodomy laws and the Supreme Court ruling upholding them (*Bowers v. Hardwick*, 1986) put the chill of criminality on gay people (Leonard, *Sexuality and the Law: An Encyclopedia of Major Legal Cases*). You hear it again in almost every gay-related issue: "This person is a habitual sodomite. . . not the kind of person you want kids exposed to." Today twenty-one states, mostly in the South, still have these laws. There is a tendency to think of gay men when thinking about sodomy. But the law is so broad that it could include married heterosexual couples and mutual masturbation. The religious right wing has turned its attention to these laws, attempting to shore them up and to make sure that they are more vigorously enforced. Again, the association of religion and law will be used to say that homosexuality is an unhealthy and immoral choice. Those who refuse to renounce the choice should be punished under sodomy laws. For more information on this and related topics, contact www.advocate.com www.thetaskforce.org for civil rights–related updates.

The legal system in many states has criminalized many acts of sexual expression. Legal rights are denied lesbians and gay men in relation to the prerogative to marry, the custody of their children, the opportunity to provide foster and adoptive care, the liberties of inheritance and decision making as a biological next-of-kin, employment rights, housing, access to resources and services, immigration and naturalization protections, and the choice to serve in the military. Many of the organizations and institutions within the gay and lesbian community have been established to fight this level of discrimination.

AIDS and HIV Disease

The response to AIDS is evidence of widespread heterosexism and discrimination operating at the heart of national social policy and law. The AIDS epidemic heightened the sense of stigma for gay men and, by association, for lesbians. Human Immunodeficiency Virus (HIV) disease is the major cause of death among men and women in the United States between the ages of twenty-four and forty-five. HIV disease is responsible for enormous psychological, social, and economic distress. It is a disease that affects not only the individual, but their significant others, family, friends, coworkers, the community, and the society. HIV disease and substance abuse are closely related. Substance abuse, another major social problem, is both influenced by and influences the social construction of and the societal response to HIV disease.

Presently, because of homophobia and negative attitudes toward drug use and addiction, HIV disease is one of the most emotionally charged public health issues faced by society (Appleby & Anastas, 1998; Altman, 1982; Conrad, 1986). Regardless of one's source of infection, the result is stigmatization for the client and secondary stigmatization for those in his or her supporting social systems. Stigma, in turn, affects HIV-related policy development, service delivery, and funding. Infected women, some lesbians and bisexual women, and their children experience public fear and discrimination. Family and friends have abandoned many of those infected. Some health care and social service practitioners, including social workers, in violation of the Code of Ethics, have refused to provide care to patients with HIV disease (Appleby, 1995).

HIV disease affects all areas of biopsychosocial functioning. Its literature is therefore enormous, drawing on a broad spectrum of academic and professional disciplines, including the arts and sciences, education, health care, law and advocacy, social services, and mental health. Each has chronicled the hopelessness and despair, as well as the resilience and the heroism of people living with HIV disease. Social workers have contributed significantly to the psychosocial and mental health literature related to HIV. Christ and Wiener (1985), Leukefeld and Fimbres (1987), Shernoff and Scott (1988), Appleby (1989), Dilley and Goldblum (1987), Land (1992), Reamer (1993), Dansky (1994), Lynch, Lloyd, and Fimbres (1993), and Odets and Shernoff (1995) are a few of the many who have published practice-oriented texts on this topic. These authors and many other social workers have addressed HIV disease in all of the leading professional journals. It is beyond the scope of this chapter to do justice to all that has been written on HIV disease in the United States. Review the references at the end of this chapter and professional journals in social work and other allied professions, specifically *Focus: A Guide to AIDS Research and Counseling, AIDS Education and Prevention, The Active Voice* (published by people with AIDS), *HIV Frontline, Journal of Gay & Lesbian Social Services,* and the *Journal of Gay & Lesbian Psychotherapy* for the depth of understanding necessary to serve HIV-infected gay, bisexual, and lesbian people and their affected children and families. This literature will document the tremendous jolt to family, interpersonal, occupational, and life situation role functioning. The patient's psychological and physical response to this disease may result in a wide range of social interaction problems. The severity and the duration of these issues will, at best, heavily tax his or her, as well as friends' and family's, coping ability.

The HIV epidemic has had a profound impact not only on many gay, lesbian, and bisexual individuals but also on the gay, lesbian, and bisexual community. In fact, the HIV epidemic presents a serious danger to the functioning and survival of the gay and lesbian communities. Early in the epidemic, serious discussions in the gay community ensued about whether the gay male population was doomed for extinction. Rofes (1996) reminds us that gay men found solace in two oft-repeated beliefs: (1) A treatment which would save their lives would be found soon, and (2) Gay men in urban centers had implemented safe sex practices and halted sexual transmission in the population. "These beliefs became the theoretical and spiritual foundation of our collective lives in the health crisis" (p. 2), providing the focus for community activism and mutual aid efforts. Often subtle and secondary discrimination will affect the environmental systems with which the infected client must deal. While discrimination is illegal (Americans with Disabilities Act), it insinuates itself at some level in every system. The practitioner may assess a low level of discrimination in any given system, but cumulatively, in all systems, this may be experienced as severe.

Overshadowing everything is the terrible tragedy of AIDS with the inexpressible personal sorrow it has brought to so many. Paradoxically, however, there have simultaneously been significant improvements in the social, legal, and political place of gays and lesbians in America. The HIV epidemic has galvanized the gay and lesbian community to adopt more of a political action agenda not only for HIV-related services and research but also for a full range of civil rights. Many previously closeted individuals realized that they had little to lose in light of the epidemic and decided to come out to family and coworkers and to fight for legal protection of their constitutional rights. Thus the fight against homophobia and heterosexism has made some of its most important advances while the nation was confronting the HIV epidemic (Berzon, 1992).

After several years of decline in new HIV cases in the gay, bisexual, and transgender communities attributed to successful safe-sex prevention campaigns, the rates are again rising among young gay men and minorities of color. The prevailing erroneous assumptions are that AIDS is a chronic disease, reasonably managed by medication, and that infection can be avoided by not having sex with older men (thirty and over). The sociopolitical context of AIDS education has shifted. A politically conservative Christian right wing has forced public policy to emphasize abstinence in place of evidenced-based, explicit, and targeted safe-sex programs, and to use faith-based initiatives, which are often anti-gay and supportive of reparative therapy.

AIDS resources on the Internet are extensive: AIDS Action Committee, www.aac. org; Centers for Disease Control, www.cdc.gov/diseases/aids.html; and the Gay Men's Health Crisis, www.gmhc.org.

Popular Culture and Attitudes

Popular culture, specifically mass media, is an important purveyor of social construction, norms, and values. Recall previous discussions of the treatment of minorities in films, music, and television in Chapters 4 and 5. There are no formal or informal social sanctions for using gay men or lesbians as the butt of jokes or using blatantly stereotypic images when making a reference. Although lesbian, gay, and bisexual stigmatization is widespread in the general population, there is great variability among individuals in their attitudes toward lesbian, gay, and bisexual people. As with racism, sexism, and other prejudices that are supported by the culture at large, the fact that heterosexism and homophobia are institutionalized in a variety of ways does not mean that every person in the society shares in those attitudes to the same degree. It is important to know what can make a difference in individual attitudes toward lesbian, gay, and bisexual people in order to create positive change.

There are several factors that have been consistently shown to make a difference on average in how people feel about gay and lesbian people. People who believe that they personally know a gay or lesbian person are consistently less likely to oppose gay rights than those who do not (Nava & Dawidoff, 1994; Herek, 1995). Conversely, those who hold strong and/or traditional religious beliefs, traditional beliefs about gender roles, and/or who live in regions of the country where such beliefs are common are more likely on average to have negative attitudes toward gays and lesbians. In addition, those who are older and who have less education are also likely to be more negative in their views. On average, heterosexual women are less likely to express negative attitudes toward gay and lesbian people, especially gay men, than heterosexual men do (Herek, 1995). Some of these factors, like having prior, pleasant contact with a person from the oppressed group, have been found to hold true for racism and other prejudices as well.

Health and mental health professionals, including social workers, are not immune from the negative attitudes toward gay, lesbian, and bisexual people that other Americans share. Their attitudes are especially significant in that these are the professionals who have responsibility for assisting gay, lesbian, and bisexual clients to cope with the personal and social consequences of homophobia, to work through the shame and guilt imposed by a homophobic and heterosexist society, to develop a positive lesbian or gay identity, and to help with the management of stigma and stress. Nonjudgmental attitudes are necessary to support social change and to end individual and organizational prejudice. Gay men and lesbians have not always been well served by the health, mental health, and social service professions.

The homophobia of health and mental health professionals has been well documented (Moses & Hawkins, 1982; DeCrescenzo, 1985). In these studies, homophobia was most prevalent among social workers. Because homophobia and heterosexism are social forces that permeate all aspects of social life, social service agencies and social work professionals are not immune to them. The belief that sexual minorities could change their orientation if they wanted is still a prevalent notion within our society. Other misconceptions that force lesbian, gay, and bisexual people to remain in the closet are that gays should not be teachers, should not have custody of their children, should be excluded from the military, are child molesters, and have a choice to act on their preference. These misconceptions, shared by both the lay and professional public, make it difficult for lesbian and gay clients to seek help. As with all minorities, peer and practitioner validation are crucial to healthy identity development.

Although attitudes about homosexuality in the helping professions as a whole have begun changing for the better since the 1970s, unfortunately both workers and clients may still be affected by the residue of outmoded psychological theory that until recently viewed homosexuality as pathology. For example, the history of gay and lesbian forced psychiatric hospitalization, imprisonment, socially sanctioned violence, and discrimination is not a solid foundation for institutional trust, but rather, for cynicism and healthy paranoia. The elimination of homosexuality from the nosology of the DSM-III did not eliminate homophobic attitudes. As Forstein (1988) and Dulaney and Kelly (1992) note, this elimination has not changed the personal opinion of the majority of the professional mental health community. Unfortunately, the most recent studies continue to suggest that negative attitudes toward homosexuality and homosexual clients persist among some social workers and social work students (Greene, 1994; Harris, Nightingale, & Owen, 1995; Eliason, 1995). Prejudice

toward lesbian, gay, and bisexual social workers has also resulted in discriminatory personnel practices in health and social service agencies, which leads to unnecessary stress.

A survey of counseling students regarding attitudes toward minority clients found
average to high homophobia despite positive attitudes toward racial and ethnic minorities.
Students with more experience with sexual minorities, however, demonstrated lower levels
of homophobia (McDermott, Tyndall & Lichtenberg, 1989). Social workers' and other
helping professionals' feelings, attitudes, and level of comfort with gay or lesbian orientation must be examined; they require self-exploration over time.

Unfortunately, the AIDS epidemic has had a negative effect on attitudes. Douglas,
Kalman, and Kalman's study of homophobia among 91 physicians and 261 nurses found
that 31% of the respondents admitted they have felt more negatively about homosexuality
since the emergence of AIDS (Eliason & Raheim, 1996). Wallach (1989) reports similar
findings among physicians and nurses in a major New York teaching hospital, with 9% of
the respondents agreeing that AIDS is God's punishment to homosexuals and 6% agreeing
that patients who choose homosexuality deserve to get AIDS. Dupras, Levy, and Samson
(1989) found that negative attitudes about AIDS were better predicted by homophobia than
by other measures.

In a recent comparative study of MSW students and age-matched lesbians living in
urban Connecticut, progress is seen. While lesbians scored lower on the Index of Homophobia than did MSW students, both groups on average were not homophobic (Thompson,
1991). In a study of undergraduate and graduate social work students, Appleby (1996)
found graduate students to be significantly less homophobic than undergraduates. These
negative attitudes, however, changed over time with greater exposure to affirmative lesbian
and gay content in their coursework.

The Committee on Lesbian and Gay Concerns of the American Psychological Association conducted an extensive study of biased practice with lesbians and gay men (APA,
1991). They found that 58.2% of therapists reported personally knowing about incidents of
professional bias against gay and lesbian clients. Examples of bias were reported in three
broad therapeutic areas. "First, examples of bias in strategies of assessment and intervention included a therapist who attributes a client's problem to his/her sexual orientation
without evidence that this attribution is accurate, a therapist's failure to recognize that a
client's psychological symptoms or distress can be influenced by the client's own negative
ideas about homosexuality, and a therapist who seeks to change the sexual orientation of a
client when not requested to do so" (pp. 10–14). A second set of examples of bias included
therapists who viewed gay identity solely in terms of sexual behavior or who interpreted a
client's identity as a "phase" that they will go through. Third, they reported examples of
bias in expertise and training where a therapist taught inaccurate information or expressed
anti-gay attitudes to colleagues or students. These observations of psychiatric or psychological practice serve as additional evidence of what Herek refers to as cultural heterosexism. Without a significant effort to expand affirming mental health services, the emotional
needs of gays and lesbians will not be adequately met in formal health and mental health
service systems, leading many to rely instead on self-help efforts (Berger & Kelly, 1986;
Appleby & Anastas, 1992).

Nicolosi's (1991) *Reparative Therapy of Male Homosexuality* is offered by Drescher
(1998) as an example of how contemporary religious intolerance of homosexuality can fuse

psychoanalytic theories that pathologize homosexuality with pastoral counseling for homosexuals. The power to marginalize is an ever-present possibility in the act of labeling, assessing, or diagnosing.

The reparative or conversion therapy (ex-gay ministries) movement has gained momentum among religious political extremists. Many ex-gay ministries are grounded in cultlike practices. The consequences of their therapies can be devastating: long-term depression, anxiety, lack of self-esteem, self-destructive behavior, loneliness, and alienation. Reparative or conversion therapies are based on a cynical lie: that gay people choose their sexual orientation and that with prayer and treatment they can change. Treatment includes prayer, counseling, meditation, twelve-step-like programs, and sometimes drugs or shock therapy. The website of the Human Rights Campaign reports that the NASW (1999), the American Psychological Association (1999), and the American Medical Association (1998) have all condemned conversion therapy, declaring it scientifically ineffective and even harmful. The APA in 1999 reaffirmed "that there is nothing wrong with homosexuality, there is no reason that gay, lesbian, or bisexual people should try to change their orientations." The American Psychiatric Association says there is no evidence that a person's sexual feelings for others of the same sex can be changed (www.hrc.org, 1999). All mental health professions are called on to respect the rights of individuals, including sexual minority clients, to privacy, confidentiality, self-determination, and autonomy.

Social stereotypes of sexual minorities lie at the heart of why sexual diversity is a psychological issue of such significance to both individuals and their families. Because the social stereotypes of homosexuality are so negative and so false, gay, lesbian, and bisexual people must reject them in order to establish a self-affirmed, psychologically adaptive identity (Weinberg & Williams, 1974). Their families, who may experience similar processes, may also need help in resisting these negative social constructions. They must reject their own stereotypes and develop new values about homosexuality that do not stigmatize their gay, lesbian, or bisexual relative. Most lesbians and gay men and their families will work out these issues on their own with the support of friends and families of choice. However, there is a significant minority who need the assistance of a professional helping person to address the pain and hurt arising from these complex processes. In addition, like all people, they may need help for reasons totally unrelated to their sexual orientation but may fear getting it because they are uncertain about how they will be viewed. Because many gay men and lesbians remember or learn through oral tradition the vigor with which they have been pathologized by those who offered help, the social worker may find developing an effective working relationship with these clients a challenge. However, whatever the sexual orientation of the social worker, gay, lesbian, and bisexual people respond well and will benefit from knowledgeable and affirmative practice. The social worker needs a framework for understanding and a framework for doing, a theory for practice and a theory of practice.

Violence and Gay Bashing

People whose sexual partner is of their own gender have long been subjected to physical brutality. Gay and lesbian historians note that violence has often represented official governmental policy; for example, sodomy was punishable by castration, torture, and death in Colonial America (Boswell, 1980; Katz, 1976). In Germany before and during World War II, approximately 15,000 homosexuals were forced to wear the pink triangle before they were slaughtered in Nazi concentration camps (Adam, 1987). Twentieth-century observers detail the collusion of police who often looked the other way while young men preyed on gay people. In everyday life, family members, coworkers, and schoolmates have harassed and brutalized lesbian and gay people.

Anti-gay/lesbian violence was frequently a subtext in the gay and lesbian literature of the 1970s and 1980s. Comstock (1991, pp. 31–32) described this as a recurring theme in autobiographical and biographical statements, political and social commentaries, novels, short stories, poetry and plays, and articles in the social sciences. Columnists reported incidents of violence in great detail, and editorialists disapproved of the leniency with which the criminal justice system tended to treat perpetrators. This information tended to be anecdotal and descriptive without sufficient data to make general observations. However, in the 1980s, lesbian and gay organizations and anti-violence projects, lesbian and gay scholars, and service administrators devoted significant attention to the task of systematically collecting data on this violence. More recently, the media has blamed the pervasiveness of anti-gay violence on the fear and hatred associated with AIDS. However, AIDS is probably less a cause of anti-gay sentiment than it is a new focus and justification for expressions of anti-gay prejudice (Herek & Glunt, 1988).

Unfortunately, violence against gay and lesbian people can occur at any age. One mother and her live-in boyfriend reported an example of extreme anti-gay violence nationally in a Chicago court transcript of a murder of a four-year-old boy. During the summer the boy was starved, burned, stuck with pins and needles, beaten with various implements, scalded with steaming water, tied up and hung upside down, and gagged for hours because he was perceived to be homosexual. His brother was tortured for the same reason. A blow to his head eventually killed the boy (*St. Louis Post-Dispatch,* 1990). The irrationality of acts like these makes it clear that violence against gay and lesbian people (or those who are thought to be) must be understood as manifestations of heterosexism and homophobia.

The National Education Association in 2005 reported that a third of GLBT students drop out of high school because of harassment and that four out of five face daily verbal and physical harassment at school (Archibald, 2005). Gay youth attempt suicide 30–40 times out of 100, well above the national average, according to the Gay Lesbian Straight Educational Network, while 25–35% of homeless youth are GLBT (GLSEN, 2005). The U.S. Surgeon General Report on Youth Violence (2001) noted that in schools, interventions that target change in the social context appear to be more effective on average than those that attempt to change individual attitudes, skills, and risk behavior.

Gregory Herek and Kevin Berrill (1992) in *Hate Crimes: Confronting Violence against Lesbians and Gay Men,* probably the most thorough study of anti-gay crime, suggest that victims have often been prevented from reporting these crimes because of stigma of not only the victim but of family and friends. Public officials and law enforcement personnel have often remained indifferent to the problem. Comstock (1991) suggests that assault has been the price paid for visibility, and trying to remain invisible has been a common strategy of the vast majority of lesbians and gay men to avoid stigma and violence.

Since the Stonewall rebellion in 1969, the modern birth date of the Gay Liberation movement, gays and lesbians have organized around the demand for political and social equality and have attempted to advance public education so as to counter negative stereotypes.

With these actions came public visibility and the increasing probability of becoming a target of those who hate and hope to harm. In this last decade, as gay men and lesbians became more visible than ever before in U.S. society, an unprecedented number of attacks against them have been reported.

During the 1980s and 1990s, anti-gay violence paralleled the increased attacks against women and against ethnic, religious, and racial minorities. These attacks included episodes of murder, arson, bombings, assault, vandalism, cross burning, and harassment. The National Institute of Justice reported that the most frequent victims of hate crime were blacks, Latinos, Southeast Asians, Jews, and gays and lesbians—gays and lesbians in fact being the most frequent victims (Finn & McNeil, 1987). During this same period, the AIDS epidemic inflicted considerable losses on gay people. Stigma was assigned to those who were infected with the virus, those thought to be infected, and often those who were the caregivers of the infected. The increase in prejudice, discrimination, and violence against lesbian and gay people was justified because of society's fear of AIDS. Violence against gay and lesbian people does not just affect the individual victim; it affects all gay and lesbian people.

> Every such incident carries a message to the victim and the entire community of which he or she is a part. Each anti-gay/lesbian attack is, in effect, a punishment for stepping outside culturally accepted norms, that is the prevailing pattern of power and privilege, and a warning to all gay and lesbian people to stay in their place, the invisibility and self-hatred of the closet. (Herek & Berrill, 1992, p. 3)

More recently, gay men and lesbians have refused to tolerate the anti-gay attacks and, in so doing, have refused to collude in the enforcement of the cultural codes of silence and invisibility.

Internalized Homophobia

Gay men and lesbians must contend with psychological assault associated with stigma throughout life. Sexual minorities have all grown up in a world where same-sex or nonconforming sexual activity has often been considered morally repulsive and psychologically damaging. Lesbians and gay men have been taught to hate themselves, that is, to internalize homophobia or homonegativity. To internalize these negative attitudes means to take these negative attitudes into the self as conscious and/or unconscious beliefs. Internalized homophobia is defined here as a set of negative attitudes and affects toward homosexuality in other persons and toward homosexual features in oneself. These features include same-gender sexual and affectional feelings; same-gender sexual behavior; same-gender intimate relationships; and self-labeling as lesbian, gay, homosexual, or queer. While this term seems to exclude bisexuals and transgender people, this is not the intent. Sexually diverse people react to heterocentrism in similar ways, thus, while the word or phrase is awkward, the concept is relevant.

Internalized homophobia is a core construct in understanding gay and lesbian affirmative psychology and often in developing a focus for clinical intervention. First, the internalization of homophobia is a normative developmental event experienced to some degree by almost all gay men and lesbians in a heterosexist society. Second, it is a significant cause of psychosocial stress and pain. Third, reduction of internalized homophobia can be considered a successful outcome of ameliorative or preventive mental health intervention. "Similarly, conversion therapies that increase internalized homophobia can be viewed as psychologically damaging to gay persons" (Shildo, 1994, p. 176).

Studies suggest that between 33% and 25% of lesbians and gay men (and possibly a larger proportion of black gay men) may have negative attitudes or feelings about their homosexuality at some point in their lives (Shildo, 1994). For example, in a study concerning attitudes of homosexuals about gay men, participants agreed that gay men are promiscuous, not effeminate, incapable of forming stable relationships, and should not be employed in schools. Cass (1979), Troiden (1979), and Sophie (1986), among others, suggest that successful lesbian and gay identity development, or coming out, involves a process of neutralizing internalized homophobia.

The internalization of these negative attitudes often starts with an awareness of being different at an early point, at adolescence or even earlier. These negative feelings about sexual orientation may be overgeneralized to encompass the entire self. No one is totally protected from internalizing these negative attitudes, neither straights nor gays. Symptoms may range from a tendency toward self-doubt in the face of prejudice to unmistakable, overt self-hatred (Gonsiorek, 1993). Responses may include total denial of one's sexual orientation, contempt for the more open and obvious members of the community, distrust of other gay people, projection of prejudice onto others, sometimes marrying someone of the other sex to gain social approval, increased fear, and withdrawal from friends and relatives. Some even attempt to change their sexuality by entering into reparative or conversion therapy. The high rates of suicide and substance abuse among lesbians and gays are thought to be indications of this self-hate (Bradford & Ryan, 1988; Shernoff & Scott, 1988). Shildo (1994) summarized the observations of many other writers who suggest that internalized homophobia is related to distrust and loneliness, difficulties in intimate and affectional relationships, under- and overachievement, impaired sexual functioning, unsafe sex, domestic violence, avoiding coping with AIDS, alcoholism, substance abuse, eating disorders, fragmentation, and borderline-like features and suicide. The psychosocial task is to manage the stigma and to develop a healthy sexual identity (Cain, 1991; Crocker & Major, 1989; Levi, 1993).

Malyon (1982), viewing internalized homophobia from a psychoanalytic perspective, hypothesized that internalized homophobia causes depression and influences identity formation, self-esteem, the elaboration of defenses, patterns of cognition, psychological integrity, object relations, and superego functioning. He views the pathogenic effects of internalized homophobia as a (usually temporary) suppression of homosexual feelings, an elaboration of a heterosexual persona, and an interruption of the process of identity formation. Malyon (1982) proposed that negative attitudes are incorporated into one's self-image, causing a fragmentation of sexual and affectional facets of the self that interferes with the developmental process. The specific psychosocial processes shared by other minorities to some degree were discussed in detail in Chapters 1, 3, and 4. The significant difference is the lack of expected support from families of origin whose function it is to teach coping strategies and to help buffer the impact of societal rejection and discrimination.

Case Study

The theory for practice presented in this chapter has been reframed as components of Factors I and II of the PIE system. This was done to give clearer direction to the social worker's assessment and intervention function. The following case study will help show how we might use Factors I and II of the PIE system when assessing a gay client with several presenting problems. A synthesis of several models of gay and lesbian development may be helpful in formulating an assessment of this case. Most models identify stages of development.

1. *Sensitization:* a general feeling of marginality and perception of being different from peers. This is usually a preadolescent experience.
2. *Identity Confusion:* an altered perception of self, heterosexual/homosexual arousal and behavior, stigma awareness, inaccurate knowledge. The behavior associated with this stage may include denial, passing as a heterosexual, repair, avoidance, and acceptance. Lesbians often experience this stage at age 14 or 15, while gay boys are often 12 or 13 years of age.
3. *Identity Assumption:* beginning to assume a gay/lesbian self-identity and presented identity. This often occurs among lesbians between ages 21 and 23 and among gay youth between ages 19 and 21.
4. *Commitment:* adopting lesbian/gay way of life, fusion of same-sex sexuality with emotionality, relationships, self-identity and disclosure, stigma management. Ages 20 through 24 are most common for lesbians, while ages 21 to 24 are most common for gay men.
5. *Identity Synthesis:* ongoing identity development. This stage is common for lesbians between ages 24 and 29 and for gay men between ages 22 and 26.

Jack, a thirty-year-old gay Muslim, second-generation Egyptian American, came to the local AIDS Service Organization wanting specifically to talk with me. I had worked with his family one year earlier while a clinical social worker at a Family Service Agency. A school guidance counselor referred his younger sister to the agency because of truancy. Jack said when I met with him this time that he tracked me down from my previous employer because I had shown great respect for his family's traditions and beliefs. All I remembered of Jack from our initial encounter was that he was very protective of his family and committed to helping his sister in any way possible. I remembered that he appeared to be a pretty together young man. His English was excellent, and he seemed to have a solid understanding of white Anglo American culture.

At this meeting he was quite nervous. He didn't know when or how he contracted HIV. He said that he would never forget the words of his general practitioner, when the doctor broke the news of illness by saying "'You have got AIDS.' It felt like the end of my life, black clouds covered my vision, heavy air surrounded my breathing, I just saw darkness." He repeated the doctor's accusation several times. Jack asked, "How can this happen? I can't forgive him. He did not offer me any sort of counseling or any other information." Jack continued to describe his ordeal, the pain and sadness. He said, "I felt as if the ground opened up, like a dark endless hole to suck me in. I left the doctor's office not knowing where I was going. I kept walking in the city streets without feelings whatsoever. I didn't hear any sound. I saw people without really seeing them. I just kept walking through the streets. The whole city of New Haven seemed dead."

The next day Jack resigned from his job. He locked himself in his room preparing to die. He said every morning he would look in the mirror waiting to shrink and vanish. "I didn't know what to say to my parents," he said. "I just told them I am not feeling well and kept to myself. I couldn't tell a soul. . . how could I? I couldn't believe this could happen to me. I thought I was doing it safely. Obviously I was not," he added.

After a long silence, he began to ask a series of questions without pausing for an answer, "How can I tell my parents? What would they think? That I have HIV and I'm gay, how can they face it. How would they look in other people's eyes? It's not my death I'm worried about, it's my parent's feelings, their reputation, especially when the rest of my relatives find out." I could imagine how difficult his situation was. It was incredible that he could still smile and keep his sense of humor. He was happy; he still wants to be happy in spite of the shadow over his life.

After a while he continued, "It took me some time to find you, all my friends can't understand what I'm going through with my parents. My boyfriend says why don't I leave my parent's home. How can I do that? I think you understand. I can't leave home before getting married. I just can't do that." His face reflected the heaviness of his feelings. He said, "My boyfriend expects me to tell my parents about my sexuality. He thinks it is as easy as talking to his own parents. How can I do that?"

He talked about his friends and how they couldn't understand his difficulties and his culture, particularly in relation to homosexuality. He said, "As you know, homosexuality is practiced in our culture but it is not talked about. It is not homosexuality itself but the way it is being expressed, the way you practice it. I am in a dilemma; I can't make my friends understand that the whole issue of homosexuality is entirely different in my culture. I find it hard to get support from my friends." Again after a long pause, "That's not entirely true of course, I get support from my friends; I love my boyfriend and I love my friends too. Simply sometimes I can't make them understand. I cannot change the way my parents think. I can't tell them I am gay. I just can't do that. There is only one person in my family who knows about me being gay and my HIV status; it's my younger sister. I had to tell someone in the family. She already knew about my sexuality, which made it easier for me to break the news to her. She broke down; we both broke down and cried for a while. She is different from my parents, she understands what I am going through, she knows all about the cultural conflicts which both of us have to deal with on a daily basis. She's married now. My parents' home is very large; my father let her and her husband stay with us so they can save to buy their own house. My brother-in-law works very hard."

After he stopped sobbing he said, "That doesn't make it any easier in my situation with my parents, especially my mother. She is a sweetheart; she is so giving and always there. They don't understand me. I don't enjoy the company of the people of my background. I try very much to run away from it all. I just don't want to know about it. I can relate to my parents' way of living, but I don't enjoy it. You see, I love my parents and I wouldn't do anything which may hurt their feelings."

"I can't let this overtake my life. I must live. I must live well, my years are numbered. I know I am not sick yet. I see my doctor regularly and I take my medication religiously.

I like meditating. I love the water and when I go swimming it revives me, it cleanses my thoughts and takes me away from the world into the unknown. . . I find life in the unknown much easier to deal with but I can't stay there for long, I have to come back to reality."

After a very long pause he continued, "I can't help thinking about my parents, about the weight of their feelings. If only they knew about mine. I can't imagine how my mother will take it. I want to tell them. I must be prepared, when I am sick, when I have to go to the hospital. When I start losing weight. What do I tell them when I can no longer work? I don't know what to tell them when I become really sick. I know my mother will not let anybody be beside my bed except her. She won't sleep and she will be around me all the time. You see I'm the only son.

"Sons in my culture mean a lot. Hopes and expectations are important in my culture. The son must carry the name of the family, he must keep the blood of the family living, children when they grow up are expected to marry and have children. The parents always want to see their grandchildren. If they die, they die in peace after seeing their grandchildren. My father keeps asking me why aren't you married by now. I keep creating excuses and reasons, sometimes I tell him I'm not ready to get married. My father asks me with questioning eyes, ready for what? You just do it. You don't need to be ready to get married. You are thirty years old, you should have a couple of children by now, look at your cousins, they are all with nice jobs, married with children, why not you? What is different about you? Normally I change the subject or leave, sometimes I pretend I have an appointment with a friend or create any excuse. I am rarely at home. I go there to sleep. Whenever I come home my mother is always up and waiting for me, whatever the time, she is always there to heat the food for me and stays until I am ready to go to bed and says, sleep well son. I hope one day to see your children.

"This is my story and I have to live with it. I am so pleased to have someone to come to and listen and to relate to what I am saying."

At this point in Jack's development his identity as an Egyptian Muslim and a gay man are in conflict. He is caught between the stages of Identity Confusion and Identity Assumption, which requires incredible psychic energy to maintain some degree of balance. This conflict in development leaves little coping skill to address his crisis and his problems in living. If his developmental issues were settled, he would be able to draw upon his social support network and his coping abilities to problem-solve more effectively.

Jack's Factor I: Problems in Social Functioning assessment may change in relation to his sibling role, significant other, lover, friends and neighbor roles because he has not come out to his family, he has not developed a healthy sexual identity, nor has he developed same-sex relationships that are not superficial. If his family and ethnic community reject him, his options are limited because his gay friendship circle is limited, he has not formed a needed support system or family-of-choice, nor has he coupled, much of which has been achieved at this age.

If Jack lived in another community, one that has a less well organized gay community in a university town with numerous health and social services, macro interventions related to gay community development, social action, alliance building, and resource development would be needed. As we can see, the use of the PIE classification system forces us to complete a thorough assessment of both the person and his environment, which then directs our energy to developing strategies for interpersonal and/or macro intervention. The knowledge of specific

PIE Assessment of Jack

Factor I: Social Role Problems

1. Familial Roles: Child (1380.444)

Type: Mixed Responsibility (parent expectations); Dependency (anticipated role change, economic problems, need for health, mental health, and social services); and Loss (anticipated loss of lover, friends, family, and worker role)

Severity: High Severity (impaired general functioning because he is not meeting his parents' role expectation and will become dependent on them)

Duration: One to six months (anxiety has become overwhelming in more recent months, he is no longer able to deny the implications of AIDS or stigma of being gay in his culture)

Coping: Somewhat inadequate coping skills (ability to solve problems but has major difficulties solving the presenting problems, acting independently, and using ego strengths, insight, or intellectual ability)

Recommended Interventions: Crisis Intervention (cultural and family reaction to sexuality and AIDS, internalized homophobia, stigma management); Psychoeducation (the psychosocial and medical course of the disease, personal, family and community reaction); Communication Training (skill asserting personal and resource needs); Role Playing (changing family-cultural role expectations); possible family mediation and counseling if coping does not increase

Factor II: Problems in the Environment

1. Social System: Affectional Support System (10102.54)

Subcategory: Support system inadequate to meet affectional needs (great demand for interpersonal support and environmental resources but little knowledge where to start and crippling denial in terms of family, lover, and friends)

Problem: Discrimination: AIDS and Sexual orientation (10205.54) (has no sense of what his new status will beget in terms of role functioning)

Severity: Very high severity (changes in key and multiple areas of social role functioning and the environment)

Duration: AIDS awareness (one to six months), Sexual Orientation—out to self and friends (more than five years)

Recommended Intervention: Consultation (with client) and Mediation (with family) because family and friends become the most effective support system

2. Social System: Economic/Basic Needs Problems (5301.46)
    Subcategory: All areas as the disease progresses

Problem: Lack of resources (changes over the course of the disease); Discrimination (5605.46) related to Sexual Orientation and Disability Status (5610.46) will develop over time

Severity: Will increase as the disease becomes acute

Duration: All resources are available and can be accessed in short time

Recommended Interventions: Possible case management (if personal coping skills diminish or needs become great; possible client advocacy if client is too overwhelmed to connect with social supports and services or if service providers fail to respond

marginalized group helps us to look for social role functioning and environmental problems from the group's perspective, to see where there are cultural strengths and barriers, and how institutional discrimination has been expressed and experienced.

Conclusion

Heterosexism, heterocentrism, and homophobia form the context of oppression in which gay, lesbian, transgender, and bisexual people live their lives. These prejudices affect all people, including those who provide health, mental health, and social services. The ecological perspective of social work practice, with its emphasis on the life processes of adaptation and reciprocal interaction between people and their physical and social environments, supported by a diversity framework, seems well-suited as a foundation for work with this diverse population. Basic practice and applied research studies are needed to better understand how clients cope with life transitions and environmental problems, develop competent interpersonal processes and effective social role functioning, and how these then influence or are influenced by the larger social and environmental forces. Effective interventions that focus on change in both the environment (Factor II) and the individual (Factor I) should be based on systematic practice research. With the exception of transgender people, there is a substantial social science knowledge base related to sexual orientations that can be applied successfully to social work; too little research, however, related to social class differences, the unique adaptations of people of color, or multiple marginalizing statuses has been conducted. Building this knowledge is the challenge of this and future generations of social workers.

References

Adam, B. D. (1987). *The rise of the gay and lesbian movement*. Boston: Twayne.

Advocate. (1998, 12 Nov.). Viewpoint: Christopher Bagley Study (p. 44). Author.

Altman, D. (1971). *Homosexual: Oppression and liberation*. New York: Outerbridge & Dienstfrey.

Altman, D. (1982). *The homosexualization of America*. Boston: Beacon Press.

American Psychiatric Association (APA). (1980, 1994). *Diagnostic and statistical manual of mental disorders (IV–R)* (4th ed.). Washington, DC: Author.

American Psychological Association (APA), Committee on Lesbian and Gay Concerns. (1991). *Bias in psychotherapy with lesbians and gay men* (Final Report). Washington, DC: Author.

American Psychological Association (APA). (1999, 20 Aug.). *APA resolution on "reparative therapy" delivers a blow to adherents, HRC asserts*. Online: Michael.Grantham@mail.hrcusa.org.

Andersen, M. (1983). *Thinking about women: Sociological and feminist perspectives*. New York: Macmillan.

Appleby, G. (Ed.). (1989). *Teaching AIDS to adults: A resource guide for acquired immune deficiency syndrome instruction*. Hartford, CT: State of Connecticut, Department of Education.

Appleby, G. (1995). AIDS and homophobia/heterosexism. *Journal of Gay and Lesbian Social Services, 2*(3–4).

Appleby, G. (1996). Homophobic attitudes of MSW and BSW students: A longitudinal study of SCSU students. Unpublished paper.

Appleby, G., & Anastas, J. (1992, 1995, 1998). Social work practice with lesbians and gays. In A. Morales & B. Sheafor (Eds.), *Social work: A profession with many faces* (pp. 347–381). New York: Allyn & Bacon.

Appleby, G., & Anastas, J. (1998). *Not just a passing phase: Social work with lesbian, gay, and bisexual people*. New York: Columbia University Press.

Archibald, G. (July 8, 2005). NEA bolsters gays on policy, practice. *The Washington Times,* B12.

Barzan, R. (1995). *Sex and spirit: Exploring gay men's spirituality*. San Francisco: White Crane.

Bayer, R. (1987). *Homosexuality and American psychiatry: The politics of diagnosis*. Princeton, NJ: Princeton University Press.

Bayer, R. (1989). *Private acts, social consequences*. New York: Free Press.

Berger, R. M., & Kelly, J. (1986). Working with homosexuals of the older population. *Social Casework, 67*(4), 203–210.

Berube, A. (1990). *Coming out under fire: The history of lesbian and gay men in World War Two*. New York: Free Press.

Berzon, B. (1992). *Positively gay: New approaches to gay and lesbian life*. Berkeley, CA: Celestial Arts.

Blumenfeld, W. J. (Ed.). (1992). *Homophobia: How we all pay the price*. Boston: Beacon Press.

Blumenfeld, W. J., & Raymond, D. (1993). *Looking at gay and lesbian life*. Boston: Beacon Press.

Boenke, M. (1999). *Transforming families: Real stories about trangendered loved ones*. New York: Waterford Press.

Bornstein, K. (1994). *Gender outlaw: On men, women and the rest of us*. New York: Routledge.

Boswell, J. (1980). *Christianity, social tolerance, and homosexuality*. Chicago: University of Chicago Press.

Boswell, J. (1995). *Same-sex unions in pre-modern Europe*. New York: Vintage Books.

Bowers v. Hardwick, 478 U.S. 186 (1986).

Bradford, J., & Ryan, C. (1988). *The national lesbian health care survey*. Washington, DC: National Lesbian and Gay Health Foundation.

Brown, M. L., & Rounsley, C. A. (1996). *True selves: Understanding transsexualism for families, friends, coworkers, and helping professionals*. San Francisco: Jossey-Bass.

Bullough, V. L., & Bullough, B. (1993). *Cross dressing, sex, and gender*. Philadelphia: University of Pennsylvania Press.

Bullough, V. L., Bullough, B., & Elias, J. (1997). *Gender blending*. New York: Prometheus Books.

Bushong, C. W. (1995). *The multi-dimensionality of gender*. Tampa, FL: Tampa Stress Center, Inc.

Cain, R. (1991). Stigma management and gay identity development. *Social Work, 36*(1), 67–73.

Cass, V. C. (1979). Homosexuality identity formation: A theoretical model. *Journal of Homosexuality, 4,* 219–236.

Centers for Disease Control (CDC). (1995). *HIV/AIDS surveillance: U.S. cases reported through August 1995*. Atlanta, GA: CDC.

Chauncey, G. (1994). *Gay New York: Gender, urban culture and the making of the gay male world, 1890–1940*. New York: Basic Books.

Christ, G., & Wiener, L. (Eds.). (1985). *AIDS: Etiology, diagnosis, treatment, and prevention*. Philadelphia: Lippincott.

Chung, Y. B., & Katayama, M. (1996). Assessment of sexual orientation in lesbian/gay/bisexual studies. *Journal of Homosexuality, 30*(4), 49–62.

Clark, J. M. (1989). *A place to start: Toward an unapologetic gay liberation theology*. Dallas, TX: Monument Press.

Clark, J. M. (1990). *A defiant celebration: Theological ethics and gay spirituality*. Garland, TX: Tanglewood Press.

Comstock, G. (1991). *Violence against lesbians and gay men*. New York: Columbia University Press.

Conrad, P. (1986). The social meaning of AIDS. *Social Policy, 17*(1), 51–56.

Countryman, L. W. (1988). *Dirt, greed and sex: Sexual ethics in the New Testament and their implications for today*. Philadelphia: Fortress Press.

Cox, S., & Gallois, C. (1996). Gay and lesbian identity development: A social identity perspective. *Journal of Homosexuality, 30*(4), 1–30.

Crocker, J., & Major, B. (1989). Social stigma and self-esteem: The self-protective properties of stigma. *Psychological Review, 96*(4), 603–630.

Cruikshank, M. (1992). *The gay and lesbian movement*. New York: Routledge.

Dansky, S. F. (1994). *Now dare everything: Tales of HIV-related psychotherapy*. New York: Harrington Park Press.

D'Augelli, A. R., & Patterson, C. J. (Eds.). (1995). *Lesbian, gay, and bisexual identities over the lifespan: Psychological perspectives*. New York: Oxford University Press.

DeCecco, J. (Ed.). (1988). *Gay relationships*. New York: Harrington Park Press.

DeCrescenzo, T. A. (1985). Homophobia: A study of attitudes of mental health professionals toward homosexuality. In R. Schoenberg, R. S. Goldberg, & D. A. Shod (Eds.), *With compassion toward some: Homosexuality and social work in America* (pp. 115–136). New York: Harrington Park Press.

D'Emilio, J. (1983). *Sexual politics, sexual communities: The making of a homosexual minority in the United States, 1940–1970*. Chicago: University of Chicago Press.

Dilley, J. W., & Goldblum, P. B. (1987). AIDS and mental health. In V. G. Gong & N. Rodnick (Eds.), *AIDS: Facts and issues* (pp. 246–277). New Brunswick, NJ: Rutgers University Press.

Dougherty, T. (2005). *Economic benefits of marriage under federal and Connecticut law*. National Gay and Lesbian Task Force (NGLTF) Policy Institute. Access: www.thetaskforce.org.

Douglas, C. J., Kalman, C. M., & Kalman, T. P. (1985). Homophobia among physicians and nurses: An empirical study. *Hospital and Community Psychiatry, 36*(12), 1309–1311.

Drescher, J. (1998). *Psychoanalytic therapy and the gay man*. Mahwah, NJ: The Analytic Press.

Dulaney, D., & Kelly, J. (1992). Improving services to gay and lesbian clients. *Social Work, 27*(2), 178–183.

Dupras, A., Levy, J., & Samson, J. M. (1989). Homophobia and attitudes about AIDS. *Psychological Reports, 64*(1), 236–238.

Eliason, M. J. (1995). Attitudes about lesbians and gay men: A review and implications for social services training. *Journal of Gay & Lesbian Social Services, 2*(2), 73–90.

Eliason, M. J., & Raheim, S. (1996). Categorical measurement of attitudes about lesbian, gay, and bisexual people. *Journal of Gay & Lesbian Social Services, 4*(3), 51–65.

Evans, A. (1978). *Witchcraft and the gay counterculture*. New York: Fag Rag Books.

Faderman, L. (1991). *Old girls and twilight lovers: A history of lesbian life in twentieth-century America*. New York: Columbia University Press.

Fellows, W. (1996). *Farm boys: Lives of gay men from the rural Midwest*. Madison, WI: University of Wisconsin Press.

Finn, P., & McNeil, T. (1987). *The response of the criminal justice system to bias crime: An exploratory review*. Cambridge, MA: Abt Associates.

Fitzgerald, F. (1986). *Cities on a hill: A journey through contemporary American culture*. New York: Simon & Schuster.

Forstein, M. (1988). Homophobia: An overview. *Psychiatric Annals, 18*(1), 33–36.

Garnets, L. D., & Kimmel, D. C. (Eds.). (1993). *Psychological perspectives on lesbian and gay male experiences*. New York: Columbia University Press.

Gay Lesbian Straight Educational Network (GLSEN). (July 11, 2005). *E-Newsletter*. Access: www.glsen.org.

Germain, C. B. (1991). *Human behavior and the social environment: An ecological view*. New York: Columbia University Press.

Germain, C. B., & Gitterman, A. (1980). *The life model of social work practice*. New York: Columbia University Press.

Goldberg, S. B. (1996). No special rights: Supreme Court's Amendment 2 decision has long-range implications. *HRC Quarterly* (summer), 4–5.

Gonsiorek, J. C. (1993). Mental health issues of gay and lesbian adolescents. In L. D. Garnets & D. C. Kimmel (Eds.), *Psychological perspectives on lesbian & gay male experiences* (pp. 469–485). New York: Columbia University Press.

Greene, R. R. (1994). *Human behavior theory: A diversity framework*. New York: Aldine De Gruyter.

Halifax, J. (1979). *Shamanic voices*. New York: Dutton.

Harris, M. B., Nightengale, J., & Owen, N. (1995). Health care professionals' experiences, knowledge, and attitudes concerning homosexuality. *Journal of Gay & Lesbian Social Services, 2*(2), 91–108.

Helminiak, D. A. (1994). *What the Bible really says about homosexuality*. San Francisco: Alamo Square Press.

Herdt, G. (Ed.). (1992). *Gay culture in America: Essays from the field*. Boston: Beacon Press.

Herek, G. (1990). The context of anti-gay violence: Notes on cultural and psychological heterosexism. *Journal of Interpersonal Violence, 5*, 316–333.

Herek, G. (1992). The social context of hate crimes: Notes on cultural heterosexism. In G. Herek & K. Berrill (Eds.), *Hate crimes: Confronting violence against lesbians and gay men* (pp. 89–104). Newbury Park, CA: Sage.

Herek, G. (1993). Sexual orientation and military service: A social science perspective. *American Psychologist, 48*(5), 538–547.

Herek, G. (1995). Psychological heterosexism in the United States. In A. R. D'Augelli & C. J. Patterson (Eds.), *Lesbian, gay, and bisexual identities over the lifespan* (pp. 321–346). New York: Oxford University Press.

Herek, G., & Berrill, K. (1992). *Hate crimes: Confronting violence against lesbians and gay men*. Newbury Park, CA: Sage.

Herek, G., & Glunt, E. (1988). An epidemic of stigma: Public reaction to AIDS. *American Psychologist, 43*, 886–891.

Israel, G. E., & Tarver, D. E. (1997). *Transgender care: Recommended guidelines, practical information, and personal accounts*. Philadelphia: Temple University Press.

Katz, J. (1976). *Gay American history*. New York: Crowell.

Katz, J. (1995). *The invention of heterosexuality*. New York: Dutton.

Klein, F. (1993). *The bisexual option*. New York: Harrington Park Press.

Kramer, L. (1989). *Reports from the holocaust: The making of an AIDS activist*. New York: St. Martin's Press.

Land, H. (Ed.). (1992). *AIDS: A complete guide to psychosocial intervention*. Milwaukee, WI: Family Service of America.

Leukefeld, C., & Fimbres, M. (Eds.). (1987). *Responding to AIDS: Psychosocial initiatives*. Silver Spring, MD: NASW.

Levi, A. J. (1993). Stigma management: A new clinical service. *Families in Society, 74*(4), 226–231.

Lloyd, G. A. (1992). Contextual and clinical issues in providing services to gay men. In H. Land (Ed.), *AIDS: A complete guide to psychosocial intervention* (pp. 91–105). Milwaukee, WI: Family Service of America.

Lukes, C. A., & Land, H. (1990). Biculturality and homosexuality. *Social Work, 35*(2), 155–161.

Lynch, V. J., Lloyd, G., & Fimbres, M. F. (Eds.). (1993). *The changing face of AIDS: Implications for social work practice*. Westport, CT: Auburn House.

Lynn, D. (1966). The process of learning parental and sex-role identification. *Journal of Marriage and the Family, 28*, 466–470.

Mallon, G. P. (1997). *We don't get the welcome wagon: The experiences of gay and lesbian adolescents in North America's child welfare system*. New York: Columbia University Press.

Mallon, G. P. (Ed.). (1998). *Foundations of social work practice with lesbian and gay persons*. New York: Harrington Park Press.

Malyon, A. (1982). Biphasic aspects of homosexual identity formation. *Psychotherapy: Theory, Research, and Practice, 19*, 335–340.

Maniaci, T., & Rzeznik, F. M. (1993). *One nation under God*. (Video). New York: First Run Features.

Marcus, E. (1992). *Making history: The struggle for gay and lesbian equal rights, 1945–1990*. New York: Harper-Collins.

McDermott, D., Tyndall, L., & Lichtenberg, J. W. (1989). Factors related to counselor preference among gays and lesbians. *Journal of Counseling & Development, 68*, 31–35.

McIntosh, P. (1988). White privilege and male privilege: A personal account of coming to see correspondences through work in women's studies. Wellesley, MA: Center for Research on Women, Wellesley College, 1–19.

McNaught, B. (1988). *On being gay*. New York: St. Martin's Press.

Moses, A. E., & Hawkins, R. O. (1982). *Counseling lesbian women and gay men: A life-issues approach*. St. Louis, MO: C. V. Mosby.

National Association of Social Workers (NASW). (1999). Reparative and conversion therapies of lesbians and gay men. Position statement: National Committee on Lesbian, Gay, and Bisexual Issues. Washington, DC: Author.

National Gay and Lesbian Task Force (NGLTF) Policy Institute. (2005). *Marriage and partnership recognition.* Access: www.thetaskforce.org.

Nava, M., & Dawidoff, R. (1994). *Created equal: Why gay rights matter to America.* New York: St. Martin's Press.

Neisen, J. H. (1990). Heterosexism: Redefining homophobia for the 1990s. *Journal of Gay & Lesbian Psychotherapy, 1*(3), 21–35.

Nicolosi, J. (1991). *Reparative therapy of male homosexuality: A new clinical approach.* Northvale: Aronson.

Odets, W., & Shernoff, M. (Eds.). (1995). *The second decade of AIDS: A mental health practice handbook.* New York: Hatherleigh Press.

Pierce, D. (1990). Who speaks for lesbian/gay adolescents: Voices to be silenced, voices to be heard. *Women and Language, 13*(920), 37–41.

Reamer, F. G. (1993). *AIDS and ethics.* New York: Columbia University Press.

Reiter, L. (1989). Sexual orientation, sexual identity, and the question of choice. *Clinical Social Work Journal, 17*(2), 138–150.

Rofes, E. (1996). *Reviving the tribe: Regenerating gay men's sexuality and culture in the ongoing epidemic.* New York: Harrington Park Press.

Rubin, G. G. (1984). Thinking sex: Notes for a radical theory of the politics of sexuality. In C. S. Vance (Ed.), *Pleasure and danger: Exploring female sexuality* (pp. 267–319). Boston: Routledge & Kegan Paul.

Scroggs, R. (1983). *Homosexuality in the New Testament: Contextual background for contemporary debate.* Philadelphia: Fortress Press.

Shernoff, M., & Scott, W. (1988). *The sourcebook on lesbian/gay health care.* Washington, DC: National Lesbian and Gay Health Foundation.

Shildo, A. (1992). AIDS related health behavior: Psychosocial correlates in gay men. Ph.D. dissertation, SUNY at Buffalo.

Shildo, A. (1994). Internalized homophobia: Conceptual and empirical issues in measurement. In V. Greene & G. M. Herek (Eds.), *Lesbian and gay psychology: Theory, research, and clinical applications* (pp. 173–205). Thousand Oaks, CA: Sage.

Shilts, R. (1987). *And the band played on: Politics, people, and the AIDS epidemic.* New York: St. Martin's Press.

Sophie, J. (1986). A critical examination of stage theories of lesbian identity development. *Journal of Homosexuality, 12*(2), 39–51.

St. Louis Post-Dispatch. (1990, 18 February). Story of boy's torture rocks courtroom (p. 72G).

Storr, M. (Ed.). (1999). *Bisexuality: A critical reader.* New York: Routledge.

Strommen, E. (1990). Hidden branches and growing pains: Homosexuality and the family tree. In F. Bozett & M. Sussman (Eds.), *Homosexuality and family relations* (pp. 9–34). New York: Harrington Park Press.

Sullivan, G., & Jackson, P. A. (Eds.). (1999). *Lady boys, tom boys, rent boys: Male and female homosexualities in contemporary Thailand.* New York: Harrington Park Press.

Swan, W. (1997). *Gay/lesbian/bisexual/transgender public policy issues: A citizen's and administrator's guide to the new cultural struggle.* New York: Haworth Press.

Szasz, T. (1970). *Ideology and insanity.* Garden City, NY: Anchor Books.

Thompson, C. P. (1991). Homophobia: A comparison study: MSW students and lesbians. Master thesis, Southern Connecticut State University School of Social Work, New Haven, CT.

Townsley, J. (2001). *Health risks of gay youth.* IUPUI. Access: www.jeramyt.org.

Transgender Education Network. (1999). Online: www.GLBTHEALTH.org

Tripp, C. A. (1975). *The homosexual matrix.* New York: McGraw-Hill.

Troiden, R. (1979). Becoming homosexual: A model of gay identity acquisition. *Psychiatry, 42,* 362–373.

Tully, C. T. (2001). Gay and lesbian persons. In A. Gitterman (Ed.), *Handbook of social work practice with vulnerable and resilient populations,* New York: Columbia University Press.

U.S. Surgeon General (2001). *Youth violence: A report of the surgeon general.* Access: http://www.surgeongeneral.gov/library/youthviolence/

Vaid, U. (1995). *Virtual equality: The mainstreaming of gay and lesbian liberation.* New York: Anchor Books.

Wallach, J. J. (1989). AIDS anxiety among health care professionals. *Hospital and Community Psychiatry,* *40*(5), 507–510.

Weinberg, G. (1972). *Society and the healthy homosexual.* Boston: Alyson Publications.

Weinberg, M. S., & Williams, C. J. (1974). *Male homosexuals: Their problems and adaptations.* New York: Oxford University Press.

Weinberg, M. S., Williams, C. J., & Pryor, D. W. (1994). *Dual attraction: Understanding bisexuality.* New York: Oxford University Press.

Wilchins, R. A. (1997). *Read my lips: Sexual subversion and the end of gender.* Ithaca, NY: Firebrand Books.

11

Ableism

Social Work Practice with Individuals with Physical Disabilities

P. Minou Michilin and Silvia Juarez-Marazzo

Once, when I was in third grade, my physical education teacher decided to change the running relay into a walking relay, which meant that I could also participate. She teamed me with the fastest girls in the class and my team won. I felt like a million dollars! I was part of the winning group! When I came home, before I could share my success and excitement with my mother, I overheard my older brother, who attended the same elementary school, speaking to my mother. He was crying and asking my mother to take me out of the physical education class. Apparently, while I had been participating in the relay race, a group of boys in the playground had been laughing and pointing at me and saying, "Look at the weirdo walk." Although my mother refused to give in to my brother's pleas, saying that it was those boys' problem and not ours, to this day when I am walking in front of other people, I hear them thinking, "Look at the weirdo walk." The concept of "weirdo" has never left me.

These comments are from a woman who has limited mobility as a result of childhood polio.

As we "become," our personality is the locus for change of both our internal and our external reality. However, we cannot dismiss the powerful and oppressive forces beyond our control that will influence our thinking, our feeling, our behavior, and our adaptation to the environment.

The opening vignette introduces us to some of the limitations and the ramifications experienced every day by those with physical disabilities. However, what left a blueprint on this woman's self-image? Was it her internal experience of that day of feeling "like a million dollars," before hearing her older brother talking to their mother? Was it the permanent internalization of judgment of those who called her "the weirdo" and then feeling like a "weirdo," or living with the responsibility of her brother's shame? Or was it her mother's strong and conflicted perspective on the episode? Had this woman become ill later in life or met difficult challenges, would her psychological response be in accord with one of those possible choices, based on that early formative experience? What is the greater limitation: her real physical disability or the external mirror that home and different levels of society impose? These questions are to be taken up in the exploration of some of the guiding concepts of which we should be aware as practitioners when assessing and working with clients with physical disabilities. Addressing those guiding concepts is the purpose of this chapter.

The poignant experience of this woman is moving. It is more profoundly moving to think that individuals with physical disabilities experience a variety of oppressions and distortions of their true being by simply moving through their everyday environments, in addition to the concrete aspects of physical limitations and discomfort in their daily life. The uniqueness of individuals with physical disabilities will determine to a considerable degree the way they adapt to their roles and the way they cope with their environment. Personal resilience, which may in part derive from that uniqueness, will play an essential part as it will generate the energy to adapt, relate, and cope. Many not able to function at a high enough level are likely to experience deep layers of shame and painful social isolation as a consequence. It is certain that all of them will experience personal, emotional abuse and/or ridicule by their peers at some point in the life cycle. This is in addition to the difficult challenges of forming an internal self-image that, in part, comes from a sense of one's body. These experiences are recurring and can be experienced at any time without warning.

These are, to varying degrees, common to all individuals with disabilities. Reality can be merciless; society can oppress at many different levels. Disability is not an abstract concept as the introductory vignette serves to show us.

What happens when a committee schedules a meeting in a physically unacceptable room? The committee member with the disability has to remind the committee chair that he or she cannot attend; naturally, the chair gives reasons why the meeting has to be held in that location. A single woman with an adolescent in a wheelchair inquires about an apartment. The landlord refuses to rent it to them, stating privately that he is concerned about increased liability while publicly he gives an excuse such as lack of availability. The scenarios are many, and the human suffering for individuals with physical disabilities in the hands of a unaccommodating environment and unenlightened society is without measure.

Prejudice, oppression, stigmatization, marginalization, isolation, and discrimination are in varying degrees long-lasting companions of people with disabilities (Engel & Frank, 1996). Charlton (1994) states, "The reality for most people of the disabled community is extreme isolation, rampant unemployment, poor education, and continuing discrimination, neglect, abuse, institutionalization, self-pity, and so on" (p. 4).

The ramifications of physical disabilities on individuals and their interactions with their environment are expansive and convoluted. Not only do they belong to one or more of the oppressed populations mentioned in earlier chapters, but they must also deal with the same issues of life adaptation as everyone else in addition to the superimposed limitations and natural consequences of their physical disability (Charlton, 1994). Thus assessing and working with individuals with physical disabilities deserves careful framing and specific considerations. In this sense, as we explore the pivotal environmental variables impinging on the adaptation and role performance of individuals with a physical disability, we will give meaning to the assessment by following the guiding concepts introduced with the opening vignette, namely, functional disability and socially imposed disability, early age of onset and later age of onset.

Finally, a few words about translating the assessment of some of the cases we will present into the descriptive person-in-environment (PIE) classification system for social functioning (Karls & Wandrei, 1994). The managed care era has driven clinical practice and its most important aspect, the human connection between the helping professional and the client, in a very different direction. When we read a DSM-IV for diagnosis, which helps to communicate one aspect of the assessment, we need to remember that its only intention is to give a general frame of the client's presenting problem in order to plan the appropriate interventions. Following the same framework, PIE addresses another aspect of assessment, which looks at the way our client and the environment are adapting and coping. In that sense, PIE is a step beyond as it tries to cluster definite aspects of the human experiences, the interpersonal roles, and the problems encountered by the individual in his or her environment. Effective assessment uses the understanding of the individual with the physical disabilities to empower the practitioner to maximize his or her intervention. Yet, only a meaningful assessment, which does not miss the multidimensional richness of what the client is saying to us, is helpful. Finally, effective assessment uses the understanding of the interactions of the individual with the physical disabilities and the environment to empower him or her to a higher level of functioning.

Historical Overview

A brief historical overview will help us understand how bigotry, oppression, social stigma-tization, marginalization, and isolation are linked to the lives of individuals with disabilities in the United States. If we look at the evolution of the way in which individuals with dis-abilities have been perceived by U.S. society, we will see how this perception is defined as the product of a social-cultural process founded on the value system brought from Europe during colonial times and rooted in the Judeo-Christian tradition. The European value sys-tem also evolved; it did not happen in a vacuum. What would it have been like to have a dis-ability in the early days of history? Were people with disabilities part of early society? Different cultures and times looked at those with disabilities in a variety of ways, though it is quite astonishing how familiar some of these views will sound to our modern ears. In "People with Disabilities and Social Work: Historical and Contemporary Issues" (1996), we are reminded how the Greek philosopher Plato, who continues to influence Western thought and ethical framework, viewed those with disabilities. He saw them as standing in the way of a perfect world, suggesting that they be "put away" in some mysterious place, "as they should be" (p. 1). The same article reveals that the belief of the Judeo-Christian tradition in the European Middle Ages held similar thinking and continues to cast a pall of shame on people with disabilities with its view that the disabled were expressions of God's displeasure and an indication of their own or their parents' sins. As the seventeenth century unfolded, the Poor Laws of Elizabethan England neatly classified those with disabilities as "the deserving poor" (Di Nitto, 1995), reducing their identity and worth to objects of char-ity, thus augmenting their social stigma and isolation. By the mid-eighteenth century, the Enlightenment was beginning its sweeping and lasting impact on American and European thought. The Enlightenment's radical optimism and its belief that humans could be perfect led to the emergence of a model that defined people with disabilities by their biological inadequacies. Thus, professional intervention focused on curing these inadequacies, or at least enabling those with disabilities to perform socially or vocationally in an acceptable manner. Although the old Elizabethan social value system was partially neutralized by the Enlightenment, people with disabilities became identified by their disabilities, rather than as people. Thus they moved on the scale from morally and spiritually imperfect to creatures defined by defective structure.

The advent of Darwin's theories in the nineteenth century had a profound effect on the social science of the time. Social Darwinism and eugenics viewed people with disabilities as innately unproductive and thus endemically unfit and without worth (Martinelly & Dell Orto, 1999). Consequently, significant attempts were made to prevent them from propagating their imperfections through marriage or childbearing, and they were often institutionalized in iso-lated and, at times, subhuman conditions.

The social constructs that equated those with disabilities as objects of shame and dis-grace persisted into the early twentieth century. Therefore, people with disabilities continued to be socially isolated and institutionalized. The devastating aftermath of World Wars I and II redirected the social consciousness and awareness toward a more humanistic view of disabil-ities as society needed to confront the reality of war veterans. So, after World War I, for the first time, federal legislation was introduced to address some of the issues confronted by the disabled veterans with the Vocational Rehabilitation Act of 1920 (Asch & Mudrick, 1995).

During World War II, the philosophy of the Axis powers severely affected the disabled population of Europe, considering them unfit, defective, retarded, and so forth. They were the first groups to go to the gas chambers, regardless of whether they were adults or children (Bock, 1983). In the United States, at the end of the war, feelings of moral and social obligation toward war veterans were again stirred. There was a national response leading to the introduction of some federal legislation to provide funding for rehabilitation.

The end of the twentieth century saw the disability movement make great strides in breaking barriers, culminating most recently in the Americans with Disability Act (ADA), a comprehensive civil rights law, which was signed in 1990. This provided the disabled legal protection against discrimination on the basis of race, national origin, color, sex, and religion parallel to that which is already available to individuals addressed by Title VII of the Civil Rights Act of 1964 (Asch & Mudrick, 1995, p. 758).

As we have seen, cultural and social beliefs are powerful forces in shaping and perpetuating the negative perceptions of people with disabilities. Not surprisingly, our culture is full of stereotypes and social resistance. So, whether people with disabilities were perceived as the "curse of God," the "deserving poor," "the disabled," or "the unfit and unwanted," the fact is that the identification of a social problem and the response to it is caught in and determined by the ideological and political web of the moment. In any case, if the social trend is guided by moralistic and Darwinistic principles or individualistic and economic ones, the boundaries between people with disabilities and people without them still exist. Over time, the mainstream community has been educated to a more compassionate view of people with disabilities and cardinal changes at the level of policies have been made to do what is necessary for this essentially powerless group. Yet, as we enter the third millennium, keeping alive the social consciousness toward people with disabilities is not a small task.

Bioethics

Bioethics is formally defined as the field of study concerning the moral and ethical choices faced in medical research and in the treatment of patients, especially when the application of advanced technology is involved. It takes up the issues of the rights of those receiving or refusing treatment under the auspices of the medical profession. This is especially relevant to those who are disabled or chronically ill because so much of their time is spent interacting with the world of medicine and its technologies. As certainly as bioethics influences the lives of the disabled whenever they encounter medical personnel or establishments—doctors, nurses, rehabilitation centers, medications, or the physical paraphernalia of specific conditions—it just as certainly figures in and prominently influences the fields of disability studies and disability rights. The questions of life and death (when is someone so seriously injured that the resulting disablement will impinge too critically on quality of life, or be of such cost that society deems it unaffordable?), the question of who decides what constitutes quality of life (research scientists, the medical profession, the government, or the individual with the disability?), the question of the right to attain or refuse treatment, and the question of society's responsibility to the needs of the disabled, including everything from equal access rights to sensory aids for those with visual or auditory impairment, are examples of the many concerns in the ongoing bioethical debate, which affects both social attitudes and social policy.

Bioethical inquiry continues to escalate and change as medical/technical advances outpace society's ability to process and implement therapeutic innovations that have already entered into the mainstream. At the same time bioethics is also charged with anticipating and influencing research and development and providing ethical guidelines at the cutting edge of medical science (for example, should more resources be allocated for one disease or disability at the expense of others?). Those in the fields of disability rights/disability studies and the disabled and their advocates must continue to be informed of, and help determine the nature of, the bioethical dialogue.

One important contribution of those in the disability field has been to reshape the "dominant message of disability studies" that was constituted along the lines of a medical model, and replace it with a "social" or "minority" model where the medical model "failed to question traditional understandings of impairment, illness, or disability" (Asch, 1995). The corrective concepts in the social/minority model that all social workers must be cognizant of include the need to evaluate the environment in which their clients are immersed as a factor influencing the clients' well-being and affecting their ability to cope with and respond to that disability; the recognition that a disabled person is first and foremost a person, and not a disability; the necessity of the disabled and their advocates to have the right to be involved in decisions about care and treatment; the right and duty of the disabled to give voice to the nature of their experience; the understanding that disability is as great a sign of diversity as sex, nationality, or religion; and the recognition that living with a disability does not exclude the possibility that a fulfilling, contributory, and highly meaningful life is possible.

The Nature of Disability

"Forty-three million Americans have one or more physical or mental disabilities, a number that marks persons with disabilities as the single largest minority group, larger even than the population of elderly and black people" (Black, 1992, p. 4). Further, those with a disability are more likely to be poor, black, female, and to live alone. The ADA currently provides the most comprehensive definition of disability, addressing the functional as well as the social dimensions of disability (Black, 1992). According to the ADA, a person is disabled if he or she meets one or more of the following criteria: "a. A physical or mental impairment that substantially limits one or more of the major activities of such individual; b. A record of such an impairment; c. Being regarded as having such an impairment" (Black, 1992, p. 5).

Although there are certain phenomena that individuals with disabilities have in common with one another, there are also many situational variables that bring about unique adaptation experiences to each person. These variables are the specific nature of the disability, the age of onset, the person's inherent character, the family and the larger environment system, the socioeconomic status, the ethnic group, and the cultural and societal interaction. Any or all of these can influence the individual's coping and adaptation. Undoubtedly, as these unique and situational variables dynamically interact, the individual's interpersonal world is redefined not only by the disability itself but also by the perceptions others have of the disability. As we have seen in the brief historical overview, the powerful winds of cultural and social beliefs are at the basis of the negative perceptions of people with disabilities, thus forming the core of oppression. The comments those children made about the girl in the walking relay in the opening vignette, while based on the visible physical differences, were oppressive in a subtle way. But how is it that the "subjective certainty" of these children, "that girl is a weirdo," was transformed into an "objective truth" for this girl, "I am a weirdo"? The reciprocal recognition for relatedness is essential; it is at the foundation of identity, self-worth, and dignity. When these reciprocal validations are endangered, the oppressed surrenders to the oppressor, internalizing the negative images projected by the oppressor, "oppressor without," and becoming the "intra-oppressor, or oppressor within" (that is the process of "subjective certainty" becoming "objective truth" [Bulhan, 1985]). The natural consequence of these internalizations will significantly impact the social functioning of the individual with disabilities. Depending on the cultural and social context, the nondisabled majority will or will not sustain social policies and cultural practices that will create a "more able-ing or disabling" environment in which the individual with disabilities must function.

To not give serious consideration to the diversity of life experiences of persons with disabilities would be a disservice. Hence, this chapter attempts to honor some of these distinctions and the importance of understanding them in order to be effective in assessing and working with this population.

Functional Disability versus Socially Imposed Disability

There are two main concepts for structuring the guidelines for assessment and intervention: functional disability versus socially imposed disability. Functional disability refers to the nature and extent of the disability and its functional ramifications for the individual. It is perhaps best described as the actual physical ramifications of the disability that translate into the inability to perform certain functions. It is the aspect of disability that perhaps receives most attention and acknowledgment both from a medical perspective and a cultural one. Because of its physical nature, it is easier to see and assess. A person with spinal injury, for example, is mobility impaired and is functionally unable to walk.

However, the extent of an individual's functionality is greatly influenced by what we will refer to as his socially imposed disability. This term refers to the person's own perception of his abilities or disabilities, which is a result of his interaction with the environment, and, to some degree, determines the adaptation of the individual to that environment. The assessment of socially imposed disability is concerned with the actual experiences, the individual's feelings, and the emotional experiences the person has had as a result of bigotry, discrimination, oppression, and isolation. What does the individual feel about himself, and how is his self-image influenced by his disability as part of who he is? As we have seen, the negative perceptions of individuals with physical disabilities are part of the social fabric, expressed in the maintenance of a disabling environment. Their reality is isolation, marginalization, frequent unemployment, poor education, neglect, and abuse. So, their experience about themselves is connected with feelings of worthlessness, self-pity, and so on. The following case of a woman with a genetically elongated and dislocated jaw will demonstrate the different dimension of socially imposed disability and its role in the person's adaptation.

After many operations to correct the problem, this woman's face remains somewhat different. She has full physical function; yet, she talks about how her face is an obstacle to her life, and how she experiences stigmatization and social isolation. While growing up, her parents were always concerned about her lack of attractiveness and her inability to ever attract a man. "What would become of her?" they worried. "Could an ugly girl have a healthy social life?" She felt haunted and made fun of by her classmates, did not have close friends at school, and suffered from low self-esteem and depression. Although she has become a self-supporting, professional woman, the feelings of inadequacy and ugliness linger. Socially imposed disability is related to the reactions of others or to the self-perceived idea of others to the disability than to the disability itself.

At the opposite end of the spectrum is the case of a young man who has severe congenital cerebral palsy. He has impaired mobility and cannot feed himself without spilling his food due to sudden spasms. From an early age, his parents told him that while they were there to help, he must, and could, find ways to cope with his functional disability. Both he and his parents became active in social and political organizations to remove barriers and to fight for legal rights. He successfully graduated from high school and moved across the country to attend college. Functionally, he was very limited, but socially he felt very capable. His high level of social adaptation helped him to deal with his functional disability and to develop practical coping skills. His self-image and abilities have not been destroyed by his disability, whereas the woman in the earlier case feels bitter, oppressed, and discriminated against. Note that the degree of disability one feels is not necessarily related to the functional aspects of the disability, as much as to one's interaction with the environment and society. In this sense, the cultural expectations and role performance as defined for each sex have tremendous weight. In traditional cultures, the roles for women are those of dependent and nurturing caretakers, and their value is related to concepts of physical beauty. Men's roles are related to action and achievement in the world. These societal constructs informed specific aspects of the personal and interpersonal experiences in the cases previously described, the man with cerebral palsy and the woman with the elongated and dislocated jaw. The man has learned to use society's resources to his advantage and make things work for him by using his strengths. The woman has become socially disabled, unable to relate. Her personal feelings of isolation and her feelings about herself as "damaged goods" are not offset by her professional achievements.

Early Age of Onset

Clearly, functionally and socially imposed disability, as well as the age of onset, deeply affects the development of the individual with disability. The response of the immediate family, along with that of society at large to the individual's disability, will have a great impact on other aspects of the individual's development. When not handled properly, a disability may impair the individual far more traumatically and pervasively than it should. The disabled individual may feel that she is a burden and may carry feelings of guilt and shame, especially if the disability develops at a later age.

In the case of a child who is born with a disability, or who develops it quite early, it is initially the parents' responses that will affect crucial stages of the child's development. The parents, who have been expecting a "perfect" baby, experience a sense of loss at the death of this expectation; so do the parents whose child becomes disabled later in childhood. Mourning the loss of a normal child becomes then part of the parents' experience.

Based on crisis theory, they may respond to this loss in three basic patterns: (1) as a challenge, (2) as a loss, or (3) as a threat (Golan, 1978, p. 65). The parents of an infant with disabilities will probably experience all three patterns at different times; however, one of them will give the direction to the bulk of the parent-infant's adaptation and interactions.

Furthermore, the oppression, isolation, and marginality that an individual with physical disabilities might feel becomes the family's issue also. This is a crucial factor in the child's development, because case studies and program evaluations indicate that the earlier the intervention, the more progress can be made in the child's development, as well as greater compensation for areas that are not functional.

When family and society respond to the disability as a challenge, the individual, as well as the family and community, is empowered. In a very real sense, they can do something about the disability rather than be helpless victims or ineffective and passive bystanders. They can fight in a positive, constructive way. They may not be able to cause a deaf child to hear, but they may be able to enhance other aspects of the child's abilities and to find alternative means of communication that will, as much as possible, fill the void of sounds in the child's life. When the parents' and society's response is primarily to view disability as a loss or as a threat, the self-esteem of the parents, as well as of the child, is affected. Frequently, the parents believe they are faced with questions such as "What have I done that I am being punished?" or "What is wrong with me?" Their own unresolved issues of self-esteem then affect the child.

When the disability happens at a young age, much of its effects on the child's personality development and the child's coping ability is dependent on the response of the family and the community. These in turn are influenced by ethnic, cultural, socioeconomic, and religious factors. Certain ethnic groups may be more tolerant and supportive of disability than others. The way the general culture either ignores or misrepresents the experiences of individuals with disabilities is part of their oppression. In the early years, the child will learn who she is as a human being and whether her concept of self revolves around her disability or whether she sees herself as a human being who has a disability. If the family, school, and society do not handle the disability as a challenge, it will have an impairing impact on other aspects of development that is only compounded by the society, as the child becomes an adult. For these powerful reasons, early intervention with biopsychosocial programs is extremely important for children with disabilities.

Parents have developmental expectations for their growing child, be it smiling at a certain age, walking at a certain time, learning to read or write, and so on. Although there is a range of time expectation for all this, caregiving parents take pleasure in their children's biopsychosocial development. When a range of disabilities and medical complications accompany some aspect of this development, this child cannot function in his or her assumed role. The parents then need to reassess their parenting role as well as consider the additional demands of physical, medical, special education, rehabilitation, psychological, and social care that are made on both the family and the child.

So, what leads to a specialized assessment of the family with a child with disabilities? The social work practitioner should assess first the strengths of the individual and his family as a whole; second, the level of the functional disability of the individual and the limitations it places on the family; third, the subjective and socially imposed interpretations of the situation by the individual and his family; fourth, the degree of the discrepancy between functional, subjective, and social disability; fifth, the resources available in the environment, which should include health care rehabilitation services, educational services, judicial and legal resources (with special consideration of ADA); sixth, the kinds of limitations the culture imposes on the individual and the family. Evaluating these fundamental aspects will help support a thorough assessment and achieve a biopsychosocial assessment of the person-in-environment system.

Golan (1978) considers it important to assess if the family's current coping patterns correspond with those that have occurred prior to the disability (p. 188). If the family is using the customary patterns, are they an appropriate response to the situation, or are those that have worked in the past not effective for the current situation? If new patterns and adaptations have been developed, are they effective in improving the functioning of the individual with disability?

The identity of the individual with disabilities is always affected by the stigma that society imposes on him or her. We briefly mentioned the dynamics operating behind the psychology of oppression. Stigma represents a spoiled identity, the idea that somehow one is imperfect in regard of the standards of the society in which one lives (Goffman, 1963). It is a "mark or characteristic that distinguishes a person as being deviant, flawed, limited, spoiled, or generally undesirable. The deviating characteristics of the person are sufficient reason for the occurrence of the stigma" (Lewis, 1992, p. 42).

The feeling of being stigmatized rises from interaction with other people, or through anticipation of interaction with other people. For a person with physical disabilities, the stigma can be felt because of society's emphasis on physical perfection and beauty, but also because of society's emphasis on activity and physical performance. Allport (1958) identifies a list of negative responses to stigmatization: obsessive concern resulting in the feelings of deep anxiety and insecurity, in addition to the denial of actual conditions and membership in groups, resulting in social withdrawal and passivity. When the stigma felt by the individual with physical disabilities is profound, it can result in emotions such as anger, sadness, humiliation, shame, embarrassment, and low self-esteem. The individual who has been disabled since early childhood has experienced this range of feelings and developed an identity similar to a racial or to an ethnic identity that is recognized and acknowledged from birth or early years. For example, a professional woman who has been wheelchair-bound and severely disabled from birth, comments that "I knew I was different from others as far back as I can remember. This is who I am."

Another issue facing families with disabled children is that of mainstreaming. When a child who is mobility-impaired becomes part of regular school activities, the child will experience marginalization and isolation. Often, the child is only accepted in a peripheral way into the community. However, being with the nondisabled community allows him to develop social skills and varied relationships. The dilemma for the parents is whether they should protect their child from the emotional pain of mainstreaming, or let him learn coping mechanisms through the experience. The mobility-impaired woman in the introductory vignette was mainstreamed as a child. For her, the price of discrimination and oppression was worth the socialization and integration, but only because she had an extremely supportive family structure. Even with their love, along with wonderful teachers, she never forgot the pain of not being chosen by her classmates to be on a team during physical education. Years later, although she is a successful businesswoman with a family of her own, the picture of the unwanted child crying lonely tears on the playground has never left her consciousness.

On the other hand, if the child is only in the company of other children with disabilities, there will be an inescapable sense of isolation from the general society, although there is commonality with those other children. These feelings and patterns of marginalization may last into adulthood. A student of one of these writers, who was deaf, would relate only to his interpreter during a seminar course. He had received most of his education in programs for deaf individuals. He believed that being part of the deaf community enabled him to become who he was and that with them, his disability was not important. After several sessions, I told him, "I am sorry we cannot seem to socialize with you." "That's okay, I do my own socializing," he responded. He carried on an animated conversation with the signing interpreter. This pattern was broken when he was asked to do a presentation for his class and educate his fellow classmates about the life and the struggles of individuals with no hearing or with hearing impairment. During this presentation, he revealed how it felt to be deaf and how he expected others to respond to him. Once he was given the opportunity to talk in the role of teacher/presenter, he was empowered, and the other students were able to respond to him. This was a turning point for him in that the other students began to treat him as a colleague rather than as a special but separate person. He became an integral part of the class.

This student and other students with physical disabilities identified and emphasized the vital importance of the university's special services not only as an advocate on their behalf but also as a center for socialization. As one student with a congenital birth defect who is wheelchair-bound said, "All through high school I was isolated and had no friends, but in college there were so many like me, I was not alone. I developed lifelong friends whom I met at special services."

In the case of the young man with cerebral palsy, as is the case for many other children, very early intervention addressed his unique needs by providing him with a separate and special education school. Only when he gained social and psychological education, competence, and strength was he mainstreamed into high school. The decision, therefore, of whether and when to mainstream has to be made on an individual basis. Motivation, desire, and the advantages and disadvantages for each child must be weighed. The more different or extreme the disability, the more discrimination and oppression, and, as well, the greater the challenge to the individual, the family, and the practitioner.

Later Age of Onset

When a physical disability occurs later in life, it has different implications for the individual, because there has been the experience of normal functioning. Now, because of accident or disease, the individual has lost some function. This creates a major crisis for the individual and her family and impacts on their functioning and their social role performance. The three basic patterns identified during earlier onset by the Crisis Theory (challenge, loss, threat [Golan, 1978, p. 65]) are also true for later onset. How the individual and her family cope with the physical disability will be influenced by how they perceive the loss of the physical functioning.

"They talk about me as if I am not there, and I get very angry at them. Then I scream. So they treat me as if I am out of my mind . . . and I start wondering if I am going crazy. Then I can't even think clearly, which has nothing to do with my body's deterioration." These are the comments of a forty-five-year-old woman with advanced stages of a neuromuscular disorder who cannot forget her first conscious awareness of the social oppression imposed on her by her family since she has become physically disabled.

One of the emotions common to individuals experiencing disability later in life is the loss of identity. A physician whose professional practice is his identity who has to stop his practice because of progressive and advanced stages of multiple sclerosis needs to renegotiate who he is after he mourns the identity that he has lost.

The actual personality of an individual is certainly a factor in how he will deal with his disability. During the assessment phase of an individual who became quadriplegic at the age of thirty-six, it was necessary to determine what resources he had before the incident, which led to his total paralysis. It became very clear that he did not have any significant relationships, intimate friends, or social contacts on which he could count. His acerbic personality discouraged all caregivers from establishing an intimate relationship. He indicated that his personality had always been vitriolic, even before the accident. In this case, the history of the person was important, as that knowledge was used to ascertain his adaptation and coping mechanisms for dealing with disability.

When pain accompanies a disability, the coping is even more difficult. A woman with mobility limitations accompanied with severe arthritis pain talked about how with every function and activity she plans, she has to think of how to minimize the pain. "There is not a moment in my life that my difficulty in walking and pain management is not at the forefront of my thinking."

In both of these examples, the spousal social roles have to be reevaluated and renegotiated, as the disability occurred after the relationship was established. In this sense, careful attention must be given to the unique impact of the medical components and the physical pain that accompany the physical disability as they will constantly challenge the ability of the individuals to readapt to the relationship.

Vulnerabilities and Risk Factors versus Resilience and Protective Factors

Children and adults suffering either from disabilities or impairments due to chronic illness will experience and endure, at some point in their lives, redefining psychological and social difficulties of a transient or permanent nature. These individuals, whether they are children or adults, will be vulnerable across disease and disability. The attuned social worker must identify and clarify the individual's degree of vulnerability. Level of vulnerability is a central determinant to understanding to what degree the stress imposed by the chronic illness and/or disability shapes that individual's experience of the self, the world of relationships, and the world in general, and thus the ability to interact and adapt. Only with this knowledge will the social worker be able to design and plan interventions that may buffer the forces exacerbating the vulnerability, thereby maximizing the individual's possibilities for adaptation.

Christ, Sormanti, and Francoeur (2001) identified the following seven risk factors:

1. demographic factors
2. illness and treatment experience
3. psychological symptoms
4. personal coping style

5. social support networks
6. illness appraisal and attributions
7. concurrent stresses (p. 133)

Naturally, the degree of vulnerability imposed by a chronic illness and/or disability will be heavily influenced by the degree of oppression experienced by the individual in the context of race, socioeconomics, and cultural group. For example, consider the contrast between an African American single mother from the inner city with a chronic illness or disability who has limited medical coverage and no other benefits, and a limited understanding of the interaction of systems and bureaucratic layers, and an educated Caucasian single mother from the suburbs who has private medical insurance and benefits and, because of her education, can advocate for herself and her family. Their level of access to benefits and medical care will differ profoundly. Compounding this, the stress of pursuit of care and the weight of disappointment increase the vulnerability index.

Age is another important factor in defining vulnerability. Each developmental stage carries its own challenges that will demand a reorganization of overall adaptive capacities. A child in latency age may not possess the cognitive and emotional abilities to comprehend, cope with, and adapt to disability and/or chronic illness and may have difficulties in the restructuring of his relational world without the benefit of life experience. The child may have difficulty seeing himself or herself as a person with a disability and instead may see himself or herself as intrinsically flawed. A mature person, who may have the cognitive and emotional equipment to understand and process the experience and re-adapt, may be more vulnerable to the vicissitudes of humiliation and shame because of age. Imagine having to depend on a spouse, family, friends, or coworkers for mobility and for assistance with bodily needs. Not infrequently this leads to withdrawal and isolation. Also, if an individual who has been responsible for supporting or caring for others has his or her independent and autonomous functioning challenged temporarily or chronically, the degree of vulnerability is influenced by the loss of competence and responsibility (letting others down). When self-identity and social identity are insecure or diminished, vulnerability and risk escalate.

As well, it is important that the social worker factors into the assessment of vulnerability and risk the following: the powerful dynamics generated by the interaction of critical physiological and medical treatment dimensions, the personal and societal stigma attached to the particular chronic illness and/or disability, the attitudes and responses of the individual's family and social systems (such as friends and coworkers), the individual's capacity to adapt to the reality imposed by the condition, and, because we tend to identify self with the body, the impact of the degree of visibility of the disability or chronic illness. All these considerations combined create a synergy that challenges the individual's ability to use and/or develop the inner strengths necessary to constantly change and re-adapt as conditions change or deepen. The intensity and number of risk and vulnerabilities factors will also impact and challenge the family system to adapt and cope. The evaluation of these by the social worker will enable the most effective educational and supportive interventions and advocacy.

The assessment of risk factors and vulnerabilities in disability and chronic illness is only half of the equation. The other half of the human equation contains the potent forces of resilience and protective factors. Every case the social worker encounters will have risk factors and vulnerabilities intermingled with the threads of resilience and protective factors. These are the critical ingredients that social workers must identify, assess, and nurture.

The *Random House Dictionary of the English Language* (1967) defines *resilience* as; "1. The power or ability to return to the original form, position, etc., after being bent, compressed, or stretched; elasticity. 2. Ability to recover readily from illness, depression, adversity, or the like" (p. 1220). Resilience, or *strength* in the social worker's language, is the energy generated by an individual who has unique physical, psychological, and emotional qualities and/or abilities. Among these are: intelligence; creative capacity for problem solving; ability to form strong and stable attachments, so others will be interested in his state of being; ability to compensate for organic and/or perceived inferiority; ability to reframe disability/chronic illness situations in positive and meaningful ways; defensive and coping skills; personal energy and temperament to engage outside resources and mobilize them for the sake of ego integrity and physical well being. Bleiberg (2001), in discussing attachment and personality development in children and the role of resilience, states, "it is a capacity that evolves over time, within the total context of biological and environmental influences affecting children's development. As Sroufe (1997) points out, 'The capacities for staying organized in the face of challenge, for active coping and for maintaining positive expectations during periods of stress are evolved by the person in interactions with the environment across successive periods of adaptation (p. 256).' This capacity for resilience does not remain static but is continuously influenced by changes in the context" (pp. 19–20). The "changes in the context" Bleiberg mentions are the *protective factors*. These are any factors that may enhance and facilitate the individual's adaptation. They range from the possession of positive genetic strength, to having a cohesive, strong family of origin system, to belonging to a caring community; from having access to efficient and adequate medical care to having financial resources; from having a strong spiritual practice to belonging to an involved religious congregation. These are just a few examples of protective factors that, along with resilience, create the opportunity to overcome some of the oppressive conditions that anyone with disability/chronic illness will face.

Christ, Sormanti, and Francoeur (2001) agree: they identified as essential protective factors for the individual with disability and or with a chronic illness the ability to cope with the situation, to keep in mind the limitations imposed by the new reality and couple it with a perspective that reframes it as a challenge, and the sense of belonging to a substantial social support structure (p. 136).

A compelling case of resilience and protective factors is best illustrated by the story of Christopher Reeve, the actor best known for his starring performances in the *Superman* films. In 1995, after being thrown from his horse, he suffered a spinal cord injury that left him completely paralyzed and totally dependent on others. Determined to walk again, he endured months of intensive and invasive procedures oriented toward his gradually achieving minimal levels of independence, including surgery to enable him to breathe without a respirator. This was achieved by implanting electrodes in his diaphragm. He then underwent electrical shock therapy to open new neurological pathways. He endured intensive and exhausting exercise therapy that first led to the possibility of moving one finger. During the initial stage of his recovery, Reeve stated that he had contemplated suicide, but he was able to overcome those thoughts and feelings by "seeing the faces of my wife and family" (Martin, 2004) and, as well, by thinking of others in his situation.

Continuing on the political path he had begun before the accident, Reeve became one of the strongest proponents and lobbyists for insurance reform for catastrophic injuries and took stands on other public health issues; he voiced his support for embryonic stem-cell research; he founded the Christopher Reeve Paralysis Foundation, raising millions of dollars for spinal cord research; he gave hope to and instilled courage in those struggling with and treating spinal cord injuries (Martin, 2004). He also continued creating: he wrote two books and directed and performed in movies. Thus Christopher Reeve, the *Superman* actor, became Christopher Reeve, the real superman, by working for independence and advocating for those who didn't have a voice. He had the resources to simply tend to his own needs and stay in a self-centered comfort zone, but his resilience led him instead onto the path of altruism. Reeve died in August 2004, but his legacy continues.

It must be emphasized that concern for others and the individual's creativity play key roles in terms of protective factors. There are psychological theories that purport that our mental health is best measured by our concern and caring for others. In religious and spiritual realms concern for our fellow beings is considered essential. The origin and nature of creativity is beyond the boundaries of this discussion, but, briefly, creativity is the ability to use the imagination to develop and actualize new and original ideas and contemplate unusual outcomes. The following vignette, in its contained prose that cries to burst forth in outrage at injustice and man's inhumanity to man, will demonstrate the role of resilient creativity that can come only from the humanizing power of restraint.

"My mother, Little Seyyedeh, was not only a hero, she was endowed with an intelligence bordering on genius. As she used to say, measles did not destroy all her hearing nerves at once; it gave her leave to perfect her speech and vocabulary. During school days, her hearing diminished gradually. 'My classmates did not like to play with me because they did not have the patience to speak loudly enough so that I could understand.' Therefore Little Seyyedeh began to teach herself lip-reading. 'At nights, I used to lower the flame in the oil-burning lamp and watch my own shadow on the wall. Then I repeated words and letters and watched the shape of my own lips. That's how I taught myself lip reading.'

"The most important characteristic of my mother was accepting the reality, and she was proud of this acceptance. During her life, she never complained about her lack of hearing. Even when I was seven years old and she went to a famous specialist in Paris with my grandfather and came back disappointed—as my father had predicted—she never complained. 'If I have one regret about my lack of hearing, it would be the fact that I cannot hear your laughter.' That was it. Her dignified nature had made her a perfect example of contentment" (Kowssar, 2004).

This too-brief exploration of resilience and protective factors versus vulnerabilities and risk factors reminds us of Marc Antony's speech to the crowd after the murder of Julius Caesar: "If you have tears, prepare to shed them now."

Person-in-Environment Assessment

The person-in-environment classification system (Karls & Wandrei, 1994) helps the practitioner to identify and describe the areas of social functioning (Factor I) and the nature of the problems in the environment (Factor II) our clients need to understand and address. It also helps the practitioner in planning the range of intervention that may help to alleviate these problems.

Now, let's take a closer look at the case of the young woman with the genetically elongated and dislocated jaw and the case of the man who became quadriplegic when he was thirty-six years old. These are short vignettes, but they give a snapshot of these clients' difficulties in major areas of social functioning (Factor I). Although the woman had early onset and the man later onset, their interpersonal problems and the way in which these interfered with their coping and adaptation to the environment were similar. Both functioned and experienced their interpersonal role of friend as powerless and ambivalent. It seemed that both did not have reciprocal and fulfilling relationships, did not have friends, and were unable to consider having a more intimate relationship with a sexual partner. Their isolation from any social resources is not a surprise. While the woman felt victimized, blaming the whole failure of her social disability on the discrimination and oppression she experienced, the man was able to admit that he always had a bitter personality. This man's insight is a point of strength that might help the social worker in defining the course of intervention. The woman's strength is that she was able to maximize her adaptation to her occupational roles.

When using PIE in the assessment of individuals with physical disabilities, the practitioner will notice that usually the problems in areas of social role functioning and performance will be centered around the same type of problems: loss of power, ambivalence, dependency, loss, isolation, and victimization as a natural consequence of the socially imposed disability, the disability itself, and the individual's perception of his disability. In other words, social roles emerge from and are sustained by the dynamic interaction of the social system, which is moved by the cultural values and expectations, the level of oppression and discrimination, and other larger social forces. However, an understanding of strengths, inner resources, and those other resources that can be activated by the social worker is of paramount importance.

Case Study

Ms. S. is the forty-five-year-old woman with an advanced stage of Parkinson's disease (a progressive neuromuscular disorder), introduced at the beginning of the discussion of late onset. The onset of this disease, which changed her life, took place at the age of thirty-five. By the age of fifty-five, she could not perform her traditional roles, including that of grandmother. Gradually, she grew apart from her son and from her husband, losing her feeling of closeness to them. As a natural consequence of her illness, she needed assistance to take care of herself, thus becoming more and more dependent on them. The husband had accepted early retirement with the idea that he could spend more time taking care of his wife. The illness affected her intimate connection with her husband and, in spite of their loving relationship, they had to sleep in separate bedrooms. Her son felt guilty and responsible for his mother and relating to her grew very difficult and conflictive. Ms. S. had a network of friends with whom she had a rich cultural life. Prior to her illness, they went to concerts, theaters, and movies together. Ms. S. felt like a burden to her friends, too. Their demonstration of love and support encouraged her to keep connected to them; yet, she found this challenging and painful. Because Ms. S. could not work anymore, their economic situation deteriorated, and she and her husband had to sell their house and move in with their son. Ms. S.'s medical insurance denied her services and she didn't know how to activate Social Security.

At the age of forty-five, Ms. S. commented:

> Before, I used to love to cook. I enjoyed being a housekeeper. I took care of my grandchildren, now I can't do any of the household work. The other day I tried to dust the house and I fell down three times. . . . When I start shaking violently my grandchildren get frightened of me. What upsets me the most is that I have to become nobody. My children relate to me as a burden and perceive me as a responsibility. My friends try to be nice, but I have nothing in common with them. I cannot participate in activities with them. I do not want to burden them with my medical problems. So, slowly I have moved away from them. . . . I do not bring in an income anymore, and I need personal assistance for everything. I am afraid of what is coming next.

Ms. S. needs to be supported in mourning the loss of her physical functions and her identity. She needs help in accepting the reality of her condition. Working through the process of loss will help her to appreciate her other strengths, including her intellectual, emotional, and social abilities and skills. Becoming aware of them will help Ms. S. to redefine her sense of self, her identity, and her relationships, empowering her to function at a higher level.

The Social Worker's Role

The social worker needs to accept and understand the implications of the functional disability while knowing that the individual himself is not disabled. She has to help the client to use his abilities to minimize the subjective implications that the self is disabled. The challenge for the worker in her role of helper will be to support the client to become realistic about his disability while maintaining empathetic understanding of the disability. In situations where the client uses denial as an adaptation, it is important not to reinforce that denial and not to push the client before he is ready to accept his condition. The client needs help in separating the functional disability from the socially imposed and subjective disability. As one client put it, "My leg is amputated, but my brain is not." This does not mean, however, that society at large does not view the person in terms of his disability.

As we have seen, society often does devalue the individual by equating him with his disability. But the meaning of the disability to the individual can decrease the impact of oppression. Typically, cultural icons of the disability are connected to the absence of the disability. When Franklin D. Roosevelt was confined to a wheelchair, no photographs or film footage indicating his disability were shown publicly. His wheelchair was seen as a symbol of weakness. The media protected the president from negative images by making them absent rather than by proving them to be untrue. Similarly, when President Clinton injured his knee in 1996, he was advised to limit his public appearances in his wheelchair. Yet, President Clinton, throughout his recovery, continued working and appearing in public, showing that strength, dignity, and productivity are parts of individuals with physical disabilities (Stanglin, 1997). Thus the task for the social worker is to assist the client in transforming the negative, stigmatized identity into a positive, affirming one.

The role of the social worker in practice with an individual with physical disabilities is to help to identify her inner resources and understand her position in the family and in the environment.

PIE Assessment of Ms. S.

PIE Analysis	Intervention`
Factor I: Social Role Problems	
Family Role	
1120.424 Parent role	Family therapy
(ambivalent type, high severity, one to five years, somewhat inadequate coping skills)	
1210.525 Spouse role (power type, very high severity, one to five years, somewhat inadequate coping skills)	Couples therapy
Other Interpersonal Roles	
2260.424 Friend role (isolation type, high severity, one to five years, somewhat inadequate coping skills)	Support group
2530.424 Grandparent role (responsibility type, high severity, one to five years, somewhat inadequate coping skills)	Support group
Occupational Role	
3250.624 Worker role (loss type, catastrophic, high severity, one to five years, somewhat inadequate coping skills)	Support group
Factor II: Environmental Problems	
5404.42 Economic resources (Social Security assistance delayed, insurance policy problems, high severity, one to five years)	Referral to human services agency for case management and legal aid
5501.43 Transportation (inadequate special services in the community, high severity, six months to one year)	Referral to multiservice specialized clinic for people with neuromuscular disorders
8109.63 Health/Mental health (health insurance was terminated, catastrophic, six months to one year)	Referral to multiservice specialized clinic for people with neuromuscular disorders
8304.63 Social services (lack of adequate education about patients' rights, catastrophic, six month to one year)	Referral to legal aid Referral for personal care services
Factor III: Mental Health Problems	
Dysthymic Disorder, late onset	
Factor IV: Physical Problems	
Parkinson's disease	

The worker needs to be up-to-date and well-informed about the resources and modern technology that are available and help the individual function at a higher level. As well, he should also be knowledgeable about the legal rights, and about local, state, and federal government resources that are available to individuals with disabilities so that the client can be connected with the appropriate social action and self-help groups.

In essence, the goal of social work intervention is to utilize the "strength perspective" and to help the client to move from an oppressed state to that of a capable and resourceful individual with disabilities (Saleebey, 1997).

Intervention

In the life of a person with disabilities, rights can become powerful forces shaping experiences and opportunities without legal action. Rights can affirm one's identity as a capable person, they can transform everyday life by conforming legal perceptions, and they can change conceptual categories used to refer to individuals. Social workers need to be aware of the rights of individuals with disabilities. They need to familiarize themselves with the ADA and its enforcement provisions. A social worker needs to be an educator who will inform the client of his legal rights, not in order to take legal action necessarily, but so that the client can discern the internal and external ways in which rights become active throughout life. The goal of the ADA is to provide equal opportunity; it is not a warranty of success. A disabled person's willingness to accept and assert these rights is dependent on personal factors, not on the law.

Conclusion

Individuals with physical disabilities face physical, psychological, and sociocultural challenges of the most daunting kinds. They are constantly in front of a mirror that reflects back to them an image that seems to show them as lacking in a way that is obvious to the world. In order to integrate them into society for their benefit, for their family's benefit, and for the good of society as well, we need practitioners who are in possession of an inner understanding and all the skills of the profession.

The practitioner who works with individuals with physical disabilities needs to have sound knowledge of social worker values, theory, and legal rights for the disabled (ADA). Only when supported by these can his skills for practice help the client to maximize his potential, to improve his psychosocial and interpersonal functioning (specifically, his social role functioning), and to develop a positive self-identity. Also, the social worker must understand the meaning of the disability for the individual's culture; having that understanding will illuminate the individual client and his family's understanding of the meaning of the disability and the way they have experienced it.

Thorough assessment should address if the disability had an early or later onset and should include an understanding of the reality of the functional disability versus the familial and cultural oppression that may be superimposed on the disability.

The PIE model for assessment will help the social worker to define with clarity those aspects of the client's social functioning that need work and those areas of her relationships with the environment that need to be addressed. Further, PIE will help the practitioner identify obstacles and locate the environmental resources that will allow empowerment, not only of the individual, but also of the environment.

Finally, intervention with individuals with disabilities is multidimensional, but its first and most important dimension is the sociopolitical (Goldstein, 1995). The task for the social worker then is to become an advocate for legal rights and an educator for the individual with physical disabilities and for his community. Assuming this challenging responsibility will enhance the visibility of persons with disabilities in the sociocultural and political arena and ensure the permanent transformation of the environment. The strength of a society is in its entire people and their ability to function in their social roles to the fullest of their potential.

References

ADA, The Americans with Disability Act: A guide for Connecticut business employing and accommodating people with disabilities, focusing on Title I and III of the Americans with Disability Act of 1990. Resource Guide Development Committee.

The Americans with Disability Act, (1991). Equal Opportunity Committee.

Allport, G. (1958). *The nature of prejudice.* Garden City, NY: Doubleday.

Asch, A., & Mudrick, N. (1995). Disability. In *Encyclopedia of Social Work* (19th ed.). Washington, DC: NASW.

Berube, M. (1997). The cultural representations of people with disabilities affect us all. *The Chronicle of Higher Education. 5,* B4–B5.

Black, R. (1992). Diversity and populations-at-risk: People with disabilities. In F. Ramer (Ed.), *The foundation of social work knowledge.* New York: Columbia University Press.

Bleiberg, E. (2001). *Treating personality disorders in children and adolescents: Relational approach.* New York: The Guilford Press.

Bock, G. (1983). Nazism and sexism in Nazi Germany: Motherhood, compulsory sterilization, and the stage. *Signs: Journal of Women and Culture and Society, 8,* 207–294.

Bulhan, H. (1985). *Frantz Fanon and the psychology of oppression.* New York: Plenum Publishing.

Charlton, J. (1994). The disability rights movement and the left. *Monthly Review: An Independent Magazine, 46*(7/10), 77–86.

Chenowith, L. (1996). Violence and women with disabilities. *Violence Against Women, 2*(93), 391–422.

Christ, G., Sormanati, M., and Francoeur, R. (2001). Chronic physical illness and disability. In A. Gitterman (Ed.), *Handbook of social work practice with vulnerable and resilient populations.* New York: Columbia University Press.

Di Nitto, D. (1995). *Social welfare: Politics and public policy* (4th ed.). Boston: Allyn & Bacon.

Editorial. (1996). People with disabilities and social work: Historical and contemporary issues. *Social Work, 41*(1), 7–15.

Engel, D., & Frank, M. (1996). Rights and remembrance and the reconciliation of difference. *Law and Society Review, 30,* 7–54.

Goffman, E. (1963). *Stigma: Notes on the management of spoiled identity.* Garden City, NJ: Prentice-Hall.

Golan, N. (1978). *Treatment in crisis situations.* New York: Free Press.

Goldstein, E. (1995). *Ego psychology and social work practice* (2nd ed.). New York: Free Press.

Greene, G., Jensen, C., & Harper Jones, D. (1996). *A constructivistic perspective on clinical social work for social functioning problems.* Washington, DC: National Association of Social Workers Press.

Karls, J. M., & Wandrei, K. E. (1994). *Person-in-environment system: The PIE classification system for social functioning problems.* Washington, DC: NASW Press.

Le Maistre, J. (1995). *After the diagnosis: From crisis to personal renewal for patients with chronic illness.* Berkeley, California: Ulysses Press.

Lewis, K. (1992). *Shame: The exposed self.* New York: Free Press.

Livneh, H., & Antonak, R. (1997). *Psychological adaptation to chronic illness and disability.* Frederick, Maryland: Aspen.

Martin, D. (2004, October 13). Christopher Reeve, 52, symbol of courage, dies. *The New York Times,* A1.

Martinelly, R., & Dell Orto, A. (1999). *The psychological and social impact of disability* (4th ed.). New York: Springer Publishing.

Saleebey, D. (Ed.). (1997). *The strengths perspective in social work practice.* New York: Longman.

Social Work Magazine. (1996). People with disabilities and social work: Historical and contemporary issues. *Social Work Magazine, 41*(1), 7–15.

Sroufe, A. L. (1997). *Emotional development: The organization of emotional life in the early years.* Cambridge, MA: Studies in Social and Emotional Development.

Stanglin, D. (1997). Setting an example. *U.S. News & World Report, 122*(13), 22.

Wells, S. (1998). *A delicate balance: Living successfully with chronic illness.* New York: Plenum Press.

12

Religious Bigotry and Religious Minorities

Constance L. Mindell

One day while driving to work, I was listening to a talk-show hostess interviewing a photographer who had just published a book on ballet dancers. The photographer, when asked how she was able to capture the dancers' exact moment of perfection, responded that she had learned to "breathe their breath." This, she explained, was what the dancers said was an important, vital part of their learning to dance together—to breathe each other's breath, to become one with the other and yet retain their individual selves. This, I mused, was what we, as social workers, need to learn to do as we work with our clients. We need to be able to become one with them, to understand as much as possible what has created them, what has formed them, what has produced this individual who sits before us. We need to join them in order to understand their past and present experiences and influencing forces but still maintain our individual professional selves. One of those experiences that continually influences and forms an individual is religion. This chapter will focus on those whose religion is different from the dominant groups and address how social workers can develop a greater sensitivity and understanding of those whose religion differs from theirs. Perhaps then it will be easier to "breathe the breath" of those who are different from us.

Religion is becoming mainstream—social workers are now realizing that social work is not the only "belief system" to be used in working with clients, but that clients' religious and spiritual beliefs play an integral role in their lives. Religion provides a framework in which to cope with adversity; it provides roots, a sense of identity, and a sense of belonging. The Council on Social Work Education (CSWE) "revised its curriculum policy statement in 1995 to say that spirituality should be addressed along with other kinds of diversity in education" (*NASW NEWS,* Sept. 1999, p. 3). It behooves social workers to be aware of the religious beliefs and language of their clients and to incorporate that understanding into assessment and intervention. This chapter will provide a framework for understanding the impact of historical, cultural, and individual experiences on religious groups and how that influences their interactions with the dominant culture. Such factors are necessary parts of the assessment process, as is "collecting and ordering relevant information that can produce a comprehensive assessment of a client's problems in social functioning" (Karls & Wandrei, 1994, p. 3). To fully understand the person, one must take into consideration the entire system and how each part of that system contributes to the functioning of the whole. This concept is an important component of the person-in-environment (PIE) classification system, and although religion is not specifically addressed, without an understanding of the meaning of religion in the life of the client, we will not be able to understand that "whole." Religion is now "relevant information" that is beginning to be brought out of the closet. To work well with clients, clinicians need to remember that it is necessary to be aware of not only clients' religions but also their own religious and spiritual beliefs and their own biases. Also, it is necessary to have a familiarity with different belief systems and practices. One should remember that for some, their religion is no religion—this too needs to be understood and respected.

Religious Minorities

The literature on cultural diversity has focused on differences in sexual orientation, race, and gender. Religious differences as a diversity have received far less attention and have not been addressed as fully as other areas. If one is to start where the client is, a basic premise of social work, and to understand the world from the clients' perspectives, then the assessments need to be expanded to include religion. The understanding of the clients' worlds needs to be consciously extended to include those who are of the religious minority—those who are not part of the religious majority and the religious establishment, no matter how integrated they seem to be. Clients must be asked about their religious beliefs, how they think others see their religion, what their experiences as a minority have been like, and how they adjust within a world that can be hostile to them because of their religion. This leads to the question of how clients see the world as well as how they see themselves. Growing up in a culture that stereotypes and maintains myths and discriminatory behavior that perpetuate the stereotype and marginalization of the minority religious group cannot help but impact on the behavior and functioning of the members of that group. How one functions in the outside world, the roles that are taken on in work, school, shops, and all facets of life, can differ greatly from the roles executed in the security of one's own group. One is not judged with such harshness and misunderstanding as one is in the dominant culture. The social worker should be able to appreciate the defenses that marginalized clients use in their interactions with those of the majority—they have been socialized to be apprehensive and to be excluded and, thus, can exclude others from their lives. Can we change society to allow for the appreciation of religious differences, even if one does not agree with those beliefs? I question if we can bring about such a major metamorphosis; however, through corrective emotional experiences with the professional, through education of others and ourselves, and by confronting injustices in systems, we can be part of a slow but continual movement toward acceptance of religious differences.

For clinicians to execute a complete and pertinent assessment, religion cannot be an afterthought. Religious oppression has been an ingredient in how clients see the world, themselves, others, and their future. Religion provides a framework for living within that world, which can be hostile, helps to make meaning out of adversity, and represents a path to finding comfort when hurt. Social workers, who historically have worked with those who have suffered painful experiences, must recognize religious bigotry as yet another adversity experienced by clients. The chapter will provide guidelines for understanding the importance of religion in assessing, understanding, and working with our clients. To accomplish such tasks successfully, social workers must understand the impact and influence of their own religious beliefs on how they respond to the world and to others. Such understanding, such conscious use of self, will allow them to appreciate and to understand the influence of religious oppression in how clients see and respond to the world and the dominant culture. The history of social work has been one of working with oppressed populations—and the religiously oppressed are part of that history.

This chapter puts forth a view of diversity that includes an often forgotten group—the religious minority. It is meant to be a starting point from which you can do further research and develop fuller understanding of different religions and the impact that the majority culture has on the marginalized. The chapter provides a framework for assessing clients whose religious belief systems differ from what is practiced in the main culture. It looks at the experience with religious bigotry in defining how clients respond to and interact in the world, how their role in the larger society is often modified by being the outsider, and the importance of the role of historical, community, and individual experiences in helping to shape each individual's interactions with that larger society. The use of person-in-environment assessment tools will be discussed as a vehicle for further refining the assessment process in working with religious minorities. And finally, this chapter hopes to instill in you the importance of acknowledging your own prejudices and how such bigotry influences how you assess and work with clients. By being open to the client's historical and life religious experiences, the social worker will be able to enter into the world of the client and develop a therapeutic relationship truly based on respect and appreciation of those differences. Perhaps then we can help the client to bring order out of memory—to begin to see and appreciate the world, or expanded parts of the world, as safer and kinder than the remembered past and what those past experiences had offered.

The Role of Religion

Diversity has become a word that those in the majority use to identify others as being different. *Diversity* has become a label that is applied to populations who have observable differences, such as skin color or physical limitations, and not to those whose differences are not outwardly visual, such as the religious minority or those with certain chronic medical conditions. It is important for the social worker to be keenly aware of those differences that are not seen, the hidden parts of the client's being that have separated him or her, or make the individual feel separated, from the majority. Unfortunately, religion often becomes a subtopic, is ignored or addressed in a superficial manner, and is not fully incorporated into the social worker's assessment or the intervention plan. Slowly, social work has acknowledged that religion is an important component of the assessment process and that the client's religion, one of the hidden differences, must be acknowledged and understood in order to work with the complete person. It is vital to acknowledge that the religion and the religious group of the client continue to influence the client's view on life and how the community and the world is perceived. To work with the complete person, the social worker must appreciate that the religious upbringing and the religious community have a profound impact on the self-identity of those with whom they work. This must be consciously acknowledged as an important component of the individual and understood that those perceptions and experiences influence, if not mold, how that person sees and identifies him- or herself. Marty and Appleby (1997) identify religion as a vital component of the concept of self-identity. Religion is connected with "almost anything on the scene, for examples, the blessing of cannon, the development of institutions, the education of the young in the ways of war and peace, the nurturing of philosophies of tolerance and intolerance, or the customs of tribes" (p. 4). Religion helps make sense of group life and helps in the struggle with the difficult questions, such as "How do groups find and express their identity? What holds them together? What motivates the actions, including their internal and external conflicts? What happens when such an identity is blurred or its holders are made insecure by what is here designated as 'transition,' change occurring within the social forms they had known?" (pp. 4–5). Such questions underline the importance and the influence that religion has on the group, the individual, and the social and personal identity of the person.

Each religion creates a system of common understanding among its people that serves to bond them together and prescribe the manner in which the members interact with the larger society. An approach to understanding this interaction with the environment is that of structural-functionalism, which emphasizes the importance of social structure, the network of social relationships within a particular society (Crapo, 1993). How do social workers use this in assessing and working with clients of different religious beliefs than those of the majority? Each individual is formed and developed by the values, beliefs, customs, religion, and views of life as defined by the community in which she or he lives. Religion plays an important role in defining how people are expected to treat each other, how to conduct their lives, and how members are to fulfill their roles in the family, in the community, and in the larger society. Religion also defines restrictions regarding diet, sexual activity, clothing, and behavior that define, if not mandate, a moral life. Through the ideology of religion, the rituals, and the community involvement, people seek a sense of meaning beyond themselves and a sense of identity. By teaching the guidelines as to how life should be properly conducted and what values are important to hold, religion helps motivate people to follow the customs and the rules of the society in which they live. Religion provides an avenue by which people can cope with circumstances over which they have no control. When there are crises, or frightening situations, religion and prayer provide a source of strength for people and allow them to face such fears. When there is a loss, religion and the religious community console those who grieve. Religion is an integral part of the culture and the belief system that is transmitted through the family. The religious beliefs of the family are taught through their religious rituals, home conversations, the interactions with family, friends, and acquaintances, even the foods prepared and shared, and through the social and religious interactions with their houses of worship. The children are infused with and formed by their family's view of the world, which influences their views of them, and their views of others as they develop and mature within the family system. These views have also been formed by the collective history, the historical experiences of the religious group, and the experiences the family and the individual have had with others who are not of the same religion.

Beliefs and Customs

Religious beliefs are so varied that to present a single definition would be difficult if not impossible. Each culture has developed its own system of "symbolic beliefs and rituals that it uses to define its place in the universe" (Crapo, 1993, p. 244). Within each of these systems, however, there are characteristics common to all religions: (1) belief in supernatural beings and a view of the world supernaturally, not scientifically; (2) an organized system of shared beliefs; and (3) a system of rituals that humans use in order to gain control over themselves and their social and natural environment (Crapo, 1993). Religious rituals play an important role in emotionally uniting the religious community in that they bring people together as equals. In houses of worship, the structure and hierarchy of the prevailing and dominant society is forgotten, and all members of the group experience a sense of sister- and brotherhood. Regardless of socioeconomic position, there is opportunity for each member to partake in and lead parts of the service. Members do not feel nor are they seen as marginal members within their own religious community, a position often experienced when interacting with the dominant culture. The involvement in religious rituals allows the individual to feel a part of that specific society, to feel a sense of togetherness and unity with others who are welcoming, accepting, and understanding. Thus, there is a strong sense of belonging and a sense of identity.

People learn through their religion that they are members of a greater community and of the universe, and that there is a relationship between them and that community, that universe. The religion provides for its members guidelines of how to live, what values to cherish and abide by, and how to follow the customs important to their belief. Religion provides its followers with strength and support during difficult and fearful times and events. When there is a sense, or a reality, of no control over life events, religion provides a framework that allows for a sense of safety and reason. The repetition of rituals within a supporting and understanding environment, where others have or will experience similar events, allows for the reduction, if not the alleviation of anxiety and a growing sense of control. One needs only to look at the rituals surrounding death to understand the power and importance of religious rituals. What might not make sense to the practitioner makes perfect sense to the individual who is grieving in a way that was learned through and defined by his or her religion. The Hmong and Jews provide two examples of burial and grieving customs that are different than those of the dominant culture.

The Hmong are an ethnic minority from Southern China, Vietnam, Laos, Thailand, and Burma; approximately 120,000 Hmong refugees are now living in the United States. Ancestor worship, animism, and a strong belief in the spiritual world are integral parts of their religious belief and practices. Where there is a death, the deceased must be sent back to the spiritual world to be with his or her ancestors, and the family is responsible for giving appropriate and sufficient animal sacrifices that will ensure that these ancestors are well provided for in the afterlife (Irish, Lundquist, & Nelson, 1993). There are elaborate preparations and specific roles assigned to family and community members prior, during, and after the funeral. Proper food must be prepared, the coffin needs to be constructed according to custom, and relatives must appropriately dress the dead. In Southeast Asia, the funerals last for one week but the Hmong have had to modify this time commitment since they came to the United States. The funeral ceremony, often limited to four days, is held to honor the deceased. Relatives stay with the body for these days and nights, and prepare food for those who come to pay their respects. The meat for these meals comes from the animals sacrificed in honor of the deceased. Because funeral homes in the United States do not allow the killing of animals on their premises, creative measures have had to be developed to meet the religious requirements of the Hmong. One funeral home in Minnesota addressed this problem by tying a rope around the neck of a cow, the other end of which was tied around the wrist of the deceased. The cow was then led into the parking lot where the sacrifice was permitted to take place. The thirteen-day post-funeral activities and ceremonies following the burial ensure that the deceased's second soul stays in the body prior to the time when it is ready to join the world of his or her ancestors (Irish et al., 1993).

Judaism, regardless of denomination—Reform, Conservative, or Orthodox—has the overriding values of honoring the dead and comforting the mourners. Burial is usually within twenty-four hours after the death and the funeral service begins with the cutting of a garment or a black ribbon attached to the mourners, the immediate family of the deceased. This ritual is a visual representation of the individual being separated—cut away—from the loved one. The period of mourning at home after the burial lasts for one week. This ritual is called Shiva, the Hebrew word for seven. Friends, family, and neighbors visit the mourners in the home during Shiva, which provides the opportunity to share stories about the deceased, how his or her life touched others, and provide the bereaved a supportive environment to also share memories and to grieve. The first thirty days, referred to as Sheloshim, the Hebrew word for thirty, after the funeral is a time when the family might attend morning and evening services. Mourning ends after the first year, the anniversary of the death, when a tombstone is dedicated. At each anniversary of the death, the Yahzeit, the family lights a special twenty-four-hour memorial candle. Mourning is seen as a process that has stages and takes time. Rituals enable the living to remember the dead.

The religious customs that are practiced during the continuum of an individual's life allow one to cope with difficult happenings, experiences, and emotions, in a supportive, emotional "home" as she or he struggles to make sense out of events that seem to have no meaning. The manner in which the struggle is done, the emotions expressed, and how the community supports its members reflect the religious and cultural history of the group and help to define the identity of the members of the group. The individual is accepted and embraced by the religious community, and there is no sense of being marginal. Thus to identify with and work well with the client of different faiths, the social worker needs to understand that whole, that culture, that religion that has provided the framework for living in and understanding the world.

Person-in-Environment Assessment

Historically, social work has appreciated the impact of environment on the individual. Jane Addams (1860–1935), the founder of the first settlement house, Hull House in Chicago, addressed the intolerable living conditions of the poor and helped to change the tenet that poverty was the result of moral weakness. Mary Richmond (1861–1928) identified the effect of social relationships on the individual and his or her problems. The social diagnosis underlined the importance of studying the client's past and present social environment to understand the impact that system had on the individual's functioning. Gordon Hamilton (1892–1967) stressed the importance of focusing on both individuals and society and studying the interaction between the person and the situation. A cause-and-effect relationship was identified between the individual and his or her environment. Florence Hollis (1907–1987) recognized that efforts need to be directed toward bringing about environmental changes when the diagnosis indicates that such changes will enhance the psychosocial functioning of the client. The ecological approach, as stated in Germain and Gitterman (1996), continues the focus on the interactions between individuals and their environments and how these systems influence, impact upon, and change each other. Karls and Wandrei (1996), in their person-in-environment system, provide a "tool for collecting and ordering relevant information that can produce a comprehensive assessment of a client's problems in social functioning" (p. 3). This assessment includes and incorporates diversity. Social work prides itself in being aware and appreciative of the cultural expressions of clients and sensitive to their unique environments. If we expand the environment in person-in-environment to incorporate the environment that has been crafted by the individual's historical and personal experiences, a greater sensitivity to and knowledge about the client's coping style is developed. Also, the awareness and appreciation of what has formed the client will be enhanced. The PIE system refines the assessment process by incorporating four classes of information (Karls & Wandrei, 1996). It is not a diagnostic system, as it does not show a cause-and-effect relationship for the problems identified but "provides a tool for collecting and ordering relevant information" and a language to classify and codify the problems of adult clients (p. 3). The PIE system breaks down the clients' problems into four factors. Factor I has five categories. The first one, social role, is divided into family roles, those roles taken on in the family such as parent, spouse, child, sibling; other interpersonal roles involving interpersonal relationships with individuals outside the family, such as friend, neighbor, member role; occupational roles, paid or unpaid; and special life situation roles that are limited in time and specific to a certain situation, such as patient role, consumer role, immigrant role. The second category of Factor I looks at the kind of problems experienced by clients that are intersectional in nature. These difficulties are power, ambivalence, responsibility, dependency, loss, isolation, victimization, mixed, and other types. The remaining third, fourth, and fifth areas of Factor I were developed to help social workers determine if intervention is needed, how severe the impact of the problem is on the clients' functioning, and the extent of the impact of the problem. Three indexes were developed: the severity index, the duration index, and the coping index. Factor I provides a framework for assessing how clients function in their roles, in what role(s) they are experiencing difficulty, and with what interactional activities there is a problem.

Factor II of PIE looks at the problems clients have in regard to interpersonal relationships, specifically economic/basic needs system; educational/training system; judicial/legal system; health, safety, and social services system; voluntary association system; and affectional support system. Factor III looks at mental health problems, and Factor IV of PIE's classification system examines physical health problems.

The authors speak of social functioning problems, difficulties performing specific social roles, and realize that cultures differ in regard to how those roles are performed. PIE is sensitive to the importance of not defining roles according to the majority and considers the way that specific cultures define roles and influence how members of their group perform those roles. Each culture and religious group has its own ideology, values, and practices that reflect the beliefs of that group, and these beliefs influence role performance. The religious minorities' experience of being misunderstood and marginalized impacts on how occupational roles are played out. Jane Gross's article in the *New York Times* of September 16, 1999, titled "Young Orthodox Jews Blend Word and World," reflects how the reactions of the majority can influence the behavior of the religious minority. An Orthodox, observant, businessman decided not to wear his kepot (yarmulke, head cover) during work as "it makes me worry about looking like a stereotypic Jew who will do anything for a buck. I tell myself that I don't want to put nonreligious people in an uneasy situation" (p. B6). The man states that he wants to be "thoughtful" about the decision and hates to describe the decision of not wearing the kepot as a compromise. How can this be understood within the framework of PIE's occupational role and interactional difficulties? Although the individual might not be having difficulties performing his occupational role, there is a subtle role tension inherent in this example. The businessman is struggling with being true to the Orthodox tradition of either wearing a kepot, that would identify and label him as a "typical Jew" who is only "out for the money," or not wearing the kepot and "blending in" with and passing into the majority group. There is a role conflict that appears to exist between the role of businessman and the role of religious Orthodox Jew—between serving the business world and serving God. Marty and Appleby's (1997) questions regarding how groups find and express their identity, what holds them together, and what motivates actions are pertinent to this example. The religious identity of the businessman is blurred, and his role of Orthodox Jew/Orthodox Jewish businessman becomes changed because of the subtle, imperceptible, internalized pressures of the majority. The tensions inherent in such choices impact upon not only the occupational role but also interpersonal roles. If wearing a kepot is part of the group identity, an element that holds the group together, will the businessman experience difficulties in either his religious or worker role? Are there intersectional dynamics that the man is, or will be, experiencing? These questions are important to consider in the assessment and the intervention plan. Significant to PIE Factor I is the length of time that there has been a problem functioning in a specific role and how severe the specific role problem is to the individual's functioning. In working with individuals of different religions, their role performance might appear to be out of the norm. Without understanding why the individual functions the way he or she does, the importance of the behavior, and how that behavior reflects an entire culture, the social worker's assessment of the client and the problem will be weak, if not wrong.

Being culturally sensitive and aware and acknowledging how the specific community defines roles for its members is vital to working effectively with those outside the dominant culture. For example, the roles of women are subservient to men in the East Indian Hindu American population. The father in the family is the primary decision maker and is the spokesperson for the family. The mother, or wife, can provide input on family matters, but the final decision rests with the male. Wives do not answer questions when the husband is in the same room and avoid direct eye contact with men. PIE is sensitive to the importance of not defining roles according to the majority and considers the way that specific cultures define roles and influence how members of their group perform those roles. Each culture and religious group has its own ideology, values, and practices that reflect the beliefs of that group, and these beliefs influence role performance. Important to this concept is the length of time that there has been a problem functioning in a specific role and how severe the specific role problem is to the individual's functioning. In working with individuals of different religions, their role performance might appear to be out of the norm.

Members of the dominant culture can view the roles of children, especially the male, in the Hmong culture as inappropriate. That role is to learn how to conduct and perform many of the funeral ceremonies through study, observation, and participation in funeral rites. Through continual exposure to funerals, from childhood to adulthood, the Hmong learn the protocols for preburial, burial, and mourning periods. The social worker needs to assess with care such involvement with the dead and dying, so as not to label it as pathological. The importance of understanding one's own biases is clear in such an example. The behaviors of the Hmong could conflict with the social worker's view of what constitutes "normal," and thus the worker would not be open to the importance and meaning of the cultural and historical rites as performed by the members of this sect.

There needs to be an addition in the discussion of roles. Not all in any group adapt to or perform roles in the same way. Members of any group do not have the same level of exposure to ceremony, ritual tradition, and practices which impact upon learned behavior. One needs to take into consideration how the individual was socialized to take on roles, the extent to which the individual chooses to participate, and the ability to take on specific roles (Parry & Ryan, 1996). These subtleties of role adaptation are important to explore and appreciate in order to develop a comprehensive assessment of the individual.

The description of environmental problems focuses on the physical environment that impacts and affects the individual's social functioning and sense of well-being. There are six environmental problem areas outlined in PIE: (1) economic/basic needs system; (2) educational/training system; (3) judicial/legal system; (4) health, safety, and social services system; (5) voluntary association system; and (6) affectional support system. The religious minority, as members of a subgroup, has historically been excluded from a number of systems and has learned that the environment has not been receptive to their joining the majority, the ones in power. The movies *Gentleman's Agreement,* produced in the 1950s, and *School Ties,* a more recent film, describe how members of a religious minority are defined by the majority, how stereotyping separates, and how prejudice affects the functioning of the individual. The systems in the environment, and how those systems have interacted with someone from a religious minority, have helped to form the clients into who they are as well as their responses to systems and individuals with whom they interface and interact in the outside world.

PIE's presentation of environmental problem areas is pertinent in the discussion of religious discrimination. Access to each of these systems—economic; educational; judicial; health, safety, and social services; voluntary association; and affectional support—are necessary ingredients for healthy functioning. One must realize that there are barriers that prevent individuals from accessing such systems—barriers based not only on color, age, sex, and country of origin, but also religion. Social work appreciates the interaction of a person with his or her environment and the impact and influence that each has on shaping the other. When the social worker can identify discrimination in the social system or environment that prevents the individual from realizing his goal, she or he can determine if and when to develop an intervention plan. PIE's severity index, duration index, and coping index provide guidelines for such an assessment of the environmental problems. Although PIE provides tools for refining the classification of problems, it is, in this author's opinion, missing an important element—that of including the client as a participatory partner with the social worker in the assessment process. PIE places the responsibility for the assessment and problem classification on the practitioner, and the client does not have the input that is integral to the ecological model of Germain and Gitterman. If the assessment does not include the clients' thoughts and feelings regarding how their religious beliefs have impacted their lives, formed their reactions to others, necessitated the development of defenses, and provided them with strengths and a stronger sense of upholding their "safe" community, important and invaluable and inestimable information and insight will be missed.

Problems in the Health, Safety, and Social Services system focus on the absence of services to serve the needs of the community's residents. However, there are services available, but these are seen as marginal and have not been recognized or fully accepted by the main culture. The absence of service in such situations can be defined as that which incorporates the two, marginal and main, to allow integrated health services and still respect the religious integrity of the client. One can say there is a missing link that ties the marginal with the dominant culture. It is important to identify and support the practices of those with marginally religious beliefs and yet not ignore the strengths of the dominant culture that can be included in the plans for intervention. The Puerto Ricans who arrived in the United States in the late 1940s brought their religion (Catholicism, Protestantism, Pentecostalism) as well as their belief in *Espiritism* (spiritualism). They brought herbal folk medicine practices,

Botanicas (herbal stores), and the belief in the diagnostic and treatment skills of the *Espiritista,* who prepares prescriptions for potions that address illnesses or misfortunes (Lecca, Quevalu, Nunes, & Gonzales, 1998). Problems arise when the dominant culture ignores the beliefs of this group and does not work to integrate the belief systems of the Puerto Ricans with the health beliefs and health systems of the mainstream. Such integration has occurred as a result of Dr. Pedro Ruiz's efforts to develop a close working relationship between Lincoln Hospital Community Mental Health Center, where he is director, and the *Espiritistas* in the South Bronx in New York (Lecca, Quevalu, Nunes, & Gonzales, 1998). The acknowledgment of the important position and the role the *Espiritistas* have in the Puerto Rican community allows for the cooperation and the referral of individuals to the traditional health care services.

The strengths that individuals have and present must be incorporated into the assessment process. By identifying and focusing on strengths, social workers are less liable to "blame the victim" and, as DeJong and Miller (1995) state, discover "how clients have managed to survive even in the most inhospitable of circumstances" (p. 729). We need to discover how those who have experienced discrimination because of religious beliefs have survived and even thrived. Saleebey (1997) discusses the importance of community in developing hope, motivation, and optimism within the clients and workers. The religious community offers its members these things as well as a sense of belonging, importance, and direction—often what the larger community is unwilling or unable to provide because of stereotyping, discrimination, and maintaining power in the larger system. As Saleebey states, the community provides opportunity to participate in common practices, and a group that allows people to depend on each other, where members identify themselves as belonging to a greater whole, and where members are responsible for each other. The sense of belonging, being accepted, and not being marginalized fosters and nurtures the individual's sense of self. Religious communities provide this sense of belonging through the socialization of their members. The Hmong children and adults learn about and participate in ceremonies surrounding death and burial. There are religious rites of passage into adulthood as seen in Confirmation and Bar and Bat Mitzvahs ceremonies, or by men growing and wearing beards after marriage, as in the Amish community. The religious community provides inner and outer resources for its members that allow them to confront the larger society that may be hostile and prejudicial toward them. The internalization of the community and its values allows for the minority to bring his community with him into the world, to not feel so alone, and to allow for the development of resilience in coping with injustices. The community not only goes with the individual; the community represents the home to which the individual returns to become nurtured and validated. It is important for the clinicians to realize the role of that community in the lives of clients who are not part of the majority and realize that not all see and experience the world as they do. Religion provides a source from which to draw meaning and strength to face and cope with the vicissitudes of life. Religion provides, as Shulman (1999) states, a "'strengths-in-numbers' phenomenon (that works) to decrease (the) feelings of isolation and individual risk" (p. 312).

Compton and Galaway (1999), Wachtel (1993), Goldstein (1995), Saleebey (1997), DeJong and Miller (1995), and Shulman (1999) are but a few of the authors who recognize the importance of working with clients' strengths. The capacity to successfully deal with life, even after "prolonged experience of oppression that is used by the majority group to justify continued stereotyping and oppression" (Shulman, 1999, p. 80) reflects resiliency and strength and an ability to function well. In order to identify with and use the resiliency and strengths of the clients, it is necessary for the social workers to allow themselves to see the strengths of a client population whose religion they might misunderstand, be ignorant of, or have prejudices against. To recognize strengths, one must recognize the humanness of the clients and the tribulations they have experienced and through which they have lived—and understand, or at least try to understand, how such trials have impacted the individual, the family, and the religious community. Such an approach takes the social workers away from focusing on the pathology or disorder and allows the clinicians to recognize and build on the positives that the clients present as well as the strengths within the religious community. Saleebey reminds us that "no matter how subordinated, marginalized, and oppressed individuals and communities may appear, people, individually and collectively, can find nourishment for their hopes and dreams, tools for their realization somewhere" (p. 233). How privileged we are, as social workers, to be in the position to help clients identify the strengths that they possess in having dealt with the prejudices and antireligious encounters they and their families and communities have endured. To identify the strengths that clients use, what they have done, how they did it, and what was learned in the process of doing, and the resources that were used in that process, one needs only to listen to their stories.

Rybarczyk and Bellg (1997) discuss the use of narratives, having patients tell us the stories about their lives, in relation to helping them cope with the stresses of medical treatment. Such an approach to working with clients, the listening to life narratives, goes beyond the medical experience and allows the clinician the opportunity to learn about all unique life experiences. Stories will relate how clients have handled antireligious experiences, how being marginalized has affected their lives, and what was learned from such struggles. Further, the stories allow the social workers to see, and hopefully understand, how clients interface and interact with other systems, with other people, and why they act the way they do. Narratives provide the therapists with indicators of the positive aspects and the strengths of the clients' lives. It behooves the social workers to encourage the clients to share their stories if they want to experience, understand, and work with the total person. The storytelling allows clients to tell, and the social workers to listen, to the personal accounting of important events. Rybarczyk and Bellg comment that these stories convey not only the personal meanings of life events but also the cultural meanings as evident in the values, ideas, and feelings of the clients. Encouraging the telling of stories from the religious culture provides the therapist with a fuller understanding and appreciation of the moral values of the individual as well as the life experiences that have helped to form the clients. One needs to listen well to hear the meanings of these stories to better understand the clients' manner of coping and reacting to certain life events.

Social workers need to appreciate how the religious historical experiences have influenced the reactions of the clients. This does not only refer to the specific history of the religion, the prejudices suffered by the religious group through the centuries, but also the memories of prejudices felt and experienced and then recounted from grandparents to parents to children. The individual's history of prejudice and hurts are woven into the family's historical memory bank and can be culled out as the social workers encourage the telling of stories of what life was and is like as a religious outsider.

Historical Overview

The religious profile of the United States has been altered as a result of many factors: the increases in new immigrants who arrive in America with different belief systems, the spurring of new denominations, and marriages of partners of different faiths. The religious identities of individuals in today's world have become quite different from the colonial times when religion was more strictly defined and bounded by traditional guidelines. As professionals, we need to be able to understand and appreciate the differences and sub-tleties that are inherent in how people define their God, worship, and explicate their religious and spiritual selves. The historical, cultural, and individual history of the client that has helped shape the manner in which she or he defines and interacts with others must be appreciated in order to lead "the social worker to view the clients' responses in the context of their sociocultural circumstances . . . (and understand and be sensitive) to the totality of the life situation of the client group" (Norton, 1978, p. 3).

Religious Bigotry as Historic Context for Understanding Religion

The history of religion in this country is one that reflects an attitude of bigotry toward those who were identified as a subgroup to the dominant religion. This history has helped to shape the manner in which the minority group interacts with the dominant culture and how the majority defines those who have been marginalized because of their religious beliefs. Rabb (1964) discusses the colonial times, a time when Quakers were publicly whipped, branded, defaced, and hung. Deviant Protestant groups were oppressed and penalized by the various Protestant establishments, and anti-Catholic biases were normal behavior, although they represented only 1% of the U.S. population. The Protestant-Catholic antagonism of Europe was imported to the New World and was played out in daily life. In 1917, Catholics were excluded from public office in Rhode Island, which had been considered to be America's most tolerant colony. Catholics were hard-pressed to practice their religion freely. After the American Revolution, religious intolerance continued. "New Hampshire's laws were not granted to Baptists until 1804, granted to Catholics until 1902" (Rabb, 1964, p. 2).

The increasingly large number of immigrants in the 1880s came at a time of difficult economic adjustment for the country, culminating in the disastrous depression of 1893. Over five million immigrants entered the country during that decade, a large number being Catholic Irish, Catholic Italians, and Jews from Eastern Europe. As immigrants began to control big-city politics, the first Irish Catholic mayors were elected in Boston, New York, and other cities in the 1880s, working men began to resent these newcomers and their growing political power, and their folkways made them feel uneasy, especially because they were not Protestant. Anti-Catholic societies began to spring up and discrimination against Catholic workers and Catholic businessmen was common. There were even a number of anti-Catholic riots in the 1890s. Anti-Catholicism became focused on the individual Catholic, especially those of Italian and Irish descent, and not the Catholic church. Rabb (1964) comments that the anti-Catholicism of that day was the anti-Semitism of nineteenth-century America.

The Jewish population at the time of the American Revolution was less than 1%. This proportion increased with the immigration of Jews in the early nineteenth century and further increased with the large number of Eastern European Jews fleeing from the pogroms and from Hitler's holocaust in the twentieth century. Protestant nativism was directed toward these new foreigners, and the country's first serious anti-Jewish violence occurred in the last two decades of the nineteenth century. Stores were vandalized, houses were burned in the South and in New Jersey when Jews were hired, in 1891, and there were several days of rioting. The discrimination against Jews resembled that against the Catholics— based not so much on religious differences but on other aspects of their group identity. There were strong anti-urban, anti-industrial feelings prevalent among a certain part of the population, and the Jews became a target for those feelings. Other groups, the newly moneyed classes who expressed a sense of superiority, if not snobbery, looked down at the less powerful, moneyed group, and the new immigrants were part of that less fortunate group. There was growing political anti-Semitism evident among the old establishment, dismayed with the growing industrial urban commercialism, which was replacing the older, more comfortable American way of life to which they were accustomed and such an integral part. The visible Jewish merchant of the day represented the vulgar commercialism that the establishment found so offensive. Political and social discrimination against Jews became woven into the country's culture. It was common for Jews to be barred from living in specific neighborhoods; working in certain industries, such as banking and insurance; attending certain colleges and universities; and joining certain clubs. Restrictions that prevented Jews from attending certain universities and from staying at many hotels and resorts were prevalent. Such anti-Jewish gentlemen's agreements, which were oral agreements between parties not to allow, or strictly limit the number of Jews into positions or establishments, were prevalent and strictly adhered to until the civil rights movement in the 1960s. The author remembers the first question asked when applying for college entrance: "What is the quota?" (meaning how many Jews do they let in), the restricted country clubs and hotels, places that one knew should be avoided because one was not of the "right" religion, and neighborhoods in which one could and should never live.

As the Protestant-Catholic antagonism of Europe was imported to the New World during the early years of this country, the European ideology of anti-Semitism found its way to these shores during the 1920s and 1930s. The United States was struggling with economic unrest, and anti-Semitism became part of the ideological mainstream of the country. "There were no less than 150 organizations promoting anti-Semitism in America, drawing inspiration and often more from the evangelistic racism of Nazi Germany" (Rabb, 1964, p. 4).

The religious climate in the United States of the twenty-first century differs from that of the earlier years, yet the past discriminations and exclusions remain a part of the historical collective memory of each group. The policy of favoring mainstream Protestants of the early years has waned and discrimination against individual Catholics is hardly a topic of concern. We elected a Catholic president, the myths about a papal conspiracy are no longer considered seriously, and few question Catholic attitudes regarding the separation of church and state. There still remains, however, the folk law of anti–Semitism, that appears to be part of this culture, and the memory of the Holocaust is a profound and lasting part of the collective being of the Jewish people. The past experiences, memories, and troubled relationships continue to influence the manner in which the religious minorities view and interact with others.

The religious profile of the United States today is very different than what it was at the turn of the century. About 87% of Americans consider themselves Christians, and Catholics account for approximately 22% of the population. There has been a dramatic increase in the number of non-Christian denominations, which has changed the religious landscape of America. There are approximately 800,000 Hindus in the country, approximately 3.5 million Muslims, which is the same number as there are Presbyterians, and 750,000 Buddhists. The American Jewish population is about 5.5 million, or just over 2% of the total population, down from 3% because of intermarriages. There are approximately 1,600 religions and denominations in the United States, with about 800 founded since 1965, and churches with strong evangelism have flourished. Over the past 30 years, Southern Baptists have increased membership by 8%, Mormons, 96%, Jehovah's Witnesses, 119%, Assemblies of God, 211%, and Church of God in Christ, 863% (Shorto, 1997). There has been an increase of Pentecostalism since 1965, as well as the number of strictly Spanish Catholic parishes, Korean American churches, Chinese Protestant churches, mosques, and Hindu temples. Islam, although still a minority religion in the United States, has grown substantially. The surrounding community often equates Muslims with terrorists, leading to increased prejudice.

Kamya (1997) studied a sample of African immigrants in the United States to examine, as one purpose of the work, the role of religion in their lives. Religion plays an important role as a coping resource for this population and provides a sense of being grounded in a new land. Spiritual well-being and the role of religion provide meaning and organization to their lives.

It is evident that the religious profile of America has changed and continues to change. There is a new religious language upon the land—one that comes from and encompasses beliefs and customs very different from the dominant religious belief. We need to learn to understand, if not speak, this new language if we are to work well with our clients.

How do we incorporate this new religious language into our work with clients? Self-awareness and use of self, long an integral part of social work's tradition and belief, is a starting point for learning to work with all clients, which includes the often overlooked religiously diverse. The clients bring their history, individual experiences, and collective life issues into sessions. Social workers examine these issues and the relationships clients have with friends, spouses, parents, significant others, community, and friends. The daily travails of life, big and small, are reviewed, discussed, and addressed, and these problems that clients present often mirror similar issues with which the practitioner struggles. Because of the universality of life events, it is vital for social workers to be able to differentiate between their issues and those of their clients. Bisman (1994) discusses the concept of practitioner observation in relation to the need for social workers to be "conscious of their own feelings and reactions to clients and the problems clients present" (p. 209). Practitioner observation expands the examination process to incorporate the clinicians' observation of themselves and then to use such observations in the professional decision-making process as they interact with clients. Through practitioner observation, social workers are able to differentiate between their issues and those of the clients, their biases and those of the clients, and their prejudices and those of the clients. The clients' needs become the focus, not the social workers' needs. The importance of this concept cannot be underestimated if social workers are to practice with honesty. The definition Bisman (1994) provides clearly articulates the role that self-awareness has in developing the professional self and acknowledging one's own uniqueness. Practitioner observation is defined as

> . . . the self-examination and articulation by social workers of their personal reactions to clients and the intentional use of this awareness in practice decisions and behaviors. The self-awareness is attention to oneself; to one's thoughts, feelings, biases, and values; to one's ethnic, racial, and class background and religious traditions; to the totality of one's life experience. Feelings of wanting to relate with clients as if they are friends or family members are acknowledged. Distinctions are made between problems the social worker has experienced and those of the clients. Self-awareness is utilized and integrated with the profession's knowledge and skills in a professional use of self that is unique and responsive to each case situation. (p. 215)

Practitioners, when able and willing to appreciate their own biases, realize that they are as culture-bound as their clients. Their historical, individual, cultural, and social experiences have influenced and formed them as clearly as those experiences have impacted the clients. Crapo (1993) comments that the cultural traits of others are best understood within the context of the cultural system of which they are a part. There should be attempts to avoid the narrow bias of judging a custom, or entire culture, on the basis of one's own cultural values. If one is to understand well the meanings that behavior has, one needs to view that meaning in terms of the culture of those with whom one works. It is invalid to assess other cultures, and other religions, on the basis of the standards of the majority; each religion is best understood by its own standards, by its own meanings and values.

Religious teaching forms not only the worldview of the individual but the way in which individuals view relationships, marriage, sex, health, mental health, children, and all aspects of life and death. Asian Americans view mental illness as a stigma, and it might be close to impossible to convince one from this group to become involved in therapy. Attitudes toward children differ among cultures. Male children receive preferential treatment among Asian Americans, and Vietnamese parents are generally very permissive with their children in regard to feeding practices and toilet training. Among Native Americans children are highly valued and parents may seem permissive in regard to childrearing. It is also considered taboo to cut the child's hair. Food restrictions are part of certain denominations. Conservative and Orthodox Jews do not eat pork and shellfish, animals that do not chew their cud or do not have cloven hoofs, or meat not killed according to religious specifications. Fish must have fins and scales, and meat and dairy products cannot be eaten at the same meal. Muslims do not eat pork, and Hindus do not eat meat. These groups follow other diet restrictions, and the social worker should learn about these. There is importance to the rules and guidelines that religion dictates and teaches its members. If the social worker is unaware of such teachings, he or she will be at a loss to understand and appreciate the responses, the behaviors, and the beliefs of the client. The pieces that make up the whole will be lost.

An example of how the forming of a worldview can be developed is through the following interaction. Two brothers approached an eight-year-old boy, where all were on holiday at the beach. "My brother wants to tell you something," the older child said. There was no response from the younger boy, even after the urging of his older brother. Finally, the older boy stated, "My brother wants to tell you that you are a Kike." The child told his father about the incident, and he handled it. Not until years later did that child, now a man, realize the pain that such an interaction causes a parent. The parent could not protect the child from distasteful realities and had to prepare and arm the child to face and handle name-calling and prejudices throughout his life. The forming of a worldview for any member of a religious minority is crafted from such encounters. Understanding the interactions between those of the religious minority and their environment, and those who people the environment, is vital to understanding the client.

A young Jewish man shared with his mother that when in high school, in a suburban setting with a socioeconomically but a minimally racially diverse student population, he had experienced a number of occasions when students would throw pennies at him as he walked down the hall. In hearing this, the mother was aghast, and questioned her son why he had not told her and what he had done in response. He had not told her because he knew she would come to school and "tear the place down"; he had done nothing and lived through it. If a social worker heard this story from the mother, and in her narrative she expressed great anger, frustration, and pain, would that social worker understand the response or would the social worker consider the mother overreacting to a minor incident? In order to answer that question, the historical, individual, and social time-life experiences of the mother and her religious group must be understood. The issues involved in understanding and appreciating the reaction include the history of anti-Semitism; the stereotyping of Jews doing anything for money, even picking up pennies; the mother's experiences with slights and hurts through her childhood and perhaps adult years; the history of the religious group being marginalized in the community; as well as the inability of the parent to protect the child from the reality of pain and discrimination because of being different. All these factors influenced how the mother told her story and the emotions she felt and expressed as she told the story years later. In understanding the why, the social worker can then appreciate the normalcy of her response. Also, where are the strengths of the young man and the mother in coping with the event? How did such an event affect the young man, the parents, and the family? And should the young man and the mother trust a Christian therapist, or non-Jews? These are but some of the questions that the social workers must ponder if they are to join the clients with honesty, empathy, and openness.

There is another issue that is raised by this example regardless of the religion. How does the parent prepare the child to face prejudice? A role of parents is to protect the child and to provide tools for him or her to face the world well equipped to handle life; however, it is not possible to protect the child from the reality of prejudice. At what age does teaching the reality of prejudice begin, or does one wait for the hurt and confused child to return home? These are the difficult questions that must be addressed if the child is to grow with strength, maintain a positive sense of self, and not turn his or her back on the religion of the family and community. The answers are equally difficult. The child needs to receive the support and understanding that parents and family offer. Parents can teach and discuss with the child that she or he is not the only one who has been the recipient of an anti-religious remark or action and help the child learn coping skills to be used in future confrontations. Whatever the child learns in order to cope with prejudice, it is a painful journey—painful for the parents who were unable to protect their child and must teach him about being disliked or hated for no understandable reason, and painful for the child who comes to realize that the world is not always a safe place and that he is disliked or hated for no understandable reason.

A young Catholic girl sat in her new classroom in a Southern high school. The family had recently moved from the Northeast and she felt like an outsider. The teacher was talking, and she heard him refer to Catholics as "mackerel snappers" and the class laughed along with the teacher. The young girl did not laugh but withdrew and lost trust in the teacher and in her classmates. She realized she was the outsider and felt that she was not wanted, and her religion was disrespected. She did not trust the others. The historical discrimination against Catholics, the distrust that the religious majority had harbored against Catholics, and perhaps still harbor, and the individual and family experiences this young woman has encountered, allow for a deeper understanding as to why she would present as cautious, distrustful, and angry toward those of a different faith than her own.

A Catholic woman in her forties remembers what it was like growing up in a Protestant town. Her best friend was a Quaker, and her parents thought that there were armed Catholics who stood outside the church and harmed non-Catholics. Within her junior high school and high school there were very few Jews, who had to explain why they were not in school during Yom Kippur and Rosh Hashanah. She stated that in the Protestant culture of the town and school, no one talked about the Jews; they were marked as different, had no friends, and were totally out of the group. They were not even worth teasing. She, as a Catholic, was teased on Ash Wednesday and felt like a second-class citizen.

The clients' narratives reveal the hurts and the questions that the clients live with and bring to the sessions. The social workers must be able to ask clients if their religious faith is important to them and how it is woven into their value and belief system. In working with clients from minority religious groups, social workers must be prepared to understand that clients might not feel comfortable in working with them. Clients could wonder if it would be more work to explain to the social worker the history and the experiences associated with being religiously marginal; would the subtleties of language or behavior ever be truly understood, and would the social worker judge and stereotype such behavior or the language or the religion?

One cannot fully understand clients without exploring the little-examined issue of religious beliefs and experiences. The information gleaned from such explorations is important in the assessment process. According to Dziegielewski (1998), the issues involved with culture and race, and religion as well, should be addressed in an open manner in the assessment phase, which will allow for an open environment.

Dziegielewski outlines five considerations that would provide guidelines for the social worker in working with those who are different: "(a) the social worker needs to be aware of his or her own cultural limitations; (b) the health care social worker (and I must add, all social workers) needs to be open to cultural differences; (c) the social worker needs to recognize the integrity and the uniqueness of the client; (d) use the client's learning style including his or her own resources and supports; and (e) implement the biopsychosocial approach to practice from an integrated and as nonjudgmental a format as possible" (p. 213). The clinicians' responses and reactions to the clients' stories and experiences need to be accepting, nonjudgmental, and understanding. Focusing on the clients' strengths and helping clients incorporate them in their approach to addressing the presenting problem allows for the clients, as well as the social worker, to appreciate the resources and strengths that have been used to cope with other problems. However, to do so, social workers need to identify their own prejudices and feelings toward the religious minority. This needs to be remembered—we carry our own prejudices into the therapeutic sessions, and unless we are able and willing to recognize and address our own issues, we will not be able to work fully and effectively with those who come to us for help. If the helpers are part of the religious majority and/or have never experienced discrimination, they must have the courage not only to look into themselves but also to allow themselves to feel the history and the pain that the clients have had, and no doubt continue to have. Their religion has set them apart from the majority, and it is important that the social workers do not reinforce the clients' sense of being outsiders. The clients often test the social workers to determine if they too hold antireligious beliefs or attitudes. Weiss (1993) speaks of clients having corrective emotional experiences when the therapists are able to pass the unconscious, or conscious, test of the clients. In so passing, the clients are offered positive, accepting experiences and feedback that they are looking for by this testing. The client, as Weiss states, is "profoundly affected by his perception of how the therapist responds to his tests" (p. 66). When the social workers are able, and willing, to understand, appreciate, and validate the clients' experiences with prejudices they experienced throughout their lives, and respond in an accepting manner, the clients will begin to see the other, someone from the religious majority, in a different light. They then will begin to perceive that not all people from the majority religion are the same.

There are a number of ways that one can listen to the religious content of clients, and Goldberg (1994) defines three ways: (1) the metaphorical approach, when the "use of religious terminology is poetic, descriptive and evocative for the patient—and that is all" (p. 130); (2) the foundational approach, when the patient "is an adherent of a particular set of religious ideas . . . that gives grounding to the patient's life" (p. 131); and (3) the functional approach, "the thinking of the function of religion in the life of the patient" (p. 132). The metaphoric language used to describe one's religion and religious experiences provides, as Goldberg states, a path to the functional approach. This approach allows the social workers to look at the way the clients use their religion in their lives and the function that religion plays in their lives. She refers to William James (1902) who proposed that a functionalist or pragmatic view of religion be taken in order to understand how religion helps the individual adapt. Again, we need to be aware of how we do or do not interpret the functions of religion for the patients, as influenced by our own belief systems, or lack of them, and by our strong or ambiguous notions about the reality of a God. Goldberg states an important reality is that if we are reticent about interpreting the functions of religion to the patients, there is a "real possibility of short-changing the patient with regard to furthering her understanding of the way in which religious faith functions for her" (p. 133).

A woman, married and the mother of one, talks of her many car accidents, her anxiety, her face flushes, and her depressions. She is able to mention quickly and shyly the sexual abuse she had experienced by two relatives—one when she was nine and the other between the ages of twelve and fourteen. This then became the focus of the treatment sessions. She stated that she was religious, sent her son to a Christian school, and speaks to her pastor about the sexual abuse. Religion was important to her, as was her pastor, and this connection was supported and encouraged. She shared how her pastor had helped her: He had asked her to picture God at the times of the abuse, and she had stated that He had not been there. He then asked if you could see Him, what would His face look like? She answered, "Sad." "What would He do?" he asked. She responded that He would embrace her, say that she was not to blame, that He loved her.

The ambiance of support and acceptance of the therapeutic setting allowed the client to share this intimate story. She had been devastated by the loss of her connection to her God, but was still involved in the church and with educating her son in a Christian way. Her God, she had felt, had deserted her when she had been abused and the guilt associated with those acts had left her with a feeling that she was unworthy of God's love. Without the connection to God, the client did not feel whole. The minister, as well as I, passed the tests of the client—we did not agree with her definition of self as bad, guilty, and unworthy. The reconnection with God would allow her not to feel as though He had deserted her or judged her harshly or unworthy but would allow her to feel whole again. One must note that historically the clergy have supported the family institution at the expense of the abused. Women have been tutored to remain within relationships despite the physical, sexual, and/or emotional abuses suffered at the hands of the relatives. It is important that the clergy in this situation supported the woman and by working to address the violation with her, was able to help reconnect her to her God and to her religion.

Although I am not an expert in religious matters, I was able to understand the meaning and the importance of the client's reconnecting with her God. This reuniting with God, returning to a strong faith, allowed the client to forgive herself, to feel worthy, to feel loved, and to find meaning in her experiences. The client's relationship to God was understood on a functional basis.

Conclusion

Religion has been mostly an overlooked theme when discussing diversity. It should not be for social workers because religion plays an important role in developing an individual's self-identity as he or she responds to the questions "Who am I? What do or should I do? To whom do I belong? How shall I act? Whom shall I trust? How should I describe myself? How am I empowered?" (Marty & Appleby, 1997, p. 6).

Religion gives meaning to life, provides a sense of belonging, and connects the individual to a greater community in which she or he has worth. The stories clients tell about their experiences living as religiously marginalized by the majority and how they face and cope with prejudices is a testimony to their strengths. The history of the religion provides understanding of the community, the people, the family, and the individual and why they behave as they do. As religious diversity in the United States increases, the social workers must be prepared to work with people with different beliefs from their own. It is impossible to know the beliefs and practices of all groups, but it is not impossible to learn how to work with clients who have different religious beliefs. We must know ourselves, our prejudices, feelings, and attitudes toward other religions, and be open to the stories and beliefs of our clients. We need to practice with respect for differences and see and appreciate the strengths of our clients and their religious communities. We should be willing to learn about and value differences, grow with our clients, learn to communicate openly and honestly, and ask questions when necessary. Also, as simple as it sounds, we must be kind with our clients because they have often encountered an unkind world. Then, and only then, can we "breathe the breath" of our clients, join them, and work with them as one to help enhance their lives—while maintaining our own integrity.

References

Bisman, C. (1994). *Social work practices; Cases and principles.* Pacific Grove, CA: Brooks/Cole.

Compton, B. R., & Galaway, B. (1999). *Social work processes.* Belmont, CA: Wadsworth.

The Council on Social Work Education. (1999). *Curriculum standard on educational policy.* Washington, DC: NASW News.

Crapo, R. H. (1993). *Cultural anthropology: Understanding ourselves and others* (3rd ed.). Guilford, CT: Dushkin Publishing Group.

DeJong, P., & Miller, S. D. (1995). How to interview for client strengths. *Social Work, 40*(6), 729–736.

Dziegielewski, S. F. (1998). *The changing face of health care social work.* New York: Springer Publishing Co.

Germain, C., & Gitterman, A. (1996). *The life model of social work practice* (2nd ed.). New York: Columbia University Press.

Goldberg, C. (1994). The privileged position of religion in the clinical dialogue. *Clinical Social Work Journal, 24*(2).

Goldstein, E. (1995). *Ego psychology and social work practice* (2nd ed.). New York: Free Press.

Irish, D. P., Lundquist, K. F., & Nelsen, V. J. (Eds.). (1993*). Ethnic variations in dying, death, and grief: Diversity in universality.* Washington, DC: Taylor & Francis, Ltd.

James, W. (1902). *Varieties of religious experiences: A study in human nature.* New York: Modern Library.

Kamya, H. A. (1997). African immigrants in the United States: The challenge for research and practice. *Social Work, 42,* 2.

Karls, J. M., & Wandrei, K. E. (1994). *Person-in-environment system: The PIE classification system for social functioning problems.* Washington, DC: NASW.

Lecca, P. J., Quevalu, I., Nunes, J. V., & Gonzales, H. F. (1998). *Cultural competency in health, social, and human services: Directions for the twenty-first century.* New York: Garland.

Marty, M. E., & Appleby, R. S. (1997). *Religion, ethnicity, and self identity: Nations in turmoil.* Hanover and London: University Press of New England.

Norton, D. G. (1978). *The dual perspective.* Washington, DC: CSWE.

Parry, J. K., & Ryan, A. S. (Eds.). (1996). *A cross-cultural look at death, dying, and religion.* Chicago: Nelson-Hall Publishers.

Rabb, E. (Ed.). (1964). *Religious conflict in America.* New York: Anchor Books.

Rybarczyk, B., & Bellg, A. (1997). *Listening to life stories.* New York: Springer Press.

Saleebey, D. (Ed.). (1997). *The strengths perspective in social work practice* (2nd ed.). New York: Longman.

Shorto, R. (1997, 7 December). Beliefs by the numbers. *New York Times Magazine,* 60–61.

Shulman, L. (1999). *The skills of helping individuals, families, groups, and communities* (4th ed.). Itasca, IL: F. E. Peacock.

Wachtel, P. L. (1993). *Therapeutic communication.* New York: Guilford Press.

Weiss, J. (1993). *How psychotherapy works: Processes and techniques.* New York: Guilford Press.

13

Ableism

Mentally and Emotionally Challenged People

Jaak Rakfeldt

This chapter deals with oppression related to persons labeled as having mental disorders. It is based on the theoretical perspective broadly referred to as the societal reaction approach, or alluded to more specifically as labeling theory, and is based on the Symbolic Interactionist system of social psychology (Mead, 1934; Blumer, 1969). Theodore R. Sarbin (1969), a proponent of the societal reaction approach, describes a "transformation of social identity" that takes place when an individual is defined as mentally ill and is admitted to a mental hospital. Sarbin states, "The diagnosis 'mentally ill' is a pejorative; its use has the effect of publicly degrading a person and also of providing the basis for self-devaluation" (p. 23).

Sarbin's "transformation of social identity" notion is based on a dramaturgical model, which holds that the establishment of a social identity occurs through the enactment of social roles in specific contexts. The task is to locate oneself in a social system. This is accomplished by actors reflexively determining who they are through the images they receive from the significant other actors in the social setting. A social identity is, then, the sum total of such reflected images. Thus it follows that role relationships define one's social identity. If role relationships change, then inferences about one's social identity will also change. Because social role relationships are so important in people's identity formation and maintenance, the assessment protocol person-in-environment (PIE; Karls & Wandrei, 1994b) will be used in this chapter to illustrate the greater richness that it provides vis-à-vis the *Diagnostic and Statistical Manual, Fourth Edition* (APA, 1994).

Theoretical Framework

Based on Sarbin's earlier formulation concerning "role-taking" (1969), Erving Goffman (1961) describes the process of becoming a mental patient. In so doing, Goffman discusses the concept of a "moral career." He maintains that the value of the career concept is its two-sidedness. He states: "One side is linked to internal matters held dearly and closely such as image of self and felt identity; the other side concerns official position, jural relations, and style of life" (p. 127).

Goffman is interested in the regular sequence of changes that a career entails in a person's sense of self, or framework of imagery for judging the self and others. According to Goffman, an individual often begins a "pre-patient" career with social relationships and civil rights, and ends up at the beginning of his or her hospital stay with very little of either. The moral aspect of this portion of the career entails a feeling of "abandonment, disloyalty, and embitterment."

Goffman maintains that an important feature of the pre-patient career is its "retroactive quality," in the sense that the person's life history is revised in light of his or her current psychiatric diagnosis. In the process of doing an anamnesis (social-psychiatric history), mental health staff persons routinely seek out incipient symptoms of mental disorder and then trace them forward from the patient's childhood into the present. Goffman states that in order to make sense of the current situation, the patient must also recast all of his or her past life as that of a pre-patient with some insidious "mental illness" progressively developing. Often, patients must accept other persons' views that they are sick: that their self-images may be "false," and that the views of the staff are "true." Goffman considers this to be "conversion" to a patient identity. PIE (Karls & Wandrei, 1994b) deals with these issues by elaborating social role problems encountered by persons in inpatient (4200.XX) and outpatient (4300.XX) statuses with the incumbent loss of personal power, the ambivalence, the social regression, and dependency that often occur.

Mental Disorders as Social Roles

Social scientists are divided in their paradigms of mental disorder. Almost all accept the notion that social and developmental factors influence etiology, but some reject the clinical approach altogether. They argue that mental disorders are not diseases but deviant behaviors that have been molded and stabilized by the same forces that shape normal roles. This perspective has been termed the "social role" approach (Townsend, 1978). There are several different emphases within the social role school.

Proponents of the "societal reaction" approach, for example, study the ways in which societies' reactions to initial deviance exacerbate that behavior. Some well-known examples of these reactions are long-term hospitalization and overprescription of major tranquilizers, treatments that have definitely produced chronic deviance in some patients (Townsend, 1982; Scheff, 1966; Goffman, 1961; Wing, 1962).

Labeling theory can be considered a subtype of the societal reaction approach. Proponents of labeling theory study the effects of the labels that society applies to deviants (Scheff, 1966, 1974, 1975; Greenley, 1972a, 1972b, 1979; Townsend, 1982). Scheff (1975, p. 76) uses the following example to illustrate labeling theory.

> The key to the labeling-denial continuum . . . is the process of defining a person as essentially and *only* a deviant. Compare the attitude of denial contained in the description, "George drinks like a fish, but he is a talented, compassionate, and accomplished man," with the attitude of labeling expressed in the statement, "George is nothing but a drunk." The attitude of labeling is to reduce a complex individual with many attributes and an eventful biography to a single descriptive trait. Exclusively some single aspect of his character or behavior defines a person. The process of labeling may be seen as giving rise to a master status that excludes all other statuses from consideration. The fact that a person is a "criminal"—that is, convicted of a felony—may cause others to ignore all of his other statuses (male, father, husband, uncle, real estate broker, neighbor, Mason, and so on). The deviant role obscures and in some instances supersedes all other roles.

Ruth Benedict laid the groundwork for subsequent applications of the social role approach. She argued that the mentally ill in any culture would be those who, for hereditary or developmental reasons, did not conform to that particular culture's definition of normality (1934, p. 60). To what degree are such categories (normal and abnormal) culturally determined, or to what degree can we with assurance regard them as absolute? To what degree can we regard inability to function socially as diagnostic of abnormality, or to what degree is it necessary to regard this as a function of culture? Benedict reveals a striking fact that emerges from the study of widely varying cultures: Persons considered abnormal in one culture would be able to function quite easily in others. Benedict cites examples of trance states and catalepsy, which characterize the shamanistic calling in many different cultures. Even the content of these trance states appears to be culturally determined. Benedict also describes the Berdache, a socially accepted homosexual group within some Native American societies, and notes that paranoid ideation and self-glorification among the Kwakiutl of the Pacific Northwest are considered normal. Benedict concludes, "these illustrations . . . force upon us the fact that normality is culturally defined" (1934, p. 60).

Three decades later, the psychiatrist Thomas Szasz argued from a similar perspective of cultural relativism (1960, p. 113): "My aim in this essay is to raise the question: Is there such a thing as mental illness? And to argue that there is not. . . . I shall argue that this notion has outlived whatever usefulness it might have had and now functions merely as a convenient myth" (1960, p. 113).

Szasz maintains that mental illness is not a literal condition but a metaphor. Abnormal behavior is interpreted, Szasz says, "as if" one had an illness of the mind. After repeated use of the metaphor, the "as if" is dropped and the "reality" of mental illness emerges, he says. But when Szasz argues that mental illness does not exist, he does not suggest that the social and psychological occurrences that have generated this label do not exist. Rather, he maintains that these phenomena are merely mislabeled, and that such mislabeling clouds the issue (1960, p. 118).

The notion of mental illness thus serves mainly to obscure the everyday fact that life for most people is a continuous struggle, not for biological survival, but for a "place in the sun," "peace of mind," or some other human value. Sustained adherence to the myth of mental illness allows people to avoid facing this problem, believing that mental health, conceived as the absence of mental illness, automatically ensures the making of right and safe choices in one's conduct of life. But the facts are all the other way. It is the making of good choices in life that others regard, retrospectively, as good mental health!

Thus, according to Szasz, the notion of mental illness obscures the issue of an individual's responsibility for his or her actions in a difficult social and ethical climate.

Like Szasz, Sarbin stresses the metaphorical aspects of mental illness. The fact of bodily illnesses, he says, gave rise to the idea of illnesses of the mind, and this metaphor was eventually reified into "mental illness." Sarbin outlines some of the implications of this conception (1969, pp. 23–24).

1. The diagnosis "mentally ill" is a pejorative; its use has the effect of publicly degrading a person and also of providing the basis for self-devaluation.
2. The belief in the "reality" of mind and mental states has directed the attention of scientists to the interior shadowy mind. The effect of this concern for the "inner life" has been a systematic rejection of possible causal factors in the exterior world.
3. The force of the illness metaphor is that physicians should be the specialists of choice. . . .
4. Special kinds of illness require special treatment centers. Euphemistically called mental hospitals, such centers are managed by physicians and in the main serve merely to segregate the diagnosed mentally ill from the community.

Following these more general formulations, social scientists have attempted to pinpoint the social processes whereby particular individuals become mental patients. Mechanic (1967) stated that the reasons why persons become identified and treated as mental patients are frequently unclear. Mechanic points out that on some occasions persons exhibiting relatively mild psychiatric symptoms are so identified, while others who exhibit more severe symptoms go unrecognized and untreated. The reason for this, he says, is that generally the early definitions of "mental illness" take place in a person's primary group. If the person's symptoms are not sufficiently disturbing to these primary group members, it is unlikely that the symptoms will be brought to the attention of a psychiatric professional. According to Mechanic (1967):

> The layman usually assumes that his conception of "mental illness" is not the important definition since the psychiatrist is the expert and presumably makes the final decision. On the contrary, community persons are brought to the hospital on the basis of lay definitions, and once they arrive, their appearance alone is usually regarded as sufficient evidence of illness. (p. 27)

What factors form the basis for such lay definitions? According to Mechanic (1986), they include the following: failure to fulfill expectations, the occurrence of serious consequences as a result of the deviance, and the visibility of the behavior. Another factor is the differing levels of tolerance to deviant behavior in different communities. Mechanic lists the size of the community and the availability of hospital beds as other contingencies. He concludes by stating, "If we are to understand the 'mentally ill' patient, we must understand the situation from which he comes and the circumstances that led to the definition that he needs treatment" (p. 32).

Insight into the circumstances that lead to such definitions is offered in an article by Yarrow, Schwartz, Murphy, and Deasy (1955). The authors describe the process by which wives of identified mental patients came to view deviant behavior as being "mental illness." The noteworthy finding is the wives' tendency to rationalize and deny their spouses' deviant behavior until it could no longer be tolerated.

Similarly, Smith, Pumphrey, and Hall (1973) revealed that a great deal of deviant behavior was tolerated in the family until it "aroused feelings of fear, shame, or disgust . . . [or] until the patient was about to involve outside community members" (1963, p. 76). In short, the family often determines when a member is to be institutionalized, and these determinations are often based on lay definitions.

Greenley (1972a) found that the desires of a patient's family are related to the length of time the patient remains in the hospital. Mental patients whose families want them released have short stays in the hospital, while those whose families want them retained tend to remain in the hospital for much longer periods. This pattern holds true even when families' preferences are at variance with therapists' recommendations. Greenley (1972a) concluded:

> Societal reaction proponents note . . . that non-professionals often are the first to identify who is "mentally ill," that the behavior patterns of those hospitalized are not categorically different from the behaviors of many of those left in the community, and that the professionals do not themselves decide who is and is not to be hospitalized. In a similar manner, this research on exit from the psychiatric hospital indicates that non-professionals have much to do with when the release occurs, that the released can only partially be distinguished from those retained on the basis of measure of pathological behavior, and that the psychiatrist's evaluations are less important in the decision to release than are the families' desires. (p. 36)

In another paper, Greenley (1972b) further developed these findings. He began by detailing two alternatives to viewing the psychiatrist's role in an inpatient setting. The first view, according to Greenley, is of psychiatrists as service professionals. In this light, they are seen as experts who supply advice and directions to patients who seek it. They seem to operate in the traditional way: by observing, diagnosing, and prescribing. If decisions are made for other reasons, these are viewed as outside interferences. In the second view, however, decisions concerning patients are made not so much by the expert but through a process of complex negotiation among interested and influential parties. Greenley states that in this view the psychiatrist functions largely to supply medical-psychiatric explanations or rationales for decisions that often are made for other reasons and by other persons. Greenley calls this the "legitimizing function" (1972b, p. 45) of psychiatry. During informal discussions with the researchers, psychiatrists frequently confirmed this legitimizing function. The data show that patients' families very often have the ability to prevent a release or effect a discharge. Greenley quotes one therapist as saying, "It's hard to stand up to a family, which is quite funny since we are supposed to be a professional group" (1972b, p. 41). In official records, however, and in explanations to colleagues and to researchers, reasons for retention or release are couched in the traditional medical terminology. When a patient's family does not want their relative discharged, the therapist translates this into the patient's needing further treatment (1972b, p. 43).

When one social worker reported that a family would not accept a patient whom his therapist wished to discharge to them, the therapist concluded, "He needs hospitalization and has no place to go," and recommended transfer to a nearby Veterans Hospital for "long-term care."

The process through which one psychiatrist came to revise his diagnosis of a patient is described (1972b):

> Sometimes when a family calls and says they don't want to see someone again, I know that my (neurotic) diagnosis is wrong and that they are probably schizophrenic. If the family doesn't want them, they are usually sicker than I think, so I change and call them schizophrenic. (p. 43)

In short, the clinical staff in their legitimizing function appear to translate social realities into medical conditions.

An important focus within the social role school has been the study of the unique role of the mental patient. In his classic essay on the subject, Goffman (1961) argues that the routines and procedures within a mental hospital prescribe a deviant role for the inmates. The treatment they receive reflects a view of the patients as incompetent and mentally ill. This view is eventually internalized in the patients' self-concepts and they begin to act according to these expectations.

Goffman describes the processes of "mortification" and "stripping," which often occur when an individual is incarcerated in a "total institution" (1961). He argues that when a person is removed from the world in which a sense of self is sustained, the self often undergoes a transformation that may lead to a "moral loosening." Once an individual is stripped of dignity, previously unacceptable acts such as urinating on the floor, masturbating publicly, and cursing and spitting at the attendants no longer seem to be significant. The person is free to practice "the amoral arts of shamelessness" (1961):

In the usual cycle of adult socialization, one expects to find alienation and mortification followed by a new set of beliefs about the world and a new way of conceiving of selves. In the case of the mental hospital patient, this rebirth does sometimes occur, taking the form of a strong belief in the psychiatric perspective. . . . The moral career of the mental patient has unique interest, however; it can illustrate the possibility that in casting off the raiment of the old self—or having this cover torn away—the person need not seek a new robe and a new audience before which to cower. Instead he can learn, at least for a time, to practice before all groups the amoral arts of shamelessness. (p. 169)

In short, Goffman suggests that the way patients are viewed and expected to act in the hospital sometimes creates many of the "symptoms" associated with mental illness.

Sarbin (1969) also discusses how the chronic mental patient's role is created, but he focuses on the relationship between the patient role and "normal" roles outside the hospital. He posits that a person labeled "mental patient" undergoes a transformation of social identity. There are three dimensions composing Sarbin's conception of social role (1969, p. 24): "The status dimension, the value dimension, and the involvement dimension."

Status is a position in a social structure; as such, it is an abstraction. Roles are public modes of behavior enacted by persons who hold specific statuses, either ascribed (adult male, mental patient, son, old maid), or achieved (doctor, professor, Nobel prize winner).

The value dimension conveys the positive or negative valuation attached to role performance for various statuses. Sarbin's point is that for achieved statuses much positive valuation is attached. For ascribed statuses, however, little positive valuation is attached to proper role performance, while much negative valuation is attached to improper performance (or nonperformance).

The third component, involvement, has to do with both the amount of time a person devotes to certain role-enactments and the degree of energy expended. For achieved statuses there may be varying degrees of involvement; an individual may choose to opt out of the status. In contrast, for ascribed statuses there is a consistently high level of involvement; one is not free to drop out. A person usually does not have a choice between role performance and nonperformance. A concrete example of this is admission to a mental hospital, which often leads to lowering of self-esteem, lessened involvement with life tasks and social relationships, and increased stigma and marginalization (Towsend & Rakfeldt, 1985).

Here is the crux of the matter: Persons who have not performed in some ascribed status may become negatively valued, and a psychiatric diagnosis is a typical form of such negative valuation. The status of mental patient—which is, of course, ascribed—has a high continuous involvement and is difficult to escape. The more a person's social identity is made up of ascribed statuses with granted roles, the fewer opportunities the person has to engage in positively valued role behavior. Sarbin, as well as others (Hollingshead & Redlich, 1958; Braginsky, Braginsky, & Ring, 1969), points out that indices of social pathology are highest among populations with predominantly ascribed statuses and granted roles (e.g., the poor).

The implications of this model for dealing with persons who are mentally or emotionally challenged are that we must locate individuals and groups who are most at risk—in other words, the people who are most constrained by ascribed statuses and granted roles, which they are then compelled to enact. The person-in-environment system (Karls & Wandrei, 1994b) facilitates assessment of such at-risk populations.

Self-Concept

The concept of self dates back to the work of William James (1890) and George Mead (1934). They conceived of self as a process. The self was viewed as a reflexive phenomenon that emerges during social interaction, primarily symbolic interaction. This means that the self is based on the use of language. According to Gecas, "The concept of self provides the philosophical underpinning for social-psychological inquiries into self-concept, but is itself not accessible to empirical investigation" (1982, p. 3).

On the other hand, self-concept can be viewed as a product of this reflexive process and is perhaps accessible to empirical investigation. According to Gecas, self-concept has been defined as "the totality of an individual's thoughts and feelings having reference to himself as an object" (Rosenberg, 1979, p. 7) or "all those parts of the phenomenal field which the individual experiences as part or characteristic of himself" (Snyggs & Combs, 1949, p. 58). Turner (1968) offers a more concrete definition:

> Typically my self-conception is a vague but vitally felt idea of what I am like in my best moments, of what I am striving toward and have some encouragement to believe I can achieve, or of what I can do when the situation supplies incentives for unqualified effort. (p. 98)

Gecas reviews the work of Epstein (1973) regarding self-concept, and describes Epstein as suggesting that it is "a theory that a person holds about himself as an experiencing, functioning being in interaction with the world" (1982, p. 3). In summary, Gecas (1982) states:

> [S]elf-concept is conceptualized as an organization (structure) of various identities and attributes, and their evaluations, developed out of the individual's reflexive, social, and symbolic activities. As such, the self-concept is an experiential, mostly cognitive phenomenon accessible to scientific inquiry. (p. 4)

An important aspect of symbolic interaction theory is the notion of an interpenetration of self and society (Mead, 1934). Thus, self-concepts are viewed as identities that are negotiated during social interaction. The context of the social situation is important to this identity negotiation process, because the "definitions of the situation" that actors bring to a particular context are said to be important to the emergent fluid meaning that is created. According to the symbolic interactionists, this is how social reality is "constructed" (Berger, 1967). Therefore, the construction of social identities both for self and others in a given situation involves a somewhat tenuous consensus among the actors or participants. Thus, self-concept from this perspective is "situated," "emergent," "reciprocal," and "negotiated."

The notion of self-concept has informed studies of mental disorders in several ways. Goffman (1961) argues that the requirements of institutional life cause hospitalized mental patients to accept—or pretend to accept—the institutional staff's view of them as mentally ill. Patients thus begin to change their self-concepts, to accept the role proffered to them, and to act accordingly. In Goffman's view, institutionalization therefore consists of the process of role internalization.

Braginsky, Braginsky, and Ring (1969) attack Goffman's theory on several grounds, contending that Goffman presents patients as helpless pawns, caught and molded by the massive forces of the institution. On the contrary, Braginsky argues, mental patients are processing information and making decisions in their self-interest like anyone else. Braginsky's experiments suggest that patients do frequently engage in active impression management in order to remain in the hospital when they perceive this as the superior option. From this he argues that the mental hospital may be omissively guilty of inadequately aiding the patient to construct or maintain healthy roles needed to live outside the hospital, but it is not commissively guilty of actually promoting chronic deviance. Braginsky thus rejects Goffman's theory that changes in self-concept form the basis of institutionalization.

Townsend (1976, 1978) proposes that part of this controversy derives from the elusive nature of self-concept. People's feelings about themselves and their situations vary over time, and different methods of eliciting self-definitions may produce different responses even in the same populations, he says. For example, Townsend (1978) and Weinstein (1983) collected data on the same hospital from comparable samples but reached quite different conclusions regarding patients' evaluations of self and their hospitalization. The questions these authors asked, however, though virtually identical in content, were framed differently, and eventually elicited different responses. Townsend argues (1976, 1978) that because self-concept is such an abstraction, research concentrating on predominantly behavioral indices has been more useful in the study of institutionalization. Similarly, the abstract quality of self-concept can explain Braginsky, Braginsky, and Ring's (1969) findings. Some patients may think they are mentally ill but not admit it, while others may not think so at all. For most people, probably these feelings also vary over time. Some patients in either group, however, may engage in impression management to remain in the hospital. This interpretation allows the possibility that the hospital may have played both a commissive role in producing such impression management by inadvertently reinforcing behaviors in the hospital that are maladaptive on the outside, and an omissive role by not adequately helping the patient construct and maintain healthy roles on the outside. This interpretation has the virtue of parsimony in that it encompasses and reconciles the evidence from several discrepant studies (Townsend, 1978).

The thesis that changes in self-concept are fundamental in the development of chronicity generally assumes that, in accepting the role of mental patient, persons become stigmatized—both in their own minds and in the minds of others. For Goffman the term *stigma* involves a special discrepancy in a person's identity. This social stigma, therefore, restricts the number and types of roles that patients (or ex-patients) are allowed to play (Sarbin, 1969). If patients fully accept their degraded status, they will not feel competent to play most normal roles, nor will they want to. Goffman (1963) writes:

> While the stranger is present before us, evidence can arise of his possessing an attribute that makes him different from others in the category of persons available for him to be, and of a less desirable kind—in the extreme, a person who is quite thoroughly bad, or dangerous, or weak. He is thus reduced in our minds from a whole and usual person to a tainted, discounted one. Such an attribute is a stigma, especially when its discrediting effect is very extensive. (p. 3)

In this quotation, the flavor of the interpenetration of self and settings is clear. Phraseology such as, "while the stranger is present . . . evidence can arise," demonstrates Goffman's notion that self-concept and identity is a "staging operation," and that stigma influences self-concept and is something to be "managed." This exemplifies Goffman's metaphor of social life as theater.

Regarding these issues, Townsend (1979) has proposed that the initial recognition threshold for mental illness in the community is high; that is, a pre-patient's personal community denies and normalizes symptoms until a "last straw" is reached (e.g., Yarrow et al., 1955; Smith et al., 1963). This finding supports Scheff's proposition (1966) that most transitory deviance is denied and never comes to the attention of authorities. Once an individual is "recognized" and labeled mentally ill, however, the recognition threshold for "symptoms" may drop drastically, and otherwise neutral acts may now be interpreted as symptomatic. This, of course, is a form of stigma. In contrast to the initial recognition threshold in the community, the recognition threshold among mental health professionals is low. Townsend (1979) draws on numerous studies of psychiatric diagnosis to demonstrate that within the mental health context, professionals frequently have difficulty recognizing anybody as completely normal.

Townsend (1979) further proposes that the social stigma surrounding mental illness, and the public's extremely negative images of the mentally ill, help to maintain an initially high recognition threshold in the community. The behavior of pre-patients usually does not match the public's stereotyped images of insanity, and pre-patients' personal communities hesitate to reclassify them in such a stigmatized category. After this redefinition has occurred, however, people vary in their ability to tolerate ex-patients' deviant behavior and to be supportive (Leff, 1976; Greenley, 1979). Some people continue to rationalize and normalize patients' behavior by speaking of their "problems" (or using other euphemisms), but never mentioning mental illness. Conversely, others view the ex-patient as a "nut" and are extremely intolerant of even minor infractions. Thus, the likelihood of discrimination is greatly increased (PIE: 5200, 6200, 7200, 8400, 9300, and 10200).

The preceding suggests that stigma may play a crucial role in determining a patient's self-concept and coping behavior. During patients' initial encounters with the mental health system, stigma within their personal communities and in their own minds may reduce their options—both real and perceived. This in turn may affect their ability to "take an active role to influence individual-environment interaction" (Strauss, 1982).

A distinction Gecas draws between "self" and "self-concept" is that self may be viewed as "a process of reflexivity," while self-concept is "a product of this reflexive activity" (1982, p. 3).

According to this model, one's self-esteem, social identity, and self-efficacy beliefs produce and determine the quality of one's involvement with life tasks and social contacts. Presumably, more positive feelings lead to greater investment in life tasks and social relationships, while more negative feelings may result in an avoidance of such involvement (i.e., self as a producer of experience).

At the same time, feedback from involvement with life tasks and social contacts may change persons' subjective judgments of esteem, identity, and efficacy beliefs (i.e., self as a product of experience). This feedback cycle, of course, has a major impact on people's social roles and relationships, particularly if they are mentally and emotionally challenged.

Social Roles/Relationships and Psychiatric Disability

Social network studies have reported that people with psychiatric disabilities have fewer social contacts than others (Cohen & Sokolovsky, 1978; Davidson, Hoge, Merrill, Rakfeldt, &

Griffith, 1995), and that the number of people with whom they have regular contact, which is between six and twelve, is significantly lower than the thirty to forty people reported for the general population (Wallace, 1984). In addition, the few relationships that people with psychiatric disabilities do maintain have been described as "unidirectional," rather than reciprocal, in nature in that they appear to receive more support than they are able to give (Cohen & Sokolovsky, 1978; Tolsdorf, 1976; Wallace, 1984). As a result, family members appear to represent the primary source of social support for many individuals with psychiatric disabilities and tend to report feeling overwhelmed by the needs of their disabled relatives (Tolsdorf, 1976). In turn, people with psychiatric disabilities tend to be characterized more as being taken care of by, rather than caring for, their relatives (Cohen & Kochanowicz, 1989; Cohen & Sokolovsky, 1978).

In the postinstitutional era, such a dismal picture can no longer be attributed to the chronicity and withdrawal thought to be brought about by processes of institutionalization. Instead, clinical investigators have begun to attribute the social isolation of individuals with psychiatric disabilities to the nature of the disability itself, citing such factors as social skills deficits, affect dysregulation, and the so-called negative symptoms of asociality, anergia, anhedonia, and avolition as reasons for why it appears to be difficult for people to establish and maintain reciprocal, caring relationships (Rakfeldt & McGlashan, 1996; Davidson, Stayner, & Haglund, 1998). This literature has gone so far as to characterize people with negative symptoms as "empty shells" who can no longer "think, feel, or act," having "lost the capacity both to suffer and to hope" (Andreasen, 1984, pp. 62–63). In this view, the lack of social support experienced by people with psychiatric disabilities is seen as having been brought about primarily by the ravages of the disorder itself, leaving the person isolated, apathetic, and no longer even desiring companionship or love.

A review, however, of first-person accounts and the mental patient consumer literature paints a very different picture. These accounts are replete with poignant descriptions of loss, loneliness, and enduring but unfulfilled desires for love, warmth, and friendship (Davidson, Stayner, Rakfeldt, Weingarten, & Tebes, in press). In addition to documenting clearly the strong needs and desires that individuals with psychiatric disabilities continue to have for social relationships—despite their outward appearance at times suggesting the contrary—these accounts also describe numerous obstacles that people face in attempting to reach out to others. Consistent with the clinical literature described above, people do report difficulties that are due to the nature of their disorders, including deficits in social skills and judgment; thought disorder and other attention, concentration, and communication difficulties; hypersensitivity to negative affect and interpersonal conflict; and loss of self and fears of engulfment (Davidson, Stayner, Rakfeldt, Weingarten, & Tebes, in press). Without detracting from the extent of damage that psychiatric disorders may do to social relationships in these ways, it is important to note, however, that people also identified obstacles that do not have directly to do with the disorder itself, but with aspects of community living that have arisen outside of the institutional culture found in long-stay hospitals. These obstacles included the social stigma that continues to accrue to mental illness in the popular culture, the demoralization and "internalized stigma" that results from repeated experiences of rejection and loss, poverty, unemployment, and a lack of opportunities for establishing meaningful, reciprocal relationships with peers outside of the formal mental health system (Davidson, Stayner, Rakfeldt, Weingarten, & Tebes, in press).

This list of obstacles to relating encountered within the community provides a possible point of departure for community-based program development efforts to address the social isolation of individuals with psychiatric disabilities. That is, acknowledging that there may continue to be some degree of social disability associated with psychiatric disorder, it may be possible nonetheless to overcome these other, less directly related obstacles to social integration encountered by individuals with psychiatric disabilities living in the community. Particularly given the persistent yearning for love and companionship articulated in the first-person and consumer literatures, it may be possible to increase social support directly simply by increasing individuals' access to, and opportunities for, reciprocal, caring relationships with their peers.

Recent research focused on the early detection of and intervention in mental illness offers new and exciting options for preventing some of the social deterioration that is so common (Rakfeldt & McGlashan, 2001, 2003). Through appropriate early intervention, people may be able to maintain higher levels of self-esteem, self-respect, and self-confidence and be better able to participate in their communities as productive members of society. There is the hope that, through early treatment, individuals can complete an education, maintain stable employment in the community, develop meaningful relationships, and live independently. This process may also serve to decrease the stigma that so often afflicts persons with prolonged mental illness—the ableism.

The case study that follows, in which a person who is mentally and emotionally challenged goes to his twenty-fifth high school reunion, where people know him simply as former classmate "Steve," rather than as a mental patient, exemplifies such increased access to opportunities for caring relationships.

Case Study

In order to protect privacy, this is a fictionalized case presentation based on real clinical experience.

God, where have the years gone? Steve thinks, half out loud. A Friday night party at a lakeside retreat, to be followed on Saturday by a formal dance, kicked off the twenty-fifth high school class reunion. People swam, played volleyball, drank beer, and reminisced. It was late. The others had all gone to sleep. Steve and Susie stayed up to listen to the music, while staring into the flames in the big fieldstone fireplace.

Music fills the room. Steve sniffs the smell of the fire and the sweet scent of Susie's perfume. They recline on the couch, bare feet propped up, toes almost touching. His eyes follow the line of her legs to her short red jumper.

The CD plays *Love Songs of the Rock & Roll Era*. Someone had pushed the repeat button, and the songs went on and on, beginning with Frankie Avalon's "Why" and ending with Barbara Lewis's "Baby I'm Yours." Steve savors his satisfaction. He had just spent the whole evening with his high school classmates laughing and talking. He wishes the evening could just keep going on and on, like the CD of rock and roll oldies.

This was Steve's first class reunion. He hadn't come to the others. His mind fills with thoughts of where the years had actually gone. He had had his first psychotic break at nineteen, spent years in and out of mental hospitals. Distancing himself from his old high school friends, he hadn't risked coming to a reunion. Now he felt strong enough to face them.

He fretted for months over how he would explain away his empty years. He concocted a story of having worked in the Outback, digging mineral core samples for mining companies. He froze at the thought of people asking him more about Australia. He saw himself stammering, sputtering, as his transparent lie publicly unravels. As it turned out, nobody much cared to hear about him. They all wanted to talk about themselves instead—what they had seen, done, accomplished.

Steve's whole body senses Susie's closeness, her sweet softness. He feels stirrings he hadn't had for years, and yearns to be closer. Susie asks about him. Before he realizes, he bursts out with how he'd gone crazy in college, how he'd been hospitalized so many times, how he'd lived in halfway houses, spent time in psychosocial clubs, worked at menial tasks for meager wages. He holds his breath. Would she leave?

Chad and Jeremy's "A Summer Song" plays again. The lyrics fill the room.

Steve's mind fills with scenes of his leaving for college. This song hit the charts while he and Amy, his high school sweetheart, learned about love before departing for different schools. He listened to the LP she sent him for hours, reliving their moments. At college, he felt overwhelmed by the huge state university campus with sometimes hundreds of students in his survey classes. Back home, he had been known by the teachers, was an average student, a fair athlete, and had a few friends. He missed that.

At college, Steve began to spend more and more time alone. He came to believe that the college radio station broadcast bulletins that he was gay. He was taken to the infirmary, and then transferred to the state hospital. He sometimes spent whole days, even weeks, on the ward talking to no one, listening only to Chad and Jeremy's lyrics over and over again in his mind.

He had known Susie in high school, too. He recalls a scene from a party. Susie was already dating Brad, whom she later married. They had gathered in their usual place, off in the woods behind the town park, built a bonfire, and drank lots of beer. Susie was tipsy and when leaving, hugged and kissed Steve with her full, round lips. He was stunned and thrilled. She kissed him again, before Brad and others ushered her off. This moment stuck in Steve's mind. And now, the smell of the fire, the old songs, and Susie's physical presence brought it all back.

While Steve had been in and out of mental hospitals or living in residential programs, Susie and Brad had been married for twenty years. They had raised a family, pursued careers, and seemingly done it all.

Steve and Susie lie back at opposite ends of the couch, their feet propped up on a cushion, their toes almost touching. He notices that Susie has moved her hand toward his. There it lay, open, fingers outstretched, pointing upward. He yearns to move his hand toward hers. He sits, stiff, frozen. A scene from a Woody Allen film shoots through his mind. Allen had invited a friend's wife over and had made a move on her. She was outraged. What might happen here? How will Susie react? And yet, here it is, her hand, open, fingers outstretched, so close.

He hadn't been with a woman for years. Long ago he tried. He'd picked up a woman in a bar and took her home. Her homeliness, combined with Steve's dosage of Stelazine and ambivalence, had left him unable to perform. He felt humiliated, devastated. He never tried again.

His hand moves closer to hers. He can almost feel Susie's fingers. Will she pull away? He senses an arousal he hadn't known for years. His body tingles. He listens to the music and thinks that just being close like this is all that he really wants. Just to feel alive is enough. Neither of them moves. Neither says a word. The CD plays. The fire becomes embers. Steve savors the throbbing of the blood through his body, the pressure in his loins. So good to have these sensations again.

All at once, his fingers brush the tips of hers. She brushes back. A warm wave spreads through him, starting from below his belly, sweeping up into his back and shoulders.

Only their fingers move—softly, gently, caressing each other, exploring wrists, fore-arms, and shoulders. Steve moves closer. He softly kisses her hair. She turns her face toward his. He sees her full, round lips. He puts his mouth on hers. She draws his tongue into her. Their toes and tongues touch. Steve shudders as twenty years of pent-up passion flows from him. They lock embraced together.

Slowly, he pulls back and looks at her. He recalls having watched her in their eleventh-grade English class, acutely aware of her beautiful face, her slender curves, and her full breasts. She's plump now, but her face, her eyes, her breasts are every bit as wonderful.

"This is like a fantasy," she said.

"You've fantasized about me?" Steve's stunned, thrilled. He feels so real, so substantive.

"I've never been unfaithful to Brad," Susie whispered.

"You won't have to be now. We needn't."

He hesitated. "I'll lock this all away in my heart. No one need know." And then, the refrain of "A Summer Song" fills Steve's brain.

Steve stares at the ceiling of the cottage. He feels the fresh air from the lake as it sweeps in through the curtains. He wonders whether he'd slept at all. And yet, he's so relaxed, so refreshed, so whole. I must have slept, he thinks. But it doesn't feel like it. Images of holding Susie fill his mind. Her mouth drawing his tongue into her. His heart races.

Steve lies in bed reveling in reverie. Images of last night blend with moments he'd spent with Amy. He gets up, watches from the window as others sail or lounge on the dock.

Things were wonderful yesterday. He fears spoiling it by going out. But finally, the blue summer sky, the lake, the fresh air coax him.

He walks down to the lake. His stomach tightens as he approaches. His face stiffens. His mouth is dry. His lips quiver slightly. The people on the dock hardly acknowledge his arrival to his relief and dismay. He stands for a minute looking out over the water. He then opens his shirt, lies back against the foot of the dock, his hand across his eyes to shield the sun, and drifts into his thoughts. The lyrics of "A Summer Song" grow louder as the voices of his former classmates dim.

At times Steve hears them talking about their careers, their children, their spouses. I've never had any, he thinks as tears swell. He pulls his hand more tightly over his face. Wavelike pain swells up from his stomach through his chest. Steve shudders. A sob bursts through the corner of his mouth. God! They heard that! he thinks. He holds his breath. The pain sharpens. Silence.

"Are you snoring, Steve?" one asks.

"Are we boring you to sleep?" another chides.

"No, no. I had a late night. That's all," Steve stutters, not lifting his hand from his face. They continue.

Steve slowly and deliberately draws in air and lets it out again controlling his chest and mouth. The lyrics grow louder.

A raucous group returns from sailing, throwing bags filled with empty beer cans onto the dock. Their clatter shatters Steve's images. They offer him a beer. Squinting from the sun, he looks up at them and shakes his head.

He gets up and slowly walks up the hill toward his cottage.

I'll get ready for the formal. That'll make me feel better, he thinks.

He'd brought along his double-breasted suit that he'd gotten for his uncle's wedding twenty years ago. He hadn't worn it much. It's tight. It's got some tiny moth holes. Steve holds it up by the window.

They're small. You only notice them close up. No one's going to get that close to me anyway, he says to himself. Steve put on the dress shirt that a salesman had assured him was chic, with multicolored ruffles in front of red, yellow, blue. The same guy had sold Steve a black silk bowtie in preparation for the reunion.

As he finishes dressing, he looks at himself in the tall mirror tacked to the bathroom door. The buttons pull tight across his stomach, the ruffled shirt, the bowtie.

Too much? he wonders. Then he turns and leaves for the dinner dance at the main house.

As Steve walks into the room, he meets Betty who had been on the dock earlier. As she sees his tight suit with the ruffled shirt and bowtie, she stops, stares, her mouth slightly open. Finally, she says: "Hi, Steve."

Her stares pierce him, wounding.

Steve moves toward the big punch bowl at the end of the room. He stands next to a group talking about how wonderful it will be to get together again in five years. They don't notice him. Steve's relieved.

He stands watching, wondering what it would have been like to have had a life like theirs, filled with places to go, people to see, things to do, and real relationships—sex perhaps, even love.

The dinner is a chicken breast stuffed with cheese and ham covered with gravy—not bad. At one point someone next to him asks: "So whatcha been doin', Steve?"

He stops chewing, grabs his water glass, takes a long sip. Silence.

"Not much really. I've worked in the Outback for a mining company, digging core samples. Down Under, you know. Gaday and all that." He says slightly stiffly.

"That's neat! God. All I've done is work with my father. We're accountants, do taxes."

"That's really great, Steve. Do the Aussies sound like Canadians?"

Steve sat. "Well. Well, not like Canadians. (pause) But not like us either. (pause) Something in between. (pause) You know." His mouth is dry. He drinks more water.

As he sips, he sees Susie walking toward him. She's wearing a deep purple dress and looks lovely. Brad walks several steps behind her.

Steve tries not to look at them, but his eyes are drawn back to Susie. He feels whole, no guilt, just that it was so right.

They come over to him. Susie looks Steve over. Her eyes stop at the ruffled shirt. Brad reaches out to shake Steve's hand. He's tall, lean, square faced, broad shouldered. He smiles as he greets Steve. They talk.

Soon, Susie asks Steve to dance. He hesitates. Brad says, "Go ahead."

"I haven't danced much," Steve says.

They go out onto the floor. As they move to the music, Steve feels Susie's body against him. It's good, but he's awkward. He wonders whether others are watching him—whether others notice his stiffness.

Susie whispers: "I feel so good about last night."

The warmth returns to his stomach and chest.

"I do, too," he responds.

Susie looks into Steve's eyes. She leans forward and kisses him lightly. His thoughts turn to the beer party. The words a quarter century lost echo through his mind. His chest tightens. Tears swell. He sobs. Susie wipes his tears with her fingertips.

The music has stopped. They're the only ones left on the dance floor.

"I've got to go. Brad's waiting," Susie says.

Steve looks at her and nods. He turns and slowly walks toward the door, his thoughts race, his mind fills with the lyrics of "A Summer Song."

Steve stumbles back toward his cottage, unbuttoning his suit as he walks. Sobs escape as the pressure's released. He lurches forward, eyes tear-filled, heart aching, chest convulsing.

He pushes open the door to his room, steps in, stands, and looks at himself in the mirror tacked to the bathroom door. His belly protrudes over the tight waistband. His ruffled shirt balloons, the bowtie tilts to the left. His mouth turns downward—Bozo the sad clown, he mutters.

He sits on the bed. His mind fills with images of the reunion—Susie's sweet softness, locked together, her mouth on his. He lies down. Off in the distance he hears the music from the main house. Buddy Holly sings, "Peggy Sue" and the refrain drifts into his cottage and into his mind.

As a kid, he'd loved Buddy's songs. Steve had really connected with Holly, who with his glasses looked like a nerd but was loved, admired, adored. Lying on his bed, Steve dimly recalls pieces of that fateful night. Buddy was out West, traveling in an old converted school bus with some other rock stars for a three-week tour. For one leg of the trip, they got a chance to hire a private plane, a four-seater. They had to decide who got to fly and who had to endure the long, cold bus ride. Holly flipped a coin and won a seat on the plane. The pilot was a young man named Petersen. The weather report listed a 10,000-foot ceiling with light snow, some squalls.

Blinding snow hit right after takeoff. "Don't trust instincts, trust instruments," Petersen's flight instructor had admonished. That night, Petersen stared at the bank of instruments in front of him: the magnetic compass, airspeed, altimeter, turn-and-bank, directional gyro, rate-of-climb, and the gyro-horizon. This four-seater was older than the plane he'd trained on. The dials were different. The gyro-horizon was upside down. Below the line was climb, above dive. Petersen's gut sensations and the tingling in his buttocks felt like he was falling. But the gauge showed "climb." "Trust your instruments!" rang through him again. Petersen panicked. His gaze fixed on the gyro-horizon. He never noticed the air speed surge, the altimeter plunge. They flew, full throttle into the ground.

Like Petersen, Steve had dreamed of flying too. He had read all about planes and pilots. Getting sick ended this. Who'd hire a schizophrenic pilot? Who'd fly with one?

The events of the night of February 3, 1959, stuck with Steve. Petersen had been filled with hope, courage, and confidence. Buddy, Richie Valens, the Big Bopper all had had so much to live for. No one deserved to die. Buddy won the coin toss and lost his life at twenty-three. It was wild happenstance.

God, they were so young, about my age when I got sick, Steve said himself. Just wild happenstance. That's all, he repeated. Sometimes Steve thought that he must be really evil or cursed in such a way to have been afflicted. But maybe his sickness was just wild happenstance, like Buddy Holly's coin toss. Somehow, his lot in life as wild chance felt freeing. He was less dogged by "why me?"

Thinking of Buddy, Steve found solace that someone who looked so nerdy could be so revered, and he recalled that Holly's last unfinished song was called "Learning the Game."

"Learning the Game," isn't that what I'm trying to do now, so late in life, Steve thought. Others have had lots of practice. They make small talk. They just do things. They don't paralyze themselves by always watching themselves. They don't think others are always watching them either.

He sat up. Just do it, he said. He rolled out over the side of the bed. Stood for a moment. Slipped out of his tight suit pants. He pulled off his shirt and bowtie. He stood in his underwear staring at himself in the mirror. It's just wild happenstance, he muttered. No one's to blame. No one's guilty. Somehow, he felt more filled with hope.

He found dress slacks in his garment bag, a blue shirt, a red tie, and a navy blue blazer. He dressed and went to the bathroom. He looked into his red eyes. He turned on the cold water tap and let it run till the water was icy. He bent forward, cupped his hands, and splashed the water up into his face, over and over again. It took his breath away. Each time, exhilaration burst through him. He brushed his teeth, rinsed with mouthwash, looked at his eyes again. Wild happenstance, that's all, he repeated.

He left the cottage and walked up toward the main house. Again, he saw the image of Petersen piloting that plane into the ground. Steve wondered if his illness wasn't like Petersen's gyro-horizon; it left him not knowing what was up or down. Like Petersen staring at that dial, I've seen only my illness. Nothing else. I had no idea Susie fantasized about me. Or that anyone would.

As he entered the big room, he noticed Betty sitting off to the side. She'd stared at his ruffled shirt before and had been on the dock earlier while Steve sunned himself. He'd heard her tell the others about her bitter divorce, how her husband had taken off with a young woman. Betty then dieted, ate only yogurt, beans, and rice, and compulsively jazzer-cised. She dated now, even placed personal ads. Steve made his way over to her.

"Got rid of my suit and fancy shirt," he said.

"You look more real," she responded.

They talk. Mostly, Betty talks. This is fine with Steve.

When a slow one, "Mister Blue," plays, Steve asks Betty to dance.

They move to the music. Steve feels her firm thighs, tummy, and breasts. "Jazzer-cise, beans, and rice really work," he whispers in her ear. She smiles.

They spend more time talking, dancing, and chatting. It gets late.

"Why don't we buy some beer and go to my cottage? There's a nice view of the lake. We could watch the sun come up," Steve said.

"I don't have my nighty," she responded.

"You could wear my ruffled shirt," he offered.

"I bet I'd look better in it than you did," she teased.

"I bet so, too."

They get up, buy four beers from the bar, waving good-bye to the few who are still left. As they walk toward the cottage, arms around each other's waists, sweet stirrings sweep up through Steve again. He smiles.

Theories of Practice: Person-in-Environment Analysis

Steve reflects a common pattern among persons who are mentally and emotionally challenged, particularly for those with severe and profound disability such as schizophrenia, in that many years after the onset of their disability they often improve (Harding, Brooks, Ashikaga, Strauss, & Brier, 1987; Rakfeldt & MacGlashan, 1996). After more than twenty years, Steve felt strong enough to face people who had known him before his mental illness, his high school classmates. This case study reflects the often difficult and delicate negotiations that persons subjected to this sort of ableism face while attempting to regain "normal" self-definitions, social roles, and social relationships. Steve's fabrications related

PIE Assessment of Steve

PIE Analysis	*Intervention*
Factor I: Social Functioning Problems	
2260.415 Friend Role (severe, long-term, inadequate coping skills) Lacks friends, lacks reciprocal relationships, moderately severe, long duration, poor coping ability	Supported socialization, peer support
3560.41 Other Occupational Role (severe, long duration) Lacks meaningful productive activity	Supported educational program to pursue finishing college Supported vocational training
Factor II: Environmental Problems	
8109.41 Mental Health Service Systems Problem (severe, long duration) Appropriate psychiatric rehabilitation services have not been provided	Assertive community-based psychiatric rehabilitation including adult daily living skills, supported vocational, social, and living services
Factor III: Mental Health Problems	
DSM-IV, 295.30 Schizophrenia Paranoid Type (episodic with interepisode residual predominantly negative symptoms)	Continue medications, psychiatric rehabilitation, focus on efforts to reestablish meaningful social roles and social relationships
Factor IV: Physical Health Problems	
0000.00, none noted	

to account for his lost years, and his fear of being found out, are typical experiences for persons who are, like Steve, trying to pass as "normal." Significantly, his romantic involvement with Susie and Betty affirms and validates Steve's "okay-ness" in the world. His reflection on Buddy Holly's fate led to an epiphany for Steve. He no longer viewed his mental illness as some sort of punishment. He was also able to shake the "why me" that had dogged him for years. Instead, Steve now views his mental disability as merely a chance occurrence, wild happenstance, for which no one, in particular, Steve himself, is culpable.

Conclusion

Persons who are mentally and emotionally challenged, and thus oppressed by mental and emotional ableism, must be provided with opportunities to reestablish meaningful roles and relationships. For social workers, who comprise the largest group of mental health professionals, it is imperative that they be aware of the fact that the initial screening encounter and the early phases of patients' careers are times when a very delicate and tenuous balance exists among the forces in people's lives. It is at such times of crisis that a person may well ask questions such as "What's happening to me?" and "Who am I really?" It may well be a time of heightened suggestibility during which either being labeled mentally ill or being reassured that one is merely having "problems in living" may tip the balance of forces, for screened individuals, either toward feeling more incapacitated or toward a greater problem-solving potential (i.e., improved self-efficacy beliefs). But if vulnerable persons emerge from such encounters feeling less able to deal with their worlds because they now see themselves as sick or broken in some fundamental way, this may be a first step toward adopting the patient role and drifting toward the deviant career of chronic mental patienthood (Rakfeldt & Strauss, 1989; Rakfeldt, Rybash, & Roodin, 1996; Sledge, Tebes, Rakfeldt, et al., 1996; Rakfeldt, Tebes, Steiner, et al., 1997). In contrast to the typical DSM-IV diagnosis, the social role functioning assessment provided by PIE allows for these existential and identity issues to be more adequately addressed.

Given the vulnerability of people in times of emotional crisis, sensitive, affirmative, collaborative, social work assessment and intervention is essential. Using a broad ecological perspective such as that provided by the PIE system will allow social workers to seek naturally occurring supports and resources for clients in an effort to keep them engaged in meaningful social relationships and social roles that affirm their worth as human beings. This affirmative social work assessment and intervention, sensitive to issues of human diversity and oppression and based on a strengths perspective, lessens the chance that clients will be stigmatized, marginalized, and oppressed.

References

American Psychiatric Association (APA). (1994). *Diagnostic and statistical manual of mental disorders* (4th ed.). Washington, DC: American Psychiatric Association.
Andreasen, N. C. (1984). *The broken brain: The biological revolution in psychiatry.* New York: Harper & Row.
Benedict, R. (1934). Anthropology and the abnormal. *Journal of Genetic Psychology, 10,* 57–80.

Berger, P. (1967). *Invitation to sociology.* New York: Doubleday, Anchor.

Blumer, H. (1969). *Symbolic interactionism.* Englewood Cliffs, NJ: Prentice-Hall.

Braginsky, B. M., Braginsky, D., & Ring, K. (1969). *Methods of madness: The mental hospital as a last resort.* New York: Holt, Rinehart, & Winston.

Cohen, C. I., & Kochanowicz, N. (1989). Schizophrenia and social network patterns: A survey of black inner-city outpatients. *Community Mental Health Journal, 44,* 197–207.

Cohen, C. I., & Sokolovsky, J. (1978). Schizophrenia and social networks: Ex-patients in the inner city. *Schizophrenia Bulletin, 4,* 546–560.

Davidson, L., Hoge, M. A., Merrill, M. E., Rakfeldt, J., & Griffith, E. E. H. (1995). The experiences of long-stay inpatients returning to the community. *Psychiatry, 58,* 122–132.

Davidson, L., Stayner, D., Rakfeldt, J., Weingarten, R., & Tebes, J. K. (in press). Friendship and the restoration of community life. In P. Stastny & J. Campbell (Eds.), *Social supports and psychiatric rehabilitation.*

Davidson, L., Stayner, D. A., & Haglund, K. E. (1998). Phenomenological perspectives on the social functioning of people with schizophrenia. In K. T. Mueser & N. Tarrier (Eds.), *Handbook of social functioning in schizophrenia* (pp. 97–120). Boston: Allyn & Bacon.

Epstein, S. (1973). The self concept revisited, or a theory of a theory. *American Psychologist, 28,* 404–416.

Gecas, V. (1982). The self-concept. *Annual Review of Sociology, 8,* 1–33.

Goffman, E. (1961). *Asylums.* New York: Doubleday, Anchor.

Goffman, E. (1963). *Stigma.* Englewood Cliffs, NJ: Prentice-Hall.

Greenley, J. R. (1972a). The psychiatric patient's family and length of hospitalization. *Journal of Health and Social Behavior, 13,* 25–37.

Greenley, J. R. (1972b). Alternate views of the psychiatrist's role. *Social Problems, 20,* 22–29.

Greenley, J. R. (1979). Familial expectations, post-hospital adjustment, and the societal reaction perspective on mental illness. *Journal of Health and Social Behavior, 20,* 217–227.

Harding, C., Brooks, G., Ashikaga, T., Strauss, J., & Brier, A. (1987). The Vermont longitudinal study of persons with severe mental illness: Methodology, study sample, and overall status 32 years later. *American Journal of Psychiatry, 144*(6), 718–726.

Hollingshead, A. B., &. Redlich, F. C. (1958). *Social class and mental illness: A community study.* New York: John Wiley.

James, W. (1890). *Principles of psychology.* New York: Holt.

Karls, J. M., & Wandrei, K. E. (1994a). *PIE Manual: Person-in-environment system: The PIE classification system for social functioning problems.* Washington, DC: NASW.

Karls, J. M., & Wandrei, K. E. (Eds.). (1994b). *Person-in-environment system: The PIE classification system for social functioning problems.* Washington, DC: NASW.

Leff, J. P. (1976). Schizophrenia and sensitivity to the family environment. *Schizophrenia Bulletin, 2*(4), 566–574.

Mead, G. H. (1934). *Mind, self, society.* Chicago: University of Chicago Press.

Mechanic, D. (1967). Some factors in identifying and defining mental illness." In T. J. Scheff (Ed.), *Mental illness and social processes.* New York: Harper & Row.

Mechanic, D. (1986). The challenge of chronic mental illness: A retrospective and prospective view. *Hospital and Community Psychiatry, 37,* 891–896.

Rakfeldt, J., & McGlashan, T. H. (1996). Onset, course and outcome of schizophrenia. *Current Opinion in Psychiatry, 9*(1), 73–77.

Rakfeldt, J., & McGlashan, T. H. (2001). Identification of vulnerable individuals before a first schizophrenic psychotic episode. *Directions in Psychiatry, 21,* 335–342.

Rakfeldt, J., & McGlashan, T. H. (2003). The nature of the prodrome in schizophrenia. In W. S. Stone, S. V. Faraone, & M. Tsuang (Eds.), *Early clinical intervention and prevention of schizophrenia.* Totowa, NJ: Humana Press.

Rakfeldt, J., Rybash, J. M., & Roodin, P. A. (1996). Affirmative coping: A marker of success in adult therapeutic intervention. In M. L. Commons, J. Demick, & C. Goldberg (Eds.), *Clinical approaches to adult development* (pp. 267–288). Norwood, NJ: Ablex.

Rakfeldt, J., & Strauss, J. S. (1989). The low turning point: A control mechanism in the course of mental disorder. *The Journal of Nervous and Mental Disease, 177*(1), 32–37.

Rakfeldt, J., Tebes, J. K., Steiner, J., Walker, P. L., Davidson, L., & Sledge, W. H. (1997). Normalizing acute care: A day hospital/crisis residence alternative to inpatient hospitalization. *The Journal of Nervous and Mental Disease, 185*(1), 46–52.

Rosenberg, M. (1979). *Conceiving the self.* New York: Basic Books.

Sarbin, T. R. (1969). The scientific status of the mental illness metaphor. In C. S. Plog & R. B. Edgerton (Eds.), *Changing perspectives in mental illness.* New York: Holt, Rinehart, & Winston.

Scheff, T. (1966). *Being mentally ill.* Chicago: Aldine.

Scheff, T. (1974). The labeling theory of mental illness. *American Sociological Review, 39,* 444–452.

Scheff, T. (1975). *Labeling madness.* Englewood Cliffs, NJ: Prentice-Hall.

Smith, K., Pumphrey, M. W., & Hall, J. C. (1973). The "last straw": The decisive incident resulting in the request for hospitalization in 100 schizophrenic patients. In R. Price & B. Denner (Eds.), *The making of a mental patient* (pp. 70–78). New York: Holt, Rinehart, & Winston.

Sledge, W. H., Tebes, J. K., Rakfeldt, J., Davidson, L., Druss, B., & Lyons, L. (1996). Crisis respite care vs. inpatient care: Part I. Clinical outcomes. *The American Journal of Psychiatry, 153*(8), 1065–1073.

Snyggs, D., & Combs, A. W. (1949). *Individual behavior: A framework of reference for psychology.* New York: Harper & Row.

Strauss, J. S. (1982). The course of psychiatric disorder: A mode for understanding and treatment. Unpublished paper.

Strauss, J. S., Rakfeldt, J., Harding, C. M., & Lieberman, P. (1989). Psychological and social aspects of negative symptoms. *British Journal of Psychiatry, 155*(7), 128–132.

Szasz, T. S. (1960). The myth of mental illness. *American Psychologist, 15,* 113–118.

Tolsdorf, C. C. (1976). Social networks, support, and coping: An exploratory study. *Family Process, 15,* 407–417.

Townsend, J. M. (1976). Self-concept and the institutionalization of mental patients: An overview and critique. *Journal of Health and Social Behavior, 17,* 263–271.

Townsend, J. M. (1978). *Cultural conceptions and mental illness: A comparison of Germany and America.* Chicago: University of Chicago Press.

Townsend, J. M. (1979). Stereotypes of mental illness: A comparison with ethnic stereotypes. *Culture, Medicine and Psychiatry, 3,* 205–229.

Townsend, J. M. (1982). Psychiatric versus social factors: An attempt at integration. *Human Relations, 35,* 356–367.

Townsend, J. M., & Rakfeldt, J. (1985). Hospitalization and first-contact mental patients: Stigma and changes in self-concept. In J. R. Greenley (Ed.), *Research in community and mental health: A research annual, volume 5* (pp. 269–301). Greenwich, CT: JAI Press Inc.

Turner, R. H. (1968). The self-conception in social interaction. In C. Gordon & K. Gergen (Eds.), *The self in social interaction.* New York: Wiley.

Wallace, C. J. (1984). Community and interpersonal functioning in the course of schizophrenic disorders. *Schizophrenia Bulletin, 10,* 233–257.

Weinstein, R. M. (1983). Labeling theory and the attitudes of mental patients: A review. *Journal of Health and Social Behavior, 24,* 70–84.

Wing, J. K. (1962). Institutionalism in mental hospitals. *British Journal of Social and Cultural Psychology, 1,* 38–51.

Yarrow, M. R., Schwartz, C. G., Murphy, H. S., & Deasy, L. C. (1955). The psychological meaning of mental illness in the family. *Journal of Social Issues, 11,* 12–24.

Social Work Practice with Immigrants

Silvia Juarez-Marazzo

As Americans, when we think of immigration to our country, we conjure up the image of the Statue of Liberty, of the United States with its arms opened wide to the "huddled masses." Although the United States has defined itself as, and even prided itself as being, a land of immigrants, in reality its receptivity toward the immigrant has often been less than welcoming. The many waves of foreigners to its shores have been met with, at best, an ambivalence that tilts toward suspicion and, at worst, xenophobia. This discrepancy between fact and fiction has arisen from many sources. After all, it is not from the works of history, sociology, psychology, or the annals of social work that our concept of immigration and immigrants have been shaped, but from page-turning works of fiction and epic Hollywood movies that present ideals and images ranging from the grand expanses of the wagon-train Westerns to the mean streets of America's cities. As a result, there is much myth and misinformation about this phenomenon and social force. It is to address and correct some of this misinformation that this chapter is dedicated. Because the social work practitioner has been a vital resource for the immigrant, and immigration itself was a major factor in the beginnings and evolution of social work, it is crucial that those entering the field have a knowledge base from which to achieve a perspective, as well as develop policy and practice. Who is there to guide the immigrant through the tribulations of entry into a new world? Not an Ingrid Bergman or a John Wayne, but the humble and helpful social worker. Let's begin by expanding our knowledge with a brief historical overview and some compelling demographics.

The Contributions of Social Work to Immigration

In 1882, barely one hundred years after the founding of the nation, immigration became federally controlled. This was the first comprehensive attempt to have a migratory policy, based on exclusion, selection, and deportation (Brown, 1969.) At that time, some forty million European-born immigrants resettled in a not-very-populous United States. During the first decade of the 1900s, nine million southern and eastern Europeans arrived. The volume and composition of immigrants introduced new racial and cultural elements at a time when the United States' concerns regarding immigration policy were already growing. Urbanization and transition from a rural to an industrialized economy created problems of urban congestion, poverty, and periods of unemployment. This process transformed the United States, particularly its cities, with resultant social issues and problems.

From the immigrants' point of view, there was a change from a predominantly rural experience to the complexities of a new urban culture, and also to the chaos and impersonal tone of the big cities (Brown, 1969.) It was from these circumstances that the settlement house movement arose in 1886. Among the first pioneers in the fight against racial discrimination, settlement-house workers were not only advocates for blacks and immigrants alike, but also cognizant of the unique challenges immigrants confronted in their resettlement (Trattner, 1994). The services they offered for domestic migrants (migrating from rural areas to urban areas) and to international immigrants were in the areas of childcare, counseling, education, and employment aid. Specifically targeting international immigrants, the settlement houses offered school in citizenship for new immigrants, aiming to introduce them into their new civic role (DiNitto, 1994.) It was from these roots that social work emerged as an autonomous profession, and social workers became professionally trained "caseworkers." After World War I, the settlement-house movement expanded into new areas: It created youth groups, senior services, neighborhood development projects, and services for immigrants and migrant workers (Trattner, 1994). Today, United Neighborhood Center of America, Inc. (UNCA), a voluntary, nonprofit, national organization with neighborhood-based agencies, continues the work of the original National Federation for Settlement and Neighborhood Centers founded by Jane Addams (a Nobel Peace Prize winner) and the settlement-movement workers of 1911.

The Council of Social Work Education and the National Association of Social Workers continue to respond to the dilemmas of the immigrant population by encouraging and supporting a curriculum and continuing-education courses for social workers that address core issues inherent in a pluralistic society. Social work arose from the challenges of immigration, and now it is both fitting and necessary that its focus return to the needs of immigrants again.

Demographics

The whole world is on the move. Though it has always been that way, both the size of populations and advances in modes of transportation and communication have profoundly accelerated migratory conditions. Corp Watch cites United Nations data that 150 million people worldwide are on the move each year. War, famine, excessive population growth, economic failure, political and social breakdown, and environmental ills are some of the leading causes. The effect on migrant-destination countries, such as the United States and European nations, has been intense. This pressure has led to an increase in anti-immigrant and racial tensions, as well as political actions to restrict immigration and diminish rights for immigrants already being processed. When people feel threatened, they direct their fears at the perceived threat. Throughout the world, in those countries receiving immigrants and refugees, political movements are arising or solidifying to curb or eliminate immigration, and to restrict, control, and deport those already there. Thus racism, discrimination, and other acts of oppression are on the rise. And, since September 11, 2001, fears of terrorist actions by Middle Eastern fundamentalists have affected even the most reasonable members of educated and liberal society, who are ordinarily the compassionate friends of the marginalized.

This degree of antipathy toward immigration was not always so, particularly in the United States. The level of opposition to immigration was, in the past, generally related to the level of threat to economic conditions, or to how familiar or unfamiliar the given immigrant populace was to the U.S. population at the time. The fear of having a job taken, having to support strangers with new or increased taxes, the sense of being overwhelmed by the unfamiliar, or losing a sense of the way things were has always influenced policies on immigration. Yet the United States from 1901–1910 admitted 8,795,000 people, a rate of 10.4 immigrants per thousand citizens. From 1991–1998, 7,605,000 immigrants entered, at a rate of 3.6 per thousand Americans. Though there was a drop over these nine decades, the doors were still open; for some citizens that door was open too wide; for others the door was not open enough. This immigration data comes from the *Statistical Year Book of the Immigration and Naturalization Services,* published annually by the Naturalization Services, a unit of the Department of Justice (U.S. Census Bureau, 2001, p. 10). The data are obtained from entry visas and change-of-immigration-status forms.

One way to quickly map the concerns of the people of the United States with regard to the numbers and kinds of immigrants is to examine the legislation that has been enacted. The number of immigrants admitted from 1921 to 1930 was 4,107,000. The Immigration and Naturalization Act of 1924 imposed the first permanent numerical limit on immigration, establishing national-origins quota systems in which northern and western European countries were favored (Balgopal, 2000, p. 10). During the Cold War, the Immigration and Naturalization Act of 1952 imposed quotas to attract skilled aliens whose services were needed in the country, maintaining the national-origin quota (Balgopal, 2000, p. 10). The number of immigrants admitted between 1951 and 1960 was 2,515,000. With the focus on Asia in the 1960s, the Immigration and Naturalization Act Amendments of 1965 (Balgopal, 2000, p. 10) dismissed the national-origin quota and established a seven-category preference system based on family unification and skills, setting a limit of 20,000 immigrants per country in the Eastern Hemisphere. The number of immigrants admitted between 1961 and 1970 was 3,322,000. The Immigration and Naturalization Act Amendments of 1976 extended to 20,000 the per-country limit of Western Hemisphere countries (Balgopal, 2000, p. 10). The number of immigrants admitted between 1971 and 1980 was 4,493,000. The Immigration and Naturalization Act Amendments of 1980 established permanent, systematic procedures for admitting refugees; removed refugees from the preference system; defined refugees based on international versus ideological standards; and established a process of domestic resettlement and a codified asylum status (Balgopal, 2000, p. 10). The Immigration Reform and Control Act of 1986 established employer sanctions for knowingly hiring illegal immigrants, created legalization programs, and tightened border enforcement (Balgopal, 2000, p. 10). The number of immigrants admitted between 1981 and 1990 was 7,338,000. The Immigration Act of 1990 increased legal migration ceilings by 40%; tripled employment-based immigration, based on skill; created a diversity admissions category; and established protected status for those immigrants in the United States at risk due to armed conflict and natural disaster in their native countries (Balgopal, 2000, p. 10). The Personal Responsibility and Work Opportunity Act of 1996 negatively impacted legal and illegal immigrants and refugees, making legal immigrants ineligible for SSI and food stamps until becoming citizens (Balgopal, 2000, p. 10).

The Outsider

To get an overview, we have started with a historical sweep and a review of the data. Beyond the realm of these statistics, however, lies the great concern to the social worker: the individual immigrant, the outsider. Each immigrant must face the daunting challenges of a new, unfamiliar, and possibly hostile world, as well as the poignant loss of all that was familiar at home, and each person must face it essentially alone. And who, at some point in his or her life, has not been an outsider? Even as a child, in a new play group or at a new school, one may look around in vain for the familiar. An immigrant is defined as an individual who leaves one country to resettle in another; a migrant is a person who leaves one part of a country to live in another part. Yet, whether immigrant or migrant, the stories, the songs, the paintings and photographs of displaced people bespeak the loneliness, the sadness, the fear, the hope, and the courage of so many. For what is an immigrant but an outsider, a stranger in a strange land? Even in the most favorable circumstances, the host environment defines the immigrant as the outsider. The degree of spatial and temporal distance between the immigrant's ideological, cultural, and spiritual values and experiences and those of the host country's are in direct proportion to the sense of *otherness* and subsequent possible oppression.

Whether it is the biblical reference, "Ruth in the alien corn," or the early classical concept described in the Greek word *xenophobia* (derived from *xenos,* which means stranger, and *phobos,* which means fear), the stigma of being the outsider is as ancient as human history. Historically, the outsider is stigmatized and easily exploited because of lack of connectedness, poor familiarity with the system and norms, and limited financial and social power. In a country where the values and the very social fabric are defined, as Appleby (2001) reflects, by oppression rooted in Western-based ideologies, societal xenophobic attitudes and sentiments, stigmatization and marginalization of the "outsider" are not the exception, but the rule. Except in the rarest cases, the immigrant is vulnerable to all the oppressive ills that a fundamental lack of power creates. This vulnerability to exploitation is in direct proportion to the physical, linguistic, religious, cultural, and educational differences between the immigrant and the dominant culture.

The Circumstances

For the social worker the immigrant's predeparture phase and the journey phase are important in terms of strengths assessments. If physical or psychological injuries occurred in those periods, a therapeutic assessment may be indicated, and these experiences are important to integrate into the immigrant's sense of personal history. By definition, these two earlier phases are prior to arrival, and thus it is obvious that it is the postjourney phase that is the real scope of the social worker. It is in this phase that the social worker must appraise the conditions of the individual/family and make determinations and judgments about what elements must be integrated in the treatment plan: language barriers, physical health, mental health, legal status, housing, finances, appropriate employment appraisal and placement, schooling for school-aged family members, and connections to resources in the community (religious, social, and ethnic).

Within the realm of multiple circumstances that surround the individual's decision to migrate, the predeparture, journey, and postjourney phases shape how the individual/family will use their strengths and will cope with the stresses of uprooting and resettling in the new society. Attention to and understanding of the details of each phase is an important part of the assessment; as well, it is a process which binds the social worker and the client.

The significance of each situation may differ: Are there differences when the immigrant is resettling on a temporary or a permanent basis? Will laborer immigrants confront different societal and work resistances and stresses than professional or student immigrants? Is there a shift in psychosocial dynamics that is determined by whether the immigrant came voluntarily or was compelled, as is the case for millions of exiles, asylum seekers, refugees, adopted children, and trafficked immigrants? Do stress and trauma color the experience?

Acculturation versus Adaptation: A Framework

In most practice settings, social workers are familiar and knowledgeable in the use of psychosocial assessments that guide their understanding of the client's presenting problem in the context of personal and family history. It is from the final formulation of the assessment that the treatment plan will emerge and upon which all interventions will be grounded. When the client is an immigrant, it is critical that the social worker is cognizant of the intertwined social, cultural, and intrapersonal-interpersonal processes that are reshaping that individual's sense of self and his relation to his social environment, for they will cast light on the nature of the problems, define the tasks, and indicate the needed approaches of the intervention.

The integration of a new individual into a society is an organic event; it is critical that the social worker have an understanding of the parallel processes of assimilation, adaptation, and acculturation, so as not to lose sight of the logical progressions of each. Park and Burgess (1921, p. 735) defined assimilation as follows: "Assimilation is a process of interpenetration and fusion in which persons and groups acquire the memories, sentiments, and attitudes of other persons or groups, and, by sharing their experiences and history, are incorporated with them in a common cultural life." Gordon (1964) describes assimilation in passing stages. These stages are initiated at the behavioral, superficial level, followed by structural assimilation—that is, the minority individual becomes part of the society within which he works and lives—and the final stage is the "marital" assimilation, a description of total internalized assimilation.

Brody (1970) explains that adaptation, in the psychological sense, is the process of establishing and maintaining reciprocal transactions between the individual and his environment. Grinberg and Grinberg (1989), through their extensive work with immigrants, view the immigrants' process of adaptation as developmental: as the reintegration of the sense of self and the ego, reborn in a new sense of identity, vis-à-vis the degree of restored mutuality between the immigrant and the host environment. Germain and Gitterman (1996, p. 9) state that adaptation is the goal-oriented movement of the individual toward *adaptedness,* that is, "a favorable person-environment fit that supports human growth and well-being, and preserves and enriches the environment."

The immigrant's adaptation is an intrapersonal-interpersonal developmental process that unfolds as unique aspects of the individual immigrant and of the host environment interact. The unique aspects of the individual emerge from his ego strength and resilience, coping strategies, emotional plasticity, cognitive style, Weltanschauung, social interest, and sense of competence prior to migration. The migration circumstances must be considered, as well. The host environment's unique aspects are related to the openness of the host society and its communities to foreigners and to the preparedness of the legal, educational, welfare, and public-health systems. The pivotal aspect is the host environment's openness measured by the degree of xenophobic and racist sentiment.

All of the above elements are based on language. Communication is so basic it sometimes escapes the scrutiny and importance it deserves. The languages we speak translate our outer and inner worlds into meanings and transform us as meaning-making beings. Language is a "unique human possession" (Chomsky, 1972, p. 70); a creative activity "inseparable from any critical phase of human existence, personal or social" (Chomsky,

1972, p. 100). The immigrant who has no ability to speak the new language has lost the contextual validation of himself, his history, and his known experience of the world. Adult immigrants are instantly regressed to childhood; they become dependent on others, perhaps a stranger or a younger family member, and until they become competent in the new language, they are defined and self-marginalized by this limitation. Because their history and values, their very selves, are linguistic in nature and reside in another language, they can't be converted and thus actualized in the new situation: the immigrant like a ghost, waiting to take his or her place in the new society.

The adaptation and assimilation of an individual into the host country's life is predicated on the degree of readiness of both to encounter each other and to change. Let us assume that both are ready; the host is not too limited in terms of acceptance of the foreigner, and the immigrant is capable of communication and commitment. When that occurs, the force of acculturation is effectively engaged.

Acculturation, according to Kroeber (1948), is a gradual process of change in a dominant culture as a consequence of its direct interaction with another minority culture. As the individuals of a minority culture learn the language, the nuances of socialization and customs codes, and the layers of values of the dominant culture, they begin to live and function in the host society as part of it; they *assimilate.* That the individual initially changes in the cultural ocean of the new society is obvious, but less obvious and infinitely subtler is the parallel process, whereby the host society changes in response. Thus, something new is perpetually being created, so long as a society is willing to open itself, and so long as someone is willing to give up everything to take a chance.

Having understood the basic processes that all immigrants must go through to enter and become a citizen of a new country, and understanding the host country's responsibilities as a part of an organic holistic construct, the social worker needs one more tool to be able to assess and make a proper intervention with regard to the immigrant/environment equation.

PIE Analysis

We began this chapter by looking at the macrocosm, a world of shifting populations of refugees and immigrants. We now narrow our focus to view the microcosm, the individual. PIE analysis is the integrator of these two worlds. The PIE model provides the social worker with a tool of assessment that looks at the individual's situation from a holistic perspective, addressing the different dimensions of the individual's adaptation to his environmental situation. PIE identifies the individual/client's problems and strengths; it includes an understanding of the dimension of the client's social role performance; it defines the environmental (community) barriers or obstacles that prevent his or her adaptation and change; it also reflects any mental and/or physical health issues. Because immigrant clients present with a multiplicity of problems, all of them complex and most of them urgent, social workers and other practitioners tend to look at the immigrant's problems and their solutions in a compartmentalized way, even in a vacuum, losing sight of the immigrant's strengths and struggles. In this sense, PIE is a helpful and fitting way to approach, organize, and integrate the information about the immigrant's adaptation and his problems without overlooking and minimizing basic intrapersonal-interpersonal processes and without missing the totality of interactions that are preventing adaptation.

Although PIE focuses on adult-client problems only, children and families can be assessed by accurate evaluation of the caregiver, as that assessment will help clarify the child's problem and the nature of interventions needed to effect change.

Case Study 1

When Alicia came to see me for the first time, she could not stop crying. We spent most of the following two sessions in a sacred silence. She needed to grieve both trauma and loss. By the fifth session she said, "I know you can listen to me. I think I have lost my mind. I have seen horrible things. I do not know if anybody will believe me. I don't know where to begin. Lately, I can't sleep; I can't eat. I remember my life and I do not understand where I got so lost. I had dreams. I fell in love and I thought I'd be OK. I realized that there is only one thing I do well; I work and work and work. The girls in the factory are good to me. The boss, you know, he is a pure American; he is gentle and appreciates that I am reliable and fast; he keeps the other girls on their toes. In the laundry, I don't know what to do when I have to answer the phone. I left the English classes; the pronunciation of the vowels killed me. Now, all the money I make goes to my husband. He lost his job. I still hide away enough to send to my children. My mother takes good care of them and we talk and write each other often; it is not the same. But it is not like before! I was paying for school and everything else. Besides he has to pay the IRS, otherwise my legal situation can be jeopardized. I miss going to mass in my hometown. You would have loved it, everybody singing and helping each other. I don't know any church like that here; there are so many! Sometimes I feel like I am on another planet. It is worse than what I saw in movies . . . I have these migraine headaches for days and backache."

Alicia is a forty-two-year-old Mexican, Catholic woman, mother of two adolescents who are enrolled in Catholic high school in Mexico City. A certified teacher, Alicia is an articulate, well-educated woman who directed a public elementary school for children with unique emotional and educational needs in a small town close to Mexico City. As the economy in Mexico went through upheavals over a period of six years, Alicia's school was closed by the Regional Board of Education. Alicia, who was the breadwinner for her two children and her elderly mother, fell into despair. The school system would not rehire her because of her age. She tried to work as a waitress, as she did in her twenties, but couldn't earn as much because her looks "were of an old woman."

Alicia began to think about coming to the United States. She attempted to obtain a visitor visa, but was denied. As the new school year approached, Alicia, who wanted to see her children succeed, decided to cross the border. She paid $2,500 to a "coyote" (a person who smuggles people across the border). She walked through a desert for four days with four other women, with a small supply of water and food. Upon arrival within the United States border, the women were locked in a house for almost two weeks, with the demand that they pay $2,500 to released. Alicia did not have money; neither did the other four women. Alicia witnessed the repeated rape of the two youngest women, while she and the other two older women were cursed at and beaten for being "ugly and old." In the desperation and confusion

PIE Analysis of Alicia

Factor I: Social Role Problems

Familial Roles	Code	Type	Severity	Duration	Coping	Recommended Interventions
Parent	11	Responsibility Loss	Moderate	One to five years	Above average	Support group for parents separated from their children; referral to individual psychotherapy
Spouse	12	Power Ambivalence Dependency	Very high	One to six months	Somewhat inadequate skills	Couples therapy
Other Interpersonal Roles						
Friend	22	Isolation	Moderate	One to five years	Adequate	Referral to Latino community center; connection to Spanish-speaking Catholic church
Occupational Roles						
Worker, Paid Economy	31	Victimization	High	One to six months	Above average	Connection to bilingual advocate; education of employment rights
Student	34	Ambivalence	High	One to six months	Somewhat inadequate	Reconnection; school advisor; ESL classes
Special Life Situation						
Immigrant— Legal	46	Mixed	High	Six months to a year	Adequate	Connection to bilingual legal services to seek second opinion

PIE Analysis of Alicia

Factor II: Problems in the Environment

Religious Group	Code	Type	Severity	Duration	Coping	Recommended interventions
	9101	Lack of religious group of choice	Moderate	One to five years	Average	Connection to Spanish Mass; connection to prayer group
Community group	9201	Lack of community support group of choice	Moderate	One to five years	Adequate	Referral to Latino community center
Affectional Support System	10101	Absence of affectional support system	High	One to five years	Somewhat inadequate	Psychoeducation and advocacy

of one of these nights of torture, Alicia was able to escape with the two older women. The two younger women were never seen by the older women again. One of the women who escaped with Alicia had relatives in another state. These relatives helped the three women, providing shelter and safety. Alicia married one of the relatives, who was an American citizen.

Alicia was happy; her husband was gentle and treated her well, in contrast with the father of her children, a well-known surgeon who had abused her physically and emotionally for almost twenty years. Alicia filed immigration papers and began to work in a factory, where she met a group of women with similar stories. To supplement her income, Alicia began to sell fruit salad, coffee, and soup to her coworkers, sending all her money to her children. Six months ago, Alicia's husband lost his job. She began to work in a laundromat, with no days off. Now, she works a total of eighty hours a week. Her husband did not find a new job; he became depressed and began to drink.

Case Study 2

Muny is a twenty-year-old Bangladeshi, Muslim woman. She was referred to me by the emergency room, where she had been admitted for an alarming asthma attack. The physician who triaged her thought she looked depressed and "numb" to her surroundings. Her parents were open to the idea of Muny talking to a social worker. For the first encounter, Muny came with both of her parents. She remained silent for most of the session. When I said that I love Bangladeshi food, Muny became interested and smiled when I said I did not cook. I learned that the family had moved to the United States almost ten years ago, with the assistance of the mother's brother, who was an American citizen. I also learned that they came from a rural area, that they were peasants, and that they had the support of extended family on the maternal side. Finally, I learned that Muny's parents were desperate. They shared that Muny was an outspoken and articulate young woman, engaged in learning and helping, and full of energy and life. However, when she turned eighteen she transformed: she stopped eating with the family, her self-care was poor, she did not sleep well, she did not want to go to the community college where she was taking computer classes, and sometimes she even talked about dying. Muny came to the next appointment with her parents and her nineteen-year-old sister. At the end of the session, her father said that Muny would only bring her mother.

At the next session, Muny's mother was very interested in knowing how I survived without cooking and what it was like to be a professional. She shared that in her country and in her culture a woman who did not cook would end up alone. At some point, Muny's mother stated that she would feel comfortable if Muny talked to me by herself. When we were left

PIE Analysis of Muny

Factor I: Social Role Problems

Familial Roles	Code	Type	Severity	Duration	Coping	Recommended Interventions
Child	11	Ambivalence, power, dependency	Very high	One to five years	Inadequate	Family and individual psychotherapy, referral for assessment for psychiatric services
Sibling	12	Ambivalence	High	One to six months	Inadequate	Family therapy
Other Interpersonal Roles						
Friend	22	Isolation	High	One to five years	Inadequate	Mediation with family
Occupational Roles						
Student	34	Power, ambivalence	High	One to six months	Inadequate	Reconnection to college counselor and, through the International , Center to a mentor or Muslim women's group

PIE Analysis of Muny

Factor II: Problems in the Environment

Affectional Support	Code	Type	Severity	Duration	Coping	Recommended Interventions
	10101	Absence of affectional support system	Moderate	One to five years	Inadequate	Consultation with client and family; psychoeducation about client's split loyalties in an environment that considers women as autonomous and independent, with the right of choice

alone Muny said, "Silvia, I know I am a Muslim, Bangladeshi woman. I respect my parents and love them very much. I have dreams! I want to study in college and go to law school. They do not think that that is important. I would like to be independent. I know they want to see me married; well, they have to; that is my culture. In Bangladesh, when I was ten, my father promised his best friend that he would marry me to his oldest son. I learned this more than a year ago. The time is coming. Now the voices tell me bad things about my parents; they contradict everything. The voices do not let me alone. I have to pray."

Case Study 3

"This house is a mess. Look! Everything is flying around. Dinosaurs are eating the house. Nothing is left! The children are scared in a corner. The moms do not know what to do. Too much work! There are no sounds. Silence! The daddies are nervous; they do not know how to cook. The tornado came. Look! The world is ending! Mom, dad, you have to see this! The world came to an end."

Six sessions later, "I have an idea now we have to construct the house of the witches and the house of the good people. The children are safe inside the house of the good people. The house needs a flag. Do you have one? Oh! Yes! The North American flag is very nice. It looks good. I do not think that the children inside would mind. They know that the good people inside the house are friendly. Now, we need to build this big house for the monsters. This house will not have a flag. A house of witches full of scary things for the children does not deserve a flag. None!"

Carolina is a seven-year-old Venezuelan girl. Her mother, a young artist, was sponsored by an American fellowship just in time to escape President Chavez's tyranny. Carolina's mother's visa allows only her to work in the United States. Her husband, Carolina's father, was a prosperous Venezuelan professional. In view of the political and socioeconomic instability in Venezuela, he decided to support his wife's opportunity. Upon arrival in the United States, Carolina had difficulty eating and sleeping, becoming oppositional and enuretic. In school, the teachers became concerned because she was silent all the time, in spite of being surrounded by Spanish-speaking children. At home she would cry for hours, calling for her "other mom." For Carolina, Venezuela "is my other mom. It's OK to have two moms, Silvia."

PIE Analysis of Carolina's Father

Factor I: Social Role Problems

Familial Roles	Code	Type	Severity	Duration	Coping	Recommended Interventions
Parent	11	Power, responsibility, ambivalence	High	Six months to one year	No coping skills	Support group; fathers parenting classes; referral to individual psychotherapy
Spouse	12	Dependency, power, ambivalence, loss	Very high	Six months to one year	Somewhat inadequate skills	Couples therapy
Other Interpersonal Roles						
Friend	22	Isolation	High	Six months to one year	Somewhat inadequate skills	Referral to Latino community center
Occupational Roles						
Student	34	Ambivalence	High	One to six months	Somewhat inadequate	Reconnection; school counselor and ESL classes
Special Life Situation						
Immigrant— Legal	46	Power	High	Six months to a year	No coping skills	Connection to bilingual legal services to seek advice on acquiring a working permit; referral to an occupational workgroup or to art workshops

PIE Analysis of Carolina's Father

Factor II: Problems in the Environment

Affectional Support	Code	Type	Severity	Duration	Coping	Recommended Interventions
	10104	Support group system is undergoing a deep realignment in terms of hierarchy and roles	Moderate to high	One to six months	Somewhat inadequate	Family therapy; connection to support group for immigrants through the immigrant hotline

With the exception of concerns regarding Carolina's adjustment, the family was doing well. They had the support of the church in their community and the support of some family members on the paternal side. Six months after resettlement, Carolina's parents began to feel the stress of the financial situation, as the scholarship money would not cover all their family's basic needs. Carolina's father realized that since he could not work he had to become the main caregiver. This difficult role reversal (considering his cultural norms and values), the financial constraints, and Carolina's emotional and behavioral difficulties caused him to sink into a depression. He became irritable and argumentative. He stopped taking English classes and engaged in unnecessary arguments with Carolina and her mother. The father will be considered for the PIE Analysis.

Conclusion

The social worker has to guide the immigrant through the emotional and logistical challenges of integration into a new world. Beyond the sensitivity to the immigrant's vulnerability to all forms of oppression, and the loss of the basic power base, the central roles of the social worker are those of mediator and advocate for the immigrant in contact with a new society. As the immigrant gradually experiences the process of adaptation and assimilation, the nature of the problems changes, and so does the social worker's role. Working with immigrants demands that the social worker be knowledgeable about policy and core issues of working within a complex, pluralistic society. Yet, a most critical concern is that the social worker be open to and respectful of the immigrant's unique sociocultural and spiritual background and circumstances, for these may be contributions and treasures. The goal is always to strive to guide and maximize adaptation over assimilation. Pushing the immigrant to adopt the new, without integrating the truth of his other experiences and values, is equivalent to fostering the denial of the immigrant's past self, to sacrificing the richness and complexity of the past, on the altar of conformity. Such a loss is oppressive in its strongest sense to both the individual who has entered a new society and, in a crucial sense, to the culture that has welcomed the possibilities of the new vitality and varied perspectives that diversity brings.

Eleven Recommendations

- An immigrant may not be familiar or comfortable with the language, values, and norms of U.S. society; do not assume ignorance or incompetence on the part of the client.
- Be considerate of the immigrant's reactions and do not jump to conclusions. The tendency in an age of managed care and conformity is to understand problems of human functioning as rising from pathology, and not from environmental challenges. It takes time to adapt.
- Social work values and ethics demand that social workers be aware of personal biases and how they affect their work and their relationships with clients. This awareness particularly is needed when working with immigrants, especially clients who have markedly different cultural orientations. Do not overidentify with the position of the dominant culture. Do not become the oppressor. Supervision, consultation, and education are invaluable.
- Let your immigrant clients educate you about their culture, belief system, and values.
- Educate your clients about their legal rights and available services.
- Educate your clients regarding social rules and acceptable conduct. Be specific when possible. For example: a South American mother, who has just arrived in the United States, spanks her seven-year-old child because she is disobedient. The mother tells the school social worker about the incident. The social worker calls DCF immediately. The whole situation is evaluated in a vacuum: nobody takes the time to educate the mother about the consequences of both the action and the information sharing. If the social worker is educated about cultural differences, other outcomes are possible, with less resultant trauma for the entire system.
- Whenever possible, work with an interpreter.
- If a translator is used, address the issue of confidentiality.
- Research and utilize the ethnic resources in your community and develop alliances with them: religious centers, community ethnic centers, social clubs, legal services, and ethnic markets, restaurants, and businesses.
- Be open and flexible. Don't be afraid to initiate social work models when appropriate.
- Create opportunities to help restore your immigrant client's inner locus of control.

References

Appleby, G., Colon, E., & Hamilton, J. (2001). *Diversity, oppression, and social functioning: Person-in-environment assessment and Intervention.* Boston, MA: Allyn and Bacon.

Balgopal, P. R. (2000). *Social work practice with immigrants and refugees.* New York: Columbia University Press.

Berger, R. (2001) Immigration and mental health: Principles for successful social work practice. In R. Perez-Koening & B. Rock (Eds.) *Social work in the era of devolution: Toward a just practice* (pp. 159–176). New York: Fordham University Press.

Brody, E. B. (1970). *Behavior in new environments: Adaptation of migrant populations.* Beverly Hills, CA: Sage Publications.

Brown, L. G. (1969). *Immigration: Cultural conflicts and social adjustments.* New York: Arno Press and The New York Times.

Bruno, K., & Karliner, J. (2002). *From Rio to Johannesburg: The globalization decade* (pp. 1–8). Retrieved August 12, 2002: http://www. corpwatch. org///article.php?id=3190.

Chomsky, N. (1972). *Language and the mind* (enlarged ed.) New York: Harcourt Brace Jovanovich.

DiNitto, D. M. (1994). *Social welfare: Politics and public policy* (4th ed.) Boston, MA: Allyn and Bacon.

Germain, C., & Gitterman, A. (1996). *The life model of social work practice: Advances in theory and practice* (2nd ed.) New York: Columbia University Press.

Gordon, M. M. (1964). *Assimilation in American life: The role of race, religion, and national origins.* New York: Oxford University Press, Inc.

Grinberg, L., & Grinberg, R. (1989). *Psychoanalytic perspective on migration and exile.* New Haven: Yale University Press.

Karls, J. M., & Wandrei, K. E. (1994). *Person-in-environment system: The PIE classification system for social functioning.* Washington, DC: NASW.

Kroeber, A. (1948). *Anthropology: Race—language—culture—psychology—prehistory.* New York: Harcourt, Brace and Company.

Park, R. E., & Burgess, E. W. (1921). *Introduction to the science of sociology.* Chicago: University of Chicago Press.

Trattner, W. I. (1994). *From poor law to welfare state: A history of social welfare in America* (5th ed.). New York: The Free Press.

United Neighborhood Center of America, Inc. (UNCA). Retrieved August 26, 2002: http://www.unca.org/about_unca.htm.

U.S. Census Bureau. (2001). *Statistical abstract of the United States: 2001.* Retrieved August 12, 2002: http://www.census.gov/statab/www/

15

Appearance Discrimination

Esther Howe

Appearance Discrimination: Lookism

> If eyes were made for seeing then beauty is its own excuse for being.
> —Ralph Waldo Emerson

Park's article (2004) on appearance discrimination includes the wry joke: "You may be forgiven for having a bad heart or personality, but you cannot be forgiven for being ugly." Discrimination based on appearance is neither new—Emerson wrote the quote above in the early 1800s—nor limited to one culture—the joke comes from Korea. Not only do the beautiful need no further justification for their lives than just showing up, but society ascribes to them a variety of socially and professionally desirable traits, based solely on looks. Lack of physical attractiveness is seen not only as an affront to the observer, but also as an indicator of a deficit of competence and other socially desirable traits, again based only on appearance.

"Lookism," defined as "discrimination or prejudice against people based on their appearances" (Park, 2004) or "appearance discrimination" has entered public consciousness and discourse even as society has become ever more inundated with standards of physical perfection. Social psychology has made clear the important role that physical attractiveness plays in our social cognition (Yela & Sangrador, 2001). The attractive are favored both in the realm of personal relationships and in employment opportunities. We "know that physical attractiveness is a major asset in sexual exchange and is associated with upward economic mobility in particular for females, and we know that it brings substantial economic gains in the labor market" (Mulford, Orbell, Shatto, & Stockard, 1998). Further, exchange theory demonstrates that physical attractiveness enhances opportunities as much in ordinary, everyday exchanges as it does in exchanges that involve sex or employment (Mulford et al., 1998, p. 30).

While the other forms of discrimination addressed in this volume arguably may be on the wane, discrimination based on appearance is growing. Experts both nationwide and internationally agree that appearance is becoming more valued than ever. As the service sector continues its dominance of Western economies, face-to-face contact becomes more important (Valenti, 2004; Sessions, 1995; Henss, 1992). Along with the face-to-face encounter, the value placed on and the benefits deriving from good looks increase. People like to be served by and interact with people whom they enjoy looking at.

Federal civil rights law protects individuals from discrimination based on disability, race, gender, and age. At this time, however, there is no federal law that prohibits discrimination based solely on appearance. Looks discrimination "must be linked to some characteristic already protected under anti-discrimination law before the courts will recognize it" (Sessions, 1995). Often the only recourse for those who feel they have been discriminated against based on their appearance is to prove that the discrimination was based on other factors.

In the following pages we look at (1) possible bases for the widespread preference for attractive others and what role race plays; (2) the advantages that accrue to the physically attractive; (3) the disadvantages and negative consequences suffered by those deemed unattractive; (4) the law as it pertains to discrimination based on appearance and whether laws should be passed to legislate against "lookism"; and, (5) the psychosocial consequences suffered by those discriminated against. Finally, we will present a case study, using PIE as the diagnostic tool.

Beauty Is and Beauty Does

Physical attractiveness brings multiple advantages. First, "beauty as taste" speaks to the preference people have for surrounding themselves, whether in personal encounters or in business situations, with the good-looking. But beauty is not only an aesthetic advantage; it also brings with it the assumption of virtues. Referred to as the "halo effect," it implies that what is beautiful is also good. Repeated experiments have shown that people ascribe a variety of socially desirable attributes to those whom they find attractive. As a consequence, good looks bring a double advantage and those less fortunate suffer doubly, through loss of opportunities, both personal and professional in nature, and through discrimination that ascribes negative characteristics, wholly unrelated to appearance, to those whose physical looks are deemed unattractive.

Jackson (2002) in her chapter on the sociocultural perspective on physical attractiveness (PA) uses three theories to elucidate the effects of PA and, by extension, the effects of non-PA: (1) social expectancy theory, (2) implicit personality theory, and (3) status generalization theory. Underlying all three theories is the prediction "that people hold more positive expectations for attractive than unattractive others"; "that people behave more favorably toward attractive than unattractive others"; and "that more favorable treatment results in more favorable self-concepts for attractive people" (p. 15). Some have sought to argue that evaluation of attractiveness is influenced by cultural values, but research findings indicate that there is significant cross-cultural agreement on attractiveness and lack thereof (Henss, 1992). Research studies also have thrown into dispute the folk wisdom notion that "beauty is in the eye of the beholder" (Jackson, 2002). There is evidence that there is "a high degree of agreement among people in their ratings of other people's physical attractiveness" (*Harvard Law Review,* 1987).

Along with the evidence of agreement both within and across cultures on what is attractive and unattractive, there is also a growing consensus that looks are more significant that ethnicity in the distribution of societal rewards. Kuran and McCaffrey (2003) in their research on discrimination were surprised to find that respondents reported that appearance discrimination was *more* significant than ethnic discrimination. Respondents also reported that they themselves had been discriminated against more based on their appearance than their ethnicity. The authors write: "Although this result surprised us, perhaps we should have expected it. . . . Apparently, many Americans consider appearance a critical determinant of the treatment they receive" (pp. 17–18). It is an arena of discrimination that needs more attention from academia and the media than it has heretofore attracted.

Does Appearance Discrimination Exist in the Workplace?

The facts and figures on both income and marriage rates bear out the truism that "looks matter." As reported in Kuran and McCaffrey's study, Biddle and Hammermesh in 1998 found that there was also a "plainness penalty" in salaries for those with below-average looks. As compared to their average-looking colleagues, those who were considered plain earned 5 to 10% less. In addition, the researchers also found a "beauty premium" for those with above-average looks of almost the same value. Thus, the pay differential between a plain employee ("plainness penalty") and an attractive employee ("beauty premium") doing the same job could approach 20%.

While the possible pay differential is significant, there is also a much greater likelihood that the unattractive will not even be hired. Sessions (1995) reports on an ABC *20/20* program in which two pairs of applicants, one set of women and one of men, were sent out on job interviews. These were actors, given similar resumes, and coached to act and answer questions in specific ways. The only distinguishing characteristic was their appearance. In each set one actor was better looking. The result was that in five out of five interviews, the more attractive woman was offered the job. With the men, three out of five times the more attractive man was offered the position. While the employers denied that "looks had any bearing on the hiring decision" (25–27), experts agree that the experiment bears out the "halo effect" theory discussed earlier. What is beautiful is clearly thought to be good.

Physical attractiveness increases an applicant's chances of being hired, of earning more money for the same job as someone less attractive, and of being evaluated more positively in job performance evaluations. "When copies of the same essay were evaluated with a photograph of an attractive person or an unattractive person attached, the essays with the more attractive purported author were judged" more positively (*Harvard Law Review,* 1987, p. 2039).

In addition, not only are better-looking executives subject to the benefits described previously, it also seems that they bring in more business for their companies. In a study of a Dutch advertising agency, the researchers concluded that managers' beauty contributed to the overall performance of the company.

Appearance on a Personal Level

Those perceived as unattractive suffer on the personal level as well. From the beginning of their lives, those perceived as unattractive suffer. Parents respond more lovingly to children they see as attractive. Contemporaries prefer to play with more attractive playmates. Further, both parents and teachers have higher academic expectations for children they see as physically attractive, thus setting up a life of reduced expectations for their unattractive offspring and students (*Harvard Law Review,* 1987). The attribution of other socially desirable traits to the physically attractive leads to the obverse, the attribution of negative attributes to those found wanting in physical appearance. Hence, they sometimes lack for friends as well as for romantic opportunities.

Obese women and short men suffer the highest level of prejudice in our society. Obese people, "especially obese women, are highly stigmatized in all sectors of American society" (NEA, 1994). Fat people are rated last as potential marriage partners, after criminals and others with significant disabilities such as blindness. Moreover, obese people suffer from a barrage of fat jokes and personal discrimination throughout their lives.

John Stossel of *ABC News* conducted an experiment in which women were asked to choose between short men with outstanding resumes and tall men with less stellar backgrounds. With no exceptions the women consistently preferred the tall men as possible suitors (Stossel, 2004). Evolutionary biologists argue that some of these preferences are "hardwired" into our brains. Studies have shown that infants react more favorably to attractive caretakers. In an experiment at Massachusetts General Hospital conducted by MIT, researchers were able to pinpoint the part of the brain that lights up when men are shown a picture of a beautiful woman. It is the same part of the brain that lights up when a hungry person sees food or an addict sees a "fix" (Stossel, 2004).

Can such seemingly naturally occurring prejudices be overcome? What position does the law take? What recourse and redress do the physically disadvantaged have? Should the law intervene?

The Law

Discrimination against those perceived as unattractive is not new. The following excerpt from a legal brief argues that the law should provide protection for those suffering from such discrimination.

> The most physically unattractive members of our society face severe discrimination. People who are regarded as unattractive are, for example, perhaps the only non-criminal, non-contagious group in America ever to have been barred by law from appearing in public. (So called "ugly laws" imposed fines on "unsightly" people who were seen in public.) The unattractive are poorly treated in such diverse contexts as employment decisions, criminal sentencing, and apartment renting. Although appearance discrimination can have a devastating economic, psychological, and social impact on individuals, its victims have not yet found a legal recourse. (*Harvard Law Review,* 1987, p. 2035)

While conceding that to discriminate is to be human, the position taken in the foregoing legal brief is that discrimination based on appearance in many employment situations is not legitimate. There are some ways to circumvent the naturally occurring bias for the good-looking. As an example, almost all symphony orchestras conduct auditions behind a screen. The purpose is clear—to assure that hiring is done based on the merits of the performance, not the looks of the performer.

In most situations it would not be so easy to rule out the advantage of appearance. As discussed earlier in the chapter, there are clear benefits that accrue to businesses employing good-looking persons. The law has ruled differentially in these matters. Stewardesses (and, by extension, stewards) won the right to work beyond the originally mandated retirement age of thirty. Age was judged not to be a valid criterion for job performance, and people discriminated against on the basis of age are protected by law (*Harvard Law Review,* 1987 pp. 2046–2047). On the other hand, Hooters (Barror, 1998) won the right to continue to hire only young, attractive women because looks were considered to be a "*bona fide* occupational qualification" due to the nature of the Hooters business enterprise.

One legal recourse open to the unattractive would be to have themselves declared a minority group. Then they too would get protection under the law. But, as the *Harvard Law Review* (1987) points out, "the physically unattractive do not constitute a cohesive group: a thin person with an unattractive face, for example, may feel little kinship with an obese person. . . . Physical attractiveness is a continuum . . . and neat determinations are impossible" (p. 2037).

While some are of the legal opinion that there should be protections provided for the unattractive, even if these protections would be limited in their purview, others argue that the government should stay out of this arena entirely. Barro, a professor of economics at Harvard University, argues, "A worker's physical appearance, to the extent that it is valued by customers and co-workers, is as legitimate a job qualification as intelligence, dexterity, job experience, and personality" (1998, p. 18). Arguing that good looks are a matter of good fortune, similar to intelligence, he sees as illegitimate any attempt by the government to redistribute society's rewards.

At this time the courts have made strides in carrying out a number of ways to combat looks discrimination by linking this condition to other protected handicapping conditions. For example, obesity can be interpreted as a medical condition and thus be considered a protected status. Sessions encourages people to take heart: "Appearance discrimination is real, but not always legally recognized. It does not have to remain that way. Many of the rights we enjoy today are the result of an individual challenging the status quo" (1995).

Still, many of those discriminated against will have to struggle individually to get society's recognition. Hammermesh is quoted (in Valenti, 2004) as saying: "We insist on being treated by somebody that we enjoy looking at. The solution is getting all of us to realize that this isn't so important." Until that day arrives, this discriminated-against group will endure.

Psychosocial Consequences for the Individual

As we have discussed previously, people who endure discrimination because of their appearance suffer very real negative consequences, both professionally and personally. In addition, due to the less favorable treatment accorded them, the unattractive are prone to negative self-concepts (Jackson, 2002). "Negative self-perceptions . . . can have life-long consequences" (Kiyak & Reichmut, 2002, p. 343). People with negative self-concepts "view themselves as less outgoing, less popular, and socially less skilled" than their attractive acquaintances (Kiyak & Reichmut, 2002).

Not only does the world discriminate against them, the unattractive discriminate against themselves. Allport (1958) refers to these phenomena as "persecution produced traits." Foremost among the characteristics described by Allport, people subjected to appearance discrimination suffer from social isolation and withdrawal as well as an acquiescence in society's judgment of them, which is seen as a form of self-hate. Clients suffering from discrimination based on their appearance present special challenges to the clinician who must try to help empower the client within an environment that dismisses the unattractive as socially undesirable and offers little legal recourse to address these wrongs.

Case Study

Patty, clearly distraught, came to the community mental health center asking to be seen by "someone, anyone." She is a 21-year-old Caucasian woman, overweight but not obese, who states that she has no friends. Her circle of relationships is composed only of her mother, father, uncle, and maternal grandparents. Her education has been sporadic due to frequent moves by the family. And she never finished high school. She seems to be of average intelligence. Her knowledge of the world outside her family has been gleaned from television news and newspapers. Patty has never worked and, in fact, is discouraged from looking for work by her mother, who warns her against the "evil out there."

By her account, this separation from all outsiders occurred after some negative experiences in school. Patty was often mocked due to her appearance. She was called fat and weird. In truth, her appearance is somewhat unusual due to her eyes, which squint and are somewhat crossed. Her mother, in an apparent attempt to protect her from the name-calling, started keeping her home from school. At first Patty was relieved to be allowed to stay home. But as the months became years and as she became older, Patty has come to see her home as a prison. Television shows demonstrate that "there is a world out there." And Patty wants help getting into that world. While she has occasionally been out of the apartment, this occurs only in the company of her mother. Twice she has "escaped" alone from the confines of the apartment. Both times she has had to call home to be rescued from situations she was totally unfamiliar with. Her mother then castigates her for these attempts, insisting that "only your family can love someone who looks like you." Patty longs for friends her own age, but her experiences with rejection while in school have made her afraid. Nonetheless, her developmental needs and some innate strengths have led her to seek help at the community mental health center.

This situation presented the agency and the therapist with a complex challenge: how to empower Patty to achieve and master age-appropriate developmental tasks given her home situation and the very real possibility of rejection by potential peers and employers based on her appearance. Some of Patty's problems emanated from her appearance—the initial social withdrawal and the fear of strangers generated by her experiences of rejection in school. Other issues had to do with her family's, particularly her mother's, reaction to Patty as well as their own psychosocial issues. The PIE diagnostic assessment was useful in determining where to intervene.

PIE Assessment of Patty

Factor I: Social Role Problems

1. *Familial Roles:* Patty has a child-role problem of the dependency type. Very high in severity and lasting more than five years. Her family is the sole source for meeting her emotional and social needs. And Patty's coping skills are inadequate.

    Recommended Interventions: A support group of people in Patty's age range. Family therapy to help Patty and family recognize Patty's need for some separation and independence.

2. *Other Interpersonal Roles:* Patty has a friend-role problem of the isolation type. It is very high in severity and has been so for over five years. Patty has inadequate coping skills.

    Recommended Interventions: A support group to provide a possible resource for finding age-appropriate friends. Referring Patty to a volunteer opportunity at a local hospital. There she may find others who also need more social contact and, through joint endeavors, may develop opportunities for socialization.

3. *Occupational Roles:* While the two following problem areas are listed here under Problems in Social Functioning/occupational roles, they could just as well be included under Factor II: Problems in the Environment. Patty's situation demonstrates the interpenetration of problems in social functioning with problems in basic-needs acquisition.

    (A) Patty has problems in the student role. It is high because, at age twenty-one, she does not have a high school diploma. The severity index is high and it has lasted over five years. Her coping skills appear to be adequate because, despite her sporadic education, Patty seems quite literate and knowledgeable.

    Recommended Interventions: Patty is to be referred to GED classes offered at the local YMCA. Transportation will be provided initially by the agency outreach worker.

    (B) Patty also has a worker-role problem in the paid economy. It is moderate because she is currently cared for by her parents. But she will have to overcome this if she continues in her aspirations to go out on her own. Having never held a job, Patty's coping skills are unknown.

Recommended Interventions: Patty is to be referred to the state vocational training agency, where she can acquire employable skills and where she will be assigned to a job coach to help her find gainful employment.

(C) Special Life Situation. Patty lives in extreme isolation. This has been going on for over five years. She has no friends and no access to the world outside her family. The severity is very high, but her coping skills are beginning to emerge.

Recommended Interventions: Weekly therapy to help Patty understand her situation and begin to develop her nascent coping skills and to formulate a plan for improving her situation in accord with her own wishes.

Factor II: Problems in the Environment

1. *Economic/Basic Needs:* Patty currently is provided for by her family. But if she is to pursue her desire to leave the confines of her family, she will have to find a place to live and provide her own food. This is predicated on her ability to find employment and to learn how to navigate the transportation system. All of these tasks are characterized by Patty's ambivalence about whether she will be able to leave home against her parents' wishes and whether she will be able to function on her own. While she has not confronted discrimination in the past few years due to her isolation from the community, she is afraid of what awaits her if she ventures out. Even PIE is inadequate for assessing appearance discrimination. The only place it can be entered is under Discrimination Code "Other." The assessment of discrimination is a putative one, given the lack of this experience in the recent past.

   Recommended Interventions: Although economic/basic needs system problems are not yet in the forefront, they can be anticipated. The agency has access to a "halfway house" for which Patty's situation would qualify. Patty's name is placed on the waiting list. This would ease the transition from total dependence to autonomy by providing an intermediate stage—when Patty is ready.

2. *Voluntary Association System:* Patty lacks a community support group of choice. This lack is of high severity and has gone on for many years.

   Recommended Interventions: Patty should join a socialization group at the agency. Most members of this group have suffered some form of mental illness which led to a loss of social connection. Members are seeking to develop some social ties as they attempt to reestablish their lives. In dealing with this issue, it is often difficult for those suffering from appearance discrimination to accept membership in a such group. They do not want to identify themselves with others whose handicapping situation has made them social outsiders. Because of Patty's extreme isolation and lack of social ties, it is thought that she might be accepting of such a group and the group would be welcoming of her.

3. *Affectional Support System:* Patty's affectional support system is of the excessively involved type. It has been so for all of her life and its severity is very high. The clinician worries that it could become catastrophic when the mother becomes aware of Patty's plans to leave home.

   Recommended Interventions: Family therapy, if parents are willing. Attempts should be made to have Patty reach out to family members other than her mother. From her telling, they seem aware that all is not right with this situation. Patty should engage in individual empowerment therapy. She needs to follow up on both the GED classes and the vocational training to enable the next stage of her life. Patty needs to develop strong ties to her support group because she may lose the familial affectional support system, at least for some time if she leaves home. Through participation in psychoeducation classes at the community center, Patty can learn that her desires for a life of her own are normal and developmentally appropriate. She can learn and understand the impact appearance has made on her life's course and learn to improve what can be improved and accept what cannot be changed.

Conclusion

This chapter has shown that appearance discrimination is real in its consequences for its victims both in personal life and in the workforce. And, as Patty's story demonstrates, appearance discrimination can have ramifications beyond the immediate suffering occasioned by the feeling of not being accepted: one can only speculate how different her life would have been had she been a pretty girl and well-liked in school. Clearly there were other issues involved, both in the family dynamic and in the personal mental health of the individual family members. But, as is often the case, the appearance discrimination served as a tipping factor that set this family off course.

We are now capable of altering our appearance due to the advances in plastic surgery. This increases the pressure to become physically "perfect" and further disadvantages the poor who cannot afford such interventions. One can foresee an era in the not-too-distant future when to remain unattractive will be to imply that one is poor as well. Before that prediction becomes a reality, perhaps we should heed Sander Gilman's words, quoted in the *Harvard Law Review* (1987),

> The need for stereotypes runs so deep that I do not think it will ever be thwarted; nor do I think that it will ever be converted to purely harmless expression. But I believe that education and study can expose the ideologies with which we structure our world, and perhaps put us in the habit of self-reflection. (p. 2052)

References

Allport, G. (1958). *The nature of prejudice*. New York: Doubleday.

Barro, R. J. (1998). So you want to hire the beautiful. Well, why not? *Business Week, 3569,* 18.

Harvard Law Review. (1987). Facial discrimination: Extending handicap law to employment discrimination on the basis of physical appearance. *100,* 2035–2052.

Henss, R. (1992). Spieglein, spieglein an der wand . . . *Geschlecht, Alte: physische Attraktivitat* [Online]. Available: www.uni-saarland.de/fak5/ronald/publicat/abstract/mirror.htm.

Jackson, L. A. (2002). Physical attractiveness: A sociocultural perspective. In T. F. Cash & T. Pruzinsky (Eds.), *Body Image* (pp. 13–22). New York: Guilford Press.

Jones, R. M., & Adams, G. R. (1982). Assessing the importance of physical attractiveness across the life-span. *Journal of Social Psychology, 118,* 131–132.

Kiyak, H., & Reichmut, M. (2002). Body image issues in dental medicine. In T. F. Cash & T. Pruzinsky (Eds.), *Body image* (pp. 342–351). New York: Guilford Press.

Koo, J., & Yeung, J. (2002). Body image issues in dermatology. In T. F. Cash & T. Pruzinsky (Eds.), *Body image* (pp. 333–342). New York: Guilford Press.

Kuran, T., & McCaffery, E. J. (2003). Expanding discrimination research: Beyond ethnicity to the web. Unpublished article.

Mulford, M., Orbell, J., Shatto, C., & Stockard, J. (1998). Physical attractiveness, opportunity, and success in everyday exchange. *American Journal of Sociology, 103,* 1565–1592.

Park, J. (2004, June 15). The crimson report: Skin deep. *The Korean Times.*

Scribner, J. D. (1994). *The study of educational politics: The 1994 commemorative yearbook of the politics of education association (1969–1994)*. Washington, DC: Falmer Press.

Sessions, D. D. (1995). If looks could kill: Looks discrimination in employment [Online]. Available: www.job-law.com/articles-discrimination.shtml.

Stossel, J. (2004, August 23). Lookism: The ugly truth about beauty. *Commentary* [Online]. Available: http://abcnews/go.com/2020/?id=123853. No longer available online but available through the Mission Viejo Office of Sessions and Kimball, LLP, (949) 380-0900.

Valentini, C. (2004, May 13). Appearance vs. reality. *ABC News* [Online]. Available: http://abcnews.go.com/sections/business/US/looksdiscrimination.

Yela, C., & Sangrador, J. K. (2001). Perception of physical attractiveness throughout loving relationships. *Current Research in Social Psychology, 6*(5), 1–15.

16

Affirmative Practice with People Who Are Culturally Diverse and Oppressed

Edgar Colon, George A. Appleby, and Julia Hamilton

A key concept for understanding the relationship between social oppression and diversity is recognition of the centrality of diversity as a reflection of the worldviews of diverse people, the nature of multiple diversities, the power of personal experience, and the interrelatedness and interconnectedness of human experience. The authors of this text contend that diversity is central to alternative paradigms to building practice knowledge for addressing human problems in social functioning resulting from social oppression. This chapter describes important concepts for social work practice based on an affirmative approach within the person-in-environment framework. The discussion of these concepts provides a conceptual model for the application of the PIE classification system. The chapter also discusses the practice implications of this intervention approach for working with the following diverse groups: women, gays and lesbians, Latinos, African Americans, Native Americans, and the chronically mentally and physically challenged, and immigrants.

A Paradigm for Affirmative Practice

There are many avenues to understanding the complex relationship between diversity, oppression, and social functioning. The most effective way for social workers to understand human experience in this context can be found in the elements of the worldviews of diverse peoples. Social workers must concern themselves with a search for new ways to answer complex questions of social oppression and the resulting human behavior of individuals, groups, communities, and organizations. An important beginning point for this search is in examining one's view of the relationship between culture and diversity.

Culture and Diversity: A Transactional View

Pinderhughes (1982) argues that the concept of culture is too often viewed as a static phenomenon. This view of culture suggests that the unique characteristics of a diverse group are unchanging. Moreover, a static view of culture leads to labels and other symbols of cultural belonging as fixed and not altered by the changing reality of group development. Greene (1994) proposed a view of culture and therefore diversity that focuses on the transactional nature of culture. This view involves active attending to the ways in which cultural symbols and group processes of identity development are maintained through interaction with the environment.

This view is premised on the belief that culture is continually being modified through the constant interaction of a group with its environment, including other ethnic groups and the social structures that influence the development of those groups. It is consistent with the ecological perspective that the necessary fit of the individual and the family environment is assured when resources such as food, shelter, and clothing are supplied in the appropriate way. It posits that culture serves as a mediator in the individual and group interaction. This mediator therefore functions as a marker for differentiation and as a coping response to stratification.

In sum, the practice of social work with culturally diverse and oppressed populations requires the use of affirming intervention approaches. These approaches must take into account the daily social realities confronted by the members of these populations. Social work practitioners must seek to develop alternative paradigms of knowing these realities to enhance their ability to assist clients in the telling of their powerful stories of personal experience as a diverse people (Everett, Chipunga, & Leashore, 1991).

The Power of Personal Experience

Alternative paradigms of concern to social work must include the importance of power and personal experience and action to understand the elements of the worldviews of diverse groups. It is therefore important that social workers understand that the personal day-to-day experiences, accomplishments, and struggles of diverse peoples have meaning and importance. Moreover, it is also important to appreciate that, as people share their personal stories, similarities and differences between the teller's world and that of the listener are discovered.

Miller (1986) suggests that through the connection created as a result of the sharing of personal stories the true development of the individual and social relationships can occur. Ruth (1990) found that the process of consciousness raising and transformation learning holds great promise for affirmative practice in social work. They argue that such an approach enables people to make connections between adverse conditions in the fabric in society and the problems experienced by them in everyday life, and, through action, to overcome those conditions. For diverse people, a sense of self is very much organized around being able to make and maintain affiliations and relationships, within the rich context of their worldview.

Diversity and Worldviews

The human experiences of diverse peoples emerge from worldviews that are quite different from that of the dominant society. It is at the crossroads where the diverse worldview meets that of the dominant society that the social worker must explore the realities of diversity. The success of such explorations can result in the development of a more holistic understanding of how to intervene with culturally diverse and oppressed populations.

The social work practitioner must also understand the nature of social oppression as a contributor to a set of values, family roles, adaptive responses, and coping strategies which combine with the traditional, historical values of diverse peoples. As a consequence of the ravages of discrimination, racism, sexism, homophobia, and other social manifestations of human psychological and emotional oppression, Pinderhughes (1982) argues that a set of values emerge as "victim values." These values can be characterized as survival values, combat values, street values. These values are quite different from those that traditionally comprise the values of diverse peoples, which often include the values of cooperation and harmony (Scott, 1988).

The social worker using an affirmative practice approach must of necessity be concerned with the human experiences of gender, color, sexual orientation, religion, age, disabling condition, culture, income, social class, and social status. These experiences translate into values and perspectives that shape a worldview quite different from that which emerges from dominant societal paradigms (Everett et al., 1991). The search for an alternative paradigm is at the core of the search for the source of strength, creativity, wonder, and power inherent in the everyday lives of diverse people.

One example of why the development of new insights into the experiences and perspectives of diverse peoples is essential to affirmative practice is that of the Latino population in the United States. In U.S. society, there are many who believe that Latino individuals are unable to both adopt the values and beliefs of the dominant culture and still retain Latino norms and values. However, Latinos have historically been able to develop the ability to be bicultural (Rodriguez, 1996). The Latino's ability to maintain an affinity with his or her cultural values, language, and tradition, while assimilating into the ways of U.S. society, has been a central feature of the historical experience of this group.

Fong, Spickard, and Ewalt (1996) argue that the social worker engaged in affirmative practice must address the impact of a historical binary system on societal views of diverse people. Historically, the method for determining the ancestry of diverse peoples in the United States has been based on a singular system of racial identification. Daniel (1992) noted that during the early history of the United States, the white-Caucasian-European race was considered pure. People with any known African ancestry based on the rule of hypodescent ("one drop of black blood") were placed in the African ancestry category. Those individuals who were neither black nor white were placed on the margins (Daniel, 1992). This binary approach to the identification and therefore categorization of diverse peoples has several implications for understanding the multiple racial realities of diverse peoples.

This binary tendency to deny multiple racial realities is most clearly reflected in the historical census-taking practices of the U.S. Census Bureau. During the 1940s, the U.S. Census Bureau used two racial categories: white and nonwhite. The individual that did not fit into one of these categories was marginalized. Daniel (1992) notes that we are fortunate that 1980 and 1990 Census Bureau reports have included the counting of individuals within forty-three racial categories and subcategories. These now include white, black, Native American, Eskimo, Asian or Pacific Islanders, with eleven Asian subcategories and four Pacific Islander subcategories, and Latinos with an origin grid that includes Mexican, Puerto Rican, Cuban, and other Latino multiple diversities.

The recognition of multiple diversities in terms of race, culture, and ethnicity is based on recognition of the fact that among diverse groups there is no unitary social status. The inherent variability within and between diverse groups includes membership in multiple diverse groups. Pinderhughes (1982) notes that to examine issues of gender and sexual orientation, social workers must recognize that there is greater variability within gendered categories than between males and females as gender groups.

Given the multiplicity of memberships in diversity categories that diverse people have to maintain, social workers have a responsibility to consciously reverse the historic binary system, enforced against ethnic groups, women, gays and lesbians, Native Americans, and vulnerable populations such as the physically challenged, the immigrant, and the chronically mentally ill.

The social worker must therefore seek to develop a comprehensive understanding of the client's background, perceptions of his or her identity, as opposed to allocating them into preconceived racial, class or social status categories (Fong et al., 1996).

An affirmative practice approach must also consider creative approaches to the exploration of diversity that goes beyond the constraints of recent theories and social work treatment approaches that assume that racial, ethnic, gender, and other diverse groups are monolithic (Brown, 1989). For example, many diverse peoples such as Native Americans,

Asians and Pacific Islanders, Latinos, and African Americans share similar belief systems about the relationship of humans to the natural environment. A primary shared belief is that humans exist in harmony with all the elements of the natural world—human, animal, or inanimate.

Therefore, these individuals share a deep respect and concern for preserving the natural world. The social worker can appreciate how this sense of interconnectedness and mutual responsibility is consistent with core concerns of social work. The recognition of the relationship between this belief and social work practice may provide an avenue for engagement and active helping.

Brown (1989) suggests that the trend within gay and lesbian communities to develop their own health and social service institutions is indicative of appropriate help-seeking behaviors for living in a homophobic world. Social workers should note that this approach to self-empowerment resonates with the ecological strengths-based model. This model is premised on the importance of understanding client issues of relationship and human connection among diverse peoples.

Interrelatedness and Interconnectedness of Human Experience

Another concept central to affirmative social work practice approaches concerns the recognition by social workers of the interconnectedness and interrelatedness of all human beings (Guba & Lincoln, 1981). An important aspect of interrelatedness especially significant to social work practice is the mutuality of partnership between the client and the social worker. While involved in human interactions, the social worker does model problem solving and other significant behaviors for the client; however, the social worker is not immune to the influence of client behaviors.

In essence, social workers are not separate from the persons with whom they interact and work. Social workers are instead partners in a mutual process of seeking meaning and understanding. Ideally, out of this mutual process the social worker and the client can work to reach their fullest potential as human beings.

Theorists of alternative paradigms to thinking argue that there is an intrinsic and ineluctable interconnectedness of all phenomena, human or otherwise (Guba & Lincoln, 1981). They suggest that new perspectives in physics have significant implications for our understanding of the human sciences, and that the most important implication for the practice of social work is that these perspectives support the view that the world is made up of harmonious interrelationships among the components of the natural world.

Interlocking Systems of Oppression

Beyond recognizing the importance of taking into consideration the concepts of interconnectedness and interrelatedness when engaged in affirmative practice, Collins (1992) suggests that social workers must seek to understand the role of interlocking systems of oppression. Pharr (1988) studied the interconnectedness of oppressions. She found it impossible to view one oppression, such as sexism or homophobia, in isolation because they are all connected. Moreover, she argues that oppressions share a common origin that includes issues of economic power and control.

This conception refers to the interrelatedness of oppressions and the interconnections between oppressions and the other dimensions of both traditional, dominant, and alternative paradigms. The social worker must therefore recognize that oppression in any institution directed toward any individual or group is connected with and results in oppression in other institutions and of many other individuals and groups. This interrelated and multifaceted conceptualization of oppression will require a significant change in the way social workers think about practice.

Clearly, in order to further understand the interlocking dynamics of oppressive systems, it is important to consider the relationship between the oppressor and the oppressed. Pharr (1988) notes that an oppressor's belief system perceives everything as an object of domination. On the other hand, the oppressed cannot perceive the oppressive system and instead identifies with the oppressor. Moreover, the oppressed may internalize the opinion the oppressor holds of them (Myers & Speight, 1994). Spence (1997) adds that devaluation of self results from the internalization of ambiguity and rejection of self, which can lead to internalization of racism and oppression. The following sections describe several practice implications that the clinician must consider when attempting to integrate his or her practice wisdom with an understanding of human diversities.

Practice Implications: Women

The traditional and dominant paradigm that informs social work approaches with women emphasizes masculine and patriarchal dimensions. The emphasis on these aspects of human relationship has resulted in a set of perspectives and institutions that represent the embodiment of masculine ideals and practices (Ruth, 1990). Westkoff (1979) observed that the male character structure and patriarchal culture mutually reflect and support one another through social, political, and economic institutions. Moreover, given the powerful interlocking nature of positivistic, scientific, objective, and quantitative dimensions of the traditional and dominant paradigm, women are subjected to oppression that is culturally devaluing.

The gender role socialization of women can lead women to perceive men as superior and therefore dominant. This may lead to internalization of sexist and oppressive views resulting in self-abnegation. Brown (1989) argues that given the power of an oppressive gender role socialization on the relations between men and women, the male comes to believe in his superiority and therefore his right to dominate. The act of rape and other forms of sexual assault is a natural outcome of such male beliefs.

Collins (1992) argues that white males control fundamental social processes that validate knowledge and suppress other voices of knowing such as those of women and ethnic minorities. The social worker must therefore first and foremost recognize that women may have internalized the voice of male oppression. From an affirmative practice perspective, he or she must help women to reconnect with the unique diversities that comprise their gender role in all spheres of their lives.

The social worker must also allow women the opportunity to create relationships that feminist research suggests are important in the lives of women (Westkoff, 1979; Collins, 1992). Lastly, it is important for the social worker to join with women in the creation of feminist knowledge, the affirmation of female attributes, and perspectives and standards that interconnect with the multiplicity of worldviews held by the female gender.

Leigh (1998) suggests that the empowerment approach to social work practice is effective in understanding the diversity issues that influence the lives of women. Within this framework, he argues that the practitioner can come to understand the institutional, systemic, and interpersonal sexism that dominates the lives of many women through structural and psychological means. This practice approach establishes a basis for the assessment and intervention planning necessary for the application of the PIE framework, as discussed throughout this text.

Practice Implications: Gays and Lesbians

Failure to consider that a client may be gay, lesbian, bisexual, or transgendered is the most common mistake made by social workers. Despite stereotypes, most clients are not visually identifiable as gay, lesbian, or bisexual at first, especially when the problem for which they are seeking assistance may not have much to do with sexual orientation (Hall, 1978). However, the social worker is unlikely to get a full enough picture of the client's situation in order to be helpful without keeping an open mind to the possibility of a diverse sexual identity.

Effective practice requires what Hall termed a dual focus: "The practitioner must be able to see the ways in which the client's presenting problem is both affected by and separate from his or her sexual orientation" (1978, p. 380). Damage to self-esteem resulting from oppression and stigmatization must always be considered, but at the same time the client probably occupies roles, works on developmental tasks, and experiences feelings to which being gay, lesbian, or bisexual is incidental.

As competent social work practitioners, we must understand the unique experiences of lesbians, bisexuals, and gay people in relation to identity formation, adaptation and development, intrapersonal conflict, emotional support, and a wide array of psychosocial stressors throughout the life span.

Practitioners must also be reminded that internalized homophobia, a core construct in identity formation, impedes an individual's ability to cope and adapt and to change one's environment. High internalized homophobia appears significantly associated with overall psychological distress and other measures of adjustment, lower self-esteem, lower social support and satisfaction with support, less gay and nongay networks, greater loneliness, and high-risk sexual behavior (Shildo, 1994).

Because of the strong relationship between internalized homophobia and a variety of psychopathological conditions, social workers should routinely include assessment and treatment of internalized homophobia when working with lesbian and gay people (Gonsiorek, 1982; Malyon, 1982; Stein & Cohen, 1984). Placing individual needs, problems, or difficulties into a broader social fabric of oppression, power, heterosexism, homophobia, stigma, and stress management is necessary if we as social workers are to gain a better understanding of the life space of gay, lesbian, and bisexual clients.

As discussed in Chapter 1, the worker should use strategies that enable clients to experience themselves as competent, valuable, and worthwhile both as individuals and as members of their gay and lesbian cultural group. Cognitive and behavioral techniques that shift the client's sense of being trapped in a subordinate role and counter the myths and stereotypes about sexuality will change negative cultural identity and self-perception of being powerless.

These strategies are often referred to as stigma management, a lifelong process of information concerning sexual orientation and identity. It is a process of carefully controlling what others know about their sexuality. The practitioner may assist the client to share his or her sexual identity or to conceal it depending on the particular situation.

These strategies, according to Cain (1991), actually involve complex interactional negotiations. Disclosure often entails careful planning and execution, and concealment requires close attention to many details of social presentation.

Herdt and Boxer (1991) would argue, however, that the practice remedies discussed in this section represent an older, more traditional social service model, wherein pathology, stigma, contaminated self, and stigma management are core constructs. Therefore, he argues that these remedies are off the mark in terms of the needs of the lesbian, gay, and bisexual communities. He would advocate for a "queer" community, positive "queer" identity, and radical social action. The practice intervention would include community development, community and public education, consciousness-raising and self-help groups, political mobilization, and coalition building with other oppressed groups with the intent of transforming society.

Transgender people have specific health and mental health needs related to making the physical and emotional transition to their desired self. This entails funding for medical intervention, social supports, and advocacy. The age-old macro versus micro practice debate or the either/or position of social transformation versus reform and remedial change should not become a false choice. The profession historically has moved back and forth between these two positions. Many practitioners attempt to combine both approaches, leaving the philosophical and theoretical debate to social work faculty.

However, the perspective of this text suggests that the psychosocial forces previously discussed be reframed so as to inform social work practice, which focuses on policy and community change. Practitioners must understand and direct their energies to environmental pressures (homophobia translated into discrimination, violence, prejudice, and the lack of civil rights protections) into action which influences society's definition of and response to social problems, needs, or concerns of the lesbian, gay, transgender, and bisexual communities.

Practitioners must be skilled in mobilizing the political and collective will so as to transform "private troubles" into "public issues." Practice should include education for the profession and all other disciplines that work with sexual minorities; public education to dispel myths and to better understand needs; reassessment of the "fit" between client need and health, mental health, and social services; and legal and political action to remove unnecessary barriers to full participation and to ensure civil rights.

Finally, practitioners should design and implement—with extensive input from lesbians, gay men, bisexuals, and transgender people—effective laws, program policies, and community-based institutions and services. These should reflect the values of the profession and be based on sound knowledge about gay, lesbian, and bisexual people as presented in this text.

Practice Implications: Latinos

When working with Latinos, it is necessary that practitioners commit themselves to the process of self-exploration designed to overcome personal biases, prejudices, and racism, and to develop their own integrative ethnic identity. This self-exploration will allow practitioners to reach an understanding of their own personal comfort or discomfort with difference and degree of personal flexibility in relationship style and communication pattern to achieve the appropriate self-disclosure when this is therapeutically necessary.

Practitioners must therefore assess for the Latino's interaction within a dynamic environment. The assessment must include an investigation of issues in family functioning, social dislocation for the newly arrived person, and important problems arising from language differences.

The practitioner must also exercise caution in using traditional white (Anglo) models of social work and psychotherapeutic intervention.

Traditional models of helping often ignore the interdependent, mutually supportive aspects of Latino group norms and individual values. The unique diversities experienced by Latinos within their self-identified group (racial, ethnic, sexual orientation, gender, or special status—mentally or physically challenged) require the practitioner to call on his or her understanding of the cultural dictates, roles, values, and complex relationships that comprise the lives of these multidiverse people.

The diversity literature speaks of the importance of the family within Latino culture (Canino & Canino, 1980; De La Cancela, 1991; Rodriguez, 1996). The significance of the Latino family is reported as a primary source of social and economic support. The Latino family is also the medium through which individuals engage in the unique Latino cultural processes of gender role socialization and ethnic identity formation.

Within this context, the practitioner can begin to understand the importance of Latino norms and values. In particular, the cultural values of *dignidad* (dignity), *respeto* (respect), *personalismo* (personalism), and *familismo* (familism) can be best understood in the unique group and interpersonal dynamics that occur in Latino families. Furthermore, practitioners can empower the Latino individual through acknowledgment of the importance of these values in his or her worldview and that of the family and community.

Given the multidimensional and dynamic aspects of Latino culture, practitioners must be open to expand their clinical interpretations of Latino conceptions of gender, race, and class. They must be able to move beyond an exclusive intrapsychic or sociocultural view (De La Cancela, 1991). Moreover, this shift in paradigm thinking will require flexibility to reach for a collective or systemic perception of assessment and intervention as opposed to an individualistic one. This approach will allow the practitioner to integrate individual treatment with family, group, and community dynamics that are consistent with Latino culture.

In sum, the practitioner engaged in an affirmative approach to working with Latino peoples is cautioned to ensure the use of culturally sensitive assessment and intervention planning and action strategies. It is necessary that such work take into account the person-in-environment features that are characteristic of Latino daily reality. The application of an ecosystem orientation to the process of intervention must consider the cultural, linguistic, educational, economic, gender, political, and environmental context of the Latino reality in the United States.

Practice Implications: African Americans

African Americans constitute one of the largest ethnic minority groups in the nation, with a population numbering 31 million. Like other ethnic minority groups, African Americans are a very heterogeneous group, with the majority being productive members of society. However, their overrepresentation among the poor as a result of institutional racism in U.S. society places many of them under severe stress, creating an affected, at-risk, and highly vulnerable group.

One of the most silent characteristics of the African American experience is the discrimination and oppression resulting from racism. The impact of racism on the lives of members of this diverse group has caused the breakdown of the family and the weakening of community and family ties. The practitioner is alerted to the need for intervention planning with this diverse group that includes advocacy and social action.

In sum, the practice implications for working with African Americans require the social worker to assess for the results of long-term racism on the lives of African Americans. The members of this community experience many health and mental health issues that are a direct result of low socioeconomic status, poor health and mental health care, and lack of access to social services. Assess for the strengths of African American clients and recognize the value of family and community and also the role of religion in the culture. Attend to the meaning of moaning, mourning, and morning in both spirituals and the blues. Moaning refers to black pain, suffering, and grief. Through moaning or cry-on-shoulder, black people sought to bring deep-seated pain to the surface for collective affirmation of its reality. Mourning in the spirituals and, to some extent, the blues, pertains to a collective process of identification, empathy, and catharsis, whereas morning in the spirituals represents a significant breakthrough, the arrival of a brighter day, a new beginning, a transformation, or a change.

Practice Implications: Native Americans

The affirmative practice of social work with Native Americans requires a paradigm shift from the dominant Western view of society to the more holistic, spiritual conception of humans and nature that affirms Native American history, values, and culture. The group norms and values that distinguish the Native American peoples from those in the dominant culture represent more than differences. They represent cultural contrasts. Therefore, it is important for the practitioner to fully understand the reality of the Native American experience in the United States. This experience is very unique, making it difficult and, some would argue, impossible to speak of just in terms of difference (Red Horse, 1978).

The early body of anthropological literature on Native Americans describes Native American values of strength, self-control, obedience, tranquility, cooperation, and protectiveness among the Hopi, and conservatism, persistence, generosity, and deference to elders among groups of Dakotas (Yellow Horse Brave Heart, 1995).

Given these values, which the literature suggests may not be indicative of the range of norms and values inherent in Native American life across the broad spectrum of Native American families, lineage, and social networks, it is clear that the social worker must engage the Native American client in a trusting, open relationship that elicits the unique story of the personal experience. It is within this story that the values will often appear.

Lastly, the practitioner is alerted to the importance of understanding the relationship of social service and health institutions to the indigenous helping patterns and what that means for interpersonal behavior in cross-cultural settings.

Practice Implications: The Chronically Mentally Ill and the Physically Challenged

The practitioner working with individuals who are mentally, emotionally, and physically challenged and therefore oppressed by mental, emotional, and physical ableism must help to reestablish meaningful roles and relationships. Practitioners must assist these individuals with managing many events in daily problems of living that affect self-esteem and may lead to negative self-efficacy beliefs. These problems increase the individual's sense of vulnerability particularly during times of emotional crisis.

Given this reality, the practitioner must provide sensitive, affirmative, collaborative assessment and intervention planning. The person-in-environment perspective provides an important framework for the type of assistance required by this diverse group. The use of this approach will allow the social worker to identify important, naturally occurring resources and supports that can be mobilized on the client's behalf.

Micro Systems Intervention

All change starts with the client. In Chapter 4, Leigh's (1998) cultural competence model was presented as an interpersonal communication strategy to engage the client in a culturally sensitive assessment and problem-solving process. The model employs ethnographic techniques to guide the communication processes between worker and client. These include asymmetrical turn taking, expressing interest, expressing cultural ignorance, repeating, restating informant's terms, incorporating informant's terms, creating hypothetical situations, asking friendly questions, and taking leave.

These ethnographic techniques aid in the assessment phase, helping the worker to elicit information related to Factors I and II of the PIE classification system, and again during the work phase, implementing the range of interventions agreed on by both the client and the worker.

The worker's goal is to discover pertinent cultural information, which will guide this process. The culturally competent social worker will elicit an insider's view of the culture rather than imposing his or her assumed understanding of the situation, which may be the outsider's view. All professional action should be guided by principles. The following principles are associated with cultural competence:

1. Avoid assumptions
2. Respect for unique culturally defined needs of various client populations
3. Acknowledgment of culture as a predominant force in shaping behavior, values, and institutions
4. Respect for client confidentiality
5. Belief that the family as defined by each culture is the primary and preferred point of intervention
6. Acknowledgment that minority people are served in varying degrees by their natural cultural systems
7. Recognition that the concepts of family, community, and so on differ among cultures and among subgroups within cultures

8. The stage of the client's identity development may be an important indicator of his or her coping and adaptation
9. Belief that diversity within cultures is as important as diversity between cultures
10. Awareness that the dignity of the person is not guaranteed unless the dignity of his or her people is preserved
11. Understanding that minority clients are usually best served by persons who are part of or in tune with their culture
12. Acceptance that cultural differences exist and have an impact on service delivery
13. Acknowledgment that process is as important as product when working with minority clients
14. Awareness when values of minority groups are in conflict with dominant society values (Cross, Bazron, Dennis, & Isaacs, 1989, pp. 22–24).

These principles direct the purpose, style, and tone of the worker-client communication. This approach to interviewing promises to make explicit the worldview of clients.

Professional education should present the cultural knowledge that is then funneled into skill development and applied to clinical practice. One of the first steps is to improve communication. Clear, specific, and open communication between the practitioner and the client is an essential clinical skill to achieve intervention goals. Desmond (1994) offers a framework to improve communication between the human service worker and a culturally diverse or oppressed client.

1. Gain the client's trust by making small talk, perhaps showing interest in the client's country, reference group, or culture.
2. Show respect for differences among your clients with regard to beliefs about problem solving, help giving and taking, illness, problems, and care.
3. Don't assume the client dislikes you, mistrusts you, or isn't listening to you because he or she avoids eye contact.
4. Determine other resources and methods the client has used or continues to use while receiving your help.
5. Verify how the client will take medication or follow the treatment plan.
6. Don't assume that the client understands you and will follow your advice simply on the basis of his or her nod and a verbal "yes." If in doubt, use an interpreter.
7. Be aware of the basic beliefs, values, and mores of various cultures.
8. Understand the value of the family presence and role in problem solving or in the illness and recovery process.
9. Use an interpreter whenever appropriate.
10. If you don't understand an attitude, belief, or behavior, ask the client to help you understand.
11. Identify formal and informal structures.
12. Understand client legal dilemmas.
13. Recognize institutional discrimination, bias, and aggression.
14. Confront, advocate, lobby, and negotiate.

Isaacs and Benjamin (1991) compared the values of Anglo Americans with those of other ethnocultural groups and found that other cultures valued more restrained modes of expression, unlike Anglo Americans, who valued openness, directness, and individuality. In many Asian societies, an ideal person is expected to remain calm and to control his or her emotions even when upset. Serenity and stoicism are cherished, and expression of any strong emotion, especially a negative one like anger, is strongly discouraged and hence suppressed (Nilchaikovit, Hill, & Holland, 1993). Each culture will find some behaviors, interactions, or values more important or desirable than others (Cross et al., 1989).

A social worker, as do other health and human service practitioners, consciously engages "the use of self" so as to establish a relationship that becomes the basis of a "therapeutic alliance" with a client. Prior to working with a client or colleague who is different from you, answering the following questions might prove helpful:

- To what ethnic group, socioeconomic class, religion, age group, and community do you belong?
- What experiences have you had with people from ethnic groups, social classes, religions, age groups, or communities different from your own?
- What were those experiences like? How did you feel about them?
- What sociocultural factors in your background might contribute to being rejected by members of other cultures?
- What personal qualities do you have that will help to establish interpersonal relationships with a person from another cultural group? What personal qualities may be detrimental?
- While growing up, what did your parents, relatives, and significant others say about people who were different from your family?
- What aspects of your ethnic group, class, religion, age group, or community do you find embarrassing or wish you could change? Why?

The following list of do's and don'ts may be used as a guideline as well.

Do's and Don'ts of Multicultural Therapy

1. Do communicate with the client. The communication techniques suggested by Desmond (1994) and listed on the previous page are helpful. Observe body language.
2. Do gain trust of the client.
3. Do admit your ignorance of their culture and ask questions about their culture.
4. Do preserve confidentiality whenever possible.
5. Do try to learn about the client's culture.
6. Do understand that the client may have differing views about various aspects of life.
7. Do utilize both family and individual therapy when possible.
8. Do not use individuals who are related to the client as interpreters.
9. Do not overidentify with the client.

The worker's choices of interventions may include consciousness-raising group work and groups comprised of a single self-identified minority that focus on coming out, identity development, and self-help. Social isolation and the loss of cultural supports must be addressed by replacing them with new social support networks that address both cultural and affectional needs. While most of the interpersonal interventions used for majority clients may be appropriate, case advocacy and skills development related to community resource use are most important. Individual, group, or family practice targeting stigma management and psychosocial adaptation should be considered.

Mezzo Intervention

Practice on a group identity level might include strategies for enhancing identities. Watts (1994) suggests that this means deciding which social dimension will be used to differentiate the assisted group from other groups. Emphasizing positive distinctiveness, while a difficult strategy, may be a worthy start. Two other broad categories are also identified: social mobility and social change. The process of passing and becoming the "ideal minority" are examples of social mobility which have been discussed extensively in Chapters 4 and 10. Social change strategies, the grist of macro practice, emphasize transformation of societies' power, privilege, and status structures. These are covered in detail in the profession's curricula.

Often, the client's reality is poorly understood; therefore, consultation and public education designed to help communities and agencies understand their needs should become a priority. Various minority communities may require assistance in identifying and training leaders in the areas of self-help, resource development, and advocacy. The use of community development and organizing strategies might focus on political mobilization, class advocacy, and coalition building with other diverse and oppressed groups.

The health and social service agencies serving these clients need to develop cultural competence. The worker may join with several colleagues to press for agency change by implementing a program of staff development and organizational policy change. A model of cultural competence developed by the CASSP (Child and Adolescent Service System Program) based at Georgetown University is presented to help the practitioner to move her professional colleagues and her social agency toward cultural proficiency (Cross et al., 1989). The Cultural Competence Continuum identifies a range of characteristics, as shown in Figure 16.1.

Cultural destructiveness is at the most negative end of the continuum and is represented by attitudes, policies, and practices that are destructive to cultures and consequently to the individuals within the cultures. Cultural incapacity occurs when the system or

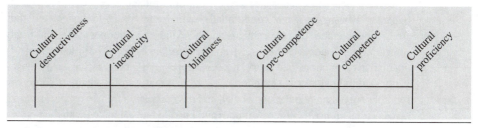

FIGURE 16.1 *Cultural Competence Continuum Scale*

Source: From *Cultural Competency in Health, Social, and Human Services,* edited by P. J. Lecca, I. Quervalu, J. V. Nunes, & H. F. Gonzales. Copyright 1998. Reproduced by permission of Taylor & Francis/Garland Publishing, http://www.taylorandfrancis.com.

agency does not intentionally seek cultural destructiveness but lacks the capacity to help minority clients or communities. Cultural blindness is the belief that color or cultures make no difference and that all people are the same. Cultural precompetence is the first step toward the positive end of the continuum. The agency realizes its weakness in serving minorities and attempts to improve some aspect of its services to a specific population. Culturally competent agencies at this point on the continuum are characterized by acceptance and respect for difference, continuing self-assessment of staff and policies regarding culture, careful attention to the dynamics of difference, continuous expansion of cultural knowledge and resources, and a variety of adaptations to service models in order to better meet the needs of minority populations. Cultural proficiency is at the most positive end of the spectrum. Culturally proficient agencies hold culture in high esteem. Culturally competent practice is enhanced by research, by treatment approaches based on culture, and by publishing and disseminating the results of demonstration projects. Specialists in culturally competent practice are hired by these agencies.

Cultural Competence and the Profession

The worker's intervention with the agency to bring about cultural competence and cultural proficiency should also be directed toward the profession. The National Association of Social Workers refined its *Code of Ethics* (1996), defining cultural competence as an ethical attribute of the professional. Conferences and in-service training by NASW chapters focusing on this expectation should become the norm of the profession. Presenting papers or workshops should be strongly requested by the membership. This educational change will take place if there is an incentive. Rewriting the various licensing regulations and testing procedures would make cultural competence more of a professional reality.

Macro Intervention

Governments too often ignore the uniqueness of diverse cultural groups when writing legislation or translating its intent into administrative policy. Legislators and policy practitioners may not know of the special needs of the people we represent. They may deny that violence and discrimination exists. It is important to assess the level of knowledge the public or legislative body has and the attitudes they hold about the marginalized group. Do they operate from stereotypes? Are their impressions based on assumptions related to negative group identity? Appleby (Chapter 10) suggests that, traditionally, when attempting to understand the attitudes of straight people about gays, lesbians, and bisexuals, practitioners would use only one global category, homophobia, to register negative attitudes. This did not leave room for important qualitative distinctions necessary to devise appropriate interventions. He notes that there are various attitudinal levels: (1) ignorance, (2) negativity, and (3) hatred. These categories hold for other oppressed populations as well and may serve as a framework to develop interventions across social group identities. Attitudes and knowledge associated with the first two categories, ignorance and negativity, are amenable to change through group exposure and education. The dynamics that support the category of hatred, however, require much more research before interventions are developed. It is important for the worker to follow the rule of parsimony by prioritizing those educational strategies that have potential for success. Building coalitions of advocates who will direct their educational efforts on solid data is an important first task.

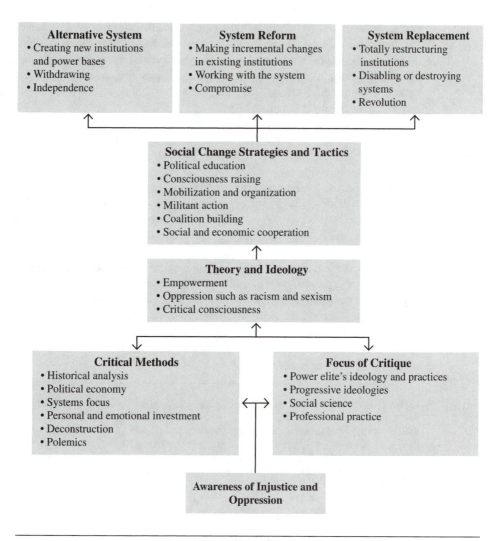

FIGURE 16.2

Source: From *Human Diversity: Perspectives on People in Context,* edited by E. Trickett, R. Watts, and D. Berman (pp. 66–67). Copyright 1994 by Jossey-Bass, Inc. Reprinted by permission of Jossey-Bass, Inc., a subsidiary of John Wiley & Sons, Inc.

Practitioners also must hold policy decision makers to task by continually asking them to assess the impact of proposed policy on diverse cultural groups. Other social institutions, such as schools and health care facilities, may need comparable intervention. A private sector that is well informed of cultural difference is more apt to be appropriately responsive. While the social worker may directly initiate an educational intervention, the group itself should be empowered to present its uniqueness, as well as their needs on their own behalf.

Watts (1994) presents an action model in Figure 16.2 that builds on personal aware-ness of injustice, introduces several methodologies for analyzing the oppression, and then moves toward the selection of social change strategies and tactics. The end result of this transformative activity may be the development of an alternative system, the implementation of system reform, or the institution of system replacement. The model incorporates a range of possibilities sought through community organizing, community development, and societal transformation efforts. The model serves as a guide for the level of analysis necessary before engaging in macro change.

Conclusion

For social workers, awareness of the concepts presented in this text and how they elucidate the dynamics of diversity, social oppression, and social functioning is only the first step toward working with diverse peoples within an affirmative paradigm. Social workers must lead their awareness to action, which in turn can lead to change resulting in economic and social justice.

Lastly, the practitioner must engage in practice that demonstrates the important relationship of theory to practice and the interrelatedness of alternative economic, political, and personal perspectives within a person-in-environment framework. The goal of such an approach must also reflect the need for multisystem analysis and action on the individual, group, organizational, community, and societal levels.

References

Brown, L. (1989). New voices, new visions: Toward a lesbian/gay paradigm for psychology. *Psychology of Women Quarterly, 13,* 445–458.

Cain, R. (1991). Stigma management and gay identity development. *Social Work, 36*(1), 67–73.

Canino, I., & Canino, G. (1980). Impact of stress on the Puerto Rican family: Treatment considerations. *American Journal of Orthopsychiatry, 50,* 535–541.

Collins, P. H. (1992). *Black feminist thought: Knowledge, consciousness and the politics of empowerment.* Boston: Unwin Hyman.

Cross, T. L., Bazron, B. J., Dennis, K. W., & Isaacs, M. R. (1989). *Towards a culturally competent system of care.* Washington, DC: Georgetown University Child Development Center, Technical Assistance Center.

Daniel, G. R. (1992). Beyond black and white: The new multicultural consciousness. In M. P. P. Root (Ed.), *Racially mixed people in America.* Newberry Park, CA: Sage.

De La Cancela, V. (1991). Working affirmatively with Puerto Rican men: Professional and personal reflections. In M. Bogard (Ed.), *Feminist approaches for men in family therapy* (pp. 195–211). New York: Hawthorn Press.

Desmond, J. (1994). Communicating with multicultural patients. *Life in Medicine,* 7–25.

Everett, J., Chipunga, S., & Leashore, B. (Eds.). (1991). *Child welfare: An Afrocentric perspective.* New Brunswick, NJ: Rutgers University Press.

Fong, R., Spickard, P. R., & Ewalt, P. L. (1996). A multicultural reality: Issues for social work. In P. L. Ewalt, E. M. Freeman, S. A. Kirk, & D. A. Poole, *Multicultural issues in social work.* Washington, DC: NASW.

Gonsiorek, J. C. (1982). The use of diagnostic concepts in working with gay and lesbian populations. In J. C. Gonsiorek (Ed.), *Homosexuality and psychotherapy: A practitioner's handbook of affirmative models* (pp. 9–20). Beverly Hills, CA: Sage.

Greene, R. R. (Ed.). (1994). *Human behavior theory: A diversity framework.* New York: Aldine de Gruyter.

Guba, E. G., & Lincoln, Y. S. (1981). *Effective evaluation*. San Francisco: Jossey-Bass.

Hall, M. (1978). Lesbian families: Cultural and clinical issues. *Social Work, 23,* 380–385.

Herdt, G., & Boxer, A. (1991). Ethnographic issues in the study of AIDS. *Journal of Interpersonal Violence, 5,* 316–333.

Isaacs, M. R., & Benjamin, M. P. (1991). *Towards a culturally competent system of care* (Vol. 2). Washington, DC: CASSP Technical Assistance Center, Center for Child Health and Mental Health Policy, Georgetown University Child Development Center.

Leigh, J. W. (1998). *Communicating for cultural competence*. Boston: Allyn & Bacon.

Maylon, A. (1982). Biphasic aspects of homosexual identity formation. *Psychotherapy: Theory, Research, and Practice, 19,* 335–340.

Miller, J. B. (1986). *Toward a new psychology of women* (2nd ed.). Boston: Beacon.

Myers, L. J., & Spieght, S. L. (1994). Optimal theory and the psychology of human diversity. In E. J. Trickett, R. J. Watts, & D. Berman (Eds.), *Human diversity: Perspectives on people in context*. San Francisco: Jossey-Bass.

National Association of Social Workers. (1996). *Code of ethics*. Washington, DC: NASW.

Nilchaikovit, T., Hill, J., & Holland, J. (1993). The effects of culture on illness behavior and medical care: Asian and American differences. *General Hospital Psychiatry, 15,* 41–50.

Pharr, S. (1988). *Homophobia: A weapon of sexism*. Inverness, CA: Chardon.

Pinderhughes, E. (1982). Afro-American families and the victim system. In M. M. McGoldrick, J. Pearce, & J. Giordano, *Ethnicity and family therapy*. New York: Guilford.

Red Horse, J. (1978). Family behavior of urban American Indians. *Social Casework, 59,* 67–72.

Rodriguez, L. J. (1996). On macho. In R. Gonzalez (Ed.), *Muy macho: Latino men confront their manhood* (pp. 187–201). New York: Anchor Books.

Ruth, S. (1990). *Issues in feminism*. Mountain View, CA: Mayfield.

Scott, J. (1988). *Gender and politics of history*. New York: Columbia University Press.

Shildo, A. (1994). Internalized homophobia: Conceptual and empirical issues in measurement. In V. Greene & G. M. Herek (Eds.), *Lesbian and gay psychology: Theory, research, and clinical application* (pp. 173–205). Thousand Oaks, CA: Sage.

Spence, L. (1997). *Popol Vuh: The mythic and heroic sagas of the Kiches of Central America*. Whitefish, MT: Ressinger Publishing Company.

Spradley, J. P. (1979). *The ethnographic interview*. New York: Holt, Rinehart, & Winston.

Stein, T., & Cohen, C. (Eds.). (1984). *Psychotherapy with lesbians and gay men*. New York: Plenum Press.

Watts, R. J. (1994). Paradigm of diversity. In E. Trickett, R. J. Watts, & D. Berman (Eds.), *Human diversity: Perspectives on people in context* (pp. 66–67). San Francisco: Jossey-Bass.

Westkoff, M. (1979). Feminist criticism of the social sciences. *Harvard Educational Review, 49*(4), 424–430.

Yellow Horse Brave Heart, M. (1995). *The return of the sacred path: Healing from historical trauma and historical unresolved grief among the Lakota*. Unpublished doctoral dissertation, Smith College School of Social Work, Northampton, MA.

Appendix A

PIE Assessment Forms for Factors I and II

Client Name: _____

Interview Date: ____ / ____ / ____

Evaluator: _____

I–4. FACTOR I:
PROBLEMS IN SOCIAL FUNCTIONING

1.	FAMILIAL ROLES	Code	Type	Severity	Duration	Coping	Recommended Intervention
☐	Parent	11					
☐	Spouse	12					
☐	Child	13					
☐	Sibling	14					
☐	Other Family Member	15					
☐	Significant Other	16					

2.	OTHER INTERPERSONAL ROLES	Code	Type	Severity	Duration	Coping	Recommended Intervention
☐	Lover	21					
☐	Friend	22					
☐	Neighbor	23					
☐	Member	24					
☐	Other (specify):	25					

3.	OCCUPATIONAL ROLES	Code	Type	Severity	Duration	Coping	Recommended Intervention
☐	Worker–Paid Economy	31					
☐	Worker–Home	32					
☐	Worker–Volunteer	33					
☐	Student	34					
☐	Other (specify):	35					

4.	SPECIAL LIFE SITUATION ROLES	Code	Type	Severity	Duration	Coping	Recommended Intervention
☐	Consumer	41					
☐	Inpatient/Client	42					
☐	Outpatient/Client	43					
☐	Probationer/Parolee	44					
☐	Prisoner	45					
☐	Immigrant–Legal	46					
☐	Immigrant–Undocumented	47					
☐	Immigrant–Refugee	48					
☐	Other (specify):	49					

| ☐ | NO SOCIAL INTERACTION PROBLEMS | 0000 | | | | | |

TYPE OF SOCIAL INTERACTION PROBLEM

10 Power
20 Ambivalence
30 Responsibility
40 Dependency
50 Loss
60 Isolation
70 Victimization
80 Mixed
90 Other (specify) _____

SEVERITY INDEX

1 No Problem   4 High
2 Low   5 Very high
3 Moderate   6 Catastrophic

DURATION INDEX

1 More than five years
2 One to five years
3 Six months to one year
4 One to six months
5 Two weeks to one month
6 Less than two weeks

COPING INDEX

1 Outstanding
2 Above average
3 Adequate
4 Somewhat inadequate
5 Inadequate
6 No coping skills

Source: Copyright 1994, National Association of Social Workers, Inc., *PIE Manual Person-in-Environment: The PIE Classification System for Social Functioning Problems,* by J. M. Karls & K. E. Wandrei.

5. FACTOR II: PROBLEMS IN THE ENVIRONMENT

ECONOMIC/BASIC NEEDS SYSTEM PROBLEMS

	FOOD/NUTRITION	Code	Severity	Duration	Recommended Intervention
❏	Lack of regular food supply	5101			
❏	Nutritionally inadequate food supply	5102			
❏	Documented malnutrition	5103			
❏	Other (specify):	5104			

	SHELTER	Code	Severity	Duration	Recommended Intervention
❏	Absence of shelter	5201			
❏	Substandard or inadequate shelter	5202			
❏	Other (specify):	5203			

	EMPLOYMENT	Code	Severity	Duration	Recommended Intervention
❏	Unemployment Employment not available in community	5301			
❏	Underemployment Adequate employment not available in community	5302			
❏	Inappropriate employment Lack of socially/legally acceptable employment in community	5303			
❏	Other (specify):	5304			

	ECONOMIC RESOURCES	Code	Severity	Duration	Recommended Intervention
❏	Insufficient community resources for basic sustenance (self/dependent)	5401			
❏	Insufficient resources in community to provide for needed services beyond sustenance	5402			
❏	Regulatory barriers to economic resources	5403			
❏	Other (specify):	5404			

	TRANSPORTATION	Code	Severity	Duration	Recommended Intervention
❏	No personal/public transportation to job/needed services	5501			
❏	Other (specify):	5502			

	DISCRIMINATION	Code	Severity	Duration	Recommended Intervention
❏	If applicable, select discrimination type from list below. Write code in box to right.	56_ _			

	NO PROBLEMS IN ECONOMIC/ BASIC NEEDS SYSTEM	0000		
❏				

DISCRIMINATION CODES

01 Age	07 Noncitizen
02 Ethnicity, color, or language	08 Veteran status
	09 Dependency status
03 Religion	10 Disability status
04 Sex	11 Marital status
05 Sexual orientation	12 Other (please specify):
06 Lifestyle	_____

SEVERITY INDEX

1 No problem
2 Low
3 Moderate
4 High
5 Very high
6 Catastrophic

DURATION INDEX

1 More than five years
2 One to five years
3 Six months to one year
4 One to six months
5 Two weeks to one month
6 Less than two weeks

6. EDUCATION AND TRAINING SYSTEM

EDUCATION AND TRAINING	Code	Severity	Duration	Recommended Intervention
☐ Lack of educational/training facilities	6101			
☐ Lack of age-relevant, adequate, or appropriate educational/training facilities	6102			
☐ Lack of culturally relevant educational/ training opportunities	6103			
☐ Regulatory barriers to existing educational/ training services and programs	6104			
☐ Absence of support services needed to access educational/training opportunities	6105			
☐ Other (specify):	6106			

DISCRIMINATION	Code	Severity	Duration	Recommended Intervention
☐ If applicable, select discrimination type from list below. Write code in box to right.	62_ _			

	Code			
☐ NO PROBLEMS IN EDUCATION/ TRAINING SYSTEM	0000			

7. JUDICIAL AND LEGAL SYSTEM

JUSTICE AND LEGAL SYSTEM	Code	Severity	Duration	Recommended Intervention
☐ Lack of police services	7101			
☐ Lack of relevant police services	7102			
☐ Lack of confidence in police services	7103			
☐ Lack of adequate prosecution/defense services	7104			
☐ Lack of adequate probation/parole services	7105			
☐ Other (specify):	7106			

DISCRIMINATION	Code	Severity	Duration	Recommended Intervention
☐ If applicable, select discrimination type from list below. Write code in box to right.	72_ _			

	Code			
☐ NO PROBLEMS IN JUDICIAL/LEGAL SYSTEM	0000			

DISCRIMINATION CODES

01 Age	07 Noncitizen
02 Ethnicity, color, or language	08 Veteran status
	09 Dependency status
03 Religion	10 Disability status
04 Sex	11 Marital status
05 Sexual orientation	12 Other (please specify):
06 Lifestyle	_____

SEVERITY INDEX
1 No problem
2 Low
3 Moderate
4 High
5 Very high
6 Catastrophic

DURATION INDEX
1 More than five years
2 One to five years
3 Six months to one year
4 One to six months
5 Two weeks to one month
6 Less than two weeks

Source: Copyright 1994, National Association of Social Workers, Inc., *PIE Manual Person-in-Environment: The PIE Classification System for Social Functioning Problems,* by J. M. Karls & K. E. Wandrei.

8. HEALTH, SAFETY, AND SOCIAL SERVICES SYSTEM

	HEALTH / MENTAL HEALTH	Code	Severity	Duration	Recommended Intervention
☐	Absence of adequate health services	8101			
☐	Regulatory barriers to health services	8102			
☐	Inaccessibility of health services	8103			
☐	Absence of support services needed to use health services (child care, translator)	8104			
☐	Absence of adequate mental health services	8105			
☐	Regulatory barriers to mental health services	8106			
☐	Inaccessibility of mental health services	8107			
☐	Absence of support services needed to use mental health services	8108			
☐	Other (specify):	8109			

	SAFETY	Code	Severity	Duration	Recommended Intervention
☐	Violence or crime in neighborhood	8201			
☐	Unsafe working conditions	8202			
☐	Unsafe conditions in home	8203			
☐	Absence of adequate safety services	8204			
☐	Natural disaster	8205			
☐	Human-created disaster	8206			
☐	Other (specify):	8207			

	SOCIAL SERVICES	Code	Severity	Duration	Recommended Intervention
☐	Absence of adequate social services	8301			
☐	Regulatory barriers to social services	8302			
☐	Inaccessibility of social services	8303			
☐	Absence of support services needed to use social services (child care, transport)	8304			
☐	Other (specify):	8305			

	DISCRIMINATION	Code	Severity	Duration	Recommended Intervention
☐	If applicable, select discrimination type from list below. Write code in box to right.	84_ _			

		Code			
☐	**NO PROBLEMS IN HEALTH, SAFETY, AND SOCIAL SERVICES SYSTEM**	0000			

DISCRIMINATION CODES
01 Age
02 Ethnicity, color, or language
03 Religion
04 Sex
05 Sexual orientation
06 Lifestyle
07 Noncitizen
08 Veteran status
09 Dependency status
10 Disability status
11 Marital status
12 Other (please specify): _____

SEVERITY INDEX
1 No problem
2 Low
3 Moderate
4 High
5 Very high
6 Catastrophic

DURATION INDEX
1 More than five years
2 One to five years
3 Six months to one year
4 One to six months
5 Two weeks to one month
6 Less than two weeks

9. VOLUNTARY ASSOCIATION SYSTEM

	RELIGIOUS GROUPS	Code	Severity	Duration	Recommended Intervention
☐	Lack of religious group of choice	9101			
☐	Lack of community acceptance of religious values	9102			
☐	Other (specify):	9103			

	COMMUNITY GROUPS	Code	Severity	Duration	Recommended Intervention
☐	Lack of community support group of choice	9201			
☐	Lack of community acceptance of community group of choice	9202			
☐	Other (specify):	9203			

	DISCRIMINATION IN VOLUNTARY ASSOCIATION SYSTEM	Code	Severity	Duration	Recommended Intervention
☐	If applicable, select discrimination type from list below. Write code in box to right.	93_ _			

	NO PROBLEM IN VOLUNTARY ASSOCIATION SYSTEM	Code			
☐		0000			

10. AFFECTIONAL SUPPORT SYSTEM

	AFFECTIONAL SUPPORT	Code	Severity	Duration	Recommended Intervention
☐	Absence of affectional support system	10101			
☐	Support system inadequate to meet affectional needs	10102			
☐	Excessively involved support system	10103			
☐	Other (specify):	10104			

	DISCRIMINATION IN AFFECTIONAL SUPPORT SYSTEM	Code	Severity	Duration	Recommended Intervention
☐	If applicable, select discrimination type from list below. Write code in box to right.	102_ _			

	NO PROBLEMS IN AFFECTIONAL SUPPORT SYSTEM	Code			
☐		0000			

DISCRIMINATION CODES
01 Age
02 Ethnicity, color, or language
03 Religion
04 Sex
05 Sexual orientation
06 Lifestyle
07 Noncitizen
08 Veteran status
09 Dependency status
10 Disability status
11 Marital status
12 Other (please specify): _____

SEVERITY INDEX
1 No problem
2 Low
3 Moderate
4 High
5 Very high
6 Catastrophic

DURATION INDEX
1 More than five years
2 One to five years
3 Six months to one year
4 One to six months
5 Two weeks to one month
6 Less than two weeks

Contributors

George Alan Appleby, MSW, DSW, LCSW, is a Professor of Social Work and Dean of the School of Health and Human Services at Southern Connecticut State University, where he teaches such courses as AIDS: A Psychosocial Response; Human Oppression and Cultural Diversity; Social Welfare Policy and Social Work Practice Evaluation; and Sexual Minorities: Gay, Lesbian, Bisexual, and Transgender Issues. Dr. Appleby is past chair of the NASW National Committee on Lesbian, Gay, and Bisexual Issues, and is active in state and local communities in AIDS service planning and evaluation, and gay and lesbian concerns. He is widely published in the areas of AIDS, homophobia and heterosexism, and GLBT issues. Along with Jeane Anastas, he authored *Not Just a Passing Phase: Social Work with Gay, Lesbian, and Bisexual People* (1998), published by Columbia University Press. Dr. Appleby is currently conducting an international study of resiliency in working-class gay and bisexual men of the United States, Canada, Mexico, England, Ireland, Scotland, Australia, and New Zealand.

Edgar Colon, MSW, DSW, ACSW, is Professor of Social Work at Southern Connecticut State University, where he teaches in the areas of social welfare administration, research, human behavior and diversity, substance abuse assessment, and treatment and social policy. Dr. Colon is also a Senior Associate Faculty/Trainer for the Multicultural Research and Training Institute at Temple University, Philadelphia. He has published in the areas of program development and evaluation in Latino communities, alcoholism issues and Latino males, and the development of intelligent organizations in health and human services. Professor Colon is also a Principal Investigator in a Southern Connecticut State University Center of School Action Research/Department of Justice Prevention Research and Evaluation Federal Grant to evaluate school and community violence initiatives within the Waterbury School District.

Jack Paul Gesino, DSW, LCSW, is an Associate Professor of Social Work at Southern Connecticut State University, where he teaches in the areas of social work practice, gerontology, and health policy. Dr. Gesino is also Chairperson of the Elder and Family Specialization. He is a consultant and trainer at the Masonic Geriatric Health Care Center, Wallingford, Connecticut.

Julia Hamilton, MSW, Ph.D., LCSW, is an Associate Professor of Social Work at Southern Connecticut State University. Dr. Hamilton teaches human behavior, where she directs her teaching and research interests to the complexities of race, racism, culture, and political power at the individual, family, and group and community levels. As a recognized diversity consultant and trainer, Professor Hamilton is extremely skillful at helping others engage in the often painful self-discovery process necessary for incorporating sensitivity to race and cultural issues germane to social work practice.

Michie N. Hesselbrock, MSW, Ph.D., LCSW, is a Professor and Director of the Ph.D. program at the University of Connecticut School of Social Work. Dr. Hesselbrock is also the Principal Investigator of a United States and Japan epidemiological study of alcoholism and serves as the technical advisor to the Japanese National Institute of Alcohol Abuse and Alcoholism. She has published extensively in the area of alcoholism research.

Esther Howe, MSW, Ph.D., is Associate Professor of Social Work at Southern Connecticut State University, where she teaches Diversity and Oppression; Social Work Practice/Theory Integration; and Social Work in Educational Settings. She is Co-director of Beyond the School House Door and chair of the School Social Work sequence.

Silvia Juarez-Marazzo, MSW, is a psychopedagogy educator from Argentina. Ms. Marazzo graduated from the Alfred Adler Institute as an NAAP Certified Psychoanalytic Psychotherapist. She has served as the coordinator of the SCSU Mentoring in the Community Project and a clinical instructor at the Yale Child Study Center Family Support Services, providing in-home services for the Intensive Family Preservation Program at New Haven Family Alliance and at the Yale Intensive In-Home Child and Adolescent Services.

Minou Michilin, MSW, DSW, LCSW, is a Professor at Southern Connecticut State University, where she teaches in the areas of social work practice, human behavior, and psychopathology. Dr. Michilin is a recognized consultant in children and family services and social work practice and physical and developmental disabilities. Her publications include a text on the care of mentally challenged children published in Iran.

Constance L. Mindell, MSSS, DSW, ACSW, LCSW (CT, NY), is an Associate Professor and Chairperson of the Health Specialization at Southern Connecticut State University. She has extensive clinical practice experience in health care settings and maintains a private practice with a focus on health and illness and the religious and spirituality issues that impact on bereavement and social coping. Dr. Mindell is on the Board of Directors of Jewish Family Services of Greater New Haven. She is also a member of the SCSU Judaic Studies Planning Committee. Professor Mindell is a recognized expert in the development of social and educational programs that address religious and bigotry issues. Presently, Professor Mindell is engaged in an international social work education-training program in the Czech Republic.

Cheryl A. Parks, MSW, Ph.D., is an Assistant Professor of Social Casework at the University of Connecticut School of Social Work and teaches graduate content in cultural diversity and lesbian and gay issues. Dr. Parks has eighteen years of clinical practice experience with diverse populations and has published widely in the area of alcoholism in gay and lesbian populations.

Jaak Rakfeldt, MSW, Ph.D., is an Associate Professor at Southern Connecticut State University, School of Professional Studies, Social Work Department, where he teaches courses in Research Methods and Psychopathology, Community Mental Health/Substance Abuse. He coordinates the SCSU-DMHAS collaboration and chairs the MSW Community Mental Health/Substance Abuse Specialization. Dr. Rakfeldt is also an Assistant Clinical Professor at the Yale University School of Medicine Department of Psychiatry, and serves as a clinical consultant, conducting seminars and colloquia at various community mental health agencies. Professor Rakfeldt has forty publications, primarily dealing with mental health issues.

Elizabeth Rodriguez-Keyes, MSW, Ph.D. candidate at Smith College, is an Adjunct Professor of Social Work at Southern Connecticut State University. She is a senior clinician and clinical instructor at the Yale Child Study Center.

Barbara Drahus Worden, MSW, Ph.D., LCSW, is an Associate Professor of Social Work at Southern Connecticut State University and Director of the Counseling Center for Families and Women. Dr. Worden teaches social work practice with an emphasis on gender being the most basic unit of diversity. She is past Chairperson of several Social Work Practice Committees of the Connecticut Society of Clinical Social Workers and is currently on the Board of Directors of the Columbia University Alumni Association. Dr. Worden recently co-authored *The Gender Dance in Couples Therapy* (1998), published by Brooks/Cole, and a professional article on salient perceptual factors in sexual harassment incidents.

Index